Disaster Mental Health

Theory and Practice

James Halpern
State University of New York at New Paltz

Mary Tramontin
Private Practice

THOMSON ™

BROOKS/COLE

Australia • Brazil • Canada • Mexico • Singapore • Spain
United Kingdom • United States

KH

THOMSON
™
BROOKS/COLE

Disaster Mental Health: Theory and Practice
James Halpern and Mary Tramontin

Senior Acquisitions Editor: Marquita Flemming
Assistant Editor: Jennifer Walsh
Editorial Assistant: Samantha Shook
Marketing Manager: Meghan McCullough
Senior Marketing Communications Manager:
   Tami Strang
Content Project Manager, Editorial Production:
   Rita Jaramillo
Creative Director: Rob Hugel
Art Director: Vernon Boes

Print Buyer: Nora Massuda
Permissions Editor: Roberta Broyer
Production Service: Matrix Productions
Copy Editor: Betty Duncan
Cover Designer: Cheryl Carrington
Cover Image: The Charlotte Observer
Cover Printer: Webcom Limited
Compositor: International Typesetting
   and Composition
Printer: Webcom Limited

Printed in Canada
1 2 3 4 5 6 7 10 09 08 07 06

Library of Congress Control Number:
2006922420

ISBN 0-534-53471-6

Thomson Higher Education
10 Davis Drive
Belmont, CA 94002-3098
USA

For more information about our products,
contact us at:
Thomson Learning Academic
Resource Center
1-800-423-0563
For permission to use material from this
text or product, submit a request online at
http://www.thomsonrights.com.
Any additional questions about permissions
can be submitted by e-mail to
thomsonrights@thomson.com.

7/20/06

To my sons, Nathan and Jordan

JH

*To Margherita and Renato Tramontin, for breaking new ground
and for your fortitude and unconditional love*

MT

Brief Contents

Contents

CHAPTER 8

Psychological First Aid   199

CHAPTER 9

Early Interventions Beyond Psychological First Aid   224

Preface

Ranging from hurricanes and floods to house fires, from plane crashes to acts of terror, disasters can rob us of our loved ones, our possessions, and our sense of well-being. Disasters can forever change life as we know it and can seriously impact our ability to function. The mental health community recognizes that advance preparation, early intervention, and appropriate follow-up can assist those whose lives are touched by disaster.

As disaster mental health practitioners, we strive to bring organization to disaster's chaos. There are currently several wonderful and informative books on disaster mental health, some of which we list at the end of Chapter 1 (our formal and detailed introduction to this field and this book), and still others that we reference throughout the course of this text. Yet we felt that there was no existing volume on this subject that brought together foundational material, core issues—including concerns regarding terminology, mission, and principles—and practical interventions, to prepare the next generation of helpers.

The need for such a comprehensive text became apparent to us as we participated in the mental health response to the disaster of September 11, 2001. It has been made ever clearer by the string of domestic and international disasters that have unfolded since then. While we were writing this text, the world experienced the destructive Florida hurricane season and the devastating Indian Ocean tsunami in 2004, followed in 2005 by the powerful earthquake in Pakistan and India, and by Hurricane Katrina in the Gulf Coast region and the subsequent flooding of New Orleans. Add to these massive events the countless smaller-scale disasters—wildfires and house fires, regional droughts and floods—and the need to train many more people to respond to those affected is evident. Hence, we hope that this book begins to address the need for a comprehensive and scholarly synthesis of theory and practice in disaster mental health.

Our book is divided into two parts, the first devoted to theory and the second related to practice issues. Naturally, this division is not a pure one, especially in such a young field. In the first part, we discuss some practice implications, and in the second part, we discuss some theoretical issues. But, overall, you will observe a shift in tone, and perhaps pace, as you move from the first to the second part of this work.

All chapters of this book are conceptually linked, but can each serve as standalone reference on a specific subject: For example, Chapter 4, "Reactions and Risk Factors," can serve as a primer for emergency management workers looking to incorporate mental health services after a disaster; Chapter 7, "The Challenges of Counseling in Chaos," provides a general guide for practitioners working at their first disasters. At the end of the text, you will also find several appendices offering useful resources on a range of topics to assist you as you explore the field further.

That being said, we recommend that you read *Disaster Mental Health: Theory and Practice* in its entirety, to best understand the complexity of disasters' impact and to appropriately apply psychological interventions in their aftermath.

Disasters change people. They scramble individual and collective understandings of reality, juxtaposing the horrific with the noble. Anything is possible in a disaster, and those who become part of one—by choice or by chance—will be touched in some way. Our best wish is that this volume will empower and equip you to negotiate the challenges of life in disaster and to assist individuals, families, and communities in their wake.

ACKNOWLEDGMENTS

Gratitude is the memory of the heart.

Jean Baptiste Massieu

Most of all, we thank those who have allowed us to be part of their lives during their personal times of disaster and afterward. We remain inspired and touched as a result of such enduring moments. For helping us to understand the impact and mitigation of disaster, we first offer our deepest appreciation to these many survivors of disasters. The case examples presented throughout the book are altered in order to protect the privacy of these individuals.

We would like to thank Marquita Flemming of Brooks/Cole for having faith in us to get this book started and supporting us with kindness and wisdom throughout its process. Karla Vermeulen deserves our most special recognition. We thank Karla for her superb, skillful, and untiring research and editorial assistance, smoothing rough writing spots with a dedicated, keen, and professional eye that blended so well with her special gift for understanding a subject dear to our hearts.

We deeply appreciate Dr. Susan Hamilton's accessibility, practice insight, and careful review of this text. She has always made the time and created the space to discuss disaster mental health issues. Given her demanding role as Disaster Mental Health Senior Associate at the American Red Cross national head-quarters in Washington, DC, we realize just how significant the continuing gift of her time and expertise has been.

We are grateful to our teachers, friends, and colleagues for their guidance, advice, and friendship. We would particularly like to acknowledge Dr. Phyllis Freeman, Dr. Gerald Benjamin, Ekpo Bassey, Liz Sarita-Hannah, Jack Herrmann, Myrna Seigle, Anne Richards-Rothe, Doris Green, Helaine Shimel, Dr. Pam Atkins, Dr. Susan Mathes, Dr. Robert Raymond, Dr. Juliana Reiss, Dr. Mark Sherman, Dottie Brier, Dr. Roger Sherwood, Nicholas Laino, Jessica Purcell, Sgt. Nancy Rosado, and Maggie Tramontin. At distinct moments, they each carried us forward with their vision and friendship.

Quite especially, we thank Gail Messenger and Dave Gusick for their care and partnership.

We thank the many disaster volunteers who we have worked with, who shared their insights and thoughts with us, and who were our companions in the trenches. All together, they have contributed to our understanding of disaster mental health. We are particularly grateful to our comrades, disaster workers from the American Red Cross in Greater New York and Ulster County.

If there's a book you really want to read but it hasn't been written yet, then you must write it.

Toni Morrison

Introduction

CHAPTER **1**

Every disaster is unique, yet there are distinct commonalities in people's reactions to these catastrophic events. Regardless of their cause—be it fire, flood, or an intentional terrorist act—disasters bring human suffering in their wake. Disasters are seldom neat and tidy. They carry with them the sights and sounds of devastation and multiple losses, eliciting profound emotional reactions. It can be stunning to view the level of destruction, the ruined personal belongings, and the scattered human remains we may see after an explosion, powerful storm, or airplane crash. There are the losses not only of life or health but also irreplaceable possessions, beloved pets, and a sense of control over one's destiny. Those who directly experience a disaster, as well as their families and those who try to help them, are all affected.

As such, disasters represent traumatic and potentially overwhelming events. Disasters leave people feeling powerless or in fear for their lives; survivors' fundamental sense of safety is violated as events exceed the limit of what they thought they could control. Treasured basic beliefs that have been held up to the moment of impact are challenged. Exposure to disaster stress results in physiological, cognitive, behavioral, emotional, and spiritual reactions. Given the scope and scale of individual responses, how can you, as a helping professional, assist people through the experience of disaster?

1

THE PURPOSE OF THIS BOOK

Disaster Mental Health: Theory and Practice is a book about the psychology of disasters and about how to thoughtfully help people who are impacted by such dramatic, life-changing events. Its primary aim is to support and empower those mental health students and practitioners who will be working in the trenches of disaster's aftermath. An ancillary goal is to arm disaster responders who are not mental health specialists with sufficient knowledge to consider the role of mental health and how it might be helpful. In this capacity, the book can be a tool in preparedness and planning. A third, broader goal is to further legitimize the still-developing field of disaster mental health by offering a synthesis of trends, discoveries, and related concepts.

As dedicated disaster mental health practitioners, we were eager to learn—and share—as much information as possible. Current knowledge about disaster mental health is widely spread out across different pockets, including such disparate areas as trauma studies and emergency management. So, this book is meant to gather together information into one consolidated volume. We freely acknowledge that to be fully comprehensive is an impossible ideal in such a rapidly developing field. Realistically, we have strived to capture enough of the basics to prepare readers to take an active and productive role in a specialty that needs more trained responders.

The volume ahead focuses on the theory and practice of this growing specialty. In our two main sections, we examine what disaster mental health helpers do and why we do it. Our mission is to be both informative and practical; we hope to stimulate thought and discussion and to enhance the field. Toward all these ends, we hope this book helps, now more than ever.

We begin this journey by laying down the structure of the book and clarifying some basic, core issues early on; then subsequent chapters explore each aspect of theory and practice in detail.

DEFINING DISASTER

Crisis. Emergency. Critical incident. Disaster. Terrorism. Trauma. Are all these terms interchangeable? Although related, each word has a slightly different meaning.

There are two key features that define the term **crisis.** First is the implication of a turning point or crucial stage. Second is the idea that an event functions as a crisis when it overtaxes an individual's resources and coping mechanisms. A crisis creates a time of instability as a survivor struggles to regain his or her balance; it generates difficulty or danger as internal and external shifts occur.

A disaster could qualify as a crisis, but not all crises are disasters. Crises have come to have slightly different meanings in different circumstances (though the two core features hold true). There are expected **developmental crises,** turning points around key issues that are relevant for a particular time of life, such as the identity crisis of adolescence or the challenges of adjusting to retirement. Unlike the often predictable developmental crises, **situational crises** are those events that occur unexpectedly, such as losing one's job without prior notice or facing the loss of a loved one through sudden death or some other form of unpredictable separation. A crisis is a process, and an individual's response to a crisis can be seen as existing on a continuum of adaptation. It is common to read in the literature on crisis intervention that the Chinese symbol for crisis also means change and growth. This would be the ideal outcome: mastery of a potentially crippling event so that the individual remains intact and optimistic, with new ways to push forward through life.

An **emergency** is an urgent crisis that requires immediate action. In an emergency, people's lives can be at stake. Without a response, the potential for escalation is often significant. Emergency services responders such as police and firefighters go to the scene of an event and use their skills to contain this kind of crisis. Other professionals, such as emergency room doctors and nurses, usually await the arrival of those involved at hospitals and makeshift triage areas.

A **critical incident** is a specific, formal term used in different specialty areas to connote those events that are nonroutine, unexpected, and uncontrollable; they have significant consequences and require a quick response. In the area of information security, a critical incident could be a security breach via hacking. In the world of emergency services, a critical incident might be the death of a colleague during a routine operational response. For those in a variety of industries, recent critical incidents include instances of employee workplace violence.

A **disaster** implies sudden misfortune that results in the loss of life or property or in other forms of great harm or damage. Disaster's impact extends beyond just one person, affecting, devastating, and sometimes eradicating an entire community. This wider net is a defining feature of what constitutes a disaster. This word's origins—it literally means "bad stars"—are rooted in the notion that such an occurrence is ill starred or ill fated and beyond one's control. And this is precisely the reaction that experiencing a disaster often induces: the feeling that, quite suddenly, the rug has been pulled out from underneath survivors, leaving chaos behind. The individuals impacted are left struggling to regain their footing in what for them is a changed universe.

The word *disaster* is sometimes used in other senses. For example, in the world of business, disasters may also be unforeseen events that ravage a company or industry and can create huge financial losses. Another common (if circular) definition of *disaster* includes any event that has disastrous consequences. Although experiences such as rape, domestic violence, motor vehicle accidents, or murder can hold disastrous results for those personally involved, reactions to these overwhelming events are generally contained within an individual survivor and their immediate circle. For purposes of this book, we retain the concept of disasters as having a wider impact, ranging from a local community to a specified region to an entire nation (though we do recognize that experiencing traumatic individual events can put survivors at risk for intensified reactions if they later experience a disaster). Therefore, we remain centered on the definition of *disaster* as a natural or human-caused catastrophe that causes destruction, frequently including loss of life, with permanent changes to an environment and a community.

Hence, although they are broader than a single critical incident, *disasters are both emergencies and crises*. Weaver (1995) suggests that disasters must be social occasions: A number of people are involved, and there must be public agreement regarding observable damage, social disruption, perceptions of the seriousness of the impact, official disaster declarations, and demands for action. Once a critical threshold is reached in terms of disruption, devastation, loss of life, and stability, an event can be considered disastrous, regardless of the source. The Federal Emergency Management Agency (FEMA, n.d.) describes *disasters* as "unforeseen and often sudden events that cause great damage, destruction and human suffering. Though often caused by nature, disasters can have human origins. Wars and civil disturbances that destroy homelands and displace people are included among the causes of disasters. Other causes can be: building collapses, blizzards, drought, epidemics, earthquakes, explosions, fires, floods, hazardous materials or transportation incidents, hurricanes, nuclear incidents, tornados or volcanoes."

Since the attacks of September 11, 2001, **terrorism** has received special awareness within the United States, and some experts have defined it as a specific type of disaster (Ursano, Fullerton, & Norwood, 2003). Acts of terrorism usually extend beyond the individuals who were personally impacted to severely disrupt a community and induce powerful feelings of fear while eroding a valuable sense of safety. These events are crimes. They involve violence or the threat of violence and are often coupled with specific demands. Targets are mainly civilians or noncombatants, "innocent" victims used as a means to an end. Motivation is political and actions are designed to achieve maximum publicity. Perpetrators are usually members of an organized group, and unlike other criminals, they often claim credit for what they have done. An intrinsic aim of terrorism is to produce psychological effects far beyond the immediate physical damage.

Terrorism represents the primitive face of evil. An act of terrorism is considered to be *malum in se,* or "wrong in itself." It is illegal by its very nature because it violates the natural, moral, or public principles of a civilized society. "A terrorist is a member of a group lacking in rightful authority who intentionally commits acts of violence against the citizens of a legitimate state to use the [ensuing] publicity and fear generated . . . merely as a means to alter public policy" (Fromkin, 1975). Because terrorism combines the potent risk factors of intentional malevolence, extreme disruption, and horrific depravity and destruction, its potential impact on psychological and community functioning is great. In a telling spin on the term *weapons of mass destruction,* experts are calling such threats "weapons of mass disruption."

Finally, the concept of **trauma** has evolved and gained increasing relevance and importance over time as our universal understanding and appreciation of trauma has deepened. *Trauma* is derived from the Greek word for "wounded." **Physical trauma** refers to an injury or bodily damage that is caused by violence or accident. **Psychological trauma** refers to an emotional wound or shock of lasting effect. The two are intimately related. Emergencies, crises, critical incidents, terrorism, and disasters are all potentially traumatizing due to the tremendous stress each type of event can cause. Traumatic events interfere with people's ability to be as emotionally healthy as possible. After it was finally recognized that trauma can undermine psychological functioning, the field of mental health has strived to devise ways to prevent, lessen, or even stop its harm.

DISASTERS AND MENTAL HEALTH

The goal of disaster mental health (DMH) interventions is to help sustain and support individuals and communities as they experience and integrate extremely painful and disruptive events. This assistance is valuable because, subsequent to being involved in a disaster, many individuals will manifest common post-traumatic reactions. But it will be important to remember throughout our discussion that even exposure to the most horrific of events does not consistently dictate the extent to which an individual's well-being and overall functioning will be challenged.

We should make it clear that, although we have defined which types of event that we consider to be disasters throughout this book, there is less consensus in the DMH field as a whole. As Lystad (1988) writes, "Typological categorization of disasters has been repeatedly attempted and yet the field lacks a single agreed-upon definition of disaster as well as a comprehensive typology of disaster characteristics and consequences." For example, in their major study of the reactions of survivors of a variety of disastrous events, Norris et al. (2002) exclude acts of terrorism and dislocation, stating that such occurrences, which take place within the context of ongoing political conflicts, are not discrete disasters. This question of inclusion also extends to wars and civil disturbances, which are sometimes described as "planned" disasters. Both are deeply traumatizing events with disastrous consequences for those affected. Yet the populations involved are distinguished as military and civilian, and the methods through which interventions and aid are provided are different than in "routine" DMH services delivery. The help that can be offered in such circumstances is constricted by these distinctions as well as by the very dangerous circumstances involved during conflicts where the usual rules of engagement have eroded. As a result, wars are not generally included in the events targeted by DMH professionals.

From a DMH perspective, disasters can be seen as events that (1) tend to be swiftly occurring and often have an intense and acute beginning, (2) have a community-wide, collective impact, (3) involve significant disruption of biopsychosocialcultural resources, (4) affect all those who are either directly impacted or who come to help, and (5) usually include a spectrum of losses. This description is broad and represents a way of listing disaster's common elements rather than an explicit definition. Disasters may be small, medium, or large in scale, and they may affect local, national, or international populations (Parkes, 1997). Ursano et al. (2003) observe that a disaster is not simply one traumatic event; rather, disasters incorporate multiple traumatic events occurring sequentially or concomitantly. As a result, disasters are characteristically unpredictable, even if there is advance warning. One calamity leads to another. Disaster responders never think they have "seen it all"—there is always some new and unimaginable way that events and elements combine. This is why these events are so challenging for all involved: It is tough to wrap your arms around chaos.

DESCRIBING THOSE IMPACTED

What is a good term to use when talking about those who have been involved in disasters? Shall we call them survivors? Victims? Clients? When the American Red Cross first created its Disaster Mental Health Services activity in the early 1990s, its workers initially used the term *victim,* but sensitivity regarding this term soon arose. Calling someone a victim seemed disempowering; the word also evoked images of the deceased rather than the living. *Survivor* soon gained popularity because it drew attention to a person's strength and inherent ability to heal and overcome a terrible event. But, this, too, has lost some appeal lately.

Both *victim* and *survivor* are static terms and often feel like labels. Disaster's effects are not circumscribed or neatly delimited: Everyone who is exposed to a disaster is impacted, regardless of their role or how they became involved in the event. This includes first responders, the press, medical personnel, and DMH workers. Are these people also victims or survivors? Currently there is no "best" or fully inclusive term that recognizes the seriousness and traumatic effects of a disaster while simultaneously acknowledging differences and resiliency in those impacted. While we are aware of the linguistic challenge of finding terms that do justice to those who have endured the unendurable and to those who share the experience through their responder roles, in this volume we use *victim, survivor, client,* and *those impacted* interchangeably.

Whatever the DMH field ultimately chooses to call them, we do know for certain that those directly affected by disasters, especially those who must endure great loss and exposure to trauma, need and deserve to be validated, acknowledged, and empowered. This is often reflected in the postdisaster emphasis of "never forgetting" disaster's ravages.

WHO IS MOST AT RISK FROM DISASTERS?

Amid the growing awareness of a disaster's impact on *everyone* who is in some way connected to it, the DMH field is struggling with identification of who may be viewed as more likely to experience the most salient posttraumatic effects. There have been two broad approaches to recognizing risk, one focusing on preevent characteristics and the other on the disaster experience itself.

The former approach seeks to identify **vulnerable populations** by determining which inherent or preexisting attributes may make a particular group more likely to suffer psychologically after a disaster. Candidates for this category have included children, the elderly, women, the disabled, refugees, and the seriously mentally ill. Lystad (1988) notes that socially disadvantaged groups are particularly vulnerable because disasters tend to intensify their social disadvantage. Such groups lack resources in general, and this starting deficit just gets worse after a disaster. Poorer families also have the most trouble acquiring aid and recovering from disasters (Bolin & Bolton, 1986). Ursano et al. (2003) propose that other high-risk groups include survivors who had prior exposure to trauma, those with a history of mental illness, and those who lack supportive relationships.

Ursano et al. (2003) also suggest that those who are directly exposed to disaster should be considered a high-risk group, providing support for experience as a determinant of risk. Indeed, regardless of age, gender, or role, research has consistently found a **dose–response relationship,** with greatest disaster exposure leading to greatest suffering. This means that primary victims and those witnessing a disaster directly are expected to be at greatest risk, even if they are members of populations that are traditionally viewed as resilient.

Identifying which survivors are truly at elevated risk is gaining increasing attention in the field. Some groups have fluctuated between being seen as vulnerable or not. Children are now clearly understood to be vulnerable in disasters due to their developmental status and dependency. But are the elderly at risk? Multiple studies of the psychological sequelae among this group do not demonstrate that they fare any worse emotionally than younger adults. However, the reality is that the elderly tend to underreport their problems and seek less assistance than other ages, so their reactions may simply go unnoticed. And they are a heterogeneous population that includes the "frail elderly" with impoverished health and circumstances as well as the better-functioning "well elderly"; these subsets may have very different levels of risk and resilience. Another group that appears to be of concern is that of first responders and rescue, recovery, and relief workers. Norris et al. (2002) found that first responders were among groups that had the lowest frequency of postdisaster negative reactions. Other studies have found mixed results, with certain variables such as experience, age, and type of exposure influencing outcome. Yet first responders are consistently cited to be at risk due to their regular exposure.

As these conflicting findings demonstrate, sorting out who may be at particular risk in the wake of disaster is difficult, but it is essential if DMH helpers and other disaster responders are to distribute limited resources effectively. Disasters of increasing scope and intensity may reduce individuals' and communities' abilities to respond to survivors' needs, but predisaster planning and preparedness can help identify the populations that may be prone to extreme reactions, allowing resources to be directed where they are most needed. Therefore, clarifying who is truly vulnerable is an important step in allocating DMH assistance wisely.

After all of this discussion of *who* may be at risk from disasters, let us touch briefly on *what* negative psychological outcomes they are at risk for. While generalized posttraumatic distress may be the most common reaction, clinical psychological reactions following disaster can include posttraumatic stress disorder (PTSD), anxiety, and depression. Survivors may also experience somatization (expressing emotional distress through physical symptoms) as well as complicated grief and bereavement. Disasters can wreak havoc with people's belief systems and their ability to cope. These effects can serve to undermine healthy functioning in subtle ways as well as in evident disorders. (We discuss reactions to disaster—both typical and problematic, obvious and subtle—in detail in future chapters.)

THE MISSION OF DISASTER MENTAL HEALTH

Disaster mental health is psychology in action, practically applied to disaster relief. It borrows from different branches of mental health, emergency management, and humanitarian aid principles. Because disasters are unlike any other experience, DMH is quite different from other areas of mental health practice. Disaster mental health's "clients" are not only the direct victims of disasters but also include those who offer safety, solace, and sustenance to those victims; therefore, DMH practitioners themselves are included among the impacted. The importance of self-care for DMH practitioners is emphasized throughout the book.

Given the chaos that disasters can produce, a timely and effective health-care response that includes a mental health component can be critical to a survivor's and a community's safety and recovery. Disaster relief organizations make efforts to alleviate damage, loss, hardship, or suffering, yet restoration after disasters is a complex, sensitive phenomenon. Disasters are change agents by their very nature. They test the integrated functioning of people and communities. Lives, culture, and beliefs may be altered forever, and new coping skills need to be developed. Providing the right kinds of support as individuals and groups wade through this process so that they can reassess their situations and make good decisions is an important role that DMH helpers play. As Weaver (1995) notes, "Disaster mental health is a growing field of practice designed to help victims, and the helpers who rush to their aid, to learn to cope effectively with the extreme stresses they will face in the aftermath of a disaster."

The global goals of disaster mental health are **prevention** and **mitigation,** but defining those goals more narrowly has proven difficult. *Mitigation* is a term commonly used in emergency management to imply "damage control" and alleviation of the effects of a disaster. *Prevention* generally refers to education and interventions intended to halt the development of a disorder before it has a chance to become established. Both are clearly worthy aims, yet determining how to measure our success at pursuing them is an ongoing challenge. As a subspecialty of the larger mental health discipline, DMH seeks a foundation in empirical research and outcome-based practices, but there is no current evidence as to what interventions alleviate harm or prevent the occurrence of a specific pathological outcome (although there are several interventions that can be identified as lessening general posttrauma distress). Therefore, general historical DMH objectives such as "prevent PTSD" or "return individuals and communities to predisaster functioning" have been modified in the pursuit of more concrete and verifiable ends.

Part of the difficulty in developing demonstrably effective DMH interventions stems from the fact that immediate reactions to severe disaster stress can often look like PTSD. After exposure to life-threatening events, people may have a heightened startle response, be generally anxious, and have problems sleeping. They may reexperience the event, especially when there are cues in the environment. But for most people, such reactions fade away over time, becoming less frequent and less intense. The disaster becomes a normal memory, which is accessed from time to time but which does not possess the immediacy of the original experience. This spontaneous recovery reflects the fact that humans are generally equipped to have adverse experiences, learn from them, and not be debilitated. Although this resilience is of course a wonderful quality, it does make it challenging for researchers to evaluate the efficacy of interventions meant to prevent PTSD because determining whether an individual's recovery was truly due to the intervention or whether it would have occurred spontaneously without any treatment can be difficult.

What are the elements of a DMH strategy that has prevention as a goal? Current practices "borrowed" from related fields such as public health or preventive medicine view prevention as circular, involving three interconnected stages. Each stage describes interventions and programs aimed at distinct groups of people based on their level of risk.

Primary prevention (preevent intervention) aims to reduce impact through psychoeducation, drills, advance warning systems, stress inoculation, and individual and community preparedness and emergency plans. This has been called "before the fact" intervention. Such *universal* prevention efforts are designed for general populations. The aim is to enhance protective factors and prevent the onset of particular problems.

Secondary prevention (early or acute intervention) aims to help during the crisis. Such *selected* prevention is more targeted toward specific subgroups that are expected to be at higher risk for particular problems. Secondary prevention approaches recognize the heightened risk status of the target or vulnerable group and then seek to reduce the effect of the risk.

Tertiary prevention (postevent intervention) occurs after impact and focuses on people who have been affected by a disaster. Also known as *indicated prevention,* these approaches target specific individuals who have already shown signs of specific problems. The aim in these programs is to prevent the progression of difficulties. Tertiary prevention is sometimes compared with treatment because the target group demonstrates a higher level of problems and needs more intensive services.

Prevention may traditionally refer to stopping problems before they start, but in its fullest sense, prevention has a broader meaning that also includes the promotion of well-being and health. It is about anticipating risk and taking action to avoid poorer outcomes. Framing mental health services as prevention recognizes individuals' strengths and potential for natural recovery, which is a core principle of DMH. As such, interventions from the least intensive to the most extensive can be seen as preventive. Prevention emphasizes survivors' potential to overcome adversity, in contrast to treatment's focus on disease and deficit. But despite this positive, strengths-based, health-promoting approach—and despite the typically higher cost of treatment—national policy and practice are more focused on responding to crisis than on prevention (Ripple & Zigler, 2003).

Disaster mental health is often equated exclusively with early intervention, but as the three-level prevention approach suggests, its reach truly extends beyond the acute (immediate postdisaster) phase where it usually gets the most attention. In particular, Ursano et al. (2003) note that preevent interventions are an important and overlooked component of DMH planning; DMH helpers also may continue to work with survivors well after the dust has settled. In general, DMH includes an understanding that mental health interventions have to be sensitive to survivors' changing needs at different points in time.

PRACTICE DIFFERENCES IN DISASTER MENTAL HEALTH

At a 2003 conference sponsored by the Disaster Mental Health Institute in South Dakota, trauma expert Yael Danieli (2003) explains that people experience a traumatic event like a disaster on three levels: the actual event; a community's reactions to the victims; and, later, what people tell themselves about it for the rest of their lives. Traditionally, mental health practitioners work exclusively with this third level, but DMH workers have the advantage of being able to impact people at the first two levels. At these levels, DMH helpers intervene by preparing and building resilience before disaster strikes and by providing a positive recovery environment in the immediate aftermath of disaster. They attempt to be helpful at the earliest, or acute, stages so that what survivors tell themselves over the months and years to come after the event is more helpful and less distorted.

To accomplish this, DMH providers need to be equipped with basic, traditional, good old-fashioned training in clinical work. This includes solid counseling and assessment skills, diagnostic capabilities, and self-awareness. Having training in crisis or emergency intervention is also essential because psychotherapy and crisis intervention must never be confused: To do so would be to deny people what they need at a very critical time.

DMH helpers will then be required to place much of what they have learned in traditional settings aside because the actual work involves a bit of an undoing of classical training.

IN TRADITIONAL CLINICAL SETTINGS

- Clients view clinicians as potential experts with whom they will work.
- Meetings last a defined time, in a "contained" setting, and clients usually arrive at a scheduled time.
- Often there is more then one session with a client, so over time a clinician derives an understanding of the client's presenting problems, coping style, and interpersonal dynamics. Clinicians make progress or treatment notes on their encounters.

IN DISASTER WORK

- Service settings may be chaotic, lacking in privacy and quiet, because there is tremendous need during disasters and time and space are often scarce. Interventions may take anywhere from 10 minutes to several hours. Settings may include shelters, schools, city streets, fields, churches, or hotels.
- It is not uncommon in DMH to see a client only once, so "instant" rapport and rapid assessment are integral with people who are experiencing extreme yet common stress reactions such as exhaustion, grief, and irritability.
- Because of the situation's targeted focus and intensity, DMH workers address pragmatic concerns while also using psychoeducational strategies and stress management techniques.

- Administrative decisions about DMH service delivery can change several times a day during disasters. DMH workers may have to alter their routines, locales, and the types of survivors with whom they are working instantaneously.

Disaster mental health has been described as "the field application of crisis intervention" (Weaver, 1995; Morgan, 1995), and there are indeed important similarities. Crisis intervention is an attempt to deal quickly with an immediate problem; DMH practice in the acute stages of a disaster has a similar focus. Yet at these moments, DMH requires even more concrete and tangible assistance than is found in "traditional" crisis intervention. In the acute impact stage, the DMH practitioner really has to make an active effort to provide for those impacted what they cannot provide for themselves, whether their needs are physical or emotional. Helpers lend structure and direction when self-direction is not possible.

Another distinguishing difference in DMH, perhaps most especially in the acute stages, is that workers are often exposed to unpleasant and even dangerous environments. They come up close and personal to the utter chaos that disasters bring. For example, some American Red Cross national disaster assignments are called "hardship assignments." This means that due to the nature of a particular disaster, a volunteer's living environment will be similar to that of the victims. They may not have access to running water or telephones; they, too, may be sleeping on cots in a shelter. A parallel danger occurs emotionally as well. In becoming intimate with tragedy, terrible losses, and immense heartbreak, DMH workers absorb psychological pain and despair. This can also lead to their own difficulties with self-regulation and perspective.

Disaster survivors often do not know they are in need of mental health support. They are often overwhelmed. Emotions are high but usually are channeled into intense and frenzied inquiry after loved ones or efforts to make sense of what it means that their homes are destroyed. Sometimes disaster clients may not be open to what DMH workers have to offer. This makes the clinical work very subtle. Providing assistance may require an unusual degree of tact or diplomacy.

Additionally, the range of people who DMH workers may help at disaster sites is broad: A client could be a direct survivor, a deceased victim's family member, a first responder, or a colleague. Think of concentric circles: The first would include those immediately impacted—that is, the ambulatory survivors and their families and support systems. Next, there are community members and witnesses to the horror, followed by rescue and recovery workers, relief agency staff, and volunteers. All are impacted by their experiences, and all are equally worthy of DMH services.

SO, WHAT IS IT THAT WE DO?

In a documentary about the attacks of 9/11/2001 (*In Memorium*, 2002), Rudolf Guiliani, the mayor of New York at that time, described his personal reaction in sorting out how best to help his citizens this way: "How do we figure out our way through this? How do we figure out how to give people the opportunity to let out the grief that they feel and the meaning that they need and at the same time organize themselves so they move on with their lives? There isn't a right way to do it: you just try." Sometimes, in our experience, the actual practice of DMH work feels precisely like this.

On the most basic level, DMH workers provide presence: We bear witness to horrific human experiences. How is this presence helpful? It serves as ballast in a chaotic, anxious situation. We are doing our part to bring down the anxiety level that surrounds us and to soothe the hyperarousal that keeps survivors off balance. We "join" our clients where they are.

Our presence is also active. We scan the disaster scene to identify potential signs of distress. We are continuously making assessments and identifying who may be in need. We make ourselves accessible by "walking and talking" and by being strategic in where we place ourselves. Our nonverbal behavior is unintrusive but attentive. Our goal is prevention, with a strong emphasis on early intervention.

Those directly immersed in a disaster have specific emotional needs, which are often magnified by the collectivity of the disaster scene. In crisis, people move into dysfunctional thinking. They start "catastrophizing" and generalizing from an awful experience, imagining that because their present circumstances are so terrible the rest of their lives will be equally awful. So we make efforts to restructure cognitive and physiological reactions early on. Informal, low-keyed approaches make it nonthreatening for those we are seeking to help to discuss their feelings, reactions, thoughts, and concerns, placing their reactions in perspective.

People impacted by disaster often need reassurance that their reactions make sense and will subside in time. Grief and shock are physically draining and exhausting, and so we share what we know about stressors and their effects. We describe possible methods of coping. This is part of resiliency building. Our focus is short term and wellness oriented; we do not address the client's fundamental personality. We reach into our standard bag of clinical tools and use time-tested techniques like active listening, problem solving, and advocacy. We work at building rapport and do what we can to "grease the skids" in this regard: We break bread together, make small talk, and hang out. We do what we can to weave connection, connection, and more connection. We comfort and support and listen to those who want to tell their story. We become auxiliary egos, normalizing the situation for those who are attempting to absorb larger-than-life occurrences.

CHARACTERISTICS OF A DISASTER MENTAL HEALTH WORKER

What qualities does a good DMH worker possess? DMH work takes place at a grassroots level, so the worker has to be willing and able to build comfortable relationships based on human-to-human exchanges. To accomplish this, you have to know yourself. Your perspective must be grounded in empathy, genuineness, and respect, essential qualities in counseling that can help you to establish positive relationships quickly in disasters. You also have to have the ability to provide therapeutic assistance without "therapizing" disaster survivors or workers.

You have to be genuine. Being real is essential. People in crisis have strong needs, and if you are immediately accessible, you can offer them a place to put their concerns.

Calmness is a cherished attribute in this work. At disaster sites, undercurrents of anxiety, despair, rage, and uncertainty break loose at different times as things shift in the recuperation process. DMH workers offer reassurance through their poise, voice, and measured approach.

Flexibility, a key to mental health, is also a key to disaster survival. This can become quite a challenge when you are working under dynamic conditions and things are shifting constantly. DMH workers have to be willing to take on different roles as dictated by the overall recovery mission. Yet the work also involves periods of time when you are not utilized at all, where there does not appear to be any work to do, or in the frantic activity of coordination, you are not given an assignment.

DMH work can be quite stimulating as you are challenged in ways that draw on the very fiber of your being. You are working with powerful emotions and exciting scenes. It is hard sometimes—yet essential—to step back from these and slow your pace down. You have to maintain good boundaries, despite the seeming informality of the work. Although erring on the side of being human is natural during times of disaster, you do need to possess and model good self-care and remain alert to overextending yourself. Hence, this role requires the ability to weave in and out of intense closeness while retaining a professional identity.

REWARDS OF DISASTER WORK

DMH practitioners get to be with people at critical junctures in their lives. These are extremely delicate, disturbing, and touching times for those undergoing them, and you can make an immense difference to others by your willingness to feel their pain and be with them. The affirmation of acute grief, fear, and despair; the ability to sense emotional, cognitive and physical needs; and the willingness to offer care on all these different levels—all these services can have an influence how people fare in the long run. This work is a privilege.

There is a strong sense of camaraderie that develops among disaster responders. Colleagues are often seen as kindred spirits who have shared a unique (and hard to describe to outsiders) day in the trenches. DMH workers are placed in remarkable circumstances together. In this way, despite our specialization, we are like other emergency responders and stand to learn much from their particular ways of coping that underscore bonding and loyalty.

DMH work hones clinical skills. Helpers work with a diversity of clients and use a range of techniques. They have to be culturally savvy, sensitive, and sharp.

Finally, it becomes hard to forget what is important in life after a day of doing such work. Disasters can lend perspective that is hard to obtain under less compelling circumstances.

THE STRUCTURE OF THIS BOOK: THEORY AND PRACTICE

Disaster Mental Health: Theory and Practice is divided in two sections. The first half of this volume is devoted to the theoretical foundations of DMH. Because the concept of DMH is relatively new, we hope to bring together different aspects of the field to lay a consolidated groundwork and rationale and to address the "why" of this work. The second half is devoted to practice elements. We examine common interventions in a practical manner, addressing the question of how we practice our craft. We also look at areas that need to be further refined.

In Chapter 2, "The Characteristics of Disaster," types of disasters and the terminology commonly used to describe them are elaborated. We discuss the subtleties involved in differentiating between natural and human-caused events and how these and other distinctions impact people's reactions.

Chapter 3 provides "A History of Disaster Mental Health" that contextualizes the different currents—social, political, psychological—that led to the field's inception and growth. Included is an overview of the genesis of PTSD.

A core concept underlying DMH is a belief in people's abilities to deal with disastrous experiences. Hence, much of Chapter 4, "Reactions and Risk Factors," reviews common, predictable, "normal" reactions that survivors are likely to experience as they progress through stages from impact to recovery. These stages are outlined to help the mental health responder understand a victim's evolving psychological state.

Chapter 5, "Extreme Reactions," continues to examine possible responses to disasters, with an emphasis on the more severe reactions that people can experience. Acute stress disorder, PTSD, comorbid conditions, and the psychophysiology of trauma exposure are examined. Additionally, we review the origins and diagnosis of complicated and traumatic grief.

Chapter 6, "Vulnerable Populations," examines the literature regarding the risk potential for key groups that DMH helpers are likely to encounter, including children, the elderly, the disabled, and the seriously mentally ill.

Then, having outlined the theoretical underpinnings of the field, we move into the second section of this book, which emphasizes the practice of DMH. This section begins with "The Challenges of Counseling in Chaos," Chapter 7. This is a largely practical, hands-on chapter intended to inform DMH practitioners about what they might expect when responding to a disaster. The nuts and bolts of this work are introduced.

Chapter 8, "Psychological First Aid," offers a summary of what is now considered the intervention of choice in the immediate aftermath of disaster. We elaborate on the elements of this intervention and review questions about its effectiveness.

Although psychological first aid represents an apparently solid practice in DMH work, it is just one of a variety of methods that can be used to modify the possible negative outcome of disaster experience. Other strategies that may also bolster and stabilize disaster victims are described in Chapter 9, "Early Interventions Beyond Psychological First Aid."

Chapter 10, "Debriefing and the Impact of Disaster Trauma on First Responders," offers a perspective on another specific and widely used intervention, debriefing. Originally intended to help first responders talk about particularly troubling on-the-job events in a structured and safe way, of late debriefing has become more broadly applied and more controversial. This debate about the practice is reviewed, as are the specific needs of first responders.

Chapter 11, "Long-Term Treatment: Continuity of Care," addresses ongoing mental health care for survivors. This represents the final leg of the prevention cycle of DMH, wherein disasters' long-term impact is acknowledged. Appreciating disasters' potential lasting effects helps link disaster planning at all stages to perspectives on how those most affected can be treated.

The book concludes with Chapter 12, "New Directions in Disaster Mental Health." This chapter provides a discussion of the many unresolved issues in our field as well as an introduction to new areas that might be worthy of attention in this developing specialty.

Our ultimate aim in writing this text was to produce a comprehensive, coherent guide to the previously scattered body of knowledge about DMH. As you will learn in working your way through the chapters, this is already a helpful young field that will only be strengthened by future efforts to demonstrate the effectiveness of the tools that we use. Whether you are interested in researching best practices or in applying them directly, we hope that this book equips you to help those impacted by disasters in their time of need.

References

Bolin, R., & Bolton, P. (1986). *Race, religion, and ethnicity in disaster recovery.* Boulder: University of Colorado Institute of Behavioral Science.

Danieli, Y. (2003, September 20). Presentation at the Sixth Annual Conference on Innovation in Disaster Psychology: Time for a Paradigm? Reflecting on the Past, Looking to the Future, held at the University of South Dakota, Rapid City.

FEMA (Federal Emergency Management Agency). (n.d.). Retrieved December 18, 2004, from http://www.fema.gov.

Fromkin, D. (1975). The strategy of terrorism. *Foreign Affairs, 53,* 683–698.

In memorium: NYC, 9/11/01. (2002). Brad Grey Pictures.

Lystad, M. (Ed.). (1988). *Mental health response to emergencies: Theory and practice.* New York: Brunner/Mazel.

Morgan, J. (1995). American Red Cross disaster mental health: Implementation and recent developments. *Journal of Mental Health Counseling, 17,* 291–391.

Norris, F. H., Friedman, M. J., Watson, P. J., Byrne, C. M., Diaz, E., & Kaniasty, K. (2002). 60,000 disaster victims speak: Part I. An empirical review of the empirical literature, 1981–2001. *Psychiatry: Interpersonal & Biological Processes, 65,* 207–239.

Parkes, C. M. (1997). A typology of disasters. In D. Black & M. Newman (Eds.), *Psychological trauma: A developmental approach* (pp. 81–93). London: Royal College of Physicians.

Ripple, C. H., & Zigler, E. (2003). Research, policy, and the federal initiatives for children. *American Psychologist, 58*(6/7), 482–491.

Ursano, R. J., Fullerton, C. S., & Norwood, A. E. (Eds.). (2003). *Terrorism and disaster: Individual and community mental health interventions.* Cambridge, England: Cambridge University Press.

Weaver, J. (1995). *Disasters: Mental health interventions.* Sarasota, FL: Professional Resource Press/Professional Resource Exchange.

First there was Chaos, the vast immeasurable abyss,
Outrageous as a sea, dark, wasteful, wild.

John Milton

The Characteristics of Disaster

In this chapter, we attempt to describe and classify the chaotic events known as disasters. But chaos does not lend itself easily to classification, and every disaster is unique. Each has its own characteristics that shape client reactions, and counseling interventions need to be custom-made to best serve the specific needs created by each particular disaster.

In the aftermath of disaster, survivors, plagued with confusion, ask in bewilderment, "What happened?" "How could this have happened?" "What was the cause of the fire or plane crash?" "Could I have done more to protect myself, my loved ones, and my home from harm?" "Is the disaster truly over, or will it return?" The answers are important to survivors as they try to find meaning and make sense of their postdisaster world, but they vary widely depending on the characteristics of the event experienced. Therefore, we now provide some basic information on the nature of disaster, to help you help survivors find the answers that they need. The catalog of disasters outlined in this chapter is not meant to be exhaustive. Some of what is reviewed may be familiar; other more obscure aspects, important to mental health professionals, are also discussed.

NO TWO DISASTERS ARE ALIKE

When you first begin thinking about the impact of disasters on mental health, it may seem as if the type of event would be irrelevant—that only the amount and kind of harm caused should really matter to survivors. However, human psychology is complex, and reactions are influenced by factors above and beyond sheer damage. The variety of issues involved are illustrated by the following anecdote, which was told to one of the authors by another disaster mental health (DMH) counselor who had worked with victims of wildfires in Wyoming about a decade ago:

> Residents in a small town had been warned that a raging wildfire was headed their way and an evacuation order had been given. The residents had to pack their things and leave within hours. An evacuation is not an easy thing to accomplish. What precautions do you take to protect your home? Are there places within the home to store valued possessions that cannot be removed? What are the possessions that can or must be taken? Without a moving van, choices must be made, and, of course, members of the household seldom agree as to what must be protected or saved. A few days after the evacuation, the winds changed, and the residents were able to return to their homes. They were understandably exhausted and stressed. They had barely gotten settled when once again the winds changed, and the residents were forced to evacuate for a second time. This time, they reluctantly drove out of town, but some did not pack or protect their things. Most were anxious and worn out, as well as irritated and angry. They thought this would be another false alarm. It wasn't. The town burned down, leaving all the residents homeless. Those who did not take their valuables the second time were particularly devastated, overwhelmed with guilt and regret over what they could have saved.

Guilt and self-blame are always important issues in the aftermath of trauma and disaster, but the circumstances of this disaster accentuated the problem. The initial false alarm left the residents less prepared for and more vulnerable to the actual event. However understandable their inaction was due to fatigue, many really could have done better to protect their valuables. One survivor said, "I was just too damn lazy." DMH counselors often attempt to correct or question distorted cognitions and appraisal, and they try to help survivors understand how normal it is to question themselves in the aftermath of tragedy, as individuals think "I could have done better or differently." But in this case, when survivors reflected that if they had heeded the warnings they could have saved much of their property, the appraisal was not altogether incorrect. The survivors had warning, an important characteristic of some disasters, but the warning was offset by the false alarm, which reduced their motivation to make a proper evacuation the second time. These survivors clearly could have done better, and their reactions, filled with self-blame, were harder to assuage. The counseling was more difficult because it was harder to tell survivors that they need not engage in self-recrimination. In contrast, the horrific impact of Hurricane Katrina in 2005 undoubtedly contributed to the evacuation of a million more people than expected when Hurricane Rita approached the Gulf Coast region a few weeks later. There seems to be a strong correlation between people's willingness to evacuate and the actual impact of the most recent disaster.

Other types of disaster elicit different psychological concerns. For example, when TWA flight 800 crashed in 1996, leaving 229 people dead, it was of enormous importance for the victims' survivors to know whether the crash was caused by some kind of mechanical failure, or pilot error, or weather disturbance—or if it was caused by human intent and cruelty. Answers would not change the reality of their loved ones' deaths, but they still needed to know what happened. As this example shows, as the bereaved and the survivors attempt to reconstruct their lives after any disaster, they need facts and information in order to cope.

The different issues raised by these incidents illustrate the need for mental health helpers to treat each disaster as a unique event and not to try to standardize interventions. Bear that in mind as we examine a number of ways in which disastrous events are typically categorized, including scale, cause, and other variables, following a brief overview of the different temporal stages of disasters.

STAGES OF DISASTER

A disaster can be viewed as a process that evolves through stages, *time-based phases* that reflect activity level, arousal, and emotional tone. Stage theory postulates that each phase has its own core initiative, or goal. In this section, we look at stages that reflect the overall response activities that take place during a disaster's trajectory (the hypothesized *emotional* stages experienced by victims in reaction to their experiences will be discussed in Chapter 4).

Some disaster writers (Cohen & Ahearn, 1980, for example) describe three broad stages: **preimpact** (predisaster conditions, warning, threat), **impact** (impact, inventory, rescue) and **postimpact** (recovery). Other theorists (Kafrissen, Heffron, & Zusman, 1975; Raphael, 1986) expand the list to seven specific phases: warning/alarm, threat, impact, inventory, **rescue**, remedy, and recovery. Obviously not all events include all seven stages; for example, many kinds of disasters do not offer a warning period. Preceding the seven-stage model, there is a **predisaster setting** that reflects the backdrop for the other stages. It is in this predisaster setting that **disaster preparedness** and **planning** come into play and will influence how the other stages unfold.

In the **warning** or **alarm phase**, if there is one, a community and its individual members are first made aware that a disaster is looming. This is more common with natural disasters, which often have warning signs. Examples of this would be the onset of hurricane season in the U.S. Southeast. This is a distinct period that happens yearly and permits the tracking of nascent storms that might come to shore. This tracking has gone on for many years, and meteorologists have baselines that help them understand and interpret anomalies that the public should be made aware of.

The **threat phase** describes the period of imminent danger. During this phase, people and communities conduct threat assessments as to what the disaster may have in store for them. There is a great deal of decision making as people try to determine how to remain safe, whether they should shelter in place or relocate. Oftentimes, local or state governments make this decision. People brace themselves for what will happen next. The action imperative of this stage, with its focus on preparation and mobilization, serves to harness underlying anxiety and dread about the uncertainty that lies ahead.

The time when a disaster actually strikes is known as the **impact phase.** Psychologically this has been termed the *acute trauma phase*. Fear and tension are extremely high at this time, but because the focus is on survival and on enduring an event intact, panic is often held at bay. People are mostly concerned for their own welfare and for their loved ones.

Impact is followed by an **inventory phase** in which a disaster environment becomes safe and stable enough for all involved to begin to examine and categorize the extent of their damage. The period of restoration slowly begins now.

Overlapping with the inventory stage is the **rescue phase** when efforts to help victims begin earnestly and in an organized fashion. Resources begin to pour in. Closely linked to the rescue phase, is the **remedy phase.** Here, large-scale relief efforts occur. Both morale and tension are often high in this stage as survivors and helpers focus their energies on productive but often taxing activities.

The "last" phase is the **recovery,** or restoration, **phase.** Although this is the period that those impacted may have been waiting for—when some semblance of "normalcy" or initial stability is reinstated—it is also a time when the reality of what has happened can finally begin to surface.

SCOPE, INTENSITY, AND DURATION

Disasters differ with regard to scope, intensity, and duration, all measures of the size of the event. Size matters: It is highly correlated with the psychological impact of a given disaster (Norris et al., 2002a; Weaver, 1995). An event that is large in scope is more likely to impact support systems because friends and neighbors are also affected by the disaster and may not be able to offer help. Disasters large in both scope and intensity are more likely to result in evacuation and relocation, which are very stressful life experiences. A disaster that is large in scope, intensity, and duration is more likely to cause injuries, deaths, economic losses of property and jobs, and disruption of schools and businesses. What do we mean specifically by each of these three measures?

Scope refers to the number of people and structures (rather than homes) affected. Disasters small in scope can destroy a home; those large in scope can destroy a city. For example, as Hurricane Katrina clearly demonstrated in 2005, hurricanes can be quite large in scope, up to 20 to 30 miles wide (La Greca & Prinstein, 2002). A disaster with a small scope might leave support networks in place, but after a large one, normal activities are diminished as shopping, businesses, and schools are overcrowded or destroyed. Utilities might be disrupted. There might be shortages of electricity. Telephone service might be disrupted, and both the quality and the availability of water might be affected. If a disaster is large in scope, the cleanup and recovery can go on for a much longer period of time. Rubble and debris are visible for weeks and months and serve as a constant reminder of the catastrophic experience. Obviously, when a disaster destroys a single home, it will have less impact on the survivors than if the disaster destroys all homes, schools, and hospitals in the community.

Intensity is related to scope, but it is not the same thing. A disaster that is large in scope may not cause much injury or death, whereas one that is small in scope but highly intense, like some tornadoes, can kill people. About 1000 tornadoes are counted every year in the United States (more than any other country), resulting in an average of 56 deaths per year during the 1980s and 1990s (Burt, 2004). However, a small percentage of the most intense examples, so-called violent tornadoes with winds over 205 miles per hour (mph), are responsible for 70% of the tornado deaths in the country (La Greca & Prinstein, 2002). Large-scope but low-intensity disasters may not have significant long-term psychological consequences, but the reverse is usually not the case. For example, the power blackout in the U.S. Northeast in August 2003 was large in scope, causing power outages for 40 million people in eight states plus 10 million people in Canada, but there were few reported deaths and injuries. This blackout was followed a few months later by a Staten Island Ferry accident in New York City resulting in 11 deaths and many injuries. Although far fewer people were affected by the ferry accident than the blackout, it caused more impact due to its intensity.

Duration refers to the length of time that people are affected by the disaster. Disasters of uncertain duration are particularly stressful because survivors do not know when they can let down their guard. For example, earthquakes, with their aftershocks, can create anxiety and anticipation as survivors wonder when the event will truly be over. Some weather-related events—such as extreme cold, heat waves, or droughts—can last for extended periods of time; and although individual hurricanes and storms generally have a defined beginning and end, if one event follows closely after another, their combined effects can blend together for survivors. For example, the 2004 hurricane season had an unusually long duration, with Florida struck by four major hurricanes over a period of 6 weeks. One exhausted and spent resident posted a sign on the lawn in front of his house: "1 Charley, 2 Francis, 3 Ivan, 4 SALE!" At that time, Hurricane Jeanne, the fourth powerful storm to hit the state, had not yet made landfall, yet the cumulative impact of the hurricanes over an extended period had left this resident without hope.

The effects of uncertain duration are particularly difficult to cope with in disasters caused by terrorism and weapons of mass destruction, which we discuss more fully later in this chapter. These events not only result in mass casualties (large scope and intensity) but also are caused by human intent and cruelty. Survivors are upset and distraught over what has happened, and they are also terrified about what will happen in the future. One of the most difficult aspects of the attack on the World Trade Center towers in New York City was the ongoing sense of terror and foreboding that lasted long after the actual day of September 11, 2001. There were regular evacuations of buildings and subways in New York City due to bomb threats in the months afterwards, as well as anthrax attacks and the crash of flight 587, which was initially believed by most New Yorkers to have been another terrorist attack. Thus, in addition to the wide scope and high intensity of the initial attack, the duration of the disaster went on for many months as anxious citizens awaited another assault.

The scope, intensity, and duration of a disaster are the most significant determinants of survivors' reactions to the event because these dimensions correlate with threat to life, exposure to grotesque images such as injury and death, loss of family members and friends, and loss of property. The size of the event also disrupts communications so that there can be added confusion and anxiety. In the aftermath of a large disaster, the ripple effect is so far reaching that it cannot be adequately calculated. In every disaster, there are typically "primary" victims and "secondary/indirect" victims, generally those with close family or personal ties to the primary victims (NIMH, 2002). With very large disasters, the impact can extend well beyond these groups. One study (Speckhard, 2003) reported that for Americans living abroad (in or near Brussels) the attacks of 9/11 provoked fear that they could be future terrorist targets, and this triggered significant posttraumatic distress responses.

Sometimes the ripple effect from a large disaster is so great that there is a danger that we might overlook some of the people who most need care. For example, immediately after the planes crashed into the World Trade Towers, hundreds of building tradespeople rushed to the site to help speed up the elevators to assist with a more rapid evacuation. One hundred and fifty-two of these workers died, leaving behind loved ones to adjust to their deaths without the public appreciation received by families of emergency services responders who were also killed on the job. Forty thousand men and women worked through the recovery efforts at ground zero, recovering more than 30,000 body parts—at unknowable personal costs. All these people had family and friends who were also affected by the disaster through its impact on their loved one.

NATURAL VERSUS HUMAN-CAUSED DISASTER

Perhaps the most common means of classifying disaster is to distinguish between natural and human-caused events. But even this typical distinction is problematic. If an earthquake causes a poorly made structure to collapse, is the cause natural or human? The earthquake was natural, but the building collapse may have been due to bad design or cheap construction. This is more than a philosophical distinction; its implications are important for survivor reactions. To the degree that survivors believe that a disaster was not preventable—not human caused—they seem more able to adjust and come to terms with the event. When a disaster is more clearly human caused, with a person or people to blame, it is seen as something that could have been prevented. Recovery may require learning to trust people again; it may also involve seeing justice done. Those responsible for the disaster must be discovered, apprehended, and punished. Because fairness and justice are commodities that are not easy to achieve, recovery will be more difficult if they are a requirement.

Natural Disasters

From the earliest recorded history, humans have suffered from natural disasters and have explained their vulnerability and helplessness with stories and myths (Miller, 1992b). According to Greek mythology, the first god was "Chaos," out of which everything was formed. Disasters bring us back to this most unwelcome experience. Biblical stories contain many references to disasters—fires, floods, and earthquakes—as well as the helplessness that is experienced in the face of God and nature.

Humans do not thrive in a state of helplessness. We seem always to be motivated to control the world around us. There is a need to experience "agency" or control when tragedy strikes. Thus, before there was an understanding of the science of disaster, worshippers engaged in prayer or sacrifice to influence the weather and to ward off disaster. Natural disasters were often conflated with human intention. In the aftermath of disaster, some believed (some still do) that they did not pray hard or faithfully enough, that they were wicked and deserved their fate, or that they were to blame in some other way. Some believed that others must have wished or prayed to a God to show no mercy. This allowed victims to view another person or persons as contributing to a natural disaster, giving them someone to blame as a possible target for revenge and action in place of feelings of helplessness. In our modern era, it may be no less difficult to separate nature from human agency. To be sure, human carelessness and cruelty can influence and exacerbate the impact of natural disasters. However, the natural disasters listed below continue to be described as beyond human control and are sometimes referred to as "acts of God."

The likelihood of experiencing a particular natural disaster is related to location. Within the United States, urban residents are more at risk for home fires and heat waves than wildfires or volcanoes. Californians are more at risk for earthquakes than are residents in other parts of the country, while residents of the South and the Midwest are more vulnerable to tornadoes. According to the National Weather Service, Americans live in the most severe weather–prone country on earth. Each year, Americans cope with an average of 10,000 thunderstorms, 2500 floods, and 1000 tornadoes, as well as an average of 6 hurricanes (National Weather Service, 2004).

Floods are the most common natural disaster. They can be caused by thunderstorms, hurricanes, and tornadoes, but they can also result simply from heavy rains. Every state in the United States has communities at risk from flooding. Regional floods, in which a river overflows its banks, are the most common and destructive type of flood in terms of property damage, but flash floods are the most dangerous to human life because they offer no warning time (Burt, 2004). **Landslides** also occur in every state, although some states are considerably more vulnerable to these falls, slides, and flows of rock and soil.

Hurricanes occur every year but tend to strike in select regions; they are also more seasonal than floods or landslides. A Category 3 or higher hurricane, with sustained winds of over 110 mph, is considered major. A Category 4 hurricane, considered extreme, has winds over 130 mph; and a Category 5 hurricane is considered catastrophic, with winds over 155 mph (Burt, 2004). Florida took an unprecedented hit during the 2004 Atlantic hurricane season with four hurricanes and one tropical storm making landfall in the state over a 6-week period. The 2005 hurricane season was even more devastating with Hurricane Katrina creating a path of death and destruction across the Gulf Coast region and leaving most of the city of New Orleans under water.

Hurricanes can generate multiple kinds of damage. In 1992 Hurricane Andrew produced wind gusts over 175 mph, causing an estimated $27 billion of damage in southern Florida, making it the most expensive hurricane in U.S. history (as this is written, the costs from Hurricane Katrina have not yet been calculated, but they are certain to exceed Andrew's toll). In addition to damage caused by high winds, hurricanes and tropical storms also can produce tornadoes and cause inland flooding, which can in turn trigger land or mudslides. Hurricane Floyd in 1999 brought extremely heavy rains resulting in 56 deaths, including 50 from inland floods, with 35 of them in North Carolina.

Along coastlines, hurricanes create *storm surges,* which are considered to cause the greatest threats to life and property. A storm surge is a large dome of water, often 50 to 100 miles wide, that sweeps across the coastline near where the hurricane makes landfall. When a storm surge coincides with a normal high tide, it creates a powerful *storm tide.* The storm tide rose to 20 feet in South Carolina during Hurricane Hugo in 1989 and 17 feet in Florida during Hurricane Andrew in 1992. This is not a new phenomenon: On September 8, 1900, more than 6000 people were killed when a storm surge from an unexpected hurricane hit Galveston, Texas (Cross, 1992). This is believed to have been the deadliest disaster in U.S. history.

Tornadoes can strike anywhere. In the United States, they are most likely to touch down in "Tornado Alley" (Oklahoma, Texas, and Kansas), but no areas are immune. Tornadoes have been reported in mountains and valleys, over deserts and swamps, in the Gulf Coast, Hawaii, and even Alaska. Though tornadoes can happen in any season, they generally occur during spring and summer; they can strike at any time of day, but are most likely between 3:00 p.m. and 9:00 p.m. Regardless of the location or time, if conditions are right, they occur. Over 1000 tornadoes are reported annually nationwide, and as our tornado-detection systems improve, more are being reported each year. Wind speeds can reach 300 mph in deadly F-5 tornadoes, rare but monstrous phenomena that appear to occur only in the United States (Burt, 2004).

As warning systems improve and give people more time to seek shelter, the number of tornado deaths is decreasing. In the 1920s, more than 300 Americans were killed by tornadoes each year. In the 1960s and 1970s, that number decreased to about 100 a year; during the 1980s and 1990s, the number of deaths decreased further to an average of 56 per year. However, it is still quite possible for a tornado to develop with no watch or warning, in effect leaving people vulnerable (Burt, 2004).

Wildfires occur throughout the country but are more likely to occur in western states during the summer, particularly if the summer has been hot and dry. Several hundred wildfires occur in the United States every year. Some are due to lightning; some are a result of accidents often from matches, and others are caused by arson.

Earthquakes can be one of the most destructive of natural disasters, though they occur much less frequently in the United States then the previously mentioned hazards. (Although thousands of minor tremors are recorded annually in various parts of the country, most do little damage.) Earthquakes can result in significant secondary disasters such as floods from a dam break or fires due to gas-line breaks and power-line collapses. They can also cause buildings and bridges to collapse. Because major earthquakes are often followed by aftershocks that can cause further devastation, they are the only natural disasters that regularly produce anxiety and terror as survivors anticipate further destruction—an appropriate fear, given their potential for harm.

Large earthquakes with a magnitude of 5.5 to 7.0 on the Richter scale occur every few years in Alaska and California, and other serious quakes occur periodically in many regions around the world. The year 2004 brought major earthquakes in Bam, Iran (leaving about a thousand people dead), off Sumatra in Indonesia (triggering the tsunami that left hundreds of thousands of people dead), and in Morocco, Japan, and the United States, where a 6.0 earthquake on September 28 near the town of Parkfield, California, caused no deaths. This spate of quakes around the world was perhaps no coincidence but rather the result of tectonic plates rearranging themselves, in keeping with the theory that a rupture on one tectonic boundary may result in another such rupture on another part of the planet. Perhaps demonstrating this effect, in 1906, the year that an earthquake destroyed the city of San Francisco, there were an unusually large number of major quakes around the world. Thus, survivors' concerns about aftershocks may not be misplaced (Winchester, 2004).

The United States has the dubious honor of ranking third in the world, after Japan and Indonesia, for our number of active **volcanoes**. Since 1980, as many as five volcanoes have erupted each year in the United States. Fortunately, however, large eruptions in the United States are rare, occurring only once in every 1000 to 5000 years, most likely in Hawaii or Alaska. Volcanoes erupt on a smaller scale in the Cascade Mountain Range in Washington, Oregon, and California on an average of once to twice each century; the most recent example was the powerful Mount Saint Helens eruption of 1980. Volcanoes produce a wide variety of hazards that directly destroy property and kill people. Ash clouds from large explosive eruptions can also endanger people and property hundreds of miles away and affect global climate (*Talking About Disaster*, 2004).

Droughts can occur in any region of the country, though they seem to happen less frequently than other disasters, at the rate of one every few years. However, in 2004 the *New York Times* (Johnson & Murphy, 2004) reported that the West, including Arizona, California, Colorado, Nevada, New Mexico, Utah, and Wyoming, may experience significant water shortages in the years to come as a result of overdevelopment and a miscalculation that the relatively wet weather across the region in the last century would continue. The expected precipitation has not continued, and the reporters contend that the overbuilding in the West may turn out to be a colossal blunder. From a global perspective, drought has been by far the deadliest of all disasters, causing over 500,000 deaths from 1980 to 2000, mostly in undeveloped countries (Quirk, 2005).

Tsunamis, sometimes mislabeled as "tidal waves," are gigantic ocean waves that can impact coastal areas. They are often a result of earthquakes or underwater volcanoes. As the water in a tsunami nears the shallower area near a coastline, it may rise to several feet or, in rare cases, tens of feet, and can cause great loss of life and property damage when it comes ashore. Tsunamis can also travel upstream in coastal estuaries and rivers, with damaging waves extending farther inland than the immediate coast. A tsunami can occur during any season of the year and at any time, day or night. Since 1946, six tsunamis have killed more than 350 people in the United States in Hawaii, in Alaska, and on the West Coast (Curtis, 1992).

On December 26, 2004, a powerful underwater earthquake off the western coast of Sumatra displaced trillions of tons of water in a few seconds. The water pushed outward at the speed of a jet plane. As it neared shore, the speed slowed and enormous waves formed and deluged 12 countries bordering the Indian Ocean, killing more than 280,000 people (Zanetti, Schwartz, & Enz 2005).

Heat is the number-two weather killer in this country, second only to cold waves and blizzards. Heat can kill by pushing the human body beyond its limits. Under normal conditions, the body's internal thermostat produces perspiration that evaporates and cools the body. However, in extreme heat and high humidity, evaporation is slowed and the body must work extra hard to maintain a normal temperature. The elderly, young children, and those who are sick or overweight are more likely to become victims of extreme heat.

A heat wave in Europe in August 2003 is estimated to have caused as many as 35,000 deaths in France, Germany, Spain, and Italy (Valelly, 2004). Closer to home, a heat wave in the summer of 1995 was responsible for 739 deaths in Chicago alone (Klinenberg, 2002). Extreme heat and humidity associated with heat waves directly killed an average of 235 Americans for the 10-year period from 1993 to 2002, and this number appears to be increasing.

Blizzards and **cold waves** are disasters that are often overlooked in the literature, yet they can be the most hazardous kind of events. A major winter storm can last for several days and be accompanied by high winds, freezing rain or sleet, heavy snowfall, and cold temperatures. People can become trapped at home, without utilities or other services, and heavy snowfall and blizzards can trap motorists in their cars where they can freeze to death. Every year there are also deaths attributed to people attempting to walk for help in blizzards (National Disaster Education Coalition, 2004).

A final note on extreme weather conditions: There seems little doubt that there has been global warming over the past 25 years. However, according to Burt (2004), there is no evidence that global warming has created more extreme weather than has occurred in the past. Weather may appear to be more severe, both because media reports can bring these events to our attention with great sensationalism and because more people are living in areas affected by extreme weather, but weather has always had the power to cause great destruction.

Although there is no doubt about the evidence of global warming, future research will determine if it is causing more extreme weather.

Turning to a different kind of natural disaster, an **epidemic** is an outbreak of a contagious disease that spreads rapidly and affects an unusually large number of people over an extensive geographic area. This type of disaster is not likely to result in property damage but, by definition, causes illness and possibly death. Thus, an epidemic may be the most traumatic of disasters. During a typical year in the United States, 30,000 to 50,000 people die as a result of influenza virus infection, but the number killed can grow much vaster. The 1918–1919 flu *pandemic* (an epidemic affecting people in many different countries) was the most destructive in recorded history, killing between 50 and 100 million people (Osterholm, 2005). The virus was extremely lethal, with many of the deaths occurring among young adults, a group usually not so affected by influenza.

It has been noted that the United States is woefully unprepared in almost every respect for the inevitable next flu pandemic. There is a lack of vaccine as well as insufficient industrial capacity to produce enough vaccine in time. There is no detailed operational blueprint for responding to a flu pandemic that would address the issues of a health care–system's ability to rapidly expand beyond normal services, known as *surge capacity*. There is a lack of general resources for health care, including food supplies and many other products and services that would be needed for an effective response. There is no detailed plan for staffing the temporary hospitals that would have to be set up in high school gymnasiums and community centers when the next pandemic strikes. Health professionals lack training in "risk communication," so they would have difficulty providing the facts—and acknowledging the unknowns—to a frightened population (Osterholm, 2005). This is particularly alarming given the current threat of avian flu developing the ability to spread through person-to-person contact.

Although its spread has been less rapid than the 1918–1919 flu pandemic, AIDS (acquired immunodeficiency syndrome) is likely to surpass flu as the deadliest of pandemics. The syndrome was first identified in 1981 among homosexual men and intravenous drug users in New York and California (Foege, 1983). AIDS quickly developed into a worldwide pandemic, affecting virtually every nation. By 2003 the World Health Organization (WHO) estimated that there were over 42 million people with HIV (human immunodeficiency virus) infection, and 3.1 million deaths per year from AIDS. WHO estimated that 2.5 million children under the age of 15 were living with HIV infection or AIDS. In 2003, 1 in 5 adults (over 26 million in total) in sub-Saharan Africa had HIV infection or AIDS, the highest rate of infection in the world since the epidemic began (Sanderson, 2004).

One of the most troubling and anxiety-producing characteristics of an infectious disease is that usually the precise cause is unknown at first (Sim & Chua, 2004). This was the case in 2003 when severe acute respiratory syndrome (SARS) was first identified in Toronto, Canada. Within months there were hundreds of people ill and 44 deaths. Most of those infected with SARS were health-care workers who in some cases transmitted the disease to their family members. When there is little known about the cause of a disease and how it is transmitted, uncertainty and anxiety are understandably quite high (Robertson, Hershenfield, Grace, & Stewart, 2004). Patients who were in isolation with SARS in one Toronto hospital reported high levels of stress, fear, loneliness, boredom, and anger. Staff also reported high levels of anxiety as they worried about contagion and of infecting family, friends, and coworkers (Maunder et al., 2003). Robert Ursano (2005), the noted disaster psychiatrist, observes, "The microbial world is mysterious and frightening to many people. Health care providers are faced with exposure to a life-threatening illness for which there is little protection or treatment and which can threaten their own lives as well as those of their families." Despite the obvious emotional trauma that can result from an epidemic, it has been observed that there is little information available to mental health professionals to guide their interventions as they attempt to support patients and staff (Maunder et al., 2003).

Although each disaster is unique, there is one generic reaction to natural disasters: a sense of having been betrayed by nature. Survivors realize that they are not truly safe. Although most of us acknowledge that our bodies are doomed to deteriorate, this thought can often be kept at bay. Disease and death may strike a neighbor or friend, but most people are able to remain defended and in denial about their own vulnerability. Natural disasters impact whole communities, making denial less possible, shattering a sense of safety and breaking down defenses against a sense of invulnerability. Survivors, family members, friends, and neighbors are all affected. Natural disasters are covered in the media with accompanying reports of property loss, injury, and death tolls. This increased vulnerability can lead to not only altruism and growth but also psychological symptoms and conflict.

Natural Disasters With and Without Warning

Some disasters have warning periods, and others do not. The National Weather Service (NWS) offers information (described as advisories, watches, or warnings depending on the urgency level) to alert the population when hazardous weather including floods, severe thunderstorms, hurricanes, tornadoes, high winds, winter storms, and heat and cold waves are expected or present. The NWS can provide advance warnings weeks in advance of a storm reaching land. A hurricane storm watch is issued 24 to 36 hours before landfall, and a hurricane warning is issued within 24 hours of arrival. Other natural disasters such as earthquakes, tornadoes and many fires can have little or no warning time.

People generally do better when they see trouble coming and are able to prepare for it. Early precautions can range from buying hazard insurance to having an evacuation plan ready to implement in the event of a disaster warning. A disaster with warning can allow the community to find safety and avoid the oncoming storm, including evacuating their homes, if necessary. With advance warning, residents may be able to find safety with friends or relatives or in hotels far from the danger. When residents don't have friends and family or can't afford a hotel and still must leave their homes, they may need to stay in a large shelter. Most shelters that are set up prior to disasters are established by the humanitarian relief groups such as the Salvation Army or the American Red Cross through agreements or understandings with schools, churches, and businesses.

Residents waiting in shelters for a disaster to strike are usually in a high state of anxiety, not knowing if the event will unfold as predicted or, if it does, whether their homes will be damaged. Of course, if disaster strikes without warning, residents who must leave their homes and go to a shelter will be in much more distress and could arrive before the facility is even up and running. Clients who arrive at a shelter in the immediate aftermath of a disaster that struck with no warning tend to display less anxiety but more shock and upset about known losses.

How Natural Are Natural Disasters?

"Natural" disasters such as floods, droughts, and famines are increasingly actually human caused due to poor environmental practices and resource mismanagement. Other natural disasters such as earthquakes and hurricanes can be magnified by human actions. For example, on average there are about 14,000 deaths a year due to earthquakes worldwide, but very few of these deaths occur because the ground shakes or creates an opening that people fall into. Most deaths are caused by human-made structures that collapse because they are unable to withstand the tremors. In 1989 the Loma Pietra earthquake in California resulted in 62 deaths and 3757 injuries. A year earlier in Armenia, an earthquake of about the same magnitude resulted in about 25,000 deaths and 19,000 injuries. The difference in casualties between the earthquakes in California and Armenia was due to the difference in the quality of the building construction in these two areas. Buildings, bridges, and other structures constructed by humans kill people, not earthquakes. Much suffering could be reduced if building codes required structures to withstand the shaking from potential earthquakes (Langston, 1992), though a lack of monetary resources often prevents ideal building practices.

As a rule, poor people in poor countries are the most vulnerable to natural disasters (Norris et al., 2002a). They are often forced to live in areas that are prone to destructive events, and they are more likely to live in shoddy structures or shantytowns that cannot withstand the impact of disaster and are subject to collapse. In some poor countries, lives are lost unnecessarily because there are no basic warning systems (Wijkman & Timerlake, 1988). The 2004 tsunami is an example of how a lack of warning systems in undeveloped countries can result in mass casualties. Even when there are warning systems in place, poor people may lack the most basic communication technology needed to receive the messages in time to be helpful. Within the United States, poor people are more vulnerable to disaster because it is less expensive to live in tornado-prone areas or certain floodplains, as the flooding of New Orleans in 2005 demonstrated. The deadliest heat waves are also more likely to affect those lacking in resources. The elderly who perish in heat waves do so because they are poor or neglected and alone when the weather becomes extreme (Klinenberg, 2002).

It may be that the distinction between natural and human-caused disaster allows friends and relatives, communities and officials to evade responsibility when there is a "natural" disaster and to place the blame on "mother nature." But as survivors begin to understand the more complex relationship between natural and human-caused disaster, their reactions are becoming less accepting.

Human-Caused Disasters

Human-caused disasters include airplane crashes, sinking ferries, and other transportation accidents; house fires and building collapses; nuclear, industrial, and toxic waste accidents; and acts of violence such as the terrorist attacks in Oklahoma City and on 9/11 and the anthrax mailings in the weeks following 9/11.

It appears that human-caused disaster, whether through malfeasance or malevolence, causes more psychological distress than disasters caused by nature. Disasters caused by human intent or malevolence produce the most symptomatology (Norris et al., 2002a). There is some tendency to accept natural disasters as inevitable, but that is not so for human-caused ones. A human-caused disaster is seen as preventable and is more likely to induce feelings of anger, depression, and mistrust. Because survivors view humans as apart from nature, they are more disappointed when there is betrayal. "How could a fellow human being have done this?" is the question that is asked—or sometimes screamed. Human-caused disasters create confusion and distrust of others. Other people, unlike hurricanes and other natural disasters, are always present. When a hurricane passes, the threat subsides; but when survivors become aware of the dark side of others, danger can be perceived to be everywhere.

Like natural disasters, human-caused disasters vary widely in type and impact. **Residential fires** account for 93% of all Red Cross responses in the United States. These fires occur every 79 seconds, with the majority occurring in the months of December, January, and February. (New York City firefighters refer to these months as "the winter offensive.") Fires cause an estimated 600,000 to 750,000 burn injuries and 5000 deaths in the United States per year (Snyder & Saigh, 1984). Most deaths occur in home fires and most occur in urban areas (Gillespie, 2004). Overloaded circuits, use of candles, smoking in bed, children playing with matches, and improper use of portable heaters, kerosene heaters, wood stoves, or chimneys all contribute to home fires. The majority of fatal fires occur during nighttime sleeping hours when people are likely to be less alert, with roughly 80% of all fire deaths occurring where people sleep.

Fires impact children and the elderly more than middle-aged adults. In fact, a fire at home is the disaster that children are most likely to experience. It also ranks as the first cause of death at home for children under the age of 15. Although home fires are common, studies make clear that they can be quite devastating for children and adolescents, who experience distress and higher levels of posttraumatic stress disorder (PTSD) following a fire disaster. Based on their work with 100 families with children whose median age was 12 years, researchers found that 30% of the children felt they should have been able to do something to prevent the fire, 18% thought it was their fault, and 85% stated that they had never seen anything in their lives as bad as the fire (Jones & Ollendick, 2002). We must point out here that the research on the impact of fires on families and children has many shortcomings due to two main method-ological factors: the regular failure to control for the survivor's predisaster con-dition and the fact that parents are typically the source of the report of the child's reaction (Jones & Ollendick, 2002). There seems to be a tendency for parents to minimize or underestimate the child's distress following a fire, perhaps because they themselves are too anxious to attend to the child's fears (McFarlane, 1987). This has been noted as a problem for the research.

Large **urban conflagrations** are prominently featured in mythology and reli-gious writings as well as in historical accounts. No major Western city has escaped serious and repeated fires (Schmalz, 1992). The story of Mrs. O'Leary's cow knocking over a kerosene lantern and starting the Chicago fire in 1871 may or may not be true, but it was true that winds spread fire across the city, resulting in the destruction of 18,000 homes and causing about 300 deaths. This was con-sidered to be a Type I conflagration, which is a major fire begun by accident, resulting in much property damage and little loss of life. Type II conflagrations are ignited by natural causes such as earthquakes and can lead to a "firestorm," a fire-driven tornado that can lead to much loss of life and property. A Type III conflagration is deliberately set and can lead to massive loss of property and life. These fires are sometimes set as acts of war or civil unrest and can also lead to firestorms (Schmalz, 1992).

Arson, or intentionally set fires, is sometimes intended to get insurance monies, to punish someone such as a landlord or tenant, or to exact revenge. Because fire is so powerful and unpredictable, a fire starter may not expect the fire to do as much damage as what results. For example, one spring night in the Bronx, New York, in 1990, a disgruntled man went to the Happy Land Social Club to plead for his longtime girlfriend to take him back. When she would not, he became so disruptive that he was forced to leave the club. He returned in the early morning hours with a gallon of gasoline, made a trail from the dance floor down the club's only stairs, lit a match and walked away. Eighty-seven people—who had come to the club to have a good time, to dance and socialize—died in the blaze. The arsonist-murderer was sentenced to 25 years to life in prison (Davis, 2002). When large fires are started accidentally, survivors can experience considerable distress and outrage, but the impact is even greater when a fire is intentionally set, moti-vated by revenge and cruelty, and causes death and destruction. Although victims experience a need for justice, when it is meted out there is little relief.

Moving on to transportation disasters, although on a per passenger-mile basis the safest way to travel is on a commercial airline, there are occasionally deadly **plane crashes** (Forbes, 1992). The fact that many people refuse to fly while others cope with their anxiety by self-medicating before and during the flight is understandable when you consider that once on board an aircraft there are not likely to be small accidents or fender-benders. One's fate is very much in the hands of others, who do make errors. Mistakes can be made by the people who design and build the plane, the people who service the plane, the flight controllers who direct the plane, the people who fly it, and the passengers themselves (Davis, 2002). It has been reported that there is usually more than one factor that leads to a plane crash. When Eastern Airlines flight 401 went down in the

Everglades in 1972, killing 103 of the 176 persons onboard, the crash was said to be due to two burned-out light bulbs, a moonless night making it difficult for the crew to see whether or not the landing gear had been deployed, an accidental bump of the control wheel, and a distracted crew (Forbes, 1992).

Weather is the leading cause of *general aviation,* or noncommercial, fatal accidents. Noncommercial pilots flying their own planes are less experienced than commercial pilots, and their smaller aircraft are more susceptible to bad weather such as thunderstorms, reduced visibility, fog, snow, icing, and turbulence. Sometimes even commercial pilots are vulnerable to losing control of a plane due to a microburst, a narrow and short-lived burst of downdraft and outflow, though pilots can be warned with Doppler radar to anticipate and cope better with this natural hazard (Forbes, 1992). Again, we see that the boundaries between natural and human-caused disasters are fluid.

Other transportation disasters include railway, subway, bus, and shipping accidents. Mass-transportation accidents other than air crashes rarely result in everyone aboard being killed. Ships do not sink as quickly as they did in previous decades. Modern ships have sophisticated navigational equipment and enough lifeboats for everyone in case of emergency (Davis, 2002). However, ferry disasters in poor countries are more common and more deadly because the boats can be overcrowded or not properly maintained. The 2003 ferry disaster in New York City (not considered a poor country) reminds us that a lack of safety standards, neglect, incompetence, and recklessness can lead to tragedy anytime and anyplace. About 70,000 passengers ride the Staten Island ferries daily, going back and forth from lower Manhattan to the residential borough. During rush hour, the ferries leave every 15 minutes, and the ride takes about 25 minutes. On October 15, 2003, while docking on the Staten Island side, a ferry slammed into a concrete pier, killing 11 people and sending dozens more to the hospital, some with severed limbs. The boat, which was reportedly not running a straight course, struck a pier surrounded by wooden pilings, which gashed the vessel's port side. As the ferry moved forward, the pier continued ripping through steel and windows all the way to the rear of the ship. After the crash, newspaper accounts reported that passengers made frenzied efforts to escape.

Research indicates that in the aftermath of a life-threatening mass-transportation disaster, adults and children are at heightened risk for developing PTSD or other mental health problems (Yule, Udwin, & Bolton, 2002). In this case, not only were the passengers traumatized, but also the ship's captain was obviously shocked and distraught: It was reported that right after the crash, the captain left the scene, went home, and attempted suicide. The mental health implications for those steering or driving or flying into transportation disasters have not been studied, but one would imagine that they would be severe.

In another variety of large-scale technological disaster, **buildings collapse** for many reasons. Structural engineers can diagnose whether a building fails catastrophically because it was designed incorrectly, constructed incorrectly, or used improperly. Nature often contributes to building collapse by finding the building's weakest link. However, collapse is most often due to ignorance, carelessness, negligence, greed, or corruption (Wearne, 2000).

Toxic Waste and Nuclear Accidents

We pay a price for the technological advances that have improved our standard of life when these advances create toxic and hazardous waste. Greed, mismanagement, carelessness, and error are all potential causes of the insidious disasters that contaminate the environment and the people living in it. What makes these types of accidents especially frightening is that illness resulting from exposure is not easy to detect and can remain unseen for many years. Toxic waste accidents typically cause little direct property damage or loss although they can cause economic loss by making homes in a contaminated area unsellable. However, they can result in cancers and other diseases, some stress related, which can take years to develop. And there is an especially high psychological price that is paid when people are exposed to these kinds of disasters (Edelstein, 1988; Minhnoi & Baum, 2002). Researchers have found that residents exposed to toxic waste contamination experience a loss of safety and control and feel isolated and alienated from other communities. They are plagued with worry about whether they were exposed to the contamination or if the exposure was sufficient to create health problems.

For decades the disposal of toxic chemical and biological wastes from our increasingly technological society has been overlooked. Some communities were literally built on or near toxic waste sites including Love Canal, New York; Woburn, Massachusetts; Fernald, Ohio; Times Beach, Missouri; Saltville, Virginia; and Shepardville, Kentucky, where 100,000 drums of hazardous waste were illegally deposited on farmlands, contaminating the water and soil. The story of Love Canal reads like a horror story. It is estimated that 20,000 metric tons of waste were buried in this neighborhood of Niagara Falls and covered with clay. In the early 1950s, the chemical company that poisoned the land sold it so that homes and a school could be built at the edge of the canal. The first evidence of danger was reported in 1958 when children playing in the area came home with chemical burns. The terror under the earth gradually became more evident, and by 1978 it was clear that the residents were experiencing significant health problems including high rates of miscarriages, liver damage, and birth defects. Ultimately, the government bought out and condemned 800 homes and closed the school (Miller, 1992a). It is believed that there is a growing list of other hazardous sites in need of decontamination, but progress to clean up these sites has been slow.

Although most research on Love Canal and similarly contaminated sites has examined the physical health of the communities affected, there has been some research on its psychological toll. Young children may not be adversely emotionally affected, perhaps because they do not see or understand the danger (Minhnoi & Baum, 2002). However, victims of such human-caused toxic accidents show heightened arousal and blood pressure, and they report a loss of control and greater emotional distress (Baum & Fleming, 1993).

In the Three Mile Island (TMI) nuclear accident in Pennsylvania in 1979, a combination of equipment malfunction and human error resulted in a near reactor meltdown and considerable release of radioactivity. There were no deaths or injuries from the accident, and there is still controversy over whether or not the accident caused increased infant mortality and cancer rates. But despite the lack of proof of any physical impact, there is evidence that those in the vicinity of TMI showed signs of chronic stress, long-lasting elevations of blood pressure, changes in their immune systems, and persistent symptoms of PTSD for many years after the accident (Baum & Fleming, 1993).

Terrorism and Weapons of Mass Destruction

Terrorism has been defined as "the instrumental use or threatened use of violence by an organization or individual against innocent civilian targets in furtherance of a political, religious or ideological objective" (Tucker, 2000). It is important to distinguish between terrorism and **weapons of mass destruction** (WMDs), which the FBI defines as "any weapon that is designed or intended to cause death or serious bodily injury through the release, dissemination, or impact of toxic or poisonous chemicals, or their precursors; any weapon involving a disease organism; any weapon that is designed to release radiation or radioactivity at a level dangerous to human life or any destructive device."

There is a considerable history of domestic terrorism in this country carried out with conventional weapons as opposed to WMDs. For example, during the civil rights movement, the Ku Klux Klan and other hate groups directed acts of violence, terror, and murder against African Americans and civil rights workers in order to prevent racial integration. Other domestic terrorist groups have concrete political goals and view indiscriminate mass casualty attacks as counterproductive. In the late 1960s and 1970s, a revolutionary group calling themselves the Weather Underground carried out numerous bombings on symbolic targets in response to political developments such as the shooting of four Kent State students by National Guardsman in 1970 and the killing of Black Panther Party leaders in 1970. The only injuries resulting from the 35 incidents listed by the FBI were the accidental deaths of three of the Weather Underground's own founders, who were killed in New York City when a bomb they were assembling went off accidentally. There were allegations that the group attempted to acquire WMDs, but these reports are not seen as credible (Parachini, 2000) because the group was attempting to bring about a revolution and did not view mass casualties as helpful to their cause. More recently, there have been terrorist acts, committed with conventional weapons, directed at doctors or clinics connected with abortion. Another example of domestic terror without WMDs was the bombing at the Summer Olympics in Atlanta, Georgia, in 1996 that resulted in one death and over 100 injuries.

WMDs have been a part of the arsenal of most states and nations for centuries. However, it is said that we live in a more uncertain and changed world, and there is a new threat: Groups other than nations are now more likely to possess both the motivation and the means to deliver terrorist attacks with WMDs. There appears to be a new breed of virulent terrorists who possess such moral certitude that they will use any weapon to destroy as many as they can. There are religious fanatics or millenarian sects who believe that God has ordered them to bring about an apocalypse so that the faithful will be saved and the evil will be destroyed. Osama bin Laden has stated that all American citizens are legitimate targets and that it is no crime to use "nuclear, chemical, biological weapons . . . to defend ourselves and liberate our holy land." Other extremist groups motivated by hatred and arrogance include white supremacists and radical ecologists who are convinced that in order to save the world a significant portion of humanity must be killed (Tucker, 2000). Fortunately, it is not easy, from a technical perspective, to both acquire and disseminate WMDs. However, with the exception of a nuclear attack, attacks with all of the other varieties of WMDs, which we describe next, have been attempted and accomplished.

Biological agents can be released in aerosols, in water or food, or by injection. Some agents require an incubation period, which can last from several hours to several weeks before symptoms appear. Many nations have developed and stored biological weapons including viruses such as smallpox, bacteria such as plague, and veterinary bacteria such as anthrax, but the only well-documented case of the use of biological weapons in wartime is Japan's use of plague and other bacterial agents against China in World War II (Carus, 2002).

Anthrax was successfully used as a WMD in the United States in the fall of 2001 when a series of letters containing finely powdered spores resulted in five deaths, many illnesses, and widespread panic. Targeted groups including politicians and media personnel were at risk, but many mail handlers (some of whom became ill after high-speed sorting machines forced the powder through the sealed envelopes they were handling) were terrified, and citizens throughout the country were afraid to touch their mail. Prior to this anthrax attack, the FBI had confirmed only one successful case of bioterrorism. In 1984 a religious cult known as the Rajneeshees attempted to sicken the population of Wasco County, Oregon, in order to ensure the election of their preferred candidate as county commissioner. They produced a quantity of salmonella, bacteria commonly responsible for food poisoning, and distributed it through salad bars in several restaurants. No one died as a result of the exposure, but 751 people became ill (Carus, 2002).

Hospitals and public health organizations in many cities have surveillance systems in place to monitor potential outbreaks caused by a biological terror attack (Rebmann, 2005). We have both participated in Point of Dispensing (POD) drills that are intended to provide antibiotics within hours to the entire population of New York City in the event of an attack with a bacterial agent. A drill in which we participated was intended to evaluate and treat 1000 "patients" per hour. The exercise appeared to be effective; however, it did not take into account the possible panic and emotional turmoil that might ensue from an attack of this type.

Chemical agents cause damage as a result of direct contact, inhalation, or ingestion. Chemical nerve agents attack the nervous system, and blister agents cause burns and blisters on the body or can damage the respiratory system. There are also choking and blood agents. Although there has been no evidence of any chemical terrorist attacks in the United States, it is believed that the terrorist group Aum Shinrikyo staged at least 10 biological and 10 chemical attacks in Japan. The most notorious attack by the group occurred in 1995 when they released sarin gas in the Tokyo subway system, killing 12 people and injuring more than 1000. The group, which had 40,000 devotees in Japan, Russia, the United States and elsewhere, maintained that there was a coming war between the United States and Japan. They hoped to hasten the apocalypse by perpetrating a mass-casualty disaster and blaming the United States (Kaplan, 2002). Following the sarin gas subway attack, it was reported that 9000 Japanese sought help for possible treatment and exposure. Although these citizens were physically unharmed, they were in a high state of anxiety. This finding suggests that for every person who is killed or injured in a terrorist attack there could be almost as many as 100 psychological victims of such an attack (Myers, 2001).

Explosive devices create shockwaves and flying debris. They can also destabilize structures such as buildings, bridges, or tunnels. **Incendiary devices** cause fires that create the dangers of smoke, fumes, and high temperatures. The World Trade Center bombing in 1993, resulting in 6 deaths and about 1000 injuries, and the bombing of the Alfred Murrah Federal Building in Oklahoma City in 1995, killing 168 people, are recent examples of domestic terrorism carried out with explosive devices. There have also been a number of thwarted international terrorist plots intended to blow up bridges and tunnels in the recent past.

There has not yet been an attack on the United States with a **nuclear device.** However, some evidence suggests that one such attack was planned. On June 1, 2004, the Justice Department announced that the alleged al-Qaida member Jose Padilla hoped to attack Americans by detonating a dirty bomb. A *dirty bomb* is a conventional explosive intended to disperse radioactivity in powder form, which could make portions of a city uninhabitable. It was reported that Padilla planned to detonate "uranium wrapped with explosives" in order to spread radioactivity. If Padilla had been successful, it would have done little actual damage: It happens that radiation from uranium, although potentially lethal in an atom bomb, is billions of times less intense than that of cesium-137, cobalt-60, and other radioisotopes. Most scientists believe that cesium and cobalt isotopes, substances used in medicine and industry, would be the fuels used in a more lethal dirty bomb. If such a bomb were detonated, there would not only be injuries and deaths but also considerable psychological panic because the danger cannot be easily seen and citizens would find it difficult to assess how much danger they were in ("Bomb Would," 2004).

Potential Targets of and Reactions to Attacks   Because a terrorist (T) attack can occur anywhere, at any time, the message that a terrorist intends to spread is that you can never be sure of your safety. There does, however, seem to be some predictability about the targets for T/WMD attacks. Critical infrastructure systems including power plants, phone companies, water treatment plants, mass-transit systems, and nuclear power plants could be targeted, as well as public areas such as shopping malls, churches or synagogues, and sporting or entertainment complexes. Symbolic or historical sites such as museums or controversial sites such as abortion clinics could also be targeted (American Red Cross, 2002).

The reactions to T/WMD attacks can be intense for many reasons. The characteristics of these events suggest that there are likely to be more psychological problems due to the following factors:

1. *Lack of warning and familiarity.* These events rarely come with warnings, and the general lack of preparedness predicts greater psychological problems. There is unfamiliarity with these kinds of attack, which leads to greater feelings of vulnerability and helplessness. Most Americans have had no life experience to prepare them for terrorist attacks, and emotions can be strong and overwhelming (Myers & Wee, 2005). The personal safety of citizens is seriously threatened, and the fear of being injured or killed increases the impact of the disaster.

2. *The scale of the event.* The scope, intensity, and duration of these T/WMD attacks all can be extreme. Survivors and first responders both are more likely to be exposed to gruesome or grotesque situations. First responders are at risk for significant line-of-duty loss of personnel, especially troubling for this group. Rescuers are at higher psychological risk if they are involved with the recovery and identification of bodies.

3. *Greater fear and uncertainty.* This kind of event creates a level of fear unlike other disasters. With earthquakes there can be a reaction to the damage of the quake and anxiety about an aftershock, but this is magnified with T/WMD attacks. Survivors become consumed with worry and uncertainty. They ask themselves: "Will there be another attack, and if so when and where? What are the steps I can take to protect myself and my loved ones?" In the aftermath of 9/11, every time a New York City subway stopped between stations, there was an obvious sense of apprehension among riders. Anytime the conductor announced that there was police activity, the fear and anxiety was palpable.

    That intense fear is exacerbated by the intentional nature of T/WMD attacks. "Essentially, terrorism is the 'perfect' traumatic stressor, because it combines the elements of malevolent intent, actual or threatened extreme harm, and unending fear of the future" (Miller, 2002). Victims who know that their distress was caused on purpose to further somebody's political or religious agenda face a very different type of psychological impact than those who feel that they just happened to be the unfortunate victims of an accident. As a result, the task of restoring a sense of security that was maliciously destroyed is different than restoring one damaged by a natural disaster or accident.

4. *Terrorist attacks with or without WMD are crimes.* Survivors not only have to cope with losses, but they also may have to follow or participate in criminal investigations and prosecution. As this book is being written, the anthrax attack of 2001 is still being investigated. Osama bin Laden and other organizers of the 9/11 attacks are still being sought. Criminals incarcerated for terrorist acts may become eligible for parole. The fact that someone like Timothy McVeigh, who was executed for carrying out the Oklahoma City bombing, can become a household name is insulting to the families of those murdered.

It is more difficult to learn to live with the losses while there are criminal proceedings that can go on for decades. Research from Oklahoma City revealed that every time there was a courtroom proceeding or a new development in the criminal investigation, there was an increase in distress among survivors (Tassey, 2005).

This description of the distressing potential of T/WMD attacks is by no means intended to minimize potential mental health reactions to other kinds of disasters. In their review of the impact of different types of disaster, Norris and her coauthors (Norris et al., 2002b) conclude that both natural and human-caused events can produce serious and lasting impairment in a substantial portion of the population. The effects of disaster appear to be most extreme when at least two of the following conditions are met: (1) The disaster causes extreme and widespread property damage; (2) the disaster causes extreme and lasting financial problems for the community; (3) the disaster is caused by human intention; (4) the disaster results in injuries and threat to or loss of life. Norris et al. (2002b) maintain that when such conditions are met, there will be significant need for professional level mental health services.

As this implies, the psychological power of disasters is immense. In the following section, we see that much misery and destruction can be caused even when there is no actual physical event.

HOAXES, RUMORS, AND PANICS

According to our definition of disaster, there is no disaster if a hurricane occurs out at sea and no one is affected. People need to be impacted in some way in order for us to recognize that a disaster has occurred. But when there is a **hoax,** there is no physical event, and yet there is impact because people believe that a disaster has occurred.

In some cases, a desperate individual who might derive a sense of power by instigating a fraud can perpetuate a hoax—for example, calling the police and announcing that a bomb is set to go off or the white powder they left in the street is anthrax. Other examples are less malicious. In a radio broadcast in 1938, actor and director Orson Welles vividly described hostile Martians invading Grover's Mill, New Jersey, attacking citizens with poison gas. The Martians moved on to destroy New York as well as other cities (Koch, 1970). It has been reported that there was mass hysteria nationwide in response to the broadcast. This may have been exaggerated, but there is no doubt that there was panic in many areas of the country as residents came out of their homes to look for meteors and invading spacecraft. Some New Jersey residents went to get guns and join the fight. Princeton psychology professor Hadley Cantril (1940) in his book, *The Invasion from Mars: A Study in the Psychology of Panic,* estimated that some 6 million people across the country had heard the broadcast and that over 1 million were at the very least severely alarmed. In interviews, Cantril found that some people were so terrified that they cried, prayed, became hysterical, or attempted to flee. There was a similar hoax and public reaction in Sweden in 1973 when a radio broadcast warned of an accident at a nuclear power plant that was under construction (Rosengren, Arvidson, & Sturesson, 1975).

While hoaxes intentionally misrepresent the truth, **rumors** may do so inadvertently. In the aftermath of a disaster, it is quite common for rumors to arise, most often of a negative and frightening sort, consistent with the anxiety that is experienced. Such rumors can make the real disaster worse. In the classic book, *The Psychology of Rumor* (Allport & Postman, 1947), it was found that a rumor's potential impact is related to two factors: its importance to the speaker and listener and its ambiguity. The more important and ambiguous the material, the more likely it will be spread. Rumors give people a hook to hang their fears and anxieties on, which may be soothing but may also create new anxieties. The uncertainty and fear resulting from disaster can also reduce people's ability to think critically and thus cause them to pass along the most improbable tales (Rosnow, 1991). Rumors following disaster can spread more quickly in our modern technological age via the Internet (Bordia & DiFonzo, 2004). This was exemplified in the aftermath of 9/11 when there were waves of rumors and false reports, such as the New York area reservoirs being poisoned and conspiracy theories such as Muslims or Jews who had advance warning and stayed home on the day of the attacks (Tyrangiel, 2001). (Rumor control is an important part of the DMH response and will be discussed more fully in Chapter 9.)

In some instances, a hoax or rumor has set off an episode of **mass panic.** Fortunately, the occurrence of mass panic following an actual disaster is relatively rare. Citizens are much more likely to respond to disaster in a helpful and cooperative manner than in a panicked, irrational manner (Glass & Schoch-Spana, 2002). Sometimes, however, panic can produce more than just emotional distress: It has been linked directly to catastrophe. Panicking crowds can stampede, which can result in people being trampled, crushed, or suffocated. For example, in February 2003, 21 people were killed trying to escape a nightclub in Chicago when pepper spray was used to break up a fight, and some people thought that a bioterrorist attack was underway. Believing that the number of exits was limited, patrons trampled and crushed one another in a rush to escape. This incident is consistent with the view that panics are generally caused by the view that one's life is threatened—that escape is possible but will soon disappear (Rosengren et al., 1975). The history of mass panic and stampedes indicates that they are caused by the perception of a life-threatening situation in conjunction with limited lifesaving resources that must be competed for, such as lifeboats or exits. In the following case study, we can see how considerable emotional distress can result from rumor and panic.

> On September 22, 2001, teams of Red Cross Volunteers entered Battery Park City to help residents who were returning to their homes after almost 2 weeks of not being allowed in their neighborhood after the nearby World Trade Center towers were destroyed. The weather was gorgeous as we exited the subway. From the west side of Manhattan, we could all see the Statue of Liberty and Ellis Island. Getting to ground zero on this day involved going through checkpoints and showing several types of ID.

The streets in Battery Park City had been cleaned, but there was still an awful smell and plenty of dust that caused everyone to cough a bit. Teams of Red Cross workers were assigned to the lobbies of buildings where we would inform residents of the services provided by the Red Cross and the immediate disaster-related assistance that was available to residents.

Each team had a mental health worker, but we could have used two or even three on a team. The residents were confused and dazed. They appreciated our being there, and they all wanted to talk about their experience of September 11. They seemed to want to connect, to not feel isolated or alone. Many were experiencing high levels of stress, and some appeared to be more severely disturbed as this new tragedy opened up old wounds and reactivated old traumas.

One woman I spoke with was crying and shaking as she told me her story of 9/11. She was several blocks west of the towers as they fell and made her way further west to the Hudson River. Then she was not sure whether to go north or south. She was distressed but not panicked. Then someone yelled that the smoke all around was filled with poison gas released by the terrorists and if anyone breathed they would die. There were shouts "Don't breathe! Don't breathe or you will die!" This was one stress, one rumor, too much. She tried desperately to hold her breath as she ran north, but running without breathing was not possible. She knew she could not save her own life, and she collapsed, wailing, waiting to die. Now weeks later, she was still in a heightened state of arousal. I listened to her for quite some time and provided psychological first aid. I also suggested to her that she could benefit from more help and gave her several referrals.

Although September 11, 2001, was an enormous event, individuals' perceptions and cognitions of the event were just as important in determining its impact. This woman was never actually in danger from poison gas, but the panicked screams and rumor begun by a stranger led her to believe that her life was about to end.

THE IMPORTANCE OF ACCURATE INFORMATION

Later in the book, we discuss the kinds of information that counselors can provide to survivors as part of mental health interventions in the early aftermath of disaster. In this section, we examine the importance of the population receiving accurate information from the media, public officials, and the mental health community. The mental health implications of providing accurate information need to be communicated to local and national leaders before disaster strikes as part of planning and prevention.

In the aftermath of every disaster, human-caused or natural, there is a desperate need for accurate information. People turn on TVs and radios in order to keep informed about what is happening. They want to know if there are precautions that they should take or otherwise how to handle the emergency. They also might want to find out if there is any way they can be of help—to make contributions or give blood. In the midst of chaos, people can feel grounded by knowledge. It may be that the antidote for chaos is accurate information. This is especially important for epidemics, toxic and nuclear accidents, and terrorist attacks because the public knows so little about these kinds of events. A terrorist act in particular is designed to create psychological insecurity. Its goal is to engender a state of uncertainty, vulnerability, and fear, making the mental health response to terrorism of vital importance (Everly & Mitchell, 2001).

The psychological response must be designed to create a sense of trust, calm, community, and support. Officials and mental health workers must be aware of the public's vulnerability to rumor, hoax, misinformation, and panic. In an atmosphere of uncertainty and anxiety, citizens want and need the truth, and the open sharing of information can help prevent panic (Glass & Schoch-Spana, 2002). As DMH counselors we must be absolutely sure that when we provide information we are not spreading rumors. If we are asked questions and we are not sure of the answer, we must say, "I do not know, but I will try to help you to find out." The public has an enormous need to trust officials, who should have a commitment to truth to warrant this trust. However, it sometimes appears that officials want to maintain calm at the expense of truth—or perhaps they want to engender anxiety and fear for political gain.

The public often suspects that leaders might lie to them, and unfortunately our officials have not always been credible. When Pan Am flight 103, from London to New York, exploded over Lockerbie, Scotland, in 1988, 256 people on board the plane as well as 11 on the ground died. Among the dead were 35 students from Syracuse University, coming home for Christmas break from a study abroad program. The perpetrators of what ultimately proved to be a terrorist attack included Iranian, Syrian, and Libyan terrorists. Government agencies as well as the airline had received warnings of a possible attack, but no notice was given to the general public. Some government embassy officials, privy to the warnings, took the opportunity to cancel their reservations (Davis, 2002). If the threat was credible enough for some officials to cancel their flights, why was the general public not warned? This is the type of narrative that destroys confidence and trust in officials.

In another example, in the aftermath of 9/11, New Yorkers had great confidence in their leader, Mayor Giuliani, to tell the truth. He was perceived by most as a credible leader, which provided psychological strength. He was able to acknowledge the uncertainty of the circumstances when there was little information. Therefore, when the mayor told people to stay home or go to work, they respected his authority and followed his instructions. Other officials proclaimed the air around ground zero to be safe to breathe when in fact the safety of the air quality was at best unknown. Perhaps they wanted citizens to feel comfortable about the air quality, hoping to avoid any panic. But the lack of accurate information and the inability to trust authority at that time was very destructive and raised suspicions that exist to this day. In contrast, in World War II England during the massive bombings, there was a paucity of rumors because citizens believed that they were getting the most accurate news, even if it was dire (Allport & Postman, 1947).

These examples suggest that mental health workers must be strong advocates for truth telling on the part of public officials, not only as a moral or ethical issue but also as a mental health issue. It is just one of the many roles that DMH helpers may need to serve in the aftermath of a disaster—but how did that complex role evolve? In Chapter 3, we review the history of how DMH emerged as an independent specialty, despite periods of great resistance.

References

Allport, G. W., & Postman, L. (1947). *The psychology of rumor.* New York: Holt, Rinehart & Winston.

American Red Cross. (2002). *Weapons of mass destruction/terrorism: An overview* (ARC 3070-2A). Washington, DC: Author.

Baum, A., & Fleming, I. (1993) Implications of psychological research on stress and technological accidents. *American Psychologist, 48,* 665–672.

Bomb would have been dud, scientists say. (2004, June 10). *New York Times,* A25.

Bordia, P., & DiFonzo, N. (2004). Problem solving in social interactions on the Internet: Rumor as social cognition. *Social Psychology Quarterly, 67,* 33–49.

Burt, C. C. (2004). *Extreme weather: A guide and record book.* New York: Norton.

Cantril, H. (1940). *The invasion from Mars: A study in the psychology of panic.* Princeton, NJ: Princeton University Press.

Carus, W. S. (2002). The Rajneeshees (1984). In J. B. Tucker (Ed.), *Toxic terror: Assessing use of chemical and biological weapons* (pp. 115–137). Cambridge, MA: MIT Press.

Cohen, R. E., & Ahearn, F. L. (1980). *Handbook for mental health care of disaster victims.* Baltimore: Johns Hopkins University Press.

Cross, J. A. (1992). The hurricane hazard in the United States. In S. K. Majumdar, G. S. Forbes, E. W. Miller, & R. F. Schmalz (Eds.), *Natural and technological disaster: Causes, effects, and preventive measures* (pp. 125–137). Easton, PA: Pennsylvania Academy of Science.

Curtis, G. D. (1992). Tsunamis—seismic sea waves. In S. K. Majumdar, G. S. Forbes, E. W. Miller, & R. F. Schmalz (Eds.), *Natural and technological disaster: Causes, effects, and preventive measures* (pp. 108–124). Easton, PA: Pennsylvania Academy of Science.

Davis, L. (2002). *Man-made catastrophes.* New York: Checkmark Books.

Edelstein, M. R. (1988). *Contaminated communities: The social and psychological impacts of residential toxic exposure.* Boulder, CO: Westview.

Everly, G. S., & Mitchell, J. T. (2001). America under attack: The "10 Commandments" of responding to mass terror attacks. *International Journal of Emergency Mental Health, 3*(3), 133–135.

Foege, W. (1983). The national pattern of AIDS. In K. M. Cahill (Ed.), *The AIDS epidemic* (pp. 1–17). New York: St. Martin's Press.

Forbes, G. S. (1992). Aviation disasters: Microbursts and other causes. In S. K. Majumdar, G. S. Forbes, E. W. Miller, & R. F. Schmalz (Eds.), *Natural and technological disaster: Causes, effects, and preventive measures* (pp. 176–191). Easton, PA: Pennsylvania Academy of Science.

Gillespie, B. (2004, January 23). *Residential fires sky-rocket in winter months.* American Red Cross in the News. Retrieved from www.redcross.org/article/0,1072, 0_312_2203,00.html.

Glass, T. A., & Schoch-Spana, M. (2002). Bioterrorism and the people: How to vaccinate a city against panic. *Clinical Infectious Diseases, 34,* 217–223.

Johnson, K., & Murphy, D. (2004, May 2). Drought settles in, lake shrinks and West's worries grow. *New York Times,* A1.

Jones, R. T., & Ollendick, T. H. (2002). Residential fires. In A. M. La Greca, W. K. Silversmith, E. M. Vernberg, & M. C. Roberts (Eds.), *Helping children cope with disasters and terrorism* (pp. 175–199). Washington, DC: APA Press.

Kafrissen, S. R., Heffron, E. F., & Zusman, J. (1975). Mental health problems in environmental disaster. In H. L. P. Resnik, H. L. Ruben, & D. D. Ruben (Eds.), *Emergency psychiatric care: The management of mental health crises* (pp. 157–170). Bowie, MD: Charles Press.

Kaplan, D. E. (2002). Aum Shinrikyo (1995). In J. B. Tucker (Ed.), *Toxic terror: Assessing use of chemical and biological weapons* (pp. 207–226). Cambridge, MA: MIT Press.

Klinenberg, Eric (2002). *Heat wave: A social autopsy of disaster in Chicago.* Chicago: University of Chicago Press.

Koch, H. (1970). *The panic broadcast.* Boston: Little, Brown.

La Greca, A. M., & Prinstein, M. J. (2002). Hurricanes and earthquakes. In A. M. La Greca, W. K. Silversmith, E. M. Vernberg, & M. C. Roberts (Eds.), *Helping children cope with disasters and terrorism* (pp. 107–138). Washington, DC: APA Press.

Langston, C. (1992). Too close to the tremors of the earth. In S. K. Majumdar, G. S. Forbes, E. W. Miller, & R. F. Schmalz (Eds.), *Natural and technological disaster: Causes, effects, and preventive measures* (pp. 49–61). Easton, PA: Pennsylvania Academy of Science.

Maunder, R., Hunter, J., Vincent, L., Bennett, J., Peladeau, M. L., Sadavoy, J., et al. (2003). The immediate psychological and occupational impact of the 2003 SARS outbreak in a teaching hospital. *Canadian Medical Association Journal, 168,* 1245–1251.

McFarlane, A. C. (1987). Family functioning and overprotection following a natural disaster: The longitudinal effects of post-traumatic morbidity. *Australian and New Zealand Journal of Psychiatry, 21,* 210–216.

Miller, E. W. (1992a). Hazardous and toxic waste sites: Strategies of control. In S. K. Majumdar, G. S. Forbes, E. W. Miller, & R. F. Schmalz (Eds.), *Natural and technological disaster: Causes, effects, and preventive measures* (pp. 294–308). Easton, PA: Pennsylvania Academy of Science.

Miller, E. W. (1992b). Human response to natural and technological disasters. In S. K. Majumdar, G. S. Forbes, E. W. Miller, & R. F. Schmalz (Eds.), *Natural and technological disaster: Causes, effects, and preventive measures* (pp. 14–24). Easton, PA: Pennsylvania Academy of Science.

Miller, L. (2002). Psychological interventions for terroristic trauma: Symptoms, syndromes, and treatment strategies. *Psychotherapy: Theory/Research/Practice/Training, 39,* 283–296.

Minhnoi, C. W., & Baum, A. (2002). Toxic waste spills and nuclear accidents. In A. M. La Greca, W. K. Silversmith, E. M. Vernberg, & M. C. Roberts (Eds.), *Helping children cope with disasters and terrorism* (pp. 207–221). Washington, DC: APA Press.

Myers, D. (2001, November). *Weapons of mass destruction and terrorism: Mental health consequences and implications for planning and services.* Paper presented at a conference on The Ripple Effect from Ground Zero: Coping with Mental Health Needs in Times of Tragedy and Terror. Sponsored by the American Red Cross of Greater New York, New York City.

Myers, D., & Wee, D. F. (2005). *Disaster mental health services.* New York: Brunner/ Routledge.

National Weather Service. (2004). Is your community ready? Retrieved from http://www. nws.noaa.gov/.

NIMH (National Institute of Mental Health). (2002). *Mental health and mass violence: Evidence-based early psychological intervention for victims/survivors of mass violence. A workshop to reach consensus on best practices* (NIH Publication No. 02-5138). Washington, DC: Government Printing Office.

Norris, F., Friedman, M. J., Watson, P. J., Byrne, C. M., Diaz, E., & Kaniasty, K. (2002a). 60,000 disaster victims speak: Part I. An empirical review of the empirical literature, 1981–2001. *Psychiatry: Interpersonal & Biological Processes, 65,* 207–239.

Norris, F. H., Friedman, M. J., & Watson, P. J. (2002b). 60,000 disaster victims speak: Part II. Summary and implications of the disaster mental health research. *Psychiatry, 65,* 240–260.

Osterholm, M. T. (2005). Preparing for the next pandemic. *New England Journal of Medicine, 352,* 1839–1842.

Parachini, J. V. (2000). The Weather Underground (1970). In J. B. Tucker (Ed.), *Toxic terror: Assessing use of chemical and biological weapons* (pp. 43–53). Cambridge, MA: MIT Press.

Quirk, M. (2005). Nature's wrath: A field guide. *Atlantic Monthly, 296,* 58–59.

Raphael, B. (1986). *When disaster strikes: How individuals and communities cope with catastrophe.* New York: Basic Books.

Rebmann, T. (2005, May 20). *Epidemiology of disasters and syndromic surveillance.* Paper presented at the meeting of the Association for Professionals in Infection Control and Epidemiology, Inc., Cleveland, OH.

Robertson, E., Hershenfield, K., Grace, S. L., Stewart, D. E. (2004). The psychosocial effects of being quarantined following exposure to SARS: A qualitative study of Toronto health care workers. *Canadian Journal of Psychiatry, 49,* 403–407.

Rosengren, K. E., Arvidson, P., & Sturesson, D. (1975). The Barsebäck "panic": A radio programme as a negative summary event. *Acta Sociologica (Taylor & Francis Ltd), 18,* 303–321.

Rosnow, R. L. (1991). Inside rumor: A personal journey. *American Psychologist, 46,* 484–496.

Sanderson, C. A. (2004). *Health psychology.* New York: Wiley.

Schmalz, R. F. (1992). Conflagrations: Disastrous urban fires. In S. K. Majumdar, G. S. Forbes, E. W. Miller, & R. F. Schmalz (Eds.), *Natural and technological disaster: Causes, effects, and preventive measures* (pp. 62–74). Easton, PA: Pennsylvania Academy of Science.

Sim, K., & Chua, H. C. (2004). The psychological impact of SARS: A matter of heart and mind. *Canadian Medical Association Journal, 170*(5), 811–812.

Snyder, D. D., & Saigh, P. A. (1984). Burn injuries in children. In V. C. Kelly (Ed.), *Practice of pediatrics I* (pp. 1–13). New York: Harper & Row.

Speckhard, A. (2003). Acute stress disorder in diplomats, military, and civilian Americans living abroad following the September 11 terrorist attacks on America. *Professional Psychology: Research and Practice, 24,* 151–158.

Talking About Disaster: Guide for Standard Messages. (2004). Washington, DC: National Disaster Education Coalition. Retrieved from http://www.disastereducation.org/guide.html.

Tassey, J. R. (2005, May 6). Presentation at Helping in a Time of Crisis conference held at State University of New York, New Paltz.

Tucker, J. (2000). Introduction. In J. B. Tucker (Ed.), *Toxic terror: Assessing use of chemical and biological weapons* (pp. 1–14). Cambridge, MA: MIT Press.

Tyrangiel, J. (2001). Did you hear about . . . . *Time, 158*(16), 77.

Ursano, R. (2005). Preparedness for SARS, influenza, and bioterrorism. *Psychiatric Services, 56,* 7.

Valelly, R. (April 16, 2004). What's gone right in the study of what's gone wrong. *Chronicle of Higher Education, 50*(32), B6–B8.

Wearne, P. (2000). *When buildings fall down.* New York: TV Books.

Weaver, J. (1995). *Disasters: Mental health interventions.* Sarasota, FL: Professional Resource Press.

Wijkman, A., & Timerlake, L. (1988). *Natural disasters: Acts of God or acts of man?* Philadelphia: New Society Publishers.

Winchester, S. (2004, December 29). The year the earth fought back. *New York Times,* Opinion Op Ed page.

Yule, W., Udwin, O., & Bolton, D. (2002). Mass transportation disasters. In A. M. La Greca, W. K. Silversmith, E. M. Vernberg, & M. C. Roberts (Eds.), *Helping children cope with disasters and terrorism* (pp. 223–239). Washington, DC: APA Press.

Zanetti, A., Schwartz, S., & Enz, R. (2005). *Natural catastrophes and man-made disasters in 2004: More than 300,000 fatalities, record insured losses.* Zurich: Swiss Reinsurance Company, Economic Research & Consulting.

*If I have learned anything from my contact with victims . . . ,
I have learned that it is vitally important to remember—and
honor—the lessons of the past. We have to know where we
came from if we are to know who we are now.*

Sandra L. Bloom, M.D.

3 CHAPTER | A History of Disaster Mental Health

Now that you are familiar with the characteristics of disasters,
let's turn our focus specifically to disaster mental health (DMH).
In this chapter, we delve into the background of the DMH field.
We identify its theoretical underpinnings, look at converging
trends that provided a ripe environment for its development, and
point out key historic and current figures who have played an
important role in that development. Throughout the chapter, we
focus on the evolution of DMH from the perspective of the
mental health professional, and we try to answer questions that
may have occurred to you already: What are the roots of DMH?
Is it simply the field application of crisis intervention? What is
the theory behind it, what are its parameters, and how is it
related to our understanding of trauma? How did it come to pass
that mental health practitioners are now routinely on-site at
disasters?

Mental health care formally became a common part of disaster response in the early 1990s. The growth of DMH over the
last decade has been spurred on by the incidence of mass-casualty
disasters, often in huge metropolitan areas. In the current tax-
onomy of the mental health universe, DMH lies within the more
global study of understanding the impact of traumatic events.
Some might question whether DMH merits recognition as more
than a highly specialized aspect of the study of traumatic stress,

but we believe that it does. Bloom (2000) cites Wilson, Harel, and Kahana's (1988) observation that

> The criteria for a true field of study must include a body of knowledge and standards of practice that are subsumed within (1) a history, (2) professional organizations, (3) publications, (4) theory, (5) measurement, (6) research methodology, (7) intervention technology, and (8) actions affecting policy and the judicial system.

Measured by these criteria, DMH *is* a distinct field, if a new and developing one. And with the continuing threat of additional events like the World Trade Center and Pentagon attacks of September 11, 2001, as well as devastating natural disasters like Hurricane Katrina, the need to refine, develop, and advocate for this mental health subspecialty becomes even more imperative.

That disasters bring in their wake a host of mental health consequences is not debated. What is less evident is how to best map out the range of possible human psychological responses to disaster and how to define where, when, and how to intervene. Researchers have achieved broad recognition that disasters may psychologically affect people in a negative way and that caring for others when disaster strikes can be helpful. However, there is also a recent emphasis in the DMH field on the natural human resilience that equips most people to recover from traumatic experiences with no outside intervention. This most recent trend, which runs counter to some earlier theories suggesting that everyone would benefit from debriefing or other interventions, has bolstered the need to seek evidence of efficacy. It must be determined whether our interventions not only do no harm but also serve a purpose: More sophisticated approaches to DMH must be developed.

We return to these important issues throughout this book, but first, let's set the stage for our discussion of current theory and practice with an overview of the history of trauma studies and the emergence of DMH as a specialty. We hope to make it clear in this chapter how deeply DMH's roots are planted in theories and treatments for all kinds of trauma, including those related to war and domestic violence.

CONVERGING TRENDS IN THE DEVELOPMENT OF DISASTER MENTAL HEALTH

The history of disasters goes back to the beginnings of time, but the history of DMH is much newer, driven by a number of trends that converged to produce an atmosphere of receptiveness to the emerging field. Humans have recorded disasters' enduring and life-altering power since our most ancient mythologies, yet it is only in the past two centuries that their effect on survivors' psychological health has been acknowledged. The first accounts of event-related reactions described the impact of early train accidents in 1880s England (Trimble, 1981). Before this time, significant emotional reactions had apparently not been reported in victims of natural disasters or accidents, but train wreck survivors often seemed to suffer impairments far beyond the physical injuries received in the crash.

It is significant that these first signs of widespread psychological impact coincided with the technical advances initiated during the Industrial Revolution, establishing a pattern that continues through the subsequent history of the field: Technology escalates trauma. This is true in war as demonstrated by the drastic increase in psychological damage as weaponry became progressively more destructive, most notably in World War I after the invention of dynamite (Weisaeth, 2002). This is clearly true in disasters caused directly by technology like airplane crashes, nuclear accidents, or bombings and other intentional acts of malevolence. And it is even true in natural disasters as industrialization clusters people together in higher population densities so that more potential victims are affected by a given storm, earthquake, or other event. Thus, the first significant trend in the development of DMH results from the increase in technology's prevalence in modern life: As we have grown more dependent on and benefited from technological advances, we also suffer more from the consequences when they go catastrophically wrong.

A second factor that focused attention within the mental health field on disasters was growing recognition in the 1980s that they could serve as vehicles for understanding other less directly observable kinds of trauma. As Raphael noted in 1986, examining disasters can be of tremendous heuristic value in helping us comprehend life event stressors because they illuminate how a particular incident might affect a large number of people. Disasters have a broad, sweeping impact, and practitioners can extrapolate from the range of psychological and social reactions that they can cause to consider the effects of smaller-scale or "personal" disasters and so achieve further insight into how people cope with overwhelming stress. Knowledge derived about risk and protective factors can be used to mitigate the possible negative impact of stressful events, large and small, in addition to guiding disaster management and preparedness policy. And this information can help DMH professionals determine where to target helping interventions, be they psychological or practical in nature.

The Concept of Trauma

The third major trend contributing to the development of DMH was actually a prerequisite for the first two: the consolidation of the general concept of trauma. It may seem absurd to readers today that there was ever any question that external events could produce lasting emotional effects, but the impact of trauma on a survivor's mental health has truly only been acknowledged by mental health practitioners as a bona fide, clinical diagnostic entity for the past 25 years since the addition of posttraumatic stress disorder (PTSD) to the *Diagnostic and Statistical Manual of Mental Disorders* (*DSM*) in 1980. Even today, Brewin (2003) points out, we continue to have "saviors and skeptics" on either side of a debate regarding the fallout of psychological trauma.

For decades before that inclusion, ideas about trauma were entertained but not fully embraced. The concept of an external experience causing deeply internal, harmful psychological change was novel. Mid-20th-century psychology regarded mental illness as originating in childhood deficits of maladaptation or family dysfunction. It required a dramatic adjustment even to begin to consider that persistent, detrimental psychological symptoms could develop in those subjected to extreme physical and psychological stress. Accepting the impact of external trauma constituted a change in focus from the intrapsychic to the biopsychosocial, which was a difficult shift for many practitioners to make.

It is, perhaps, understandable that the full recognition of trauma's impact faced so much resistance. After all, such a shift carries inherent social implications that may engender scrutiny of existing social realities and lead to issues concerning accountability. Accepting the concept of trauma meant that the larger impact of certain acts, such as war and physical abuse, could no longer be ignored. It also implied that people have breaking points—that, given enough stress, all individuals will succumb. This shattered belief in one's ultimate self-control. Additionally, a survivor's body took on a new, important role as a witness to what had transpired: Biological alterations signaled the presence of prolonged or persistent symptoms in response to an event.

Given these barriers to acceptance, how did trauma finally come to be recognized by mental health practitioners? Judith Herman traced how the concept of trauma has surfaced into public consciousness over the past century in her 1992 book, *Trauma and Recovery*. Herman writes that this awareness was derived from three separate historical developments: the psychological concept of hysteria, the heightened social recognition of sexual and domestic violence, and the recognition of the war phenomenon of shell shock and its successors. Let's now examine these factors.

Railway Spine, Hysteria, and Dissociation

In the early 19th century, several doctors in England wrote about lasting neurological symptoms following physical injuries. They generally attributed the symptoms to lesions, which they believed developed after a victim received a concussion of the spinal cord (Trimble, 1981). In 1882 John Eric Erichsen, a professor of surgery at London's University College Hospital, expanded on this theory and applied it specifically to victims of accidents in England's rapidly expanding railway system.

Erichsen was intrigued by cases in which the trauma was severe or of a different nature than the proximate cause—the physical injury—would lead one to expect. For example, he reported cases in which a railway accident led to problems including anxiety, disturbed sleep, distressing dreams, irritability, sudden alarm, and problems with memory and concentration (Kinzie & Goetz, 1996). These symptoms are now clearly recognizable as psychological responses to trauma, but in keeping with the beliefs of the era, they were deemed to be the result of damage to the spinal cord. Weisaeth (2002) attributes this misperception to the period's ignorance of the relationship between mind and body: "In the absence of a theory of anxiety, the physical signs of anxiety were easily misunderstood as symptoms of organic illness." Thus, Erichsen wrongly attributed the symptoms of trauma to an organic cause, regardless of how disproportionate or unrelated those symptoms were to the original injury, but his work is still noteworthy because it was the first time that disasters and trauma were explicitly linked.

A contemporary, Herbert Page, countered Erichsen's theory, recognizing that the experience of a railway accident could cause purely emotional damage above and beyond any physical injury and that this emotional damage could be responsible for the variety of symptoms reported by accident victims. Because they occurred so suddenly and often at high speeds, railway accidents included an element of horror that was lacking in less novel, nontechnologically driven events, so they were capable of causing psychological harm in addition to physical injury. Therefore, Page proposed, cases of "railway spine" could be divided into those with an organic, or physical, cause and those with a functional, or psychological, cause, and he suggested that some of the functional cases could be attributed to traumatic neurasthenia, or hysterical neurosis as defined by the concurrent work of Jean-Martin Charcot.

Charcot, a French neurologist, studied diseases of the nervous system at Paris's Medecin de l'Hospice de la Salpetriere from 1862 to 1893. He is credited with demonstrating the existence of hysteria in men, previously considered an exclusively female complaint. In **hysteria,** a disturbing psychological event or conflict is kept out of one's awareness. The conflict is not under conscious control, but it does not go away, instead signaling its existence through physical and emotional symptoms. Charcot specialized in treating patients who were suffering from a variety of unexplained physical symptoms including paralysis, contractures (muscles that contract and cannot be relaxed) and seizures. Charcot eventually came to the conclusion that many of his patients were suffering from a form of hysteria that had been induced by their emotional response to a traumatic accident in their past, such as a fall from a scaffold or a railway crash. In fact, he proposed that the symptoms of railway spine that Page wrote about were often the result of hysteria (Saretsky, 2004). These patients suffered, in his view, not from the physical effects of the accident but from the idea they had formed of it. Charcot attempted to cure the malady by eliciting the buried experience or conflict through hypnosis.

Sigmund Freud and his colleague, Pierre Janet, met while studying with Charcot in the 1880s, and both went on to expand upon Charcot's theories of hysteria. Freud, the founder of the psychoanalytic movement and a pioneer in advancing new mental health concepts, was captivated by Charcot's work. He took from it the notion that one of the principal forms of psychological disorders came about when a traumatic experience led to the process of unconscious symptom formation, a hysterical response. Janet believed that hysterical reactions to trauma only occurred in people with some preexisting mental weakness or pathology, whereas Freud, working in collaboration with Josef Breuer, believed that hysterical symptoms arose as a socially acceptable expression of repressed memories of traumatic events, regardless of any underlying psychopathology (Trimble, 1981).

Although Freud's theories had more lasting influence, it was Janet who first used the term **dissociation** and explained its role in a victim's response to trauma. He suggested that dissociation occurred as a way of splitting traumatic memories off from awareness in order to avoid the distress that the memories would otherwise cause because they were incongruent with existing cognitive schema:

"According to Janet, emotions that are far too strong cannot be deposited anywhere and thus dissociate themselves from conscious and deliberate control" (Lamprecht & Sack, 2002). Such fragmented consciousness impairs a person's functioning because mental resources are not fully available for the demands of daily life, such as handling minor conflicts, grieving, and accumulating positive experiences (Weisaeth, 2002)—limitations that closely resemble our current description of PTSD. The importance of Janet's insight into the role of dissociation during traumatic events was recognized at the time by his contemporaries but seemed to become somewhat submerged diagnostically until interest in dissociation was revived in the 1980s and as a symptom that would be included in the diagnosis of acute stress disorder (Bryant & Harvey, 2000).

Freudian Concepts of Trauma

Freud's studies of hysteria ultimately led to two separate models of trauma, the "unbearable situation" model and the later "unacceptable impulse" model (Weisaeth, 2002). In the former, developed during Freud's collaboration with Breuer in the 1890s, exposure to a situation of traumatic helplessness (typically, premature sexual experience) overwhelms the ego, and the resulting unmanageable fright leads to the development of a traumatic neurosis. In this model, the reaction is brought about by external forces, not through any action or desire of the patient—which was a remarkably progressive view given how little credibility that the mentally ill, particularly women, had at the time. Initially, Freud's therapeutic goal for the patients he diagnosed with hysteria was "catharsis" or "abreaction": By making use of the hypnocathartic method, a patient was able to reproduce what he or she had kept out of consciousness. If this was accomplished so that the unconscious mental representations were integrated into the patient's normal consciousness and associations, Freud's early assumption was that the accompanying affect and emotions would be liberated (abreaction) and discharged (catharsis). At that initial time, Freud did not seem to hold doubts about the genuineness of the trauma. Instead, he was preoccupied with the fact that the memory traces of the trauma could not be verbalized or accessed and controlled in the conscious domain.

However, Freud later retreated from this position, perhaps in the face of the devastating social implications behind such a theory; he may have been unable to confront how endemic the mistreatment of children and women appeared to be based on the prevalence of hysteria (Herman, 1992). He rejected his initial theory on the sexual abuse that he had started to expose and turned his work to exploring what he now claimed were his patients' fantasies about abuse. It was this approach that led to Freud's "unacceptable impulse" model, which asserted that hysterical symptoms are produced by defense mechanisms triggered by the patient's own inappropriate desires. This view emphasized subjective experience over external reality—leading to a tendency to blame the victim for his or her own traumatization that would continue (at least in cases of sexual assault and domestic abuse) for decades (Herman, 1992). Freud altered his therapeutic process to adopt a new method he called psychoanalysis, or "the talking cure."

In his previous period, the goal was relatively simple: Patients had to put their traumatic history into words, especially those parts that were forgotten or repressed. In this new theory, psychopathology in general and hysteria in particular had more to do with a "wrong connection" caused by a conflict between desire and prohibition than with a real traumatic event. Treatment became more complex, with a heavy intrapsychic emphasis, and had to do with repairing the right connection through free association and the process of interpretation.

Herman (1992) describes this shift in Freud's attitude toward trauma as rooted in a social and political need to deny sexual abuse that led him to reject the veracity of complaints he had previously accepted as true. As a result, the psychiatric study of the genuine aftermath of traumatic events as an individual internalizes them froze for a time—just as the focus on the impact of trauma shifted to a more collective venue.

Trauma and War

each war
gives it a new name
and each war
gives it a new treatment

D. Theis

At the same time that Freud was revising his views of hysteria and trauma, the reality of psychological trauma was gaining attention in another context: war. World War I coincided with Freudian theoretical advances that were applied in the treatment of soldiers, such as the interpretation of dreams and discussion of mental conflicts. In fact, Ben Shephard's *A War of Nerves* (2001) makes the case that psychiatry and psychoanalysis flourished in the United States and England because they were legitimized and popularized by their use in the two World Wars.

Much of our knowledge and appreciation of the psychological response to trauma and disaster has been derived from the urge to understand and manage responses to war. War has been defined as "the controlled application of violence to achieve political goals" (Silver, 2005); it can be likened to a "planned" disaster, one that unfolds over time. The conditions of battle include both human agency and mass violence, factors that are associated with higher levels of trauma (DeWolfe, 2000; Norris, Friedman, Watson, Byrne, Diaz, & Kaniasty, 2002). Yet there has often been resistance to a full admission of the psychological consequences of war. As Herman (1992) observes, "One of the many casualties of war's devastation [is] the illusion of manly honor and glory in battle." This resistance is maintained from war to war as lessons regarding the impact of combat on those fighting surface and than submerge. Let's review how views of trauma from the battlefield have changed over time.

The American Civil War   In ancient wars, warriors who faltered in battle were viewed as cowards or as possessed. The American Civil War in the 1860s appears to have been the first Western war where a common traumatic syndrome was acknowledged in a large number of soldiers; Weisaeth (2002) suggests that military authorities in previous wars could not begin to pay attention to psychological problems until other issues like infectious diseases had been brought under control through advances in medicine and hygiene practices. Affected soldiers were considered to have "neurasthenia," meaning a state of physical and mental exhaustion (Trimble, 1981) or "irritable heart syndrome," also called "soldier's heart" or "Da Costa's syndrome," after the doctor who wrote about it in 1871. Symptoms, which included rapid pulse, palpitations, cardiac pain, and respiratory problems as well as headache, dizziness, disturbed sleep, and gastrointestinal symptoms (Kinzie & Goetz, 1996), were attributed to overstimulation of nerve centers at the base of the heart. Of course, these can now be recognized as physiological reactions to stress, but because this war predated Charcot's work on hysteria or Page's on nervous shock, the symptoms were still attributed to purely organic causes—or to malingering to avoid dangerous duties, a dichotomy that would remain in place for the next several wars.

"Nostalgia" was the second major label used during the Civil War era to describe what would be thought of today as a stress disorder. Military doctors of the time recommended dealing with cases of nostalgia in different ways. One tactic was to accuse soldiers suffering from nostalgia of moral turpitude and a lack of patriotism and courage. Some suggested that permitting leaves of absence through a generous furlough policy might be useful. Others thought that idleness provoked "homesickness" and insisted that if soldiers were made to work hard, they would fare better and not have time to think of their families and the lives they left behind to engage in warfare. Battle activity and preparation for battle were also seen as curing many individuals.

World War I By the 1870s, interest in nostalgia as a medical category had all but vanished. However, in the face of compelling clinical phenomena and with the concomitant growth of medicine and psychology, military psychiatrists during the course of World War I came to acknowledge the psychological trauma resulting from soldiering. As in several other examples we have already mentioned, psychological reactions were initially attributed to physical causes. By 1914 British doctors were diagnosing soldiers with a malady they referred to as "shell shock." At first the doctors believed that a bursting artillery shell created a vacuum in the spine and that when the air rushed into this vacuum it disturbed the cerebrospinal fluid, causing an upset in the brain's functioning. This weapon-centered explanation reflected a marked change in the nature of the threat that soldiers were exposed to in this war: Artillery shelling was vastly more powerful than weaponry available in the previous wars. Tactical changes compounded this technological increase in destructive potential because the trench warfare strategies of World War I meant that soldiers were exposed, immobile, and often helpless to far greater explosive impact than ever before. Thus, symptoms of hysteria, confusion, exhaustion, and nervous collapse were at first attributed to concussive damage caused by the proximity to explosions.

Before long, though, the explanation for shell shock shifted to a psychological diagnosis that painted the condition as a kind of male hysteria. The term *shell shock* remained in use even after it became clear that the syndrome was a type of battle neurosis without an organic cause—a point that was undeniable because the condition was found in men who had not been directly exposed to shelling. Yet military authorities were loathe to abandon a physical explanation because it spared them from having to attribute a soldier's breakdown to any personal weakness or cowardice or to a lack of trust in leadership or belief in the war (Weisaeth, 2002).

Regardless of politically motivated attributions of cause, the number of afflicted soldiers was remarkable. Between 1914 and 1918, the British Army identified 80,000 men as suffering from shell shock. A much larger number of soldiers with the same symptoms were classified as "malingerers" and sent back to the front line. In some cases, men committed suicide; others broke down under the pressure, refused to obey the orders of their officers, and deserted. There were reports that some soldiers who disobeyed orders were shot on the spot, while others were court-martialed and imprisoned or executed for cowardice. Philip Gibbs (1923), a war reporter, wrote,

> The shell shock cases were the worst to see and the worst to cure. At first shell shock was regarded as damn nonsense and sheer cowardice by generals who had not themselves witnessed its effects. They had not seen, as I did, strongly, sturdy, men shaking with ague, mouthing like madman, figures of dreadful terror, speechless and uncontrollable. It was a physical as well as a moral shock which had reduced them to this quivering state.

Fortunately, methods for treating shell shock effectively began to emerge during World War I, driven by two primary principles. First, there was a recognition that collective, social aspects of corps membership functioned both as risk factors and as protective factors. Shell shock often occurred disproportionately within particular units, with incidence rates as high as 20% in some units, compared to 2% in combat troops overall (Kinzie & Goetz, 1996). This suggested that trauma had some contagious element among allies that could cause it to spread, but appealing to a soldier's loyalty to his brothers could also convince him to return to battle. Second, it was observed that keeping the affected soldier as close to the front as possible and creating an expectation that he would soon rejoin his unit often speeded his recovery. This principle became known as "forward psychiatry," and various armies created acronyms such as PIES (proximity, immediacy, expectancy, simplicity) and BICEPS (brevity, immediacy, centrality, expectancy, proximity, and simplicity) to describe it (Weisaeth, 2002). Removing a soldier from the front lines, in contrast, impaired his ability to recover by "(i) providing a primary gain by saving his life, (ii) reinforcing his sense of personal failure, and (iii) separating him from his group and the support that comes from mass-suggestion of men striving shoulder to shoulder" (Weisaeth, 2002).

World War II   With a new war, the nomenclature again changed. Soldiers in World War II suffered from "combat" or "battle fatigue" and tended to be removed from the battlefield and treated remotely at a hospital, often never to return. Psychoanalytically based explanations for battle-related neuroses flourished in

World War II, as post-Freudian theorists proposed explanations for why some soldiers developed psychological problems in response to their experiences (Kinzie & Goetz, 1996). Abram Kardiner's influential 1941 book, *The Traumatic Neuroses of War*, attributed posttraumatic damage to the ego's inability to master the traumatic event. In this view, a soldier's usual adaptive methods would become overwhelmed, leaving him unable to integrate the experience or adjust to the new external environment through corresponding internal adaptations. The ego then "contracted," an inhibitory process that resulted in symptoms such as flashbacks, amnesia, irritability, and disturbed sleep (Lamprecht & Sack, 2002).

Although Kardiner accepted traumatic neurosis as a legitimate response to overwhelming stress, he also acknowledged the existence of secondary gains that could develop if a soldier was not promptly treated and returned to the front lines:

> We know of the secondary gain in the form of compensation for illness after the war. But there is another equally important secondary gain in the form of legitimate escape from duty. The compensation issue then does not in these terms actually create the neurosis but is more of a source of resistance in treatment and rehabilitation. (Kardiner, 1941)

Kardiner and his collaborator in the 1940s, Herbert Speigel, developed a treatment method for soldiers in World War II that included hypnosis combined with talk therapy. This combination was intended to recover traumatic memories so that their attendant emotions could be integrated into normal memory; simply retrieving the memories without integrating them would not effect a lasting cure (Herman, 1992).

Vietnam: A War Unlike Any Other   It took the suffering and postconflict adjustment difficulties of Vietnam veterans to bring the impact of combat stress to the forefront of public consciousness and to dramatically expose the reality of the traumatic aftermath of horrendous and brutal events. Vietnam differed from previous American wars on several fronts, as outlined in a startling landmark article published in 1974 by a Veterans Administration social worker, Sarah Haley. "When the Patient Reports Atrocities" highlighted aspects that distinguished Vietnam from World War II and the Korean Conflict: namely, the use of guerilla tactics, the public exposure of war atrocities committed by soldiers during combat, and the fact that the war was undeclared and extremely unpopular among civilians. The Vietnam era (approximately 1961–1975) was a time of extreme social and political unrest in America. In contrast to previous wars when returning soldiers were generally welcomed home as heroes, those returning from Vietnam were stigmatized and greeted with hostility. A military of mostly drafted soldiers were spat upon and called baby killers. And veterans were unable to receive services that they needed to assist their recovery for a variety of reasons, including the fact that there was no diagnostic code for combat stress in the existing *DSM*, which was in its second edition in 1968.

With time, mental health clinicians—many of them returning veterans with their own personal experiences of the trauma of war—became increasingly socially and politically active in promoting veterans' needs. Veterans also began to advocate for themselves. A grassroots movement grew, raising social consciousness and awareness of war's aftereffect. Robert Jay Lifton, who later studied disaster's aftereffects, had served as a military psychiatrist in the Korean War and had studied and published work on the survivors of Hiroshima. He became an ardent antiwar activist and wrote about what was happening to Vietnam veterans. Charles Figley, a psychologist who eventually founded the Green Cross (an organization devoted to training mental health professionals in trauma and disaster response) and pioneered the concept of compassion fatigue, had served as a Marine in Vietnam in the 1960s. In 1978 he edited a book on Vietnam veterans and introduced a new psychosocial series that is still in existence, which recently produced a volume dedicated to the impact of disasters (Myers & Wee, 2005). John Wilson, another prominent trauma scholar, was a conscientious objector to the Vietnam War and began work on what he termed "The Forgotten Warrior" project (1977). He has written extensively on trauma and collaborated for over two decades on many works with Australian psychiatrist and disaster studies expert, Beverly Raphael.

Vietnam veterans helped mainstream the idea that horrific events can resurface even years later, to be experienced posttraumatically through a collection of equally horrific symptoms. The term *posttraumatic stress syndrome* crept into the vocabulary, labeling this latent reaction to previous trauma. After a prompt from Congress, the Veterans Administration funded research examining U.S. soldiers returning from Vietnam. It was this military research that provided the foundation for much of the initial conceptualization of the new diagnosis of PTSD (Brewin, 2003).

Combat Trauma Today   Fortunately for today's soldiers, the potential traumatic effects of combat are widely recognized, and the government makes efforts to address prevention and treatment. Current military mental health practice refers to "combat stress response," which is defined as "emotional conflict caused by the desire to perform duty while gripped by overwhelming fear of death or mutilation." Another condition, "combat fatigue," is described as "the psychological reaction manifested by a variety of physical symptoms during or immediately after combat." Military interventions now are short term, viewing the reaction as a passing one, and focused on early identification of combat stress or fatigue. Treatments include emphasizing the need for rest and offering an opportunity to talk, and social workers, psychologists, and psychiatrists are embedded in the war zone to provide services. Their emphasis is on restoration, and those they tend to are seen as soldiers, not patients; are managed, not treated; and who are fatigued, not mentally ill. When possible, soldiers are kept close to the unit so that the unit can support their own, especially because unit cohesion has proved to be the biggest protective factor against development of PTSD. However, these efforts, though commendable, cannot prevent significant psychological reactions to war stress. In 2004 Hoge, Castro, and Messer estimated that 15 to 17% of soldiers returning from combat in Iraq met the diagnostic criteria for PTSD, generalized anxiety disorder, or major depression. This research, acknowledging the psychological impact of war while a war is ongoing, is a stunning achievement.

It took nearly 10 years, for example, after Vietnam began, that its hurtful impact on soldiers was first addressed in the clinical literature.

The Legitimization of Trauma

Although there may be no more stressful setting than a battlefield, combat zones are not the only place to find evidence of posttraumatic stress symptoms. Unnerving events in day-to-day life, such as car wrecks, accidental near deaths, violent assaults—and disasters—can lead to similar symptoms. Indeed, if traumatic stress had remained relevant only in the context of war, there would be no DMH field. But during the 1970s, a zeitgeist arose in which awareness of trauma came to the fore in a variety of settings beyond combat.

A number of converging social influences were powerful in bringing trauma into public consciousness in the United States and throughout the world. Researchers began examining the effects of war on populations other than soldiers. Studies were published and conferences were held in Israel on the effects of war stress, "a logical occurrence given the unremitting nature of warfare in that region" (Bloom, 2000). Dr. Yael Danieli, whose parents were Holocaust survivors and who had served in the Israeli Defense Forces before immigrating to the United States, founded the Group Project for Holocaust Survivors and Their Children. During this time, she began her life's work of exploring the intergenerational transmission of victimization, styles of adaptation to victimization, survivor guilt, and the attitudes and difficulties of mental health professionals working with this population.

Interest in terrorism and hostage situations also grew during this period, perhaps prompted by several outstanding events in the early 1970s. In 1972 the world was riveted by the politically motivated hostage taking of Israeli athletes (whom were later killed) during the Olympics, a neutral, global event. Two years later, a hostage taken during a bank robbery in Sweden fell in love with and married the bank robber who held her captive, inspiring what became known as the "Stockholm Syndrome." In that same year, a terrorist group kidnapped Patty Hearst, the granddaughter of wealthy industrialist William Randolph Hearst. During her captivity, she was physically and psychologically tortured, yet she developed a new persona that was sympathetic to her captors, and she participated with them in criminal activities. These latter two episodes raised awareness of the powerful dynamics that can develop between victim and victimizer (Bloom, 2000). Looking at larger-scale issues, in 1975 the Department of Justice commissioned the National Institute of Mental Health to conduct an inquiry into the unique effects of terrorism, (Bloom, 2000). In separate research, a 1979 article by Sims, White, and Murphy concluded that even people who were not seriously harmed in a terrorist bombing were more incapacitated than would have been expected by what they called an "aftermath neurosis."

All these contemporaneous explorations contributed to a fuller understanding of the varied sources of trauma. But according to Herman (1992), the third principal contributor to trauma theory after hysteria and combat was the illumination of the impact of rape, domestic violence, and incest. Herman credits activists fighting for women's rights for this development: "Not until the women's liberation movement in the 1970s was it recognized that the most common posttraumatic disorders are those not of men in war but of women in civilian life." Rape in particular can lead to symptoms qualitatively akin to what soldiers may experience postcombat. Ann Burgess and Linda Holstrom (1974) described this as "rape trauma syndrome," making a case for the similarity in symptoms found in women who had been raped to the traumatic effects of war. Feminist writer Susan Brownmiller portrayed rape as an act of violence directed at maintaining control. As Herman (1992) noted, this placement of rape in a political framework allowed for discussion and cooperation among survivor groups.

THE DIAGNOSTIC NOMENCLATURE AND TRAUMA

As views of trauma evolved, so did the official terms used to describe its effects. The mental health field's primary source for diagnostic validity is the American Psychiatric Association's *Diagnostic and Statistical Manual of Mental Disorders* (*DSM*), which has been through several revisions since its inception. At the time when the first edition of the *DSM* was published in 1952, it was generally accepted that otherwise normal individuals could experience acute stress reactions as a transient response to extreme experiences (Bryant & Harvey, 2000). In the original *DSM*, a diagnosis of "gross stress reaction" applied to acute posttrauma reactions, whereas more lasting reactions were considered to reflect either anxiety or depressive neuroses—a division that reflected the opinion of the time that, although anyone could temporarily break under extreme pressure, most people would soon recover with treatment, and only those with some underlying pathology would experience long-term problems (Kinzie & Goetz, 1996).

The second edition, *DSM-II*, appeared in 1968. In this version, long-term effects were still subsumed in existing categories of neuroses (Bryant & Harvey, 2000). However, in a dramatic minimization of psychic trauma, the "gross stress reaction" diagnosis was replaced with "(transient) adjustment disorder of adult life," a description that encompassed a vast range of reactions including psychosis (Lamprecht & Sack, 2002). As Wilson et al. (2001) observed, this was striking because by that time there had been many events including wars, civil violence, and the threat of nuclear warfare, all of which should have underscored the importance of acknowledging the impact of trauma.

Fortunately, trauma was strongly reinserted into *DSM-III*, largely through the efforts of the Vietnam Veterans Working Group, which was composed of mental health experts and activist Vietnam veterans. Members worked to demonstrate to the American Psychiatric Association taskforce charged with revising the *DSM* that the reach of trauma's impact extended beyond war veterans and that other survivor groups also demonstrated posttraumatic stress responses worthy of a diagnosis. As a result, in 1980 the *DSM-III* introduced posttraumatic stress disorder as an anxiety disorder that was precipitated by exposure to an event that fell outside usual life experience. PTSD was the only diagnostic category in the *DSM* that was based on a disorder's etiology or cause, yet its description avoided theoretical discussion of cause and focused on overt symptoms (Kinzie & Goetz, 1996).

DSM-IV, published in 1994, refined the PTSD diagnosis. The rarity of the triggering event was de-emphasized, and more importance was placed on the survivor's perception of that event. Significantly, PTSD could now be diagnosed in someone who was not directly exposed to a horrific event. *DSM-IV* also addressed a vacuum that was inadvertently created by a refinement in the PTSD criteria in 1987's *DSM-III-R* (which was considered a revision of *DSM-III* rather than an entirely new edition). That change had stipulated that symptoms must be present for more than 1 month after the traumatic event, to show that they were not the result of a transitory reaction. However, this meant that there was no trauma-specific diagnosis for people suffering acute traumatic reactions within a month of the event, so they were placed into the adjustment disorder category. To correct for that imprecision, *DSM-IV* introduced a new diagnosis, acute stress disorder (ASD), to describe people suffering from significant distress immediately after a traumatic event.

According to Bryant and Harvey (2000), the ASD addition was controversial due to a lack of empirical evidence validating its diagnostic merits and because many in the field feared pathologizing normal reactions to extreme events. This new diagnosis emphasized dissociative symptoms, an onset time of 2 days to 4 weeks after a traumatic event, and the expectation that it is a precursor to PTSD. It implied the prediction of more serious, long-term sequelae.

With the establishment of these official diagnoses of posttraumatic reactions, the impact of trauma on survivors' psychological functioning was now formally recognized. This was a turning point for both trauma survivors and mental health practitioners, and it perhaps limited the general public's ability to deny the influence of the shockingly unimaginable on people. But as this review has shown, it has taken a long time to legitimize the reality of trauma's impact and people's suffering.

THE LINK BETWEEN TRAUMA AND DISASTERS

Early disaster studies paralleled the emergence of trauma studies. In one of the first studies of the effects of natural and human-made disasters on nonclinical samples, the Swiss researcher Edouard Stierlin proposed in 1911 that fright neuroses could result from violent emotions even in normal individuals with no underlying psychopathological disposition (Weisaeth, 2002). Symptoms of fright neurosis include amnesia, clouded consciousness, disorientation, hallucinations, fearful affect, and perceptual disturbances. This acute reaction usually improved within 3 days although in some cases a secondary reaction, traumatic neuroses, could develop; its symptoms include increased pulse rate or pulse lability, increased patellar reflexes, sleep disturbance, and sometimes tremor and loss of energy (Kinzie & Goetz, 1996).

Between the World Wars, two notable researchers examined the impact of disasters on civilians. Prasad (1935) studied the effects of the enormous Indian earthquake of 1934, paying particular attention to the rumors that arose as people tried to accept the immensity of their losses. Then in 1944, Lindemann wrote about the impact on survivors of the deadly Cocoanut Grove nightclub fire. Of the 46 survivors he followed for 11 months after the event, 26 were found to have developed psychiatric complications. He divided symptoms into two syndromes, general nervousness or anxiety neurosis. Those with general nervousness reported irritability, nervousness, fatigue, and insomnia; two-thirds of those cases cleared up within 9 months. In contrast, those with anxiety neurosis had uncontrollable fears and anxieties, accompanied by nightmares, and two-thirds of those patients' symptoms did not improve after 9 months. Perhaps most notably, patients who developed subsequent psychological symptoms did not experience more severe burns or more deaths of friends in the fire than those who did not develop sequelae, providing further support for the belief that everyone is susceptible to posttraumatic suffering. Building on his conclusions, Lindemann developed one of the earliest models of crisis intervention, described later.

Moving forward in time, several large-scale events during the 1970s provided an opportunity to study disaster's impact on psychosocial functioning. In 1972 the Buffalo Creek Dam broke in West Virginia, killing 125 and displacing many more. Then in 1979, the Three Mile Island nuclear reactor experienced a meltdown outside of Harrisburg, Pennsylvania. Even though no serious health consequences occurred, the population in the area was evacuated, and the incident spurred tremendous fear. Both of these events became the focus of a great deal of analysis. During the same decade, a number of noteworthy researchers and clinicians turned their attention to studying disasters. In 1979 Lenore Terr published the first of a series of papers and a book on the functioning of a group of children who had been kidnapped in Chowchilla, California, in 1976, introducing a developmental focus on the effects of trauma. In the early 1970s, Beverly Raphael, an Australian psychiatrist, began to write and publish work about disasters and bereavement. Bloom (2000) notes that Raphael established a connection early on with John Wilson, an American trauma scholar, thereby engendering an international dialogue. Other disaster studies emerged at this time, including a 1977 overview by Quarantelli and Dynes in the *Annual Review of Sociology* examining disasters as a social phenomenon.

By the 1990s the concept of psychological trauma resulting from disaster was "in the air" worldwide. Bloom (2000) speculates that the growing global communication network was alerting people to tragedy every day. Disasters are high-profile events that receive much publicity, helping to increase the general level of consciousness about the consequences of traumatic events. Accompanying this consciousness, a budding awareness began to emerge that the various forms of traumatic experience might be similar and even interconnected in some ways. The nascent body of literature on the psychological effects of disaster implied that there could be long-term consequences to overwhelming stress even in populations "generally considered by the public to be free from any culpability in their experienced victimization" (Bloom, 2000). The disaster survivor became and, is each of us.

Although the ascension and acceptance of trauma's role in psychological maladaptation and disorder provided the foundation for DMH, other streams in professional mental health also contributed to the growth of this specialty. Research on pathological responses to immense stress and on human wellness and potential also inform the practice. Hans Selye provided the groundwork for the development of the basic concepts of stress management. Abraham Maslow described the hierarchy of needs that survivors express after a disaster. Viktor Frankl, a concentration camp survivor, wrote of the existential search for meaning in the face of unimaginable atrocities, speaking to the human dynamic capacity not only for survival but also for wisdom. Their respective works contributed to the multifaceted practice of DMH.

Stress and Trauma

Shalev (2004) asks, "Does stress equal trauma?" This is a core question for DMH and one that is not easy to answer. (And the use of the word *stress* in clinical descriptions such as those of PTSD and psychosomatic illness hardly helps). Conceptually, trauma and stress have an intimate and intricate relationship that is not fully sorted out. Trauma represents the imprint of extreme stress that may be the result of a single intense blow, such as surviving a disaster, or cumulative blows, like the experience of living with an abusive partner. However, an individual's nature and biopsychosocial resources contribute significantly to where exposure to a potentially traumatic stressor will lead. One survivor might be relatively untouched by an experience, whereas the same stressor causes severe reactions and lasting impairment in a second person. A third might experience reactions that are unpleasant and upsetting but transient. And the reaction of a fourth may fall in a slightly different realm, appearing more existential and more closely related to meaning making, identity, and self-esteem than to posttraumatic anxiety. Thus, stress does not appear to be automatically equivalent with trauma, a point that is important to remember in treating disaster survivors as individuals. Still, even nontraumatic stress can take a toll.

The concept of stress is now an ingrained part of our vocabulary and daily existence, but our current use of the term originated only a little more than 50 years ago. It was essentially "coined" by Hans Selye (1956). As a medical student, Selye noticed that patients suffering from different diseases often exhibited identical signs and symptoms. They just "looked sick." Based on this observation, he later discovered and described the general adaptation syndrome (GAS), a response of the body to the demands placed upon it. The GAS detailed how stress induces hormonal autonomic responses that over time can lead to an assortment of illnesses: ulcers, high blood pressure, arteriosclerosis, arthritis, kidney disease, and allergic reactions. Selye concluded that the GAS has three distinctive phases: alarm, resistance, and exhaustion (also called, respectively, alarm reaction, whereby the body detects the external stimulus; adaptation, whereby the body engages defensive countermeasures against the stressor; and exhaustion, whereby the body begins to run out of defenses).

Selye broke new ground by demonstrating the role of emotional responses in causing or combating much of the wear and tear experienced by human beings throughout their lives. In his view, stress is the nonspecific response of the human body to any demand made upon it. Stress could be bad (*distress*) and contribute to disease, but it could also be good (*eustress*) and contribute to human well-being. Through his seminal 1936 work, *A Syndrome Produced by*

Diverse Nocuous Agents, and a more popular 1956 book, *The Stress of Life,* Selye played an indirect though major role in the stimulation of ideas concerning the sources of "wellness" as well as of "sickness." He also evolved into a sort of philosophical leader whose views on health helped change the way that the body and mind were viewed in the decades after World War II. He often spoke of the value of love. Psychosomatic research conducted by Selye's students during the 1960s fostered the development of clinical biofeedback, the growth of body–mind theories, and investigations of the role of stress in the rate of human aging. Selye underscored the importance of the physical, biological underpinnings in an individual's response to external stress. His work laid the foundation for the development of the concept and theory of stress management, a core feature of DMH.

Building on Selye's groundbreaking work, in 1977 Mardi Horowitz wrote *Stress Response Syndromes,* in which he began to provide a psychophysiological framework of how the body reacts under intense stressors and how these responses connected to a psychological manifestation. Following Horowitz's work, Bessel van der Kolk has been in the forefront of research in the psychobiology of trauma and in the quest for more effective treatments for more than 20 years. Van der Kolk's interest in this field began in the late 1970s when he became an employee of the Veteran's Administration and began to appreciate how much trauma is "incarnate"—that is, how overwhelming stress is captured in the bodies and brains of those exposed. His approach to understanding and working with trauma became increasingly holistic. Traumatic experiences, he now believes, are "relived" through the survivor's sensory modalities and behavioral actions. Similar to Freud's view of the core pathology of traumatic events, van der Kolk asserts that certain sensations, emotions, memories or elements related to the traumatic experience are dissociated. They are not psychologically processed in the same ways as other experiences are. As a result, these fragments return unbidden; they may have triggers that stimulate their resurgence but often are unpredictable and are resistant to fading over time. Physiological reactions to stress, both typical and disordered, are discussed in the next two chapters, because understanding them thoroughly is essential for understanding the experience of disaster survivors.

Wellness and Humanistic Psychology

Disaster mental health also draws strongly on the theories of humanistic psychology, which was characterized by one of its founders, Abraham Maslow, as a "third wave" that succeeded Freudian theory and behaviorism. Humanistic psychology gave rise to several different therapies, all guided by the idea that people possess the inner resources for growth and healing and that the point of therapy is to help remove obstacles to individuals' ability to achieve those goals. The most well-known humanistic approach was client-centered therapy, developed by Carl Rogers, which emphasized unconditional positive regard and "joining" one's client. Maslow's chief contribution to the field was his suggestion that human beings' needs are arranged like a ladder, or a pyramid, in a hierarchy of needs. The most basic needs were physical, for air, water, food, and sex. Then came safety needs—security and stability—followed by psychological or social needs for belonging, love, and acceptance. At the top of the pyramid were the self-actualizing needs to fulfill oneself, to become all that one is capable of becoming. Maslow felt that unfulfilled needs lower on the ladder would inhibit a person from climbing to the next step. He saw these needs as innate and essential for survival and for self-regulation. Rogers's and Maslow's theories, with their emphasis on addressing survivor's practical concerns and helping them tap their own resources, form the basis for the earliest essential DMH interventions.

We also take note of the contribution of Viktor Frankl, who built his *logotherapy,* or existential analysis, around the human quest to find meaning in pain, guilt, and death. Frankl's psychological theories depict the personal, dynamic aspects of people's response to great adversity. They were derived from his own exposure to extreme stress, which he recounted in *Man's Search for Meaning* (1946): He was a survivor of four Nazi concentration camps. His wife, father, mother, and brother all died in the camps; only he and his sister survived. The "existential" aspect of Frankl's psychotherapy maintained that humans have the ability to choose how they will ultimately respond to extreme adversity, no matter the biological or environmental forces. In his view, tragedy could also provide humans with the opportunity to turn suffering into achievement and accomplishment by deriving from guilt the opportunity to change oneself for the better and to view life's transitoriness as an incentive to take responsible action. Elements from Frankl's theories can be used to help disaster survivors find meaning in their experiences and to possibly use suffering as a touchstone for posttraumatic growth.

CRISIS INTERVENTION IN THE COMMUNITY

Moving from theoretical influences to professional responses to traumatic stressors, the mental health field of crisis intervention offered DMH a well-formulated springboard from which to leap into action. Dykeman (2003) provides a clear description of the principles of crisis intervention, which we quote at length:

> Crisis intervention provides an immediate and temporary emotional first aid to the victim, with specific interventions targeted to the victim and to the circumstances of the presenting problems. To this end, crisis intervention attempts to reduce the level of stress experienced by the crisis victim and to modulate the intensity of stressors operating in the victim's life. Timing is of crucial importance. An immediate intervention is needed to interrupt, reduce or redirect the crisis victim's maladaptive behavior. In this regard, professionals from a variety of disciplines, and non-professionals alike, often provide crisis intervention strategies . . . As such, crisis intervention is usually an immediate and temporary intrusion into the life of a person . . . the focus is directed to personality factors as coping mechanisms and individual resilience, as well as to such environmental factors as the sources of emotional support.

Theorists have divided crisis situations into different domains (James & Gilliland, 2005). Often they have been broadly placed in two categories, maturational/developmental and situational/accidental. Crises that involve the reassessment of the meaning and purpose of life may be seen as belonging to a third, existential category.

A review of the crisis intervention literature demonstrates diversity in terms of theory and techniques, but most scholars attribute the origin of modern crisis intervention methodology to the work of Eric Lindemann (1944) and his colleagues following the 1942 Cocoanut Grove nightclub fire. This fast-moving fire killed 493 people in Boston, making it the country's largest single-building destruction of human life at that time. Lindemann and others from Massachusetts General Hospital helped survivors who had lost loved ones in that event. They involved clergy and other community caretakers in helping survivors cope with their sudden grief, a collaboration that was novel for that time. Lindemann's clinical report on the psychological aftermath of the fire and the intervention strategies used became a foundation for the emergence and development of crisis theory as a conceptual framework for preventive psychiatric interventions.

Lindemann later worked with Gerald Caplan, a proponent of preventive psychiatry, to launch a community-wide effort in 1946 (Caplan, 1964). Known as the Wellesley Project, the initiative was used to study and support personal reactions to traumatic events. This early emphasis on community well-being represented an advance in deciphering how to help others during a time of crisis, and it was an approach whose popularity would soon grow. Fueled by the social activist spirit of the 1960s, a community mental health movement arose throughout the United States. The burgeoning movement received generous government support: The Short–Doyle Act of 1957 provided funding for each county throughout the United States to provide mental health clinics. In 1963 the Community Mental Health Centers Act created a comprehensive program of mental health care facilities available to all residents (Kanel, 2003). As a result of these efforts and the concomitant discovery and use of psychotropic medications, monumental deinstitutionalization of mental patients took place. Mental health centers were now located in clients' communities; initially intended to serve the chronically or severely mentally ill, these centers also began to serve less impaired and healthier clients. Serving this population became a specialty area for practitioners. Models of providing care as needed in the community came into being; these included the development of hotlines as well as mobile crisis teams, tactics that are often borrowed today by DMH practitioners.

THE ROLE OF EMERGENCY MANAGEMENT

Of course, disaster survivors are likely to have many practical and logistical needs in addition to their mental health needs. DMH helpers often work as part of or collaborate with the organizations responsible for tending to those needs, so we provide an overview of the major players in disaster response.

The Federal Emergency Management Agency (FEMA) is tasked with responding to, planning for, and recovering from disasters. FEMA traces its original roots to the Congressional Act of 1803. This act, generally considered the first piece of disaster legislation, provided assistance to a New Hampshire town following an extensive fire. In the century that followed, ad hoc legislation was passed more than 100 times in response to hurricanes, earthquakes, floods, and other natural disasters. By the 1930s, a federal approach to disasters became popular, but relief was still offered through a variety of agencies. Such a piecemeal approach led to inefficiency and drove the development of legislation requiring greater cooperation between federal agencies. The 1960s and early 1970s brought massive disasters requiring major federal response and recovery operations. A string of powerful hurricanes included Carla in 1962, Betsy in 1965, Camille in 1969, and Agnes in 1972. The Alaskan earthquake hit in 1964, and the San Fernando earthquake rocked southern California in 1971. These events served to focus attention on the issue of natural disasters and brought about increased legislation.

In 1968 the National Flood Insurance Act offered new flood protection to homeowners. In 1974 the Disaster Relief Act firmly established the process of presidential disaster declarations, and it officially recognized the roles and responsibilities of the American Red Cross in times of disaster, establishing important and influential lines of communication between American Red Cross and the federal government in the areas of disaster planning, preparedness, response, and relief. The Disaster Relief Act also included a mental health component: It authorized the National Institute of Mental Health (NIMH) to provide training and services to alleviate mental health problems created or increased by major disasters. This program is funded by FEMA and is designed to supplement the available resources of state and local governments and can support crisis counseling for months after a disaster, if needed.

Although the Disaster Relief Act provided some consolidation, emergency and disaster activities remained fragmented. When planned responses to hazards associated with nuclear power plants and the transportation of hazardous substances were added to those for natural disasters, more than 100 federal agencies were involved in some aspect of disasters, hazards, and emergencies. Many parallel programs and policies existed at the state and local level, compounding the complexity of federal disaster relief efforts. As a result, President Carter centralized federal emergency functions through a 1979 executive order that merged many of the separate disaster-related responsibilities into the new Federal Emergency Management Agency. Given the similarities between natural hazard preparedness and civil defense activities, those responsibilities were also transferred to the new agency from the Defense Department's Defense Civil Preparedness Agency. FEMA began development of an Integrated Emergency Management System with an all-hazards approach that included "direction, control and warning systems which are common to the full range of emergencies from small isolated events to the ultimate emergency—war" (www.FEMA.gov).

FEMA was faced with many unusual challenges in its first few years, which emphasized how complex emergency management can be. Early disasters and emergencies included the contamination of Love Canal, the Cuban refugee crisis, and the accident at the Three Mile Island nuclear power plant. Later, the Loma Prieta earthquake in 1989 and Hurricane Andrew in 1992 focused major national attention on the agency. Over time, disaster relief and recovery operations became increasingly streamlined, with a new emphasis regarding preparedness and mitigation and focusing agency employees on customer service. The end of the cold war also allowed FEMA's limited resources to shift from civil defense into disaster relief, recovery, and mitigation programs.

The terrorist attacks of September 11, 2001 shifted FEMA's focus yet again to issues of national preparedness and homeland security and tested it in unprecedented ways. The agency coordinated its activities with the newly formed Office of Homeland Security, and FEMA's Office of National Preparedness was given responsibility for helping ensure that the nation's first responders were trained and equipped to deal with weapons of mass destruction. FEMA was now actively directing its all-hazards approach to disasters toward homeland security issues. In March 2003, FEMA joined 22 other federal agencies, programs, and offices to form the Department of Homeland Security. The new department, initially headed by Secretary Tom Ridge, brought a coordinated approach to national security during emergencies and disasters, both natural and human-made. In July 2005, Ridge's successor, Michael Chertoff, announced a department restructuring intended to increase efficiency and responsiveness. No doubt FEMA will be part of further organizational changes in the future as the nation's emergency needs continue to change, especially in the wake of sharp criticism of FEMA's response to Hurricane Katrina in 2005.

Government disaster response does not occur entirely at the federal level; Lystad (1988) notes that the responsibility for planning emergency-related programs, including training those who will run such programs and practicing roles and responsibilities during drills and tabletop exercises, is located within public agencies at the federal, state, and local levels. Each state has an office of emergency management that coordinates emergency-related planning, with arrangements made for localities within the state based on their location and size. These offices work with larger state and federal agencies when additional resources are needed. The importance of having mental health professionals involved—hopefully with more than a consultancy role, at least in the future— in the planning processes of emergency management at the federal, state, and local levels cannot be underestimated.

Humanitarian Relief Groups

Another distinct cornerstone of disaster response is provided by humanitarian relief agencies. Humanitarian agencies are conventionally divided into three types: intergovernment or international organizations (IGOs), government or national organizations (GOs), and nongovernment organizations (NGOs). The United Nations is an example of an IGO. The U.S. Agency for International Development, an independent federal agency that provides foreign assistance and humanitarian aid to advance the political and economic interests of the United States, is a GO. In contrast, NGOs are composed of individuals with shared interests and goals. They may be paid members of an agency or volunteers offering relief efforts to clients in need.

There is great diversity to NGOs in terms of size, mission, and politics. Those concerned with health, welfare, and humanitarian matters include the Red Cross and Red Crescent Movement. Established in 1863, this movement is composed of the International Committee of the Red Cross (ICRC), National Red Cross and Red Crescent Societies, and the International Federation of the Red Cross and Red Crescent Societies. Although international, the movement is nongovernment in structure, and all of its activities have one central purpose: to prevent and alleviate human suffering, without discrimination, and to protect human dignity. Their aim is restorative, to rebuild safety and trust. The ICRC is the founding body. It promotes and guards international humanitarian law and directs Red Cross involvement with armed conflict and internal violence. The Federation coordinates assistance to victims of disasters, whether natural or human caused, outside of conflict areas. It encourages the development of National Societies within individual countries to help them plan and implement disaster preparedness programs.

Within the United States, voluntary agencies are critical partners with city, state, and federal emergency management agencies in helping communities recover from the devastating effects of disasters. These entities are involved in all four phases of emergency management: mitigation, preparedness, response, and recovery. Disaster relief agencies exemplify the "FI-LO" ideal: first in, last out. Voluntary agencies help people get back on their feet after the devastating effects of disaster; without these agencies, local, state, and federal entities could not meet all the unique needs of disaster victims. The United States has a long history of altruism in this regard, stemming from colonial times.

Today there are numerous disaster relief agencies, many of which are derived from a religious, ecumenical philosophy based on doing acts of good when people are suffering the most. Some of the faith-based groups that are active in disaster recovery work include the Salvation Army, Adventist Community Services, Church of the Brethren, and the Southern Baptist Disaster Relief.

The American Red Cross and Disaster Mental Health

The relief group that has played the largest role in the history of DMH is the American Red Cross, which was the very first disaster relief agency to formally acknowledge the need for mental health support during times of disaster in the United States. It was also the first voluntary disaster relief agency to develop standards regarding who could deliver such an important service and to create a standardized training curriculum for all of the professional mental health volunteers who would be responding under its auspices to help those experiencing disaster-related stressors.

Clara Barton, a teacher who interrupted her career to commit herself to volunteer work, founded the American Red Cross in 1881, to support soldiers during the Civil War. She received permission to volunteer at the front lines during the war, and after it was over, she began a letter campaign to search for missing soldiers. Barton suffered from exhaustion as a result of her work (perhaps making her the first helper who we may identify as suffering from compassion fatigue) and traveled to Europe to recuperate. While there she was exposed to the International Red Cross. She served with them at the front lines during the Franco–Prussian War, and she learned about the Geneva Treaty, which contained provisions for relief to sick and wounded soldiers. After returning to the United States, she plunged into the task of creating an American-based Red Cross.

Her efforts were successful: In 1881 the National Society of the Red Cross was organized, in national headquarters located one block from the White House in Washington, DC, thanks to money donated by John D. Rockefeller. During her 25 years as head of the organization, Barton personally served at many disaster sites in the United States and throughout the world; her last disaster job was the Galveston, Texas, hurricane in 1900.

Over a century after its inception, the American Red Cross began an initiative to develop a systematic and organized plan to expand its role and to help disaster victims even further by including a mental health component in its services. The pressing need to address stress levels within the organization as well as in victims became evident in the wake of two large-scale disasters in 1989, Hurricane Hugo and the Loma Prieta earthquake. High levels of worker dissatisfaction and resignations led to the distribution of an extensive study, which discovered "alarming levels of distress within the ranks of Red Cross workers, who were suffering under the strain of work overload (increasingly frequent and long term disaster assignments) in the face of insufficient support" (Weaver, Dingman, Morgan, Hong, & North, 2000). In 1990 the American Red Cross National Disaster Services evaluated their relief operations protocols and convened a task force whose purpose was to ascertain whether there was a need for a formalized, internal DMH program. Given its far-reaching activities in the seemingly endless area of disaster relief (Lystad, 1988), this task force took into account the mental health needs of both survivors and disaster workers—consideration of the latter marking an important and defining new trend.

As a result of the task force's findings, the American Red Cross Mental Health Services (MHS) was created with the goals of ameliorating acute postdisaster stress responses among both disaster survivors and Red Cross workers. In 1991 systematic training for mental health professionals in Red Cross disaster policy and procedures began. To facilitate the provision of mental health during times of disaster, the American Red Cross developed Statements of Understanding with different national mental health organizations including the American Psychological Association, the National Association of Social Workers in 1992, and the American Psychiatric Association in 1995.

The power of the program was soon recognized in the disaster field. For example, the National Transportation Safety Board designated the American Red Cross to be the "independent nonprofit organization" to provide for the emotional well-being of the families or survivors who are impacted by an aviation disaster. This appointment may have come as a result of the American Red Cross's comprehensive DMH efforts after TWA flight 800 exploded and crashed in New York on July 17, 1996, killing all on board. This event involved protracted mental health support because its cause was initially unknown. At first it was treated as a potential crime, and it took many years to conclude that the explosion was the result of a technological accident. Throughout that time, American Red Cross MHS assistance was available to victims' families for emotionally stirring moments including memorial services and visits to the hangar where the airplane was reconstructed in order to obtain intelligence about the crash. DMH support was imperative at times like that.

The continued occurrence of sizable disasters in recent years underscores the need for DMH services as a component of response efforts. Increasingly, disaster response stress appears to be intensified by highly troubling human-caused disasters, including the Oklahoma City bombing in 1995 and the attacks of September 11, 2001, as well as severe natural disasters like Hurricane Katrina. Fortunately, the DMH field is growing in response to the evident need for its services. It is a significant accomplishment that *thousands* of licensed mental health professionals are now involved with the American Red Cross MHS, which is a volunteer-fueled endeavor; the percentage of paid MHS staff is small. Weaver et al. (2000) observe, "The secret of this success can be attributed in part to the inherent nature of disaster response that elicits the highest level of humanitarianism, exemplified by the willingness of these volunteers to put their own very busy lives and agendas on hold to accept local or national volunteer assignments."

The American Red Cross model is an interdisciplinary one in which the practitioner's skills are more important than their specific professional identity. Mental health volunteers are asked to look beyond guild or political issues or theoretical alliances and focus on serving the community; this is possible because the duties performed in a disaster context are basic and universal. American Red Cross DMH volunteers deliver strategic outreach and services where those impacted by disasters are; they do not wait for people to seek them out. They are seen as facilitators and catalysts of an expected stress recovery process. DMH volunteers may respond to large-scale national disasters, and many local Red Cross chapters have used the national MHS structure as a template, establishing a capacity to include disaster mental health services in their response to local events such as fires and building collapses.

Two defining features characterize the American Red Cross model: presence and self-care. Presence on-scene parallels that of other relief workers, with DMH practitioners appearing routinely in the trenches as a disaster occurs in order to begin assisting survivors as quickly as possible. But unlike most other volunteers, DMH workers are there to help not only survivors but also other helpers who may make their own self-care a lower priority when serving those impacted.

SUPPORTING FIRST RESPONDERS

In the 1980s, an implicit belief that workers in the front lines—police officers, firefighters, emergency medical technicians, and paramedics—had psychological immunity to trauma despite being constantly exposed to tragedy and horror, had grown to be viewed as less and less plausible.

The discipline of police psychology was gaining acceptance during this time, and psychologists were increasingly present, on-scene and afterwards, to provide support to service members who had undergone a traumatic event such as a violent death of another officer. Mental health experts also became part of hostage negotiation teams, acting as consultants in order to understand the psychology of the hostage taker and making recommendations to the responders on how best to negotiate based on personality assessment. But police psychologists sometimes faced the challenge of having to conduct both posttrauma interventions and fitness-for-duty evaluations to determine whether an officer's traumatic experience made him or her unable to work—two conflicting tasks that sometimes put practitioners in the position of needing to both work with and rule against an individual. A desire to bypass this conflict and the acknowledgment that the unique experience of first responders would perhaps be best understood by one of their own led to enhanced peer-support models that offered mental health training to equip officers to help fellow officers.

Leaders of first-responder groups were beginning to pay heed to the impact of events on their personnel; certain experiences seemed to affect even seasoned responders in ways that they found hard to reconcile. Almost everyone could recall a troubling experience, and almost all could recall someone whose career or family began to unravel after exposure to a particularly poignant or gruesome event. But there were few acceptable places for troubled workers to turn for help. Veteran-to-rookie chats were sometimes held, privately and quietly, but they were never formally prescribed; support depended randomly on one's officers and comrades (Gist & Woodall, 1998).

To meet this need for assistance more systematically, in 1983, Jeffrey Mitchell developed a model, which he called *critical incident stress management,* for mitigating the consequences of responder stress specifically in first responder populations. He had been an emergency medical technician and volunteer firefighter and based his technique on his own experiences. He had responded to a car crash that injured an inebriated groom and fatally impaled his bride. The images of this scene remained with him, as he told the *Columbus Dispatch* (Pyle, 2002): "It tore at my heart. . . . For six months, I couldn't pass a wedding-dress shop without secretly crying for her. . . . The groom was swearing at me and was as obnoxious as any drunk I'd ever met. He was not even aware of what he had done. I had no one to talk to, and I didn't want anyone to have to go through something like that alone." As a result, he developed an intervention to help rescue workers deal with the constant loss of life and other hardships that they were exposed to in the course of a routine day's work.

Mitchell called his process *debriefing* to communicate a more formalized technique for postevent processing, and he used the phrase *critical incident* to avoid the possible connotation of a broader term and process such as *crisis*. Even so, as Flannery and Everly (2000) write, "The term *critical incident* is a term which is frequently confused with the term *crisis*. Contrary to the crisis response, a critical incident may be thought of as any stressor event that has the potential to lead to a crisis response in many individuals. More specifically, the critical incident may be thought of as the stimulus that sets the stage for the crisis response." Mitchell later founded the International Critical Incident Stress Foundation.

The techniques that Mitchell originally advocated became embraced by many agencies and was applied to other groups including nonprofits, relief workers, and private industry. Understandably, this model appealed to managers of workplaces and environments that were increasingly exposed to violence and unexpectedly distressing and shocking events, including disasters. In a time of increasing awareness of the consequences of traumatic stress, debriefing provided a ready tool of on-scene crisis intervention. Even American Red Cross volunteer mental health practitioners were introduced to a modified form of these methods during their training.

Mitchell's work may be seen as an accelerant to the field of DMH intervention. His efforts served to move mental health concerns to the forefront, placing the psychological well-being of *all* involved in traumatically stressful events "on the table."

DISASTER MENTAL HEALTH TODAY

What is the current state of the DMH specialty? A range of evidence suggests that it is firmly established as a specialty. Bloom (2000) notes that, "the development of . . . a field cannot come about without the simultaneous development of supporting organizations that provide the safety, mutual exchange, and collegiality that stimulates individual creativity, while also encouraging and supporting opportunities for group contributions."

Toward this end, different **professional organizations** have developed that address the theory and practice of DMH. Some of these organizations do not have an exclusive disaster focus. For example, the International Society for Traumatic Stress, founded in 1985, is devoted to promoting "advancement and exchange of knowledge" about severe stress and trauma. But it has a related special-interest group in early intervention and offers psychoeducational materials on its website (www.istss.org) for coping with mass disasters, trauma, and loss. Other groups do have DMH as their primary concentration. For example, the American Psychological Association developed its Disaster Response Network to meet the need for mental health professionals to be on-site with emergency workers to assist with the psychological care of trauma victims. Disaster Psychiatry Outreach, founded in 1998 by four psychiatrists, is dedicated to providing psychiatric services to people affected by disasters. Their mission is to provide mental health services at disaster sites in conjunction with government and private charitable organizations and also includes developing research and policy in the field of disaster psychiatry.

Government departments have also placed increasing focus on disasters and other traumatic stressors, including war. In 1989 the Department of Veterans Affairs created the National Center for PTSD to, according to its website, "serve as a resource center for, and promote and seek to coordinate the exchange of information regarding all research and training activities carried out by the VA and by other federal and non-federal entities with respect to PTSD." The center's useful website (www.ncptsd.va.gov) offers free access to the most up-to-date information on PTSD, including research studies, fact sheets, and psychoeducational materials. There are also several important documents pertaining to disasters, including a handbook on DMH.

Government agencies sometimes collaborate on DMH issues because disasters affect a range of departments. In an event in 2001 (planned prior to the events of September 11 but held later that fall), NIMH brought together significant figures in the field of early intervention posttrauma and disasters with experts from the Departments of Defense, Health and Human Services, Veterans Affairs, and Justice, along with the American Red Cross, to join forces across groups. Researchers and practitioners from academia and the private sector involved in this historic collaboration included prominent trauma and disaster scholars and experts—many of whose individual work you will see cited in this text—such as Arieh Shalev, John Tassey, Patricia Watson, Robert Ursano, Matthew Friedman, Josef Ruzek, Richard Bryant, Brett Litz, Beverly Raphael, Fran Norris, Lars Weisaeth, Terence Keane, Susan Hamilton, and Elspeth Ritchie. Participants discussed the state of the art in evidence-based practices for responding to the psychological effects of mass violence. In 2002 NIMH released their findings in a document entitled, "Mental Health and Mass Violence: Evidence-Based Early Psychological Intervention for Victims/Survivors of Mass Violence: A Workshop to Reach Consensus on Best Practices." It is a landmark publication for the field of DMH, which we will refer to throughout this text.

Additionally, **academic centers** for studying disaster psychology as well as providing practice opportunities have been created over the last 15 years. The University of South Dakota developed the Disaster Mental Health Institute (DMHI) in 1993. Gerard Jacobs helped create the institute after his involvement in helping victims in the 1989 Sioux City airline crash. DMHI is designed to bring together practice and research in DMH and to help train psychologists to deliver mental health services during emergencies and their aftermath. In addition to DMHI doctoral training, the program also offers educational opportunities for undergraduate students to learn how to serve their communities in times of disaster, including working with the American Red Cross.

The State University of New York at New Paltz established the Institute for Disaster Mental Health (IDMH) in 2004. James Halpern—director of the institute, professor of psychology at the university, and coauthor of this book—was inspired to advocate for its creation by his involvement in local and national disasters as a member of the Greater New York Chapter of the American Red Cross DMHS. The IDMH offers a minor in disaster studies, focused on training undergraduate students to deal with the effects of disasters on individuals, communities, organizations, and the nation. The institute also supports a yearly conference as well as training and education in DMH to community members and mental health professionals.

In addition to these organizational developments, **research** specifically relevant to disaster psychology has also advanced. Searching the professional literature review database, PsychInfo, for "Disaster Mental Health" now yields many articles and book chapters: 1 from 1953, 2 from the 1980s, 17 from the 1990s, and dozens more that have been published since 2000. This increase in references is not the sole indication of the field's growing importance, but it certainly suggests an expansion in professional interest in understanding the psychological aftermath of disasters. This interest continues to grow as larger and more invasive catastrophes occur: As we write this, a number of studies have been published on the effects of the attacks of September 11, 2001 and many more have been written about the Oklahoma City bombing of 1995. No doubt they will soon be joined by articles addressing the effects of the 2004 tsunami and later by those examining Hurricane Katrina in 2005.

The impact of disasters has also been recognized in the field of *journalism*. The media have played a significant role in raising awareness of how people are affected by the devastation following disasters—perhaps too much awareness, according to Moeller, whose 1999 book, *Compassion Fatigue: How the Media Sell Disease, Famine, War, and Death*, suggests that overly sensational and excessive disaster coverage that fails to explore a situation's underlying complexity may lead to public "compassion avoidance" or hardening of sympathies toward disasters and their victims. To train media professionals to avoid this mistake, the University of Washington has developed the DART Center for Journalism and Trauma, meant to support journalists who are exposed to traumatic stress and dedicated to improving media coverage of trauma, conflict, and tragedy. Instruction is offered to journalism students in the agenda of reporting and in how to be sensitive to their own reactions and responsive to the treatment of victims and survivors.

This kind of dual emphasis on self-care and service also has developed in strength over the last decade in the DMH field. There is consensus that everyone exposed to a disaster is touched by it. Caring for those who have survived a particularly stressful event can be particularly stressful in turn, and disaster responders may experience psychological distress as a result of their interactions (Figley, 1986, 1995; Nelson-Gardell & Harris, 2003; Schauben & Frazier, 1995). Charles Figley developed the concept of compassion fatigue (CF) when he began to focus on the unique work environment of trauma workers and mental health professionals (1995). The potentially adverse consequences of working with traumatized people are reflected in the growing awareness of the CF-related concepts of burnout, vicarious traumatization, and secondary traumatization as well as the counterpart concept of compassion satisfaction. DMH workers, especially those providing on-site services, will have firsthand exposure to the disaster to which they are responding, and they may need assistance themselves in handling their experiences.

In light of this current depth and breadth of professional efforts, it seems difficult to deny that DMH should be recognized as a true field of study. Let's return to the criteria that we cited at the beginning of this chapter as essential components of an established specialty:

- *History* As we have described, DMH has a relatively brief history that is increasingly becoming distinct. It is clearly rooted in the "birth" of PTSD as an established diagnostic entity. It also remains intertwined with the study of trauma and stress. Future developments will become increasingly disaster specific.
- *Professional Organizations* Disaster mental health has professional organizations established to provide both services and the development of theory, and many more general organizations in varied mental health disciplines have DMH divisions or subgroups. In addition, the American Red Cross, with its status in humanitarian relief, has paved the way for appreciating the role of mental health at times of disasters, both civilian and military.

- *Publications* Several reference volumes are now focused solely on DMH. A "short" list of references discussing both theory and practice in the field includes

  Disaster Mental Health Services (Myers & Wee, 2005)

  Disasters: Mental Health Interventions (Weaver, 1995)

  Disaster Psychiatry: Intervening When Nightmares Come True (Pandya & Katz, 2004)

  When Disaster Strikes: How Individuals and Communities Cope With Catastrophe (Raphael, 1986)

  Mental Heath Responses to Mass Emergencies: Theory and Practice (Lystad, 1988)

  Trauma and Disaster: Individual and Community Mental Health Interventions (Ursano, Fullerton, & Norwood, 2003)

  Interventions Following Mass Violence and Disasters: Strategies for Mental Health Practice (Ritchie, Friedman, & Watson, 2005)

- *Theory* At this juncture, theory is still in the process of definition, with key questions begging for illumination, including a consensual definition as to DMH's goals. Early objectives reflected a desire to prevent PTSD. Other aims include mitigation of general distress and a return to equilibrium. Perhaps the development of clearer goals, articulated in terms of the different stages of disaster intervention, may serve to elucidate both short- and long-range best practices.

- *Research Methodology and Measurement* Research in disasters, examining traumatized individuals in emergency contexts, presents several challenges. Due to disasters' unpredictable nature, pretest/posttest studies or randomized controlled designs are not easily achieved. There are ethical considerations in collecting data on individuals, organizations, communities, or countries reeling from a traumatic event. Practical considerations abound, including time (when to do assessments), cost (how to justify allocating resources for a long-term research goal when the short-term physical and emotional needs are so great), and communicating results (determining who your intended audience is and what they need to know). These remain methodological stumbling blocks in producing useful outcome studies. Fully incorporating DMH into an integrated emergency response will require far better empirical data than are currently available. Some statistics about reactions do exist, and specific interventions such as critical incident stress debriefing have been the focus of increased scientific study, leading to progress and hypotheses in how best to intervene postdisaster. The field has also benefited from literature reviews that have helped clarify the boundary between trauma and disaster-specific stress. Still, there is much work to be done, both on hypothesis-testing questions involving issues of population-based symptomatology and on theory-generating questions involving the type of social phenomena more readily studied on a small-case/sample level (Mitchell, 2005).

- *Intervention Technology* Intervention technology, meaning the actual techniques used to help people, fluctuates depending on a disaster's size, scope, and intensity; the stage at which the intervention is performed; the setting (on-site or carried out at a safer distance); individual factors in survivors; and other variables. Beyond a general agreement that low-level, soothing techniques carried out by mental health practitioners soon after a disaster can be helpful, the fluid nature of disasters means that when and how to best intervene is still striving for definition.

- *Actions Affecting Policy and the Judicial System* DMH factors have become increasingly important in emergency management. The biopsychosocial and cultural aspects of disasters have attained a much-needed awareness among public officials. Several agencies have incorporated DMH into the highest levels of emergency management. But this representation is uneven, with mental health practitioners generally serving more in a consultancy position than one of full authority. Disaster mental health plays an even less clear role in the judicial system, although survivors have sometimes acted as witnesses, providing an opportunity to reflect on their experience at different points in the criminal justice process. Survivor groups have also become advocates for disaster victim issues.

Disaster mental health represents a distinct field, if one in an early stage of development. Yet despite the growing evidence that mental health is an important component of disaster response, there are areas of significant controversy in the field that you should keep in mind as you read this book. Most notably, the widely adopted technique of debriefing has come under considerable scrutiny over the last several years, with criticism focused on the lack of empirical evidence of its efficacy and on questions of whether it can actually be harmful to participants, discussed in fuller detail in Chapter 10.

This coincides with a new emphasis in the field on natural resilience. Some observers suggest that early mental health interventions postdisaster are not entirely justified because most of those exposed can manage and recover on their own. There have been media attacks on what has been called "the grief industry" (Groopman, 2004), critiquing the swarms of mental health practitioners who now commonly descend upon disaster sites. Psychiatric professionals (for example, Satel & Sommers, 2005) have taken a public stance to challenge the mental health aspects of disasters, asserting that what people need during times of disasters is concrete and basic—medicine, food, and shelter—and not emotional, in a position that posits a dichotomy between needs that may better be viewed as interrelated and interdependent. The recent criticisms of debriefing have led to a sort of vacuum in what to offer disaster survivors initially; to fill this void, "psychological first aid" (described in Chapter 8) is often proposed as a first line of support. However, this approach in turn may become too broadly embraced as we wait for theoretical models and research to become more linked.

Part of what is transpiring today appears to echo the historical resistance to acknowledging the psychological effects of trauma. Just as there would not be a trauma field without advocacy by practitioners and others who insisted that survivors' needs be recognized in the face of societal resistance (Bloom, 1995, 2000), perhaps current controversies in DMH will put practitioners back in the position of advocating for their clients and for the relevance of the field in general. But, as Bloom asserts, this role must be handled carefully:

> There is a moral danger inherent in our work, perhaps best thought of as the medicalization . . . of what is a socially determined problem. If we fail to provide evidence-based treatment for our patients who suffer from chronic disorders related to traumatic experiences, we fail as healers. But, when we focus out attention exclusively on deciphering the complex brain processes that lead to the symptoms of posttraumatic stress, we may ignore the social context within which the traumatic stress originally occurred. (Bloom, 2000)

The DMH field can at least partially avoid this dilemma because many disasters, especially those of a natural origin, are events that can descend upon unsuspecting people at any time. But events that are human caused and intentionally harmful hold the potential of increasing polarization around issues of blame and social responsibility for practitioners and responders. We hope that you will keep these concerns in mind as you prepare to become a DMH helper.

Disaster mental health has made increasing strides in recent years as the field develops. Disaster mental health now emphasizes that preparedness—emotional as well as tactical—can be as crucial as response. The roots of DMH are richly tied to being able to recognize *both* survivors' capacity for vulnerability and their resiliency. And there is a deep connection in the field to the humanitarian provision of efficacious and compassionate support when the very worst happens. As practitioners working in often-chaotic situations, we are learning how to stay out of the way of first responders, but we also believe that the service we provide merits a presence on-scene. In this new and evolving field, it has been easier to look back at our foundation in other aspects of mental health than to say what is next on the horizon in terms of influences. Disaster mental health poses special challenges for practitioners as well as scholars, especially because the face of disaster is ever changing (Laino, personal communication, 2005). Over the remainder of this book, we continue our look at current findings and trends. And in Chapter 12, our last chapter, we look at possible future directions for the field of DMH.

References

American Psychiatric Association. (1994). *Diagnostic and Statistical Manual of Mental Disorders* (4th ed.). Washington, DC: Author.

Bloom, S. L. (1995). The germ theory of trauma: The impossibility of ethical neutrality. In B. H. Stamm (Ed.), *Secondary traumatic stress: Self-care issues for clinicians, researchers, and educators* (pp. 257–276). Lutherville, MD: Sidran Press.

Bloom, S. L. (2000). Our hearts and our hopes are turned to peace: Origins of the International Society for Traumatic Stress Studies. In A. Y. Shalev, R. Yehuda, & A. C. McFarlane (Eds.), *The international handbook of human response to trauma* (pp. 220–250). New York: Kluwer Academic/Plenum.

Brewin, C. (2003). *Posttraumatic stress disorder: Myth or malady?* New Haven, CT: Yale University Press.

Bryant, R., & Harvey, A. (2000). *Acute stress disorder: A handbook of theory, assessment, and treatment.* Washington, DC: American Psychological Association.

Burgess, A. W., & Holstrom, L. L. (1974). Rape trauma syndrome. *American Journal of Psychiatry, 131,* 981–986.

Caplan, G. (1964). *Principles of preventive psychiatry.* New York: Basic Books.

DeWolfe, D. J. (2000). *Training manual for mental health and human service workers in major disasters* (2nd ed.). U.S. Department of Health and Human Services: Center for Mental Health Services (Publication No. ADM 90-538). Retrieved February 14, 2005 from http://mentalhealth.org/publications/allpubs/ADM90-538/index.htm

Dykeman, B. F. (2003). Cultural implications of crisis intervention. *Journal of Instructional Psychology, 32,* 45–50.

Figley, C. R. (1986). *Trauma and its wake: Vol. 2. Traumatic stress theory, research, and integration.* New York: Brunner/Mazel.

Figley, C. R. (Ed.). (1995). *Compassion fatigue: Coping with secondary traumatic stress disorder in those who treat the traumatized.* New York: Brunner/Mazel.

Flannery, R. B., & Everly, G. S. (2000). Crisis intervention: A review. *International Journal of Emergency Mental Health, 2,* 119–125.

Frankl, V. E. (1946). *Man's search for meaning.* New York: Simon & Schuster.

Gibbs, P. (1923). *Adventures in journalism.* Out of Print. Quote via www.firstworldwar.com/bio/gibbs.htm.

Gist, R., & Woodall, S. J. (1998). Social science versus social movements: The origins and natural history of debriefing. *Australasian Journal of Disaster and Trauma Studies, 1.* Open access online resource. Retrieved May 13, 2005 from http://www.massey.ac.nz/~trauma/issues/1998-1/gist1.htm.

Groopman, J. (2004, January 26). The grief industry. *The New Yorker, 30.*

Haley, S. (1974). When the patient reports atrocities. *Archives of General Psychiatry, 30,* 191–196.

Herman, J. L. (1992). *Trauma and recovery.* New York: Basic Books.

Hoge, C. W., Castro, C. A., & Messer, S. C. (2004) Combat duty in Iraq and Afghanistan, mental health problems, and barriers to care. *New England Journal of Medicine, 351,* 13–22.

Horowitz, M. J. (1977). *Stress response syndromes* (2nd ed.). Northvale, NJ: Jason Aronson.

James, R. K., & Gilliland, B. E. (2005). *Crisis intervention strategies.* Belmont, CA: Thompson Brooks/Cole.

Kanel, K. (2003). *A guide to crisis intervention* (2nd ed.). Pacific Grove, CA: Brooks/Cole.

Kardiner, A. (1941). *The traumatic neuroses of war.* New York: Paul B. Hoeber.

Kinzie, J. D., & Goetz, R. R. (1996). A century of controversy surrounding posttraumatic stress-spectrum syndromes: The impact on *DSM-III* and *DSM-IV. Journal of Traumatic Stress, 9,* 159–179.

Lamprecht, F., & Sack, M. (2002). Posttraumatic stress disorder revisited. *Psychosomatic Medicine, 64,* 222–237.

Lindemann, E. (1944). Symptomatology and management of acute grief. *American Journal of Psychiatry, 101,* 1141–1148.

Lystad, M. (Ed.). (1988). *Mental health response to emergencies: Theory and practice.* New York: Brunner/Mazel.

Maslow, H. A. (1970). *Motivation and personality* (Rev. ed.). New York: Harper & Row.

Mitchell, S. G. (2005). Developing our emergency mental health research capacity: Taming the chaos in a multidisciplinary field. *International Journal of Emergency Mental Health, 7*(1), 1–4.

Moeller, S. D. (1999). *Compassion fatigue: How the media sell disease, famine, war, and death*. London: Routledge.

Myers, D., & Wee, D. F. (2005). *Disaster mental health services*. New York: Brunner/Routledge.

Nelson-Gardell, D., & Harris, D. (2003). Childhood abuse history, secondary traumatic stress, and child welfare workers. *Child Welfare, 82*(1), 5–27.

NIMH (National Institute of Mental Health). (2002). *Mental health and mass violence: Evidence-based early psychological intervention for victims/survivors of mass violence. A workshop to reach consensus on best practices* (NIH Publication No. 02-5138). Washington, DC: Government Printing Office.

Norris, F. H., Friedman, M. J., Watson, P. J., Byrne, C. M., Diaz, E., & Kaniasty, K. (2002). 60,000 disaster victims speak: Part I. An empirical review of the empirical literature, 1981–2001. *Psychiatry: Interpersonal & Biological Processes, 65*, 207–239.

Pandya, A., & Katz, C. (Eds.). (2004). *Disaster psychiatry: Intervening when nightmares come true*. Hillsdale, NJ: Analytic Press.

Prasad, J. (1935). The psychology of rumor: A study relating to the great Indian earthquake of 1934. *British Journal of Psychology, 26*, 1–15.

Pyle, E. (2002). Personal experience inspired founder of national CISD movement. *Columbus (Ohio) Dispatch*.

Quarantelli, E. L., & Dynes, R. R. (1977). Response to social crisis and disaster. *Annual Review of Sociology, 3*, 23–49.

Raphael, B. (1986). *When disaster strikes: How individuals and communities cope with catastrophe*. Basic Books: New York.

Ritchie, E., Friedman, M. J., & Watson, P. J. (2005). *Interventions following mass violence and disasters: Strategies for mental health practice*. New York: Guilford Press.

Saretsky, E. (2004). *Secrets of the soul: A social and cultural history of psychoanalysis*. New York: Knopf.

Satel, S., & Sommers, C. H. (2005). The mental health crisis that wasn't. *Reason, 37*(4), 48–56.

Schauben, L. J., & Frazier, P. A. (1995). Vicarious trauma. *Psychology of Women Quarterly, 19*(1), 49–65.

Selye, H. (1956). *The stress of life*. New York: McGraw-Hill.

Shalev, A. (2004). Further lessons from 9/11: Does stress equal trauma? *Psychiatry, 67*(2), 174–176.

Shephard, B. (2001). *A war of nerves: Soldiers and psychiatrists in the twentieth century*. Cambridge, MA: Harvard University Press.

Silver, S. (2005, June 1–2). *Long-term care of posttraumatic stress disorder*. Paper presented at the conference Psycho-Social Aspects of Complex Emergencies, sponsored by the Homeland Defense Training/Market Access International, Washington Convention Center, Washington, DC.

Sims, A. C. P., White, A. C., & Murphy, T. (1979). Aftermath neurosis: Psychological sequelae of the Birmingham bombings in victims not seriously injured. *Medicine, Science and the Law, 19*, 78–81.

Terr, L. C. (1979). Children of Chowchilla: A study of psychic trauma. *Psychoanalytic Study of the Child, 34*, 547–623.

Trimble, M. R. (1981). *Posttraumatic neurosis: From railway spine to the whiplash*. Chichester, England: Wiley.

Trimble, M. R. (1985). Posttraumatic stress disorder: History of a concept. In C. R. Figley (Ed.), *Trauma and its wake: The study and treatment of posttraumatic stress disorder* (pp. 5–14). New York: Brunner/Mazel.

Ursano, R. J., Fullerton, C. S., & Norwood, A. E. (2003). *Terrorism and disaster: Individual and community mental health interventions*. Cambridge, England: Cambridge University Press.

Weaver, J. D. (1995). *Disasters: Mental health interventions*. Sarasota, FL: Professional Resource Press/Professional Resource Exchange.

Weaver, J. D., Dingman, R. L., Morgan, J., Hong, B. A., & North, C. S. (2000). The American Red Cross Disaster Mental Health Services: Development of a cooperative, single function, multidisciplinary service model. *Journal of Behavioral Health Services & Research, 27*(3), 314–322.

Weisaeth, L. (2002). The European history of psychotraumatology. *Journal of Traumatic Stress, 15,* 443–452.

Wilson, J. P., & Doyle, C. (1977). *Identity, ideology, and crisis: The Vietnam veteran in transition: A preliminary report on the forgotten warrior project*. Cincinnati, OH: Disabled American Veterans.

Wilson, J. P., Friedman, M. J., & Lindy, J. D. (2001). *Treating psychological trauma and PTSD*. New York: Guilford Press.

Wilson, J. P., Harel, Z., & Kahana, B. (1988). *Human adaptation to extreme stress: From the Holocaust to Vietnam*. New York: Plenum.

Never say you know the last word about any human heart.

Henry James

4 CHAPTER | Reactions and Risk Factors

What happens to people when they are exposed to disasters? In this chapter, we examine how people typically respond after experiencing a disaster, leaving extreme reactions for a closer look in Chapter 5. We discuss the physiological changes that humans experience in response to perceived threats—the famous *fight-or-flight response*—as well as what the field has come to understand as "common reactions to abnormal events," including emotional, cognitive, behavioral, physical, and spiritual responses. We look at stage theories of disasters and at the impact of loss and grief on recovery. We examine the disaster mental health (DMH) field's growing understanding of risk and resilience factors, characteristics that appear to make some individuals particularly vulnerable and others particularly resistant to lasting postdisaster problems. Disasters have the potential to transform identity in ways that either increase fragmentation of the self or lead to growth and positive reorganization. So, we discuss the existential changes that such events can cause in individuals and communities.

As you read about these "normal" responses, bear in mind that an examination of individual human reactions to disasters requires a multidimensional perspective because a particular survivor's response will be affected by a number of factors. The nature of the disaster agent (whether it was natural or human caused, predictable or unexpected) will play a role, as will how a person negotiates the actual event. The sum of the characteristics and history that define an individual at the moment of exposure helps shape how he or she will fare. What happens to people immediately after the event and for some time afterwards will also affect their reactions, determining in part how they internalize and manage their experience. In short, responses to disaster vary widely, so the mental health helper should be careful not to make assumptions about any individual's likely trajectory.

As we have seen in previous chapters, disasters can be psychologically traumatic events. They are differentiated from other types of trauma in the mental health field because they are clear, external events that can transform a person's inner world as well as their mental health functioning. Disasters bring overwhelming stress in their wake; however, stress does not equal trauma or, more important, posttraumatic stress disorder (PTSD), which is the best-known psychiatric response in the trauma spectrum. Still, certain levels of stress have the potential to challenge coping abilities on many levels. When people are in crisis, such as in times of disaster, they feel stunned and put upon as they marshal their internal and external resources to cope with an event. The individual's reaction is further complicated by the collective nature of disaster because each survivor is surrounded by others who are also trying to cope with the same event, all within a changed environment.

Exposure to stress also produces a distinct physical response. We assume a biopsychosocial perspective. Stressful events impact survivors in their bodies, in their personal psychology, and in how they interact with the world. Psychological trauma disrupts homeostasis and can cause both short-term and long-term effects on many areas of functioning. Multiple factors influence whether psychosocial functioning will be enhanced or undermined, including the presence or absence of social supports and networks, the availability of needed resources, the development of comorbid disorders, and how survivors make meaning and incorporate what has happened to them. To understand the background in which these external factors interact, we first describe the hardwired physical changes that affect anyone exposed to disaster.

PHYSIOLOGICAL RESPONSES TO DISASTER

Human biology produces commonplace acute reactions to external stressors, whether they are physical or psychosocial in nature. In an effort to develop targeted interventions to mitigate the most adverse outcomes, DMH clinicians and researchers have worked to normalize and understand these shared responses and to distinguish them from any potentially pathological reactions.

Anatomically, the acute stress response is focused in the central and peripheral nervous systems, controlled by the brain and spinal cord. Perceiving a threat, such as an approaching tornado or a fire breaking out in one's home, brings about a host of automatic physiological changes that equip an individual to deal with the reality of an emergency: To survive, humans automatically prepare for fight or flight, their reactive potential boosted by a tremendous energy surge. The threatened person's heartbeat increases in order to pump blood away from the extremities (the hands and feet) to where it is needed around vital internal organs. Blood flow increases to the brain, heart, and lungs (areas that need increased oxygen to perform well) and to the major muscles to help in either fighting or running away. Blood flow is constricted to the digestive organs, shutting down the digestive system temporarily. Muscles tense for movement, and the heart works harder than it would in a relaxed state to carry oxygen and other nutrients to the active body parts (van der Kolk, McFarlane, & Weisaeth, 1996).

As the heart rate increases, so does blood pressure. Breathing becomes more shallow and rapid as the body tries to obtain more oxygen, which is necessary to continue fueling the response. The liver releases stored sugar into the bloodstream to meet the increased need for more energy. The metabolic rate speeds up to meet increased energy requirements; this generates heat, so perspiration increases to cool the body. Adrenaline and other hormones are released into the bloodstream. Blood-clotting agents are released in anticipation of possible injury. The pupils dilate to let in more light, and other senses become heightened, making the brain acutely aware of all things around the body. In this normal reaction to very stressful circumstances, bodies enter a state of physical and sensory preparedness for what might come next.

This response is not all or none but usually occurs to a degree that is adaptive to the situation at hand. In fact, the physical processes involved in the acute stress response are always present to some small degree because we need a certain amount of stress to go about our daily work and routines. For example, we have a certain level of awareness of our surroundings most of the time, and this helps us to notice changes that might constitute a threat sufficient to activate the fight-or-flight response. Additionally, humans have evolved so that the stress response can be activated by events other than physical danger. Threats to people's status, to their sense of personal security and esteem, and to their loved ones can evoke a stress reaction of a significant magnitude.

As normal and adaptive as the acute stress response is, mental and physical distress often follows its activation, especially if a person did not actually take the kind of action that his or her body was prepared for. For example, the release of reserved sugar and the tensing of muscles to help with running or fighting are productive during the fight-or-flight state. However, when extra energy is not utilized, it remains in the body and turns into lactic acid, often leading to painful muscle cramps. Similarly, the release of hormones including adrenaline, noradrenaline, and cortisol helps a threatened person focus and become alert, but these chemicals can also cause cognitive problems including aggression, pent-up frustration, loss of concentration, irritability, and hostility if not completely used in activity. Specifically, as adrenaline is released into the bloodstream, the heart beats more quickly and directs the blood supply to the major organs. However, adrenaline that remains unused in the blood can cause digestion problems, anxiety, panic, fear, withdrawal, and feelings of heart palpitations. Unused cortisol can contribute to feelings of anxiety, depression, and withdrawal (Rothschild, 2000). Additionally, because certain neurotransmitters are depleted during the acute response, exhaustion sets in afterwards. If another stressor comes along shortly after the initial activation, an individual would have less ability to deal with it because of this biochemical depletion.

Given these uncomfortable aftereffects of the acute stress response, it is important to educate disaster survivors about the process of what happens physiologically when one is under stress. That way, those impacted can understand why they are feeling the way they do or why they feel the need to do something physical to satisfy the urge that their body has so efficiently prepared them for. It is equally important for the mental health helper to understand this response in order to help people at the time of a disaster. Intense arousal does not readily go away. The original stressor may have passed, and the intense stress reaction may no longer be needed, but that does not guarantee that people can or will simply relax afterwards. Remember, those impacted may be bombarded by a tremendous number of other stressors that place them at further risk for psychological disequilibrium and undermine their chances of making an optimal recovery. This is one of the reasons why we intervene early on with low-level, nonintrusive, and reassuring techniques.

So, as you work with survivors who have recently been exposed to the acute stressor of a disaster, remember that they will have experienced a literally visceral reaction to their experience and they may still be feeling its influence uncomfortably. Next, let's look beyond the physical effects of the acute stress response to examine the full range of typical reactions experienced by disaster survivors.

NORMATIVE REACTIONS TO DISASTER EXPOSURE

Normative reactions are those that "make sense" after someone has been exposed to a horrific, life-altering event and that do not suggest that the individual is at risk of developing lasting problems as a result of their experience. In the early days of DMH, an accepted phrase in helping people after exposure to a disaster was, "You are having a normal reaction to an abnormal event." Today, we have substituted "common" for "normal" in appreciation of the uniqueness of individual responses and acknowledgment of typical or expectable but not omnipresent reactions.

Reactions are often grouped into different areas, the most common being emotional, cognitive, behavioral, and physical; spiritual is also now included more frequently. The following are some of the commonly listed reactions to disaster stress.

PHYSICAL, OR BODILY, REACTIONS

- Palpitations
- Breathlessness
- Jumpiness or edginess
- Rapid and shallow breathing
- Indigestion
- Nausea
- Diarrhea
- Constipation

- Muscle tension or pain
- Fatigue
- Headaches
- Sleep disruption
- Changes in body temperature

As we can see, many of these are directly related to the aftermath of an extended stress response.

BEHAVIORAL RESPONSES

- Dietary changes (eating less, eating more, eating less healthy foods that can perpetuate the stress response)
- Social withdrawal and isolation (perhaps to deal with hyperarousal symptoms of irritability and global overstimulation)
- Purposeful avoidance of reminders of the disaster and/or purposeful immersion in reminders and activities around the disaster
- Increases in the use of alcohol and mood-altering substances (which can be seen as ways of self-medicating and providing immediate relief from internally disturbing thoughts and feelings)
- Increased feelings of dependency on others and neediness
- A desire to overcontrol relationships
- Changes in sex drive

Note that some of these responses appear to reflect efforts at coping with post-disaster distress and some seem to have interpersonal elements.

EMOTIONAL REACTIONS

- Distress
- Tearfulness
- Emotionality
- Anxiety
- Depression
- Impatience
- Irritability
- Anger
- Hostility
- Rage
- Vulnerability
- Feeling rushed
- Panic

COGNITIONS, OR THINKING

- Worry or rumination
- Preoccupation
- Difficulties in concentration
- Forgetfulness and making uncharacteristic mistakes

The spiritual reactions that are usually noted reflect efforts to make sense of what has happened. Those impacted by disaster tend to search for an answer to the mystery of why one person's life can so swiftly be torn asunder and why another's experience is entirely different. The inclusion of spiritual reactions, centering around meaning making, reflects the developing awareness that during times of crisis people struggle to incorporate the event into their worldview. They often turn to their faith for help in this existential quest. They may experience hopelessness and wonder who is to blame for such horror and tragedy, as reflected in a news article soon after the 2004 tsunami entitled "Why Would God Drown Children?" (Haught, 2005).

Normative reactions that initially result from exposure to severe stress can look somewhat like PTSD. People may develop a heightened startle response, be generally anxious, and have problems sleeping. They may reexperience the event, especially when there are cues in the environment (for example, storm clouds after a devastating hurricane or loud noises after a bombing). Over time, such reactions fade away, becoming less frequent and less intense. The traumatic event becomes a normal memory, which is accessed from time to time but does not possess the immediacy of the original experience.

This broad range of expectable reactions after a disaster underscores the challenge of doing assessment in the immediate wake of such events. On first encountering survivors, it can be difficult for the mental health helper to understand what portion of their reaction is state or trait—that is, attributable to their recent stressful experience or due to more lasting personal characteristics. In addition, survivors' symptoms and actions change as time passes after the event, as we discuss next.

STAGES OF DISASTER REACTIONS

Disasters can be seen as events that have a beginning, middle, and end. As we reviewed in Chapter 2, they have been broadly conceptualized in terms of preimpact, impact, and postimpact stages. Because of personal safety risks, DMH responders will most likely be working with survivors or the family members of victims during the postimpact phase, either immediately after a disaster or at a later point, though there are exceptions to this rule. For example, in communities where the local disaster response has integrated DMH services, on-scene mental health support may be provided under certain circumstances, such as a fatality or severe injury, or when disaster responders may need support because a scene is particularly gruesome due to multiple casualties or the deaths of children.

Even though DMH workers are not usually present for the preimpact and impact stages, it is important to understand what survivors probably experienced and how they may have acted during those times before you arrived on the scene.

Before and During Impact

Disasters that allow warnings or advance notice let people spend some time cognitively and emotionally digesting that they may be affected. This provides the individual and the community with an opportunity to develop safety and contingency plans, efforts that bestow an important and empowering sense of mastery and competence. Still, disasters bring chaos and the moment of impact will always deliver its own vagaries, its unexpected twists and turns. If there is little or no warning before a disastrous event strikes, people will be at an initial cognitive and emotional loss as they strive to decipher what is happening. It is as if they are making their way through a terrifying maze. Communication systems may be disrupted, increasing feelings of helplessness and uncertainty and reinforcing the disaster trauma. Shock is common, with accompanying denial, numbness, and fear.

Magnified arousal levels characterize impact phase reactions and responses, with everyone involved on high alert. This increase in overall arousal sets the stage for traumatic imprinting. As described previously, the primitive fight-or-flight response is activated as the body readies for action, even if one is not at the core of impact. (Less frequently a freezing response occurs instead; this freezing, or peritraumatic dissociation, has been connected to poorer postdisaster functioning.) Efforts to process highly extraordinary, bizarre, and ghastly sights and sensations further tax the individual. When a person is caught in the middle of such an unexpected and dreadful set of circumstances, fear, a terrible sense of urgency, concerns about impending doom, hypervigilance, and strivings to survive predominate. How helpless a person feels or acts during such an event plays a key role in how he or she will accept and retain the experience.

Certain typical behaviors are frequently seen during the impact phase. Survivors who believe they are facing possible death may assume a protective posture such as hiding under an object or curling into a ball, and they may make efforts to hold on to and shield others. People tend to seek each other out and band together during disasters because closeness and affiliation is reassuring at a time of crisis. A dramatic example of this was seen in the casts of victims of the eruption of Mt. Vesuvius in 79 A.D., discovered in excavations in Pompeii, Italy. Victims, who had been buried in volcanic ash, were found huddled together, often holding onto each other, locked in an embrace. A more recent example occurred on September 11, 2001 in New York City. Several of those in the World Trade Center towers who either leapt or fell to their deaths did so in tandem, holding hands. These images are amongst the most emotionally stirring, heartrending, and disturbing sights that exist from a disaster. Finally, contrary to stereotype, panic has not been documented as a prevalent response during the impact phase. In fact, purposeful and productive acts are far more common.

In terms of an individual's mental health, the disaster impact phase is one of the most crucial stages. What happens in this phase on all levels—emotional, cognitive, physical and behavioral—will have implications for postimpact functioning and regrouping.

After Disaster: Emotional Changes Over Time

The period following a disaster can be further divided into a series of stages, each characterized by typical behaviors and emotions. According to DeWolfe (2000), emotional stages correspond to levels of activity and arousal during particular time frames surrounding a disaster. These include the heroic phase, the honeymoon phase, the disillusionment phase, and the reconstruction phase. The **heroic phase,** which occurs during and just after the disaster's impact, reflects survivors' immediate outpouring of amazing and noble efforts to help those most devastated. A collective spirit of mutually reinforcing compassion and a striving to provide relief follows in the **honeymoon phase.** At this time, those involved in the disaster, as well as those observing it, are focused and like minded, sharing a sense of purpose. Social barriers are not as pronounced, so people start to feel closer to each other, unified by a common mission. There is an increase in tolerance and hope. This period typically lasts approximately 2 weeks to 2 months or longer in disasters of large scope and intensity.

Naturally, the honeymoon period cannot last indefinitely. With increasing stabilization of a disaster scene—which is the goal of disaster relief—comes increasing withdrawal of resources and media attention, and those most impacted are eventually left on their own. This is not to imply that they are abandoned. Resources can be left in place for many years to help assist with the aftermath of disaster. But there comes a time when the community must readjust to its changed circumstances, so after the initial energy, excitement and hope that characterize the honeymoon phase start to decline, the **disillusionment phase** may set in. This is the reflective sequel that feels anticlimatic after months of community activity and passionate intensity. An estimated time frame for this phase is several months to 2 years.

Finally, the **reconstruction phase** can last for several years and perhaps the rest of a person's—and community's—life. The tasks required in this phase can be quite profound. Imagine the challenges faced by someone who has lost his or her entire family in an aviation accident or someone whose home and livelihood have been washed away in a flood. Extreme destruction is followed by extreme challenges to rebuilding and reintegration. As this book goes to press, residents of New Orleans and other areas devastated by Hurricane Katrina are only beginning to confront the long road that they face to rebuild their homes and their lives, and their mental health needs are evolving. One university professor from New Orleans wrote to us 3 months after the flood that

> People need to realize that an ongoing crisis of this magnitude is going to affect us for a long time to come. And that emotions that were frozen by the shock and grief of what happened so suddenly to our beloved city and almost all of our friends, colleagues, family members, are going to thaw and come to the surface. . . . This storm has disrupted the lives of citizens of all social and economic classes. It has caused devastation of so many homes in a city where people loved their homes. . . . New Orleans people are people of faith and that sustains us. But it is the overview of collective mental health in this kind of crisis that needs attention.

Another example of this might be the experience of the New York City Fire Department after September 11, 2001. The department suffered an unparalleled loss of life including many upper-hierarchy personnel on that day. A percentage of the surviving senior members of service were exposed to the toxic, grisly, and morbid conditions of the recovery environment for nearly 9 months as they continued the search for bodies of colleagues and other victims. Many of these firefighters subsequently developed chronic medical problems and have been or will be forced to join the ranks of the many others who retired after recovery was completed. Due to these drastic losses, the force now had a different composition of mostly younger members. Opportunities for mentoring and transmission of the unique firefighting culture through the network of relationships with seasoned members of service have been largely diminished. Myers and Wee (2005) reported that in 2002 "the retirement rate had doubled for both officers and firefighters, with 450 retirements, at the rate of 5.5 per day since the attacks, resulting in the loss of over 4000 years of experience." As this example demonstrates, some of the subtler, nonclinical but far-reaching psychological aftereffects of disaster only begin to display themselves in the months and years after the event.

Survivors' reactions to a disaster are generally expected to correspond to the stage of recovery. As a result, what they will need in terms of mental health support is different at different points along this somewhat fluid time frame. If you are working with a family who has just lost their home, asking them to sit down and emotionally process their sense of loss, grief, and whatever else they may be feeling defies common sense as well as good mental health practice. However, after this family has had some time to regain a sense of equilibrium and their basic needs have been restored, they may begin to take stock of the emotional aftermath of their experience. Supportively assisting clients to explore or understand their reactions at this time through the techniques used in DMH practice may be appropriate.

The concept of a sequence of postdisaster stages is useful because it reflects the reality that responses to disaster usually follow a progression characterized by decreasing intensity and arousal as time passes. Yet, as the examples from the reconstruction phase attest, disaster's impact remains, especially in events of significant scale and intensity. Fresh, raw reactions diminish, yet reminders can serve to conjure up defining moments, as this commentary in the *New York Times,* written 4 years after the World Trade Center attacks in 2001, observes:

> Perhaps the strangest thing about the destruction of the World Trade Center towers, for many of us who lived through the attack and its aftermath in New York, is how unreal it all seems now. Already, the events of September 11, 2001, often feel as if they took place in the distant past. And yet all it takes is the smallest reminder—a low-bearing plane, a National Guardsman patrolling Grand Central Terminal, a whiff of jet fuel like the smell that pervaded Lower Manhattan for months afterward—and one is plunged immediately into the same emotions that gripped us at the time: horror, grief, shock, rage. (Baker, 2005)

Proximity to Impact

Disasters exist in space as well as time (Raphael, 1986). Imagine casting a pebble into a still body of water. The point of impact of the pebble creates the greatest disruption, and it sets off a ripple effect seen through the formation of concentric circles. As the circles move away from the pebble's blow, they become less pronounced. This image of concentric circles symbolizes the spatial dimension of a disaster's effect on survivors, with those closest to the point of impact generally demonstrating the most needs and experiencing the greatest reaction.

Again, the attacks of 9/11 provide an example. The term *ground zero*, originally used to refer to the central point of any explosion, was quickly adopted to indicate the heart of that disaster's impact at the former World Trade Center site. Imagine concentric circles around that bull's-eye of impact: The first would include those immediately affected—that is, the survivors who escaped the building collapse and their families and support systems. Next there are direct witnesses to the horror, including community members and bystanders, followed by those whose function it is to come to disasters to help—rescue and recovery workers, relief agency staff and volunteers, and DMH workers themselves. In the ground zero example, the concentric circles of impact expanded quickly to an international level so that anyone throughout the entire world with access to television or the Internet could witness the unfolding horror.

In large disasters, certain regions are affected almost totally, others more peripherally. Most of the convergence of aid occurs within the first concentric ring where the disaster has done the most damage, which is appropriate given the significance of the dose–response relationship: Repeated studies have shown that the heavier and more intense an individual's exposure is to a disaster, the more likely it is that he or she will suffer a more significant reaction. The amount of destruction, death, and disruption diminishes as one moves farther away from the central circle. Still, experiencing a disaster, even from some distance, almost always creates some sense of grief and loss, whether it is loss of property, a person, or simply peace of mind. In some cases, merely watching a disaster on television can produce a strong emotional reaction. We discuss the characteristics of grief in detail in our next section.

THE IMPACT OF LOSS AND GRIEF

Many themes will be left with those who have experienced . . . disaster: triumph over death; loss of innocence . . . ; devastation and destruction of property and place, community and culture; dislocation; and a new view of the self and of life. These themes . . . have many variations. Statistics on deaths, injuries and destruction of home and property help to quantify the impact and reflect the experience of the individual. But the psychological themes will be significant in many different ways in the days and weeks, and perhaps even the months and years, that follow the catastrophe. Those who have known this impact will never be quite the same again. (Raphael, 1986)

Loss, trauma, and grief permeate disasters, so current themes in the study of trauma and DMH include efforts to clarify the roles these experiences play in the wake of catastrophe (Neria and Litz, 2003; Green, 2000; Prigerson, et al., 1999; Hobfoll, 1991; Rando, 1994; Horowitz, 1997; Brewin, Dagleish and Joseph, 1996 and Wortman and Silver, 1989). Before examining those roles, we present definitions of some of these terms that overlap conceptually yet have subtle but important differences:

- **Grief** is the emotional reaction to loss.
- **Mourning,** or **bereavement,** indicates the painful and thorny process of relinquishing and readjusting after a meaningful loss.

- **Normal loss** describes the death of a loved one in circumstances that allow for some preparation for or expectation of that death, and it involves the achievement of a return to full functionality after a period of mourning.
- **Traumatic loss** describes the death of a loved one suddenly, often in horrific, violent circumstances that reflect and intensify the experience of trauma. Traumatic loss is often compounded and made more complex by a shared, communal context, as in disasters.
- **Traumatic grief** is the process of dealing with traumatic loss. It is sometimes called *traumatic bereavement*.
- **Complicated grief** is the process following a loss, under traumatic circumstances or not, that is characterized by unremitting bereavement. It is sometimes called *chronic* or *difficult bereavement*.

Loss and trauma have compelling similarities that beg ongoing clarification; Neria and Litz (2003) refer to the "complex synergy of trauma and grief" in which traumatic stress and traumatic loss frequently intersect. Describing a model that frames trauma as a kind of loss, Green (2000) writes, "Traumatic stressors attack people's most basic values, occur unexpectedly, make excessive demands, and are outside the usual realm for which coping strategies have been developed." Brewin, Dagleish, and Joseph (1996) use the construct of loss to underpin their definition of trauma, emphasizing the disruption that trauma causes by undermining or destroying one's basic world assumptions, one's sense of self, and one's social and interpersonal relationships. Not surprisingly, exposure to loss involving death, especially death of a grotesque nature as may be experienced during disasters, can be especially disturbing. Lifton (1976; Lifton & Olson, 1999) writes about the "death imprint" that remains after this kind of experience, leaving the survivor spellbound by images that seem indelible and feel disturbing. We feel it is fair to state that exposure to traumatic stress almost always includes some component of loss and frequently traumatic loss.

Although our definitions specifically refer to the death of a loved one as the source of the pain, other types of disaster-induced losses can be significantly traumatic as well. Harvey (1998) notes the frequency with which loss and death are interchangeably used; for example, when he asked a population of college students to define *loss*, nearly 60% of the students associated the term with death. He speculates that this is so because death is the ultimate form of loss—simply put, death is forever. Whereas you can replace or recover from other losses, even devastating ones such as the destruction of a home, there is no chance of replacing a person lost to death.

As a result of this tendency to associate loss with death, other forms of loss during disasters may sometimes be minimized, but their impact should not be overlooked. Grief experts such as Rando (1988) suggest that there are two basic types of losses: physical (or tangible) and symbolic, which are more abstract. Disaster losses are often both physical and symbolic; they can include loved ones and pets, property, a way of life, occupation, a sense of personal invulnerability, self-esteem and identity, future hopes, and trust in God or protective powers.

As Raphael (1986) states, "Whatever the losses, the bereavements of disasters are rarely uncomplicated."

Current theories propose that loss causes a disruption in social reality that affects self-definition, so individuals may never completely return to their preloss state—and indeed, this may not be the optimal goal: "Instead, the aim is to review the loss, come to terms with the changes and integrate oneself into a new social context or identity" (Rosenblatt, 1993). Neimeyer (2000) emphasizes that active meaning reconstruction in response to loss is the central process in grieving. This is counter to earlier theory that conceptualizes stages of grief as static or stable, not dynamically influenced by culture and personal variations. Grieving is construed from this perspective as a process of relearning the self and relearning the world in response to a loss (Attig, 1996). Important issues in the interface of loss and stress for DMH helpers include identification of risk factors for complicated grief in the wake of traumatic loss and further explication of what happens to those who are directly traumatized and also suffer a traumatic loss. We spend the next few pages reviewing loss in the context of disasters in order to provide a framework of understanding for the practitioner.

Specific Issues in Disaster Loss

Disasters present unique challenges in terms of understanding loss and grief. They are traumatic events, with traumatic loss a frequent component. A survivor may have to deal simultaneously with having survived a disaster personally and with experiencing traumatic loss. The scholarship of Beverly Raphael, a true pioneer in disaster studies, in particular sheds light on why disaster loss can be so complex and excruciating, making it especially traumatic or stressful to negotiate. Let's consider some of the difficulties involved.

First, often uniquely troubling circumstances surround deaths that result from disasters. The death of others is probably the most significant and agonizing disaster loss that exists, increasing the event's potential impact on survivors, family members, and community. Sudden and unexpected deaths in particular may leave the residue of the unresolved ambivalence of everyday life: There was no time to prepare for this lasting separation, no opportunity to have said a good-bye, and there is the possibility that the last encounter with the deceased may have been rushed or even negative. People are at risk for problematic grief reactions any time they lose intimates unexpectedly, especially through malicious acts of violence.

Second, when someone dies in a disaster, the condition of the body often becomes an added complication. Whether the disaster was natural or human-caused and pernicious, there may be obstacles to obtaining a body or remains. The body may be in a foreign part of the world as in many aviation incidents, far from the family's home. Depending on bureaucracy or on the extent of damage to a given region, there may be a lengthy period of time before loved ones are able to obtain the victim's remains.

When remains are available, they may be in a devastated condition, reduced to fragmented parts or bits of bone and ash. For those involved in a disaster or its recovery, witnessing the horrific and grotesque deformation of the wholeness, intactness, and integrity of the human body may be of particular consequence. Even so, Raphael (1986) reports on early studies suggesting that family members prefer to view and have access to remains, regardless of the condition, and that this viewing is not inherently harmful. She suggests that not having such access is more problematic. In our experience, family members will discuss who should view or identify remains, often taking great care to protect those they view as the most vulnerable to distress.

In the absence of a body, a legacy of uncertainty and doubt exists (Raphael, 1986). This has been our clinical experience in our work with family members of victims of mass-fatality events, such as the crash of flight 800 and the World Trade Center attack. Those who did not receive their loved ones' bodies struggled with decisions around how to ritualize their grief; for some it was important to find even a fragment of the beloved. The terrible condition of the remains recovered at the World Trade Center site created a particular challenge for loved ones. Perhaps in an effort to counter this extraordinary assault on humanity and civilization, members of an American Red Cross Spiritual Care team blessed every body part discovered at ground zero. This team was composed of chaplains of different denominations who were available 24 hours a day, 7 days a week to perform this work, whether it was in the midst of the excavation site or at temporary morgues.

Other disaster-specific issues arise when victims have perished in violent circumstances. Family members are left with many concerns and questions that may never be answered to their satisfaction. They are often preoccupied with whether their loved ones suffered in the moments before their deaths. They agitatedly ponder were their deaths slow or quick, were they alone, were they afraid, were they in great pain or anguish? Sometimes this becomes a painful focus, as those left behind find it heartbreaking to bear the idea that their loved ones may have been in conscious agony or personal torment as they faced death. It feels like a transgression of their love, of their efforts to care for and keep out of harm's way those whom they have cherished most. It is haunting and difficult to reconcile. There are often troubling, incongruous circumstances to such tragedies that make these deaths even more irreconcilable, such as when competing contexts are juxtaposed as in the case of a young newlywed couple dying together while on their honeymoon in a plane crash. Family members often express a reassuring hope or fantasy that death was fast and suffering minimal.

Another frequent and significant loss in disasters is the loss of one's home or property and personal possessions, including those that are irreplaceable and of special emotional significance. Perhaps the worst context is when a home is completely destroyed so that a person's identity, as reflected in documents, photos, souvenirs, and ancestral heirlooms, is wiped out. Destruction of someone's home means that his or her safe, private sanctuary has been razed; one of the bottom rungs of the Maslow hierarchy of needs has been obliterated. Losing a home means being dislocated and relocated and dealing with the resulting consequences: making due in temporary settings that are often overcrowded or marginal, dealing with the pragmatic tasks of replacing belongings, relying on others for help, experiencing changes in school or work, and having one's routine social and interpersonal networks and habits disrupted. All these concomitant stressors that arise when a family's base of operations is gone provide fertile ground for heightened family disorganization and tensions. Raphael (1986) asserts that those in this situation may also experience a loss of dignity, especially for individuals who value self-reliance. Being even temporarily homeless may challenge beliefs about independence, pride, and self-esteem, producing a sense of humiliation and degradation.

There is great physical and symbolic stress in losing one's home, but grief at this loss is often repressed, denied, or postponed because it may pale in a comparison to the more penetrating loss of life. And the psychological, symbolic, intangible losses—those that shatter the individual's assumptions about the world—may be even more readily submerged. As a result, sadness and grief around such losses may become disenfranchised as the full significance of the loss is denied. This has also been called *ambiguous loss* (Boss, 1999), a term that reflects losses that lack clarity and that can lead to sharply differing assessments of exactly what has transpired. There may even be a question of whether a loss has actually occurred and what sort of response a person and a community should have. Unacknowledged losses may produce unresolved or hidden grief that can lead to an incomplete resolution of the tasks of mourning (Worden, 1982/1991). The course of the grief reaction may then be extended and will complicate adjustment now and in the future when other losses occur.

Characteristics of Bereavement

Given the extra stressors inherent in disasters, can we expect those impacted by disaster loss to grieve "normally"? The answer to this question is yes and, sometimes, no. In writing about the aftermath of unfolding trauma and traumatic loss following September 11, 2001, Miller (2003) noted, "These unique expressions of traumatic loss, like trauma itself, require a broadened expectation. Experience cannot be measured against other death, as the factors of trauma and scope of loss place this in another realm of consideration." Raphael (1986) speaks of the strong need to continue on with life that most people display. We can be faced with the losses that we never could have imagined surviving but do. The requirements of existence and the person's ongoing commitment to life draw him or her on into the future; there is an involvement in the world that is not easily relinquished, despite the pain of adjustment.

Immersion in the process of bereavement includes intense distress at separation: We yearn for a return of the dead, long for reunification and want those we loved not to be dead. Accepting the reality of loss is all consuming and takes time to sink in. One's whole being is engaged in this process. Painful affect is accompanied by waves of bodily distress (Lindemann, 1944); grief is very physical. Many people are surprised by this physical nature, but it is real and should be respected. The process is demanding and exhausting, so one of the more common physical symptoms of deep grief is low energy.

Anger is another common reaction. Those bereaved may be surprised to discover deep pockets of anger at the loss, or perhaps toward the loved one for leaving them behind, or toward their deity. This anger is frequently displaced onto others such as the authorities, the rescuers, or oneself. This is most intense when the disaster was human-caused because the bereaved can find an easy target for blame, especially if there is any suggestion that it was the consequence of intent or negligence or insufficient care.

Anxiety and panic about how to cope alone may alternate with profound sorrow. Preoccupation with the deceased is common as mourning creates an intense renewed initial connection. Recurrent images of the loved one may be intrusive but welcomed by some bereaved; others may try to repress or avoid these reminders of their loss. There is often a heightened vigilance, a secret hope that the lost person will reappear. Things that symbolically link one to the deceased, called *linking objects* (Volkan, 1988), take on special significance. One wears the deceased husband's shirt or daughter's wristwatch, especially if the body was not recovered.

Those who are bereaved often dream vividly of seeing and being with the deceased. These dreams may be very upsetting because they bring the illusion of being together with the deceased, an illusion that is painfully undone upon awakening and experiencing a renewal of loss and grief. Memories abound: moments of the relationship, the times spent together, the smells, the sights, the embraces, the loved one's voice that echoes—all these resurface and intermittently saturate the bereaved person's days, enhanced by the awareness that a tangible relationship has ended. Through a gradual process of review of these remembrances, adjustment to the loss is attained. Still, even in normal bereavement, reactions reflective of the mourning will continue to surface for some time. During the entire first year and at the anniversary of the death at the very least, there will be periodic exacerbations of sadness, mourning, guilt, and anger as new aspects of the loss are faced.

After a traumatic death, the interaction between posttraumatic stress and grief raises specific treatment implications. Figley (1995/1997) asserts that the symptoms of traumatic stress and grief are intensified when both are present, in a pairing that can significantly affect one's relationship to the deceased, issues of identification, and the processing of anger and rage. Regehr and Sussman (2004) point out that the grief literature has its foundations in psychodynamic and relational theories, so treatment has focused on resolving issues through reminiscence and developing a new sense of the relationship, whereas trauma literature has been founded largely on biological and cognitive formulations. These perspectives need to be integrated in working with those suffering traumatic loss because two tasks are presented to the affected individual: trauma mastery and loss accommodation.

The current consensus is that where significant posttraumatic symptomatology exists, treatment for the stress should take precedence over that for the bereavement (Figley, 1997). In fact, Rando (1993) asserts that complicated grief is a form of PTSD and that there is great similarity in the treatment agenda of both that

> necessitates the working through of related affects, integration of conscious and dissociated aspects, mourning of relevant secondary physical and psychosocial losses, acquisition of new ways of being to move adaptively into the new world, development

of a comprehensive perspective on the event and one's level of control therein, emotional relocation of what was lost, acceptance of fitting responsibility and relinquishment of inappropriate guilt, revisions of the assumptive world, demanded by the event and its repercussions, creation of meaning out of the experience, integration of the event into the totality of one's life, formation of a new identity reflecting survival of the event, and appropriate reinvestment in life.

Clearly this is a difficult and complex process for survivors and one that often requires professional assistance.

A Double Blow: Bereaved Survivors

It sometimes happens that those who have lost loved ones—the bereaved—may have been directly impacted by the same disaster as the person who died. They have may have been injured, or they may have been spared through some action of the deceased. Naturally, being exposed to a traumatic stressor in addition to losing loved ones adds to an already complicated grief picture, and it can be difficult to tease apart the differences between complicated grief and a severe traumatic stress response.

The degree to which grief is experienced in the days and weeks after a disaster will be greatly influenced by the extent of emotional shock and threat that was suffered personally during impact and by the subsequent need to be emotionally committed to issues of survival and basic existence. If multiple losses have occurred, the survivor may not have the opportunity for what Raphael (1986) calls the "luxury of grief." As a result, those impacted may seem to observers as if they are unaffected and coping well, when the truth is that they are simply remaining focused on the present task at hand. Because of the pressing demands of life postdisaster, those dealing with a death and with other disaster losses may suppress the normal, reactive, and noticeable grief processes. The bereaved person's emotions may be exhausted or taken up with survival or anxiety. Initially, numbness or denial may be at the fore because immediate tasks need attention: obtaining remains, dealing with bureaucracies, taking care of children and other family members. It takes some time before survivors can drop their own guard and explore the thoughts and feelings surrounding loss that need attention. Safety and survival come first.

Loss, Guilt, and Shame

After experiencing a disaster, an individual can have "wrong" cognitions, dysfunctional thought patterns: "I should have . . . ," "If I only . . . ," or "Why me?" Although survivors may eventually feel positively about how they acted during a disaster, shame and guilt represent common initial reactions. The differences between these two emotions are subtle, and indeed, they are often fused together and difficult to disentangle. Essentially, *shame* involves people's sense of the quality of their person or self, whereas *guilt* is the emotion triggered by feelings that one may have harmed someone else or violated some important code. People are vulnerable after a trauma and receptive to self-blame, to shame and guilt; this may be one reason why negative social support after an event can be extremely detrimental, constituting a risk factor for impaired recovery.

A feeling of shame often follows an exposure of the self in a way that reveals something of a hidden or personal nature. Jackley (2001) found that shame was negatively associated with hope and quality of life and positively correlated to symptom distress measures, including depression and PTSD. The experience of shame elicits a sense of a defective self. This is an extremely painful and ugly feeling that can have a negative impact on interpersonal behavior. For example, at a June 2005 conference on the psychosocial aspects of disasters, a New York City firefighter, Jimmy Brown, eloquently spoke of his actions on the day of September 11, 2001. A former police officer, he had just begun his training to become a firefighter in the firehouse closest to the World Trade Center. During the response, he became separated from the rest of his crew and eventually found himself huddling at the base of Tower One, curled into a fetal position to protect himself from further injury. Brown recalled being convinced he was about to die. He thought of his wife—and he thought of the shame and embarrassment of being found in a fetal position. This last thought mobilized him into action, and he miraculously forged his way out of a window and survived. Such is the power of shame (Lewis, 1971).

Moving from shame to guilt, many people who live through a disaster where others died experience some level of survivor guilt, often combined with feelings of numbness and loss of interest in life. Survivors often feel that they did not do enough to save those who perished or that they are unworthy relative to the dead. Survivors may feel that their lives were spared at the cost of another's.

Performance guilt is another typical emotion experienced by many survivors, who blame themselves for how they did or did not act during a disaster. Menzies-Lyth (1987) suggested that it can be harder for survivors to cope in the aftermath of disaster than even those who are bereaved or physically injured. She observes, "Bereavement gets more sympathy than survival." The impact of guilt should not be underestimated: Some survivors of disasters have killed themselves, sometimes many years after the event, partly, it is thought, because of the burden of their guilt (Levi, 1994). No matter how much survivors do at the time of a disaster or how heroically they act, they are often left with the feeling that it was not enough, and so they have no right to continue living (Hodgkinson & Stewart, 1991). Indeed, someone labeled a hero for his or her actions may feel an even heavier burden of guilt and feelings of deeper inadequacy. Although painful, such performance guilt may be protective against the even more painful feelings of powerlessness or confronting the arbitrary randomness of events beyond anyone's control.

Finally, guilt may be experienced by those who were not present at the scene of the disaster but who believe they should have been—for example, those who had traded shifts the night before or who missed a crucial plane or train that would otherwise have taken them to their death. A disaster may provide completely innocent people with an object for their guilt. In part, this reflects the collective nature of disasters, which tend to affect all members of a community to varying degrees. This shared response is discussed next.

COLLECTIVE RESPONSES TO DISASTER

One of the defining features of disasters is the social context in which they occur. Survivors experience disasters and subsequent loss and grief in a community context, and the validation received through social support is important in the resolution of grief. According to Zinner and Williams, editors of *When a Community Weeps: Case Studies in Group Survivorship* (1999), survivor groups experiencing significant losses in common are often recognized after a disaster. For group members, the loss may be a very personal one, such as the death of a loved one, or it may be a loss that is experienced either as a result of being part of the same event or through a process of identification.

Zinner and Williams (1999) write that the concept of group survivorship allows for an examination of an event by "aggregates of individuals beyond the family and friends of the deceased and promotes the exploration of ways to help groups respond positively to death." They describe four levels of group survivorship: The primary level includes family members of the deceased; secondary are those who are connected through work or dwell in the same locale; tertiary survivors share significant social characteristics with the deceased such as occupational or recreational traits; and the fourth level reflects those who have in common an ethnic, geographic, or national identification. The tasks of carrying on are shared and accomplished through an exchange of informational and affective processing within or across survivor groups that have a shared focus. It is their belief that survivor groups have certain social rights (for example, acknowledgment and recognition as having suffered a significant loss) and obligations (for example, to acknowledge publicly the group's survivorship status) that, when recognized, can help facilitate immediate and long-term well-being in relation to traumatic loss.

Rando (1993/1999) highlights two social changes that have intensified the phenomenon of group survivorship and made it more prevalent. The first is the increasing probability of death in a traumatic context, especially through human-induced disasters and terrorist actions. This, she suggests, enhances the traumatic element and adds an increased relevance to the creation and potency of survivor groups. The second change that Rando underscores is that of the role of the media. She writes,

> Here is found an example of the 'double-edged sword' effect *par excellence* . . . the media can be a positive, therapeutic agent . . it can disseminate necessary and accurate information . . if effectively used by leaders who convey messages that enable and provide direction for healthy grief. It can connect individuals to others. It can also increase the suffering of actual mourners and actually create vicarious mourners . . with graphic images and horrifying information. Secondary traumatic stress is spawned. . . . There is no other agent as valued and vilified. (Rando, 1993)

The collective nature of disaster also helps determine the external public response to events, with specific interventions shaped by cultural, political, and socioeconomic factors (Zinner & Williams. 1999). For example, the outpouring of unsolicited professional help to the Oklahoma City community after the bombing of the Alfred P. Murrah Federal Building in 1995 is contrasted with the restraint demonstrated by Finnish mental health responders who waited to be invited in by the community before intervening while a populated ferry was sinking. In Finnish culture, not waiting for an invitation would have been inappropriate. In contrast, Americans have learned to expect a certain public response to shocking violence; public grief has become part of the shared experience, especially on television.

Some of the collective responses observed in communities following a disaster or tragic event include specific local rituals or ceremonies that are used to create a container for the expression of feelings and to provide a focus for collective reflection. These can take the form of funerals, memorials, arts exhibits, community open houses, anniversary commemorations (through which time is measured), and group legal action. Indelible structures marking disasters become community landmarks and commemoration sites. Lord (1996) and Wortman (1983) surmise that, even though communities are never the same after catastrophic events, collective gatherings and action provide a forum for survivors and their communities to experience their pain and tell their story. These acts are largely viewed as supportive and therapeutic, offering permission to community members and survivor groups with a range of losses to acknowledge the extent of what they have undergone.

Looking at an even broader level of community, a shared increase in patriotism may be viewed as a form of national group identification with the actual victims. This reaction was observed in the United States after the September 11 attacks, and it was intensified, in keeping with Rando's (1993) earlier observations, by the large scale, malevolent intentionality and brutality of the events—and by a very present media. Brewin (2003) observes that when thoughts of death are prominent "the mere existence of people with different beliefs threatens our primary basis of psychological security." When people are reminded of the possibility of their own death, their worldviews are strengthened (Pyszczynski, 2004). There is an increased sense of national identity and use of cultural symbols such as flags.

Indeed, in the immediate aftermath of September 11, 2001 there was a widespread call for national unity demanding unwavering patriotism, as well as uncritical support for state policy (Brown, 2003). It was common to hear the phrase, "If you're not with us, you're against us." This collective response may have had a synergistic effect with the other widely experienced sensation of the time: terror, which was characterized for many people by feelings of impending doom, anger, panic, and fearfulness. A primary goal of terrorism is to engender mental defeat (Brewin, 2003); patriotism and nationalism can help counter this with a sense of purpose, meaning, and empowerment, as if embracing patriotism made citizens feel they were part of the effort to prevent terror's recurrence.

Finally, narrowing our focus to consider a smaller collective group, traumatic events leave an enduring legacy within a family system. Such events cast huge shadows, and in cases of extreme stress, traumatic reactions can last for many years. In one study of Nazi concentration camp survivors (Valent, 2000), many reported a continuing sense of anxiety and fear a full 50 years after they were released. Transgenerational effects have been noted in children of parents who have experienced significant traumatic events (Parsons, Kehle, & Owens, 1990). Terms such as *vicarious, empathic,* and *secondary traumatization* have been used to describe intergenerational trauma transmission whereby family members exhibit symptoms of the traumatic response. This phenomenon has been detected in children of Vietnam veterans (Silverstein, 1994) and in those of Holocaust survivors (Danieli, 1982). Silverstein poignantly states, "Clearly, the wounds of the parents impact on the children." This transmission provides a connection to previous generations because the family worldview that gets passed down is shaped by experiences of the generation before. A powerful family mythology is formed.

Tauber (1998) describes children of those who have experienced a trauma of significant scale as living in a "traumatogenic reality." In terms of those who survived the Holocaust, she lists the following as elements of a parent's experience that may have influenced their children's lives: significant deprivation, humiliation, loss of community, loss of human rights and health, and exposure to mass death. The influence on children might take the form of contamination of suffering, search for cultural background, aggression regulation, denial of wounds, a continuing impact of the overwhelming presence of death, fear of death, and difficulties in separation-individuation. In detailed interviews with second-generation survivors, Tauber identified the importance of acknowledging traumatization and its impact on the family. Second-generation survivors "absorb the intensive emotions which controlled their parents into their lives and experienced them as what they thought were their own feelings. Everything the parents ever repressed often returns in the lives of their children, who don't always understand what is happening to them." Parental communication around a traumatic event may include obsessive retelling or all-consuming silence. If the traumatic event has not been sufficiently integrated by a family system, children and the generations to follow will struggle with the unprocessed traumas of their survivor parents.

To treat those who experience intergenerationally transmitted posttraumatic stress, Kidron (2003) suggests using a support group based on narrative practice as a format for allowing descendents to fashion their own sense of self as survivors of a distant traumatic past. In this way, they can develop their own identities and fashion life stories personally constituted by this distant past, yet also separate from it.

INDIVIDUAL RISK AND RESILIENCE

So far in this chapter, we have reviewed common stress reactions after exposure to disaster, emphasizing "normal" (if powerful) responses that often affect survivors, in some cases causing them to experience nightmares, intrusive thoughts, or any combination of cognitive, physical, emotional, behavioral, and spiritual changes for the first times in their lives. This approach has shared some of the "one size fits all" quality of many of the historic mental health interventions geared toward disaster survivors.

However, the DMH field is evolving, and researchers and clinicians are beginning to focus on the role of early assessment, or triage, aimed at identifying people and groups who may be the most vulnerable to lasting mental health effects.

This change comes out of the recognition that not everyone who is exposed to trauma is at equal risk for experiencing posttraumatic symptomatology and that responses to exposure vary. An underlying belief regarding early intervention is that survivors can and will benefit from support, though most will ultimately be able to regroup with little or no assistance. But people have differing core-resilient capacities. How can we foster these capacities and identify those people who need our help to make the best recovery possible? Factors that predict risk and resilience are discussed next because appreciation of these issues will help us learn where to place our resources and how to focus our work.

According to the National Institute of Mental Health workshop on Mental Health and Mass Violence (NIMH, 2002), **risk factors** are defined as empirically validated variables related to risk for long-term adjustment problems. These may be understood as factors or circumstances that contribute to the likelihood that exposure to traumatic events will have long-term, serious mental health consequences. A risk factor, when present as a characteristic either of the event, the person, or the environment, is associated with an increase in a negative outcome. On the other side of the equation, those factors that offer sufficient protection to endow survivors with a greater ability to cope with stress can be seen as **resilience factors.** What we call risk and resilience factors are also sometimes known as *vulnerability* or *hazard* and *protective* or *preventive factors,* respectively. These factors have been examined in terms of an individual's characteristics and demographics (that is, gender, age, or marital status), the features of the event itself, and aspects of the recovery environment. Much of this research has not been exclusively on disasters but on different traumatic events including combat and war-related events, natural and technological disasters, sexual assault, domestic violence, crime, motor vehicle accidents, death of a close family member or friend, acts of terrorism, and life-threatening medical conditions.

More research is needed to pinpoint the mechanisms through which these various characteristics exert their effect, but Norris, et al. (2002) made an important contribution by summarizing results from 160 samples of disaster victims in an ambitious study that incorporated a remarkable 61,396 individual participants, hence the title of their work, "60,000 Disaster Victims Speak." Their focus was specifically on disasters and not traumas in general, so they included acute, collectively experienced events with a sudden onset. The authors examined responses to disaster involvement and identified outcomes in terms of frequency in order to determine observable risk factors. There is considerable similarity between their disaster-specific findings and those for risk factors for negative reactions found in multiple studies of other types of trauma. Table 4.1 summarizes Norris et al.'s comparison of the findings from the literature on trauma and from this specific work on disasters, highlighting the striking similarities and important distinctions (Bravin, 2003; Myers & Wee, 2005; Wilson & Friedman, 2001).

While there were significant similarities between the aftereffects of disasters and those from a range of traumatic experiences, some disaster-specific findings appear particularly noteworthy. First, among adults, those who are middle aged appear to fare the worst. Norris et al. (2002) speculate that this may be due to the burdens on this age group, especially middle-aged women who often care

Table 4.1 | Risk Factors Summary

	Trauma Studies	Disaster Studies
	Preevent	
Demographics		
Gender	Female gender increased risk.	Female gender increased risk: • Effects longer lasting, more severe. • Greater in traditional cultures. • Greater if exposure severe. • Strongest for PTSD outcome.
Age in adult population	Younger age at time of event increased risk.	Middle aged adults most adversely affected. Effects of age may vary cross-culturally according to the social, political, economic, and historical context of the disaster setting.
Socioeconomic status (SES)	Lower SES fared worse.	Lower SES (defined as education, income, literacy, occupational prestige) had greater postdisaster distress. • Effects increased with severity of exposure.
Intelligence	Lower IQ fared worse.	
Ethnicity/culture	Majority groups fared better.	Majority groups fared better. Negative effects of disasters in developing countries much greater.
Background		
Experience of prior events	Mixed findings, demonstrating both inoculation and increased vulnerability effects.	Those already exposed to disasters of smaller magnitude had reduced anxiety and increased levels of preparedness. Professionalism and training increased the resilience of recovery workers, not past trauma per se.
Psychiatric history	Prior and ongoing-psychiatric problems can lead to increase in psychopathology.	Predisaster psychiatric history disproportionately increases risk for disaster-specific PTSD. • Severity of exposure augments risk.

Continued

Table 4.1 | (Continued)

	Trauma Studies	Disaster Studies
	Preevent	
Background		
		Predisaster "neurotic" personality increases risk whereas stable, calm, and "hardy" personality decreases risk.
Family factors	Family instability and poor family functioning deleterious.	Children highly sensitive to postdisaster distress and conflict in family; parental psychopathology the best predictor of child psychopathology.
		Married status a risk factor for women and husband's symptom severity predicted wives' symptom severity. Being a parent added stress; if threat is ongoing, mothers more at risk.
	Event	
Level of exposure	The greater the severity level of exposure, the more negative is the outcome.	The greater the severity level of exposure, the more negative is the outcome.
Bereavement/ loss	Predictive of a more negative outcome.	Predictive of a more negative outcome.
Injury	Predictive of a more negative outcome.	Predictive of a more negative outcome. • Also negative if injury is to family member.
Life threat/ horror	Predictive of a more negative outcome.	Predictive of a more negative outcome.
Peritraumatic behavior	Dissociation predictive of a worse outcome.	Panic or similar emotions predictive of a worse outcome.
Relocation/ displacement		Predictive of a worse outcome.
Separation from family		Predictive of a worse outcome. • Especially salient for youth.

Table 4.1 | (Continued)

	Trauma Studies	Disaster Studies
	Postevent	
Social support	Predictive of a better outcome.	Perception of social support most important: If disaster survivors believe that they are cared for by others and can get help, they fare better psychologically.
Negative social support	Negative, critical social support, such as blame assignment, is indicative of a poorer outcome; it appears to impact more profoundly than neutral or positive social support toward a negative end.	
Additional and secondary stressors	Subsequent life stressors after the index trauma demonstrate a strong association with post traumatic distress.	The greater the amount of resource loss and disruption, regardless of the specific resource, the greater is the psychological distress.
Coping		Inconsistent findings regarding ways of coping as successful or not. • However, avoidance and blame were consistently adverse. Belief in one's coping strategies and coping abilities were more influential than the actual strategy used.

for children while caring for their aging parents. Second, the amount of resource loss, regardless of type, also contributed significantly to a more negative outcome. Finally, a belief in one's ability to cope was more important than the specific coping mechanism used, with the caveat that avoidance and blaming were consistently detrimental ways to cope with disaster stress.

Bear in mind that the presence or absence of any of the risk factors that we have outlined does not set an individual survivor's recovery course in stone because risk and resilience factors operate through mechanisms that the field is still striving to identify. In predicting survivors' outcomes, two issues appear to be especially important (Norris et al., 2002): their coping strategies and their available resources, including both internal beliefs and the external reality of emotional support systems and concrete assets. Disasters represent an assault on the integrity of both resources and coping abilities, just at the time when they are most needed. Events may limit access to normally available resources that could have been mobilized for successful adaptation. Also, demographic factors may have implications for the availability of resources. For example, those who are poorer or are members of a minority group may have less access to the resources that would facilitate recovery from trauma. Similarly, the loss of a loved one and subsequent bereavement may profoundly affect one's ability to cope because a valuable source of comfort and guidance is no longer in place. This is the intricate dance of life postdisaster in which diverse elements collide and influence adaptation. Coping is not static but an ongoing process influenced by availability of resources, by the survivor's conviction in his or her own ability to recover, and by the meaning an event has for that person. Interventions need to be geared thoughtfully, regarding context and embracing individual variance.

The developing scientific findings on risk and resilience factors have potentially significant implications for clinical interventions and for policy and preparedness decisions. As King, Vogt, and King (2004) write,

> Only recently have practitioners and planners begun to attend to the literature on risk and resilience factors for PTSD and to apply these findings to clinical and policy decision making concerning management of risk. Although the trend is encouraging, a lack of understanding about causal inferences that can be drawn from studies of risk and resilience can considerably reduce the usefulness of this information for prevention, treatment and policy and valuable resources may be squandered on interventions that fail to have the desired impact.

When Resilience Fails

Overcoming trauma can be viewed as a creative, constructive process, with personal growth possible as an optimal result. The term *resilience,* referring to people's ability to bounce back from crisis and to persevere through difficult times, has been made much of recently as an explanation for the fact that the large numbers of survivors do not experience PTSD and are able to resume functioning; related concepts include hardiness, a sense of self-coherence, and posttraumatic growth. Bonanno (2004) states that resilience is more than the absence of psychopathology and that it is characterized by "a stable trajectory of healthy functioning across time, as well as the capacity for generative experiences and positive emotions."

Although it is evident that most people do not break down even after a severe stressor, the quality of life or level of internal distress is possibly as important. Is it resilient to lead a functional life but one of "quiet desperation" after a traumatic event? For example, many veterans, especially of the wars before Vietnam where PTSD was not well recognized, adapted to their PTSD symptoms. They chose occupations that were solitary and did not involve interactions with others, such as long distance driving or construction work. In this way, they did not have to further tax hyperarousal symptoms of anger and irritability and risk interpersonal difficulties. They developed strategies to "deal" with their nightmares, such as having their spouses sleep in separate rooms. We recall one veteran who built a harness to hold him in place while he slept, and another adult child of a veteran recalling "Daddy's usual habit of screaming out in the night."

As we discuss in the next section, "Existential Reactions to Disaster," surviving a disaster can cause people to question every aspect of the changed world they now live in. Shalev (2004) asserts that what turns a stressor into a trauma is not the threat to life but, rather, "a threat to one's image of the world." He calls this witnessing the unthinkable: "Stressful events become traumatic when they include novel and incongruous experiences, such as exposure to extreme brutality, disfigured dead bodies, people jumping out of windows, or major loss. . . . They tax the brain's mapping of reality. . . . They defy internalized rules, expectations, and assumptions." In some cases, a survivor is unable to move on, to find new meaning and purpose.

Wilson, Friedman, and Lindy (2001) and other PTSD experts describe one of the core elements of the disorder as human dispiritedness, which includes "helplessness, demoralization, withdrawal, alienation, a lack of ego mastery, detachment, a loss of essential vitality, a generalized shutting down. . . . The psychic core, or soul, of the survivor is diminished and attachments to other persons and life itself are lost. . . . A capacity to experience positive emotions is enmeshed or lost in a web of depression, despair, a sense of futility—giving up the struggle to be alive, a psychological surrender . . . decompensated downward spiral toward self destructive behavior."

Brewin (2003) also captures this terrible state in his description of the phenomenon of mental defeat in those who are traumatized. *Mental defeat* means surrendering one's sense of personal agency. He notes that this extends beyond feelings of helplessness and rocks the core of one's identity. Others have reflected on this as well. Trauma has been defined as "a cut into the soul" (Elbert & Schauer, 2002), "a wound that doesn't bleed" (Zabriskie, 2004), or "a shattered soul" (Shalev, 2004).

EXISTENTIAL REACTIONS TO DISASTER

As these powerful statements suggest, people who survive a disaster often experience subsequent reactions of an existential nature, relating to issues of meaning, sense of self, and identity. Disasters penetrate the deepest core of a survivor's being, and massive readjustments in their lives occur depending on the extent of their resource loss. Relevant literature alludes to "closure," "recovery," and "healing" as goals of recovery from traumatic experiences, but Rando (1993) argues for the term *adjustment* to reflect the process more accurately and thoroughly. What is the nature of this existential adjustment?

First, traumatic stress has the potential to fragment a survivor's sense of self. Nathanson (1992) writes that the concepts of identity and self relate to the notion of consistency or sameness over time, but trauma disrupts the meaningful organization of the self and the world (Auerbach, 2000; Janoff-Bulman, 1992; McCann & Pearlman, 1990; Ulman & Brothers, 1988), leaving people feeling helpless, hopeless, and worthless. Stern (1985), a developmental psychiatrist who studied the development of the self, says, "Sense of self is not a cognitive construct. It is an experiential integration." In other words, the self is a unifying system that can become burdened under the pressures of incorporating an experience that seems to make no sense, as in a disaster. If that incorporation of experiences fails, it can result in long-term problems. For example, clinicians working with veterans have noted that PTSD is a disorder of identity characterized by a failure to integrate aspects of identity, memory, perception, and consciousness.

Second, the work of integration extends beyond managing traumatic memory, dreams, irritability, and intrusive ideation to a quest for meaning in the presence of the unimaginable. When lives have been catapulted into an unexpected and seemingly foreign territory, issues of meaning making gain prominence. Horowitz (1986) wrote that we develop schemas that represent ourselves and the most important relationships and expectations in our lives. People's functioning in the world is mediated by implicit assumptions that organize thoughts, feelings, and actions, but severe stressors lead to a reconfiguration of these self-schemas. Harvey (1998) writes, "After such colossal mental and behavioral revisions, the survivor may wonder, 'who am I anyway?'" Many turn to God in their search for meaning; others gain a new understanding of their priorities. As Susan Hamilton, the director of mental health for the American Red Cross, reflected at a 2005 conference, on September 11, 2001 when people had only a few minutes to make phone calls before possibly dying, no one called their stockbrokers.

Rebuilding the Self After Disaster

The ultimate task for disaster survivors is to integrate the experience into a changed but intact identity. After a near-death experience, it is common to take stock of one's life, reviewing what has been good and what has been hard. To remain alive after others have died can seem onerous or puzzling. To have survived is simply not fair, or, rather, part of an unfair process. A ruminative cycle can result in which initial relief and gratitude are followed by despair at having much to contend with as a survivor. One may think, "It seems easier to have died." This thought is often followed by guilt over such thoughts, and so on.

Ultimately, a survivor must come to terms with how the trauma has changed his or her self-concept, relationships, and aspirations (Shalev, 2004). Family members of soldiers who return from war often comment that their loved ones are "not the same," and a similar alteration is seen in many disaster survivors. There are issues of functional adjustment (being able to adapt to the demands of daily life) as well as issues around one's broader happiness and quality of life.

After a disaster or trauma, people are left with many questions. With proper support, both from without or within, human beings can display an amazing capacity to spring back from the deepest distress and helplessness. This capacity is very old within humanity and is potentially part of each one of us. As Raphael

(1986) writes, "Many, although stressed by their experience, will feel a renewed commitment to life and relationships. They will gain an awareness and experience personal growth. They may well view their experience as giving them a valued 'second chance' in the game of life."

Tedeschi & Calhoun (1995) list three broad categories of potential perceived benefits in connection with traumatic experience: changes in self-perception, changes in interpersonal relationships, and changes in philosophy of life. Traumatic events may reinforce a belief in one's ability to cope with adversity. One's closest relationships may become of increasing importance, and many people will give more time and thought to the purpose of life, their involvement in their community, and their investment in spiritual issues or in advocacy for charitable causes. But this kind of "posttraumatic growth" depends on an individual's successful integration of his or her disaster experience, something not all survivors can accomplish on their own.

How do we recognize people who cannot achieve this necessary adjustment but who are suffering from a deep-rooted mental devastation in response to their traumatic experience? In our next chapter, we look closely at extreme reactions to disaster.

References

Attig, T. (1996). *How we grieve: Relearning the world*. New York: Oxford University Press.

Auerbach, C. (2000). Trauma shatters the self and world. *NYS Psychologist, 12*(1), 7–10.

Baker, K. (2005, January 21). On 9/11, before the horrible became the unimaginable. *New York Times*.

Bonanno, G. A. (2004). Loss, trauma, and human resilience: Have we underestimated the human capacity to thrive after extremely adverse events? *American Psychologist, 59*(1), 20–28.

Boss, P. (1999). *Ambiguous loss: Learning to live with unresolved grief*. Cambridge, MA: Harvard University Press.

Brewin, C. (2003). *Posttraumatic stress disorder: Myth or malady?* New Haven, CT: Yale University Press.

Brewin, C. R., Dagleish, T., & Joseph, S. (1996). A dual representation theory of posttraumatic stress disorder. *Psychological Review, 103*, 670–686.

Brown, W. (2003). Political idealization and its discontents. In A. Sarat (Ed.), *Dissent in dangerous times* (pp. 23–45). Ann Arbor: University of Michigan Press.

Danieli, Y. (1982). On the achievement of integration in aging survivors of the Nazi Holocaust. *Journal of Geriatric Psychiatry, 14*(2), 81–90.

DeWolfe, D. J. (2000). Training manual for mental health and human service workers in major disasters. U.S. Department of Health and Human Services: Center for Mental Health Services (Publication No. ADM 90-538). Washington, DC: Government Printing Office.

Elbert, T., & Schauer, M. (2002). Burnt into memory. *Nature, 419*, 883.

Figley, C. (Ed.). (1995). *Compassion fatigue: Coping with secondary traumatic stress disorder in those who treat the traumatized*. New York: Brunner/Mazel.

Figley, C. R. (Ed.). (1997). *Burnout in families: The systemic costs of caring*. New York: CRC Press.

Green, B. L. (2000). Traumatic loss: Conceptual and empirical links between trauma and bereavement. *Journal of Personal and Interpersonal Loss, 5*, 1–17.

Harvey, P. (Ed.). (1998). *Perspectives on loss: A sourcebook*. Philadelphia: Brunner/Mazel.

Haught, J. A. (2005). Why would God drown children? *Free Inquiry, 25*(3), 14–36.

Hobfoll, S. E. (1991). Traumatic stress: A theory based on rapid loss of resources. *Anxiety Research, 4*, 187–197.

Hodgkinson, P., & Stewart, M. (1991) *Coping with catastrophe*. London: Routledge.

Horowitz, M. (1986). *Stress response syndromes* (2nd ed.). Northvale, NJ: Jason Aronson.

Horowitz, M. J., Siegel, B., Holan, A., Bonanno, G. A., Milbrath, C., & Stinson, C. H. (1997). Diagnostic criteria for complicated grief disorder. *American Journal of Psychiatry, 154*, 904–910.

Jackley, P. K. (2001). Shame-based identity and chronic posttraumatic stress disorder in help-seeking combat veterans. *Dissertation Abstracts International: Section B: The Sciences and Engineering, 61*(9-B), 49–86.

Janoff-Bulman, R. (1992). *Shattered assumptions: Toward a new psychology of trauma*. New York: Free Press.

Kidron, C. A. (2003). Surviving a distant past: A case study of the cultural construction of trauma descendant identity. *Ethos, 31*(4), 513–544.

King, D. W., Vogt, D. S., & King, L. A. (2004). Risk and resilience factor in the etiology of chronic posttraumatic stress disorder. In B. Litz, (Ed.), *Early intervention for trauma and traumatic loss* (pp. 34–64). New York: Guilford Press.

Levi, P. (1994). *The drowned and the saved*. London: Abacus.

Lewis, H. B. (1971). *Shame and guilt in neurosis*. New York: International Universities Press.

Lifton, R. J. (1976). *The life of the self*. New York: Simon & Schuster.

Lifton, R. J., & Olson, E. (1999). The human meaning of total disaster: The Buffalo Creek experience. In M. Horowitz (Ed.), *Essential papers on posttraumatic stress disorder* (pp. 206–231). New York: New York University Press.

Lindemann, E. (1944). Symptomatology and management of acute grief. *American Journal of Psychiatry, 101*, 1141–1148.

Lord, J. H. (1996). America's number one killer: Vehicular crashes. In K. J. Doka (Ed.), *Living with grief after sudden loss* (pp. 91–102). Washington, DC: Hospice Foundation of America.

McCann, L., & Pearlman, L. (1990). *Psychological trauma and the adult survivor: Theory, therapy, and transformation*. Philadelphia: Brunner/Mazel.

Menzies-Lyth, I. (1987). *The dynamics of the social. Selected essays, Vol. 2*, London: Free Association Books.

Miller, M. (2003). Working in the midst of collective trauma and traumatic loss: Training as a collective process of support. *Psychoanalytic Social Work, 10*(1), 7–25.

Myers, D., & Wee, D. F. (2005). *Disaster mental health services*. New York: Brunner/Routledge.

Nathanson, D. L. (1992). *Shame and pride: Affect, sex, and the birth of the self*. New York: Norton.

Neimeyer, R. A. (2000). Searching for the meaning of meaning: Grief therapy and the process of reconstructions. *Death Studies, 24*, 541–558.

Neria, Y., & Litz, B. (2003). Bereavement by traumatic means: The complex synergy of trauma and grief. *Journal of Loss and Trauma, 9*, 73–87.

NIMH (National Institute of Mental Health). (2002). *Mental health and mass violence: Evidence-based early psychological intervention for victims/survivors of mass violence. A workshop to reach consensus on best practices* (NIH Publication No. 02-5138). Washington, DC: Government Printing Office.

Norris, F., Friedman, M. J., Watson, P. J., Byrne, C. M., Diaz, E., & Kaniasty, K. (2002). 60,000 disaster victims speak: Part I. An empirical review of the empirical literature, 1981–2001. *Psychiatry: Interpersonal & Biological Processes, 65*(3), 207–243.

Parkes, C. M. (1990). Risk factors in bereavement: Implications for the prevention and treatment of pathologic grief. *Psychiatric Annals, 20,* 308–313.

Parsons, J., Kehle, T. J., & Owen, S. V. (1990). Incidence of behavior problems among children of Vietnam war veterans. *School Psychology International, 11*(4), 253–259.

Prigerson, H. G., et al. (1999). Consensus criteria for traumatic grief: A preliminary empirical test. *British Journal of Psychiatry, 174,* 67–73.

Pyszczynski, T. (2004). What are we so afraid of? A terror management theory perspective on the politics of fear. *Social Research, 71*(4), 827–849.

Rando, T. (1988). *How to go on living when someone you love dies.* New York: Bantam Books.

Rando, T. (1993). *Treatment of complicated mourning.* Champaign, IL: Research Press.

Rando, T. (1994). On treating those bereaved by sudden, unanticipated death. *In Session: Psychotherapy in Practice, 2/4,* 59–71.

Rando, T. (1999). Foreword. In E. S. Zinner & M. B. Williams (Eds.), *When a community weeps: Case studies in group survivorship* (pp. xvii–xxiv). Philadelphia: Brunner/Mazel.

Raphael, B. (1986). *When disaster strikes: How individuals and communities cope with catastrophe.* New York: Basic Books.

Regehr, C., & Sussman, T. (2004). Intersections between grief and trauma: Toward an empirically based model for treating traumatic grief. *Brief Treatment and Crisis Intervention, 4*(3), 289–309.

Rosenblatt, P. C. (1993). Grief: The social context of private feelings. In M. S. Stroebe, W. Stroebe, & R. O. Hansson (Eds.), *Handbook of bereavement: Theory, research, and intervention* (pp. 102–111). New York: Cambridge University Press.

Rothschild, B. (2000). *The body remembers: The psychophysiology of trauma and trauma treatment.* New York: Norton.

Shalev, A. (2004). Further lessons from 9/11: Does stress equal trauma? *Psychiatry, 67*(2), 174–176.

Silverstein, R. (1994). Chronic identity diffusion in traumatized combat veterans. *Social Behavior and Personality, 22*(1), 69–80.

Stern, D. (1985). *The interpersonal world of the infant: A view from psychoanalysis and developmental psychology.* New York: Basic Books.

Tauber, Y. (1998). *In the other chair: Holocaust survivors and the second generation as therapists and clients.* Jerusalem: Gefen Publishing House.

Tedeschi, R. G., & Calhoun, L. G. (1995). *Trauma and transformation.* Thousand Oaks, CA: Sage.

Ulman, R. B., & Brothers, D. (1988). *The shattered self: A psychoanalytic study of trauma.* London: Analytic Press.

Van der Kolk, B. A., McFarlane, A. C., & Weisaeth, L. (Eds.). (1996). *Traumatic stress: The effects of overwhelming experience on mind, body and society.* New York: Guilford Press.

Valent, P. (2000). Stress effects of the Holocaust. In G. Fisk (Ed.), *Encyclopedia of stress.* San Diego: Academic Press.

Volkan, V. D. (1988, May 24–26). *What the Holocaust means to a non-Jewish psychoanalyst without Nazi experience.* Paper presented at the Fourth Conference of the Sigmund Freud Center of the Hebrew University of Jerusalem.

Wilson, J. P., Friedman, M. J., & Lindy, J. D. (2001). *Treating psychological trauma and PTSD.* New York: Guilford Press.

Worden, W. (1982/1991). *Grief counseling and grief therapy: A handbook for the mental health practitioner.* New York: Springer-Verlag.

Wortman, C. B. (1983). Coping with victimization: Conclusions and implications for future research. *Journal of Social Issues, 39*(2), 195–221.

Wortman, C. B., & Silver, R. C. (1989). The myths of coping with loss. *Journal of Consulting and Clinical Psychology, 57,* 349–357.

Zabriskie, P. (2004). Wounds that don't bleed. *Time, 164*(22), 40–43.

Zinner, E. S., & Williams, M. B. (1999). *When a community weeps: Case studies in group survivorship.* Philadelphia: Brunner/Mazel.

If you gaze into the abyss, then the abyss also gazes into you.

Friedrich Nietzsche

Extreme Reactions

As described in Chapter 4, exposure to disaster stress results in reactions on all levels of a person's being: physiological, cognitive, behavioral, emotional, existential, and spiritual. Many of these reactions are transient, but some mental health consequences endure, impairing the survivor's natural recovery and necessitating treatment. In this chapter, we discuss extreme and lasting reactions. We examine the physical roots of posttraumatic stress disorder (PTSD) and the emotional, behavioral, interpersonal, and identity issues inherent in this disabling condition. We also discuss the relatively new diagnosis of acute stress disorder and its successes and failures at predicting who will develop PTSD, as well as the issues faced by those dealing with complicated grief. Finally, we look at substance abuse, depression, and the other disorders that often can follow exposure to a traumatic event.

TRAUMA STUDIES AND DISASTER MENTAL HEALTH

As we described in Chapter 4, there are notable similarities in how people react to disasters, and it is this understanding of the expected response to stress—and the subsequent return to equilibrium—that provides disaster mental health (DMH) practitioners with an initial framework with which to approach a client.

However, despite the broad commonalities, an individual's reaction to a disaster constitutes a distinct phenomenon, defined in part by

1. Who the person is in terms of strengths and vulnerabilities.
2. His or her psychiatric and prior history.
3. The support and reactions that the person receives from loved ones and community.
4. Where the person literally was at the time a disaster struck and how he or she responded.
5. The extent of loss, change, or additional stressors the person faces in the aftermath.

These variables, which reflect individual differences, underscore the complexity and delicacy of this work and the need for proffering DMH services with awareness and caution.

One of the most serious clinical outcomes for an individual following exposure to the stress of a disaster is the development of PTSD. PTSD is a relatively "new" malady in the sense that it was only established as an official diagnosis in the last 25 years, after the mental health field fully took on the challenge of understanding and acknowledging the pervasiveness of trauma's effects and became willing to treat them. Today, at last, we recognize the gravity and frequency of the disorder. Both are demonstrated by results from the National Comorbidity Survey, conducted in the early 1990s (Kessler, 2002), which showed that PTSD is a highly prevalent disorder that often persists for years. The survey demonstrated that the qualifying events for PTSD are also common, with many people reporting the occurrence of several such events during their lifetimes.

PTSD appears to be a universal disorder, which provides support for the diagnosis as a valid condition rather than a cultural construct. PTSD symptoms of intrusive thoughts and avoidance have been identified and assessed in non-Western societies (Brewin, 2003). Clinicians working with war victims from diverse crisis regions such as the Balkans, the West Nile, and Somalia (Elbert & Schauer, 2002), as well as those working with victims of the 2004 tsunami in Thailand (Leitch, 2005) have reported PTSD symptoms in the clients they have treated. Elbert and Schauer write, "We are still amazed at the ability of an illiterate survivor, who has been driven out of the bush in southern Sudan and who has little contact with the outside world, to present us with a classic report of textbook psychiatric symptoms." Although there are some culturally specific expressions of symptoms and indigenous ways in which those affected deal with them, in general, cross-cultural consistency outweighs cultural and ethnic differences.

We believe that a close examination of PTSD is crucial for understanding the full range of survivor reactions following exposure to disasters, as trends in DMH practice have paralleled and been guided by the struggles within the mental health community to develop prevention, assessment, and treatment methods for PTSD. Thus, although the global, initial, explicit goal of DMH intervention is to help people return to predisaster functioning by reestablishing the normal stress response sequence and by providing adequate social, economic, medical, and psychological resources (Raphael, Wilson, Meldrum, & Bedosky, 2000), an implicit but vital hope of DMH helpers is to prevent PTSD and other debilitating reactions. A guiding concept for DMH practitioners is the assumption that disaster survivors are essentially healthy, adaptive people who will be able to overcome what has been dramatically placed in their path. However, this may or may not be the case for particular individuals, and this assumption may have led to the overapplication of certain interventions and/or reduced appreciation for the complexity of the postdisaster response.

A parallel debate exists within the mental health community about the nature of PTSD as a response to stress. Certain experts have asserted that PTSD falls along the normal stress response continuum (Brewin, 2003; Horowitz, 1986; Myers, 2005). This speaks to a very fundamental assumption about PTSD: that anybody could develop this disorder as a result of exposure to a traumatic event. In contrast, others have postulated that PTSD is a qualitatively distinct response to extreme stress (Yehuda, 2001; van der Kolk, McFarlane, & Weisaeth. 1996), not a normative response to trauma. According to these experts, the "normal" response to stress—even extreme stress—is homeostasis, or a return to regular functioning. Trauma's customary aftermath includes immediate and intense reexperiencing, hyperarousal, and avoidance, all components of PTSD. But these symptoms eventually drop off, especially after 1 to 3 months (Brewin, 2003; Foa & Rothbaum, 1998). In PTSD, however, the individual cannot return to the expectable baseline; the biological stress response does not shut down. Therefore, in this view, PTSD does not constitute a normal reaction.

Recent scientific findings challenge the notion that traumatic events are the sole cause of subsequent symptoms. So, the idea of PTSD as a typical stress response appears to be less substantiated. How survivors respond to trauma is not random; neither is it fully predicted by the nature of the traumatic event. The importance of risk and resilience factors in mediating an individual's outcome has come to the fore, as described in Chapter 4.

How does this evolving picture affect our work in DMH? It suggests that we will need to build increasingly sophisticated approaches to our interventions that are based on evidence from the ever-growing field of traumatic stress. Only by integrating findings from the two related fields can we attain a solid clinical and theoretical grasp of PTSD. Some of the most basic techniques used in DMH interventions make even more sense when we appreciate what constitutes PTSD, the mechanisms of trauma/stress response theory, and what we can expect when interacting with a diversity of disaster survivors. Perhaps most important for the aspiring mental health helper is that the greater a practitioner's understanding of and foundation in theory, the less dependence there will be on techniques and interventions learned by rote. The helper who has a comprehensive base in theory can tailor an intervention to the person impacted by disaster rather than assuming such an individual will fit into the intervention (Rothschild, 2000). Therefore, we now discuss the theories and mechanics of PTSD in detail, to prepare you to deliver the best mental health help possible in future work with disaster survivors. We also address complicated grief, another severe outcome, and outline other commonly occurring serious disorders.

POSTTRAUMATIC STRESS DISORDER

In its most basic conceptualization, PTSD represents an inability to take in and integrate an event of unusual scope, intensity, and meaning in the usual ways that people are programmed to do. This is not from a lack of conscious effort. Rather, immensely stressful occurrences constitute special experiences that challenge people's available coping resources simultaneously on multiple levels. PTSD is "a dramatic and complex shift in the steady state of the organism" (Wilson, Friedman, & Lindy, 2001). In contrast to the eventual adaptation to and processing of tremendous stress that permits a return to homeostasis, for those who develop PTSD, fragmentation results. The development of full-blown PTSD following any trauma exposure is statistically relatively small. One study of trauma survivors indicated that 20% of those exposed to a trauma will go on to develop PTSD (Breslau, Davis, Andreski, & Peterson, 1991). Another study found that 90% recover spontaneously following a traumatic experience (Litz, 1992).

Looking specifically at the impact of disasters, let's return to the comprehensive synthesis of the disaster literature conducted by Norris, Friedman, Watson, Byrne, Diaz, and Kaniasty (2002). In addition to looking at risk and resilience factors among the 61,396 individuals from 160 distinct samples, the researchers examined the type of events experienced, dividing them into technological, natural, or mass-violence disasters. (This third category represents a current trend in the disaster literature. Both the technological and mass-violence categories represent human-caused disasters, but the category of mass violence has the additional elements of intentional malevolence and significant loss of life.) Norris and her colleagues were striving to identify what the variety of psychosocial outcomes might be, to assess the distribution of the overall magnitude of these events in order to compare the impact of different types of disasters, and to outline the typical course of postdisaster reactions by looking at changes noted in longitudinal studies.

Examining the overall severity of psychological disorders including PTSD, Norris et al. (2002) found that between 18 and 21% of participants showed severe to very severe impairment, indicative of clinically significant distress. Their synthesis also revealed that the effects of disasters could be enduring, with significant psychological symptoms detected in a minority of the participants years after the disaster occurred. These researchers found that events that were of a greater magnitude or intensity, or those in which intention to harm was a component, were related to more psychological disturbance, which is consistent with other research findings in the general trauma literature. For example, Foa and Rothbaum (1998) found that 47% of a sample of rape victims reported ongoing PTSD symptoms 9 months postassault. In contrast, a study of a natural disaster, the 1980 Mount Saint Helens volcano eruption in Washington state, found that only 3.6% of those exposed developed PTSD, and most of the symptoms resolved within 2 years (Shore, Tatum, & Vollmer, 1986).

Although the nature of the disastrous event does appear to play a part in predicting rates of extreme reactions, it is not sufficient to account for the development of PTSD in some individuals. Certain mediating factors are generally agreed upon: the preparation—or lack of it—for expected stress, successful fight-or-flight responses, developmental history, belief system, prior exposure to trauma, internal resources, and support from family, community, and social networks. All these elements must be evaluated and incorporated into the DMH helper's decision about appropriate interventions for a specific survivor.

Diagnosing Posttraumatic Stress Disorder

In the American Psychiatric Association's fourth edition of the *Diagnostic and Statistical Manual of Mental Disorders* (*DSM-IV*), diagnostic criteria for PTSD include the occurrence of a traumatic event, the individual's response to or perception of that event, clinically significant distress, and functional impairment. PTSD in its current *DSM-IV* formulation contains three core symptom areas:

1. *Hyperarousal.* Hypervigilance, concentration problems, sleep disturbances, and exaggerated startle response
2. *Reexperiencing.* Flashbacks, intrusive thoughts, nightmares of the traumatic event, and physiological reactivity on exposure to internal or external cues that symbolize or resemble the stressor
3. *Avoidance.* Efforts to avoid reminders of the trauma, inability to recall part of the event, feelings of detachment, and a restricted range of affect

In addition to exposure to a stressor and subsequent hyperarousal, reexperiencing, and avoidance phenomena, a diagnosis of PTSD includes notable impairment in key areas of functioning including work adaptation and interpersonal and social relationships. For a diagnosis of PTSD, these symptoms have to persist for longer than 1 month. *Acute PTSD* is designated if the duration of the symptoms is less than 3 months, and *chronic PTSD* reflects the existence of these symptoms for longer than 3 months. In some cases, people do not become symptomatic immediately posttrauma. Those who begin to report symptoms at least 6 months after an identifiable stressor are diagnosed with *delayed onset PTSD* (American Psychiatric Association, 1994).

Studies have raised the question of whether the three core symptoms of hyperarousal, avoidance, and reexperiencing alone sufficiently capture the essence of PTSD. For example, factor analytic and meta-analytic studies have suggested that numbing may also be a core component. Additionally, studies have shown that at least two other disorders, depression and substance abuse, frequently co-occur with PTSD, and some evidence shows that these disorders may be consequences of PTSD. (We return to these comorbid conditions at the end of this chapter.) Brewin (2003) and others point out that none of the symptoms occurring in PTSD are unique to this disorder; they all can be found in other diagnoses, too. But, as he explains, it is the existence of a credible traumatic event that transforms a set of symptoms into the ingredients of PTSD.

Physical Underpinnings of Posttraumatic Stress Disorder

Trauma is intrusive: It does not become assimilated in the same way as other events. Traumatic stress is stress of great magnitude. It taxes one's system, impacting brain chemistry and physiological functioning. Memories of traumatic events feel different than memories of ordinary and of less dramatic occurrences, even when these other events have enormous personal significance. Traumatic events have unique importance for people in the realms of meaning and identity. These life-altering experiences have profound effects on our deepest, unspoken, and core assumptions and on how we hope and project into the future. They reflect products of our mental processes resulting from the inextricable link between brain, body, and mind (van der Kolk et al., 1996).

This link means that PTSD has a neurobiological base involving multiple body systems. People with the disorder experience significant changes in physiology and memory—fundamental alterations in "hardwiring" that in turn impact their behaviors and interpretations about life. Van der Kolk et al. (1996) describes this phenomenon as *somatic memory,* the concept that the body remembers and "keeps the score" of traumatic experiences. Let's next examine the physiological changes that occur in response to overwhelming, cataclysmic stress and how the normally protective fight-or-flight response described in Chapter 4 sometimes turns harmful.

Although most kinds of mental activity (such as thinking or remembering ordinary matters) produce purely psychological processes, experiencing a strong emotion generates a physical reaction as well, beginning in the brain and traveling through multiple body systems (Gazzaniga, Ivry, & Mangun, 2002). When humans are faced with a stressor or demand, be it a disaster or a confrontation with one's boss, an arousal response intended to maintain our most basic safety takes place. As soon as a particular external stimulus is perceived—even before it reaches conscious awareness—it is evaluated as to whether it might represent a possible danger. Our bodies unconsciously prepare, in ways both primitive and complex, for the fight-or-flight response already described. An individual may also freeze in an evolutionarily programmed response intended to avoid attracting a predator's attention. How does this actually occur each time that we are faced with a demand, in response to a potential threat to safety or in response to multiple daily stressors? And what happens when the response exceeds any protective value and becomes dysfunctional, as in PTSD? Understanding fully requires a brief tour of the complex world of the human nervous system.

The nervous system consists of two main subsystems, the **central nervous system** (CNS), which is composed of the brain and the spinal cord, and the **peripheral nervous system** (PNS), which encompasses everything outside of the brain and spine and is responsible for sensory and motor responses. The PNS is further divided into the **somatic** and **autonomic systems,** describing, respectively, voluntary and involuntary reactions throughout the body. Finally, the autonomic, or involuntary, system of the PNS is divided yet again into the **sympathetic** and **parasympathetic** branches. The sympathetic branch is engaged when the fight-or-flight response is active, and the parasympathetic branch takes over to return the body to homeostasis when the emergency preparedness is no longer needed.

The brain is the control center of the CNS, receiving and processing sensory information and triggering responses as needed. In the course of the brain's evolution, different structural system areas have developed, each with different anatomical and neurochemical compositions. The cortex, the wrinkly outermost layer of the brain, is the source of higher-order mental functions and is the site of most sophisticated neural processing including language, planning, working memory, and conscious thought. Deeper, and older, subcortical areas of the brain include the brainstem and hypothalamus and the limbic system. The brainstem and hypothalamus are linked to the regulation of internal homeostasis, helping to control our most basic, vegetative functions. The limbic system maintains the balance between the internal and external world. It is the seat of survival instincts and reflexes (Rothschild, 2000). It "guides" the emotions and behaviors necessary for self-preservation and survival. Two limbic system regions, the amygdala and the hippocampus, are especially relevant in emotional processing and understanding traumatic memory. Finally, the thalamus, which flanks the limbic system, is a major relay station; all sensory pathways except the olfactory go through it on the way to the cortex.

Of course, all of these individual brain parts must be able to share messages with each other in order to respond to danger. Communication in the nervous system is achieved through electrical impulses within individual cells or through the exchange of chemicals, including neurotransmitters that serve communication between two or more nerve cells, and neurohormones that communicate with organs and glands.

After the eyes, ears, or other sensory organs have detected a potential threat in the external world, data about it are transmitted simultaneously through two distinct pathways, dubbed the "low road" and the "high road" (LeDoux, 2002), helping the brain determine how actively to respond. Information sent through the high road is processed via the sensory cortex, an area capable of more advanced decision making, before being sent on to the amygdala, which is the brain's basic threat-evaluation center. This processing takes some time to complete and is relatively slow (at least in neurological terms), but is likely to be more accurate in comparison with the low road. In this latter path, the sensory cortex is bypassed, and the stimulus is transmitted directly to the amygdala. This enables a faster response but at the cost of accuracy or detail. The amygdala essentially acts like a dispatcher, receiving a message from the environment and "deciding" what bodily responses to activate with the situation.

If the stimulus is perceived as sufficiently threatening, the amygdala triggers areas that activate the sympathetic branch of the autonomic nervous system, launching the fight-or-flight response described in Chapter 4. The amygdala also activates the hypothalamus, a small structure in the limbic system, which initiates a series of hormone releases by glands throughout the body. Known as the hypothalamic–pituitary–adrenal axis (HPA axis), this network collectively regulates the hormonal response to stress. Most notably, the adrenal gland next to each kidney releases adrenaline and noradrenaline, hormones that enhance the effects of the sympathetic nervous system by further stimulating respiration and increasing cardiac output. The adrenal glands also produce cortisol, a hormone that causes an increase in blood glucose level, making additional energy available to fuel action (Phillips, 1991).

When things are "fired up" this way, signals are continually relayed to the cortex to enable the brain to weigh new information about whether the threat continues. This evaluation helps modulate primitive emotional reactions to a perceived threat and, when the system is functioning properly, ensure that the response is appropriate for the actual degree of danger. The HPA axis reins in the stress response, returning the individual to homeostasis once the aroused and ready state is no longer needed. In PTSD, however, the brain keeps repeatedly calling in the same alert, commanding the body to prepare for fight, flight, or freeze, well beyond any utility. The outcome is reflected in the core PTSD symptom of persistent hyperarousal.

Even when the stressful exposure is not extreme enough to produce a clinical condition like PTSD, ample evidence shows that repeated activation of the stress response can be damaging. Physically, chronic stress has been linked to increased vulnerability to infection due to suppression of the immune system; to the development of insulin resistance, which is a risk factor for diabetes; to hypertension and cardiovascular disease; and to premature death. These long-term negative effects are attributed to *allostatic overload,* or an inability to fully shut off the stress response even after the need for it has ended (Kinnunen, Kaprio, & Pulkkinen, 2005). Essentially, repeated exposure to stress causes the individual's once-protective reaction to get stuck in the on position, gradually leading to a degradation of various physical systems.

Psychologically, strong emotional arousal can impair memory as high levels of cortisol disrupt activity in the hippocampus, a brain region instrumental in memory formation and in inhibition of the hypothalamus. In animal experiments, long-term experience of high-stress levels actually led to degeneration and death of the hippocampal cells. Stress hormones can also impair functioning of the prefrontal cortex, the region where judgment and decision making are focused, potentially leading to bad choices in complex situations (LeDoux, 2002).

Perhaps most disturbingly, experiencing the type of intense stress that could be expected during and after a disaster essentially establishes a feedback loop that amplifies reactions to subsequent stress in two ways. First, the cortisol released by the adrenal glands eventually travels back to the amygdala, which it stimulates for another round of hormone release, leading to yet more cortisol entering the bloodstream. Second, cortisol impairs the normal ability of the hippocampus to rein in the hypothalamus in its role in the release of stress hormones. Thus, cortisol functions like a driver moving his or her foot from the brake pedal (the hippocampus) to the accelerator (the amygdala), leading to a net increase in the stress response. Clearly, this response is powerful and susceptible to excess activation.

In working with disaster survivors, remember that nervous system responses under conditions of threat are automatic survival actions, largely beyond the control of the individual performing them. Automatic does not mean simple in this context. It means that the responses produced are not the end result of considerable cognitive or mental reflection. Still, although reactions are based on the demands of the current moment, past history and experience can have some bearing on them. An example of this would be what is referred to in soldiering or emergency service work as "muscle memory." The concept is that first responders preparing to face dangerous, life-threatening situations can practice in advance, imagining and role playing what a threat would be like. This helps them retrain their reactions so that in the face of threat they are able to push forward and perform their role, contrary to a civilian or routine biological response. But although learned and practiced responses can override instincts, some automatic reaction to danger is retained; the limbic system still makes an appraisal of whether there is time or strength or distance to escape, fight, or freeze.

Core and Related PTSD Symptoms

Now that we understand the basic physical processes that underlie PTSD, let's look more closely at the disorder's core symptoms of hyperarousal, reexperiencing, and avoidance and how they impact daily life for the sufferer.

A persistent state of **hyperarousal,** as if grave danger is imminent, makes individuals vulnerable to overreacting to sensory stimuli. Traumatized people have difficulty in evaluating external cues and mobilizing appropriate levels of physiological arousal. Their ability to discriminate what may be a true threat is undermined, so their appraisal of the world is distorted. Innocuous stimuli are misinterpreted. Because of the physiological sensitivity that results from a chronically disordered pattern of arousal, those with PTSD can immediately go from stimulus to response without being able to figure out the meaning of what is happening.

Hyperarousal can be accompanied by *hypervigilance,* the feeling that one always needs to be on guard, with increased threat scanning and appraisal. Yet, the ability to determine danger or safety accurately is impaired. It is not uncommon to find, for example, that those who have experienced combat or have been involved in gunfire exchanges prefer to sit with their backs to the wall when in eating establishments or crowded settings. Irritability and insomnia are also common, possibly a result of the strain of staying defensively alert at all times.

An exaggerated *startle response* is often part of the symptom picture. A "normal" startle response is the result of a characteristic sequence of muscular and autonomic responses elicited by sudden and intense stimuli, usually auditory cues such as loud, unexpected noises. Most people can disregard and filter out these cues, but those with PTSD may be unable to control their reactions. An example of an exaggerated startle response would be someone diving for cover when "mistaking" the sound of a car backfiring for gunshots after having been involved in a trauma that involved gunfire exchange.

The hyperarousal state of those with PTSD seems to set the stage for the existence of the second core symptom, **reexperiencing** phenomena such as flashbacks and intrusive memories. When faced with current experiences that include elements or reminders of their original trauma, those with PTSD may react as if they are living through an experience again, with the same biological systems and reactions activated as in the original traumatic episode. Those elements of the present that serve to activate flashbacks of intrusive memories are called *triggers*. Triggers can be external or internal cues. For example, the sound of a jet flying overhead may be an external trigger for a September 11, 2001 survivor. An internal trigger could be an accelerated heart rate, a sensation that could be the result of any number of factors in the present. For those with PTSD, it can initiate a cascade of associations to their traumatic response. This generates a flashback.

Flashbacks are highly disturbing replays of memories of traumatic events. This replaying is accompanied by sensations that are so strong that the person experiencing these sensations has a hard time differentiating current reality from past events. Someone enduring a flashback has a sense that he or she is reliving the past in the present. Flashbacks involve different sensory modalities: One can hear or see something that is not present now. They can be emotional, behavioral, or somatic. Because they almost always include the behavioral and sensory aspects of the original traumatic experience, they are utterly terrifying for the person suffering through them and mystifying and frightening to observers.

Flashbacks are far more intense than "normal" memories, so to explain what causes them we must return briefly to physiology. Kolb (1986) suggested that people with PTSD suffer from impaired cortical control over subcortical areas responsible for learning, habituation (the ability to become accustomed to a stimulus rather than constantly reevaluating it as if it is a new one), and stimulus discrimination (the ability to distinguish between threatening and nonthreatening cues). Those with PTSD have lost some capacity for stimulus discrimination so that both neutral and trauma-specific stimuli can serve to trigger the feeling of being in that dangerous situation once again.

Flashbacks are not the only kind of reexperiencing symptom. People with PTSD can also be plagued by intrusive memories of their traumatic experiences or elements of these events. These memories are not as intense as flashbacks, but they arise unbidden, upsetting sufferers' sense of existing in the present and keeping them captured in the past. They can also serve to initiate a chain of thoughts about what has happened, leading to rumination and speculation.

As a less obvious effect of reexperiencing trauma, nearly everyone with PTSD suffers from sleep disturbances. These can include difficulty getting to sleep, difficulty remaining asleep, nightmares, and night sweats. Sleep normally consists of a number of cycles that are experienced throughout the night; each cycle moves through several stages including rapid eye movement (REM) sleep, during which dreaming occurs. Sleep disruptions in those with PTSD can occur at any phase during the sleep cycle (van der Kolk et al., 1996). Traumatic nightmares may or may not resemble the original traumatic experiences exactly. Night sweats, in which people awaken during the night drenched in sweat from the body's autonomic reaction to terror, are common and can happen several times a night. They can accompany nightmares but can also exist in the absence of a recollected dream. Indeed, people with PTSD may or may not be able to remember their nightmares, but the significant others of those with such sleep disruption often report that their partners can be seen thrashing and shouting or crying out in their sleep. In some cases, partners have even been injured as a result of these actions.

The impact of these sleep disturbances on people suffering from PTSD should not be minimized; just imagine what it would be like to be unable to rest, especially given the context of hyperarousal, flashbacks, and intrusive memories. The purpose of sleep is not completely known, but it seems to permit processing of psychological material as well as physiological restoration. Sleep deprivation has deleterious consequences during one's daily life.

Persistent difficulty in neutralizing stimuli in the environment in order to pay attention to relevant tasks leads to the third core PTSD symptom, **avoidance.** This largely unconscious response can be interpreted as a compensation for chronic hyperarousal and subsequent reexperiencing. Behaviorally, those with PTSD will avoid stimuli that can serve as reminders, or triggers, of the original traumatic incident. They feel unable to talk about it; they will switch off the TV or radio to protect themselves from exposure to evocative images; they may even go so far as to relocate and attempt to "start over." Concentration problems are common. Emotional numbing can result. Initially, the avoidance is focused on reminders of the trauma, but it can become generalized to many other situations. This global shutting down in order to cope leads to an inability to risk new and gratifying experiences. The individual comes to minimize interactions with the outside world and to prefer isolation (van der Kolk et al., 1996).

Some typical emotional reactions also characterize PTSD. Anger or aggression stems in part from the chronic hyperarousal, which brings with it a readiness to fight; aggression is also related to the typical diminished stress tolerance and a blend of ongoing sleep deprivation, irritability, and subsequent frustration. Fear, anxiety, and tension are prevalent. Terror returns during flashbacks. There is always a feeling that a potential threat may be on the horizon. Fear persists and generalizes to more and more aspects of the environment, increasing constriction and avoidance.

Those with PTSD also may feel ashamed by what has happened to them, and they may feel guilt for outcomes that they could not possibly have controlled. They may review their performance during the traumatic event and come up short, feeling that they let themselves down, especially if their reaction included freezing. Along with the fear and pain that are associated with trauma comes an incredible sense of helplessness—that one's actions have little or no influence in the course of an event as it unfolds. Those impacted yearn for a lost feeling of invulnerability, so they desperately struggle to regain a sense of control. It is confusing and difficult for survivors to appreciate the reality that many responses made under the threat of annihilation are automatic and biologically based.

People with PTSD often also experience depressive responses. Deflated moods, feelings of hopelessness, desolation, psychological surrender, and possible thoughts of suicide may be part of their experience of depression. When people feel "trapped" in their traumatic experiences, they become more vulnerable to feeling enervated and drained, unable to muster internal resources to push forward. After a traumatic event, there is often a feeling that the future is foreshortened. This perspective can combine with the depressive view that "now is forever and there is no way out." In addition to depressive feelings, alcohol and drug abuse are often-seen forms of self-medication following exposure to a trauma, perhaps in an attempt to reduce hyperarousal and reexperiencing states as well as depressive feelings and beliefs.

Not surprisingly, given this cluster of painful and limiting symptoms, people with PTSD experience a reduced overall quality of life. The intrusive symptoms that we have reviewed restrict their ability to function. Chronic hyperarousal is exhausting because reminders or triggers of trauma can appear out of nowhere and cause panic. Sufferers learn to fear their own reactions. The ability to feel safe is undermined when so many things in the environment are perceived as dangerous. The global numbing and shutting down lead to diminished pleasures and interest in people and things. As a result, maladaptive coping ensues, and a huge toll is paid. Meaningful interpersonal attachments are disrupted. People with PTSD often appear moody, socially withdrawn, and unwilling or unable to share their stories and their lives; in turn, loved ones, friends, and family members find it challenging to be close to them. With affective numbing comes a reduction in the ability to express the range of warm and affectionate feelings needed to sustain intimate relationships and close friendships. Occupationally, those with PTSD who work may choose jobs and shifts that are solitary to reduce stressful interpersonal demands. Or they may chose occupations in which a hypervigilant, threat scanning, and suspicious mind-set might be an asset, for example, such as in a correctional setting. After they stop working, symptoms can become resuscitated, intensified, and problematic in the absence of the structure and demands of a work environment.

MEMORY AND TRAUMA

Memory is an important aspect of trauma. Rothschild (2000) writes that in PTSD, memory has gone awry: "Traumatic experiences free float in time without an end or place in history." Again, we must return to biology to understand how trauma impacts memory.

For an experience or perception to become a memory, three basic steps have to occur: encoding, storage, and retrieval. Memory begins with sensory input. This can come from the environment outside the body, perceived via the five senses: sight, hearing, touch, smell, and taste. Or information can come from the inside of the body, reflecting proprioception (one's sense of how the body is positioned) and the ability to take inventory of the internal environment including heart rate, visceral sensations (gut feelings), and vestibular information about balance and posture. This input is not stored in any one brain region or structure; that is, there is no specific place in which the various components of a memory—emotions, sensations, chronology—are collected. Instead, the brain processes perceptions and stores them as thoughts, emotions, images, sensations, and behavioral impulses that must be assembled into a cohesive whole upon retrieval.

In ordinary contexts, the brain structures that are involved in managing memories work together smoothly, but this integration breaks down when it comes to remembering traumatic events. As van der Kolk et al. (1996) write, "Trauma imprints (are) stored as fragmented sensory and emotional traces, rather than being organized into a narrative by the higher brain's autobiographical self." In particular, areas of the prefrontal cortex, which process language and symbols and which are responsible for analyzing experiences and associating them with other knowledge, function differently when a person is under siege. Even those who do not develop PTSD will recall traumatic experiences in ways that are somewhat different than other events. Memories of traumatic events often stand out more or are recalled in a piecemeal fashion. Even without PTSD, it may be hard to provide a seamless, chronologically accurate narrative of the sequence of actions during a traumatic episode.

Two of the same limbic system areas that we saw play a major role in determining the immediate physical response to stress, the hippocampus and the amygdala, are also crucial in how we remember and make sense of things experienced under conditions of intense arousal. The hippocampus seems to have an important influence on how we shape or structure a "normal" memory, organizing it with a beginning, middle, and end. However, alterations in one's focus of attention and/or extreme emotional arousal may interfere with hippocampus operations. Studies have shown that functioning of the hippocampus is suppressed during traumatic threat (Nadel & Jacobs, 1996; van der Kolk, et al., 1996) and that survivors of trauma who are diagnosed with PTSD tend to have a smaller hippocampus than the general population (Bremner et al., 1997). (It is not clear whether those with PTSD have a shrunken hippocampus due to the impact of stress or whether they began life that way.) This impairment of the hippocampus seems to lie behind the PTSD sufferer's sense of the traumatic event not concluding, leading to flashbacks and other forms of reexperiencing.

In contrast to the reduced functioning of the hippocampus under threatening conditions, the amygdala is very active both during a traumatic event and while remembering it later. The amygdala aids in the processing of intensely charged events. It is understood to be the seat of our emotions and gives an "emotional label" to an experience; this is especially true for our more negative emotions such as fear. The amygdala appears to affect sensory input storage in the cortex of the right hemisphere, which is specialized for the perception and expression of emotion. In contrast, the left hemisphere of the brain plays a larger role in cognitive analysis and language production, and the left cortex seems to have a more involved relationship with the hippocampus. Van der Kolk (1994) has found that activity in Broca's area, which is a left cortical structure responsible for speech production, is suppressed during a traumatic incident. He poignantly refers to the "speechless terror" of trauma.

Models of Memory and Trauma

Looking beyond the roles of parts of the brain, trauma researchers have proposed a number of different memory types and mechanisms. Many memory researchers differentiate between **explicit,** or **declarative, memories** about specific facts, images, sensations and behavioral impulses, and **implicit,** or **nondeclarative, memories** for more conceptual matters such as general motor and cognitive skills—the things people know without really knowing how they learned them.

Essentially, declarative memories include the individual's conscious awareness of what has happened to him or her, and nondeclarative memories include skills and habits, emotional associations, reflexive actions, and conditioned sensorimotor responses. According to van der Kolk et al. (1996), people with PTSD experience an inundation of images, sensations, and behavioral impulses arising from their declarative memories, disconnected from the context, concepts, and understanding usually provided by nondeclarative memories.

Foa and Rothbaum (1998) postulated an *emotional processing theory* based on an associated network approach. In this theory, a newly created fear network is forged that is not integrated in the same way as ordinary memory because of high levels of emotion and fragmentation. This is also known as a *single representation theory* in that traumatic memory is understood to exist in one memory system. Under extreme stress, the memory representations would be fragmented, and memories of event-specific knowledge (such as sensory details) would be poorly integrated with the rest of one's memory.

Brewin (1996/2003) proposes a dual representation approach to traumatic memory. In this model, traumatic memories are captured in two different memory systems, the **verbally accessible memory** (VAM) system and the **situationally accessible memory** (SAM) system. The VAM system holds the narrative memory of a trauma. In this memory system, the trauma can be processed on many levels: The information encoded has received sufficient conscious processing to become part of long-term memory, so the underlying event is integrated into the fabric of the individual's experiences and history. The impacted individual uses what he or she recalls in this system to generate new thoughts, conclusions, and meaning about the traumatic experience. However, the VAM system does not include everything that a person was exposed to during a traumatic episode. As a threatening event unfolds, the individual's attention is closely focused on the source of the threat and his or her arousal level is high, restricting the volume of information that can be registered. This is where the existence of the SAM memory is suggested. The SAM system contains the more extensive and lower-level processing that took place during impact, including internal and external occurrences that happened rapidly or were not consciously attended to and brought into the VAM system for processing. The SAM system holds information about the individual's physiological response as well as the sights, sounds, and smells that were involved. The SAM system does not use a verbal code, and so it is difficult to integrate these memories. This memory system is used to explain the power and nature of flashbacks.

Traumatic Memory Failures: Amnesia and Dissociation

As the variety of memory models demonstrates, PTSD experts continue to wrangle with understanding how memory is captured or encoded during traumatic events. But there is general agreement that memory is a key to understanding the impact of trauma, not only in how we remember an event after it has passed but also in terms of how present we are while it unfolds.

Those who experience trauma may not be able to remember what they have gone through; they may develop amnesia for some or all of what they have suffered.

The clinical phenomenon called dissociation is more complicated. *Dissociation* means a disconnection or splitting in awareness. It exists partially in the category of memory processing and partially as an example of psychological defensive functioning. Some theorists believe that dissociation exists on a continuum, viewing it as normative and pathological only under some circumstances. The dissociation referred to during traumatic events is *not* the extreme form referenced in other *DSM-IV* disorders. For example, dissociative identity disorder, formerly known as multiple personality disorder, describes a condition in which those who are exposed to severe abuse at an early age are able to psychologically defend themselves by "removing" themselves from moments of horror. They somehow encapsulate all of what would be experienced in being fully present to the abuse in all its terror and pain in a way that locates it outside of one's awareness.

Dissociation has remained an important concept since the early days of studying trauma. Janet, one of the first clinicians to focus on trauma, felt that traumatic memories are split off, or dissociated, from consciousness and stored as sensory perceptions, or as obsessional ruminations or behavioral reenactments.

Recent study has found that even when a personal narrative is created, intrusive sensations, sensory perceptions, and affective states still persist. Dissociation may serve a defensive function, separating elements of the experience of trauma in order to dilute their impact. Lowenstein (1993) speculates that dissociation may be the mind's way to flee when actual fight or flight is not possible. Putnam (1989) writes that there are long-term pathological consequences for the individual if dissociated elements and affects are not assimilated.

The biology of dissociation has remained elusive, though it is a well-documented clinical phenomenon. This process of splintering off elements of an experience can involve narrative, physiological, or psychological elements. Dissociation can occur in different ways, including amnesia for all or some of an experience. Alternatively, survivors can feel numb or have no access to their emotions regarding an event.

Depersonalization—feeling disembodied—is another form of dissociation. Symptoms can depend on when the phenomenon occurs. **Peritraumatic dissociation** takes place as the event is occurring, and **acute dissociation** refers to dissociation after a trauma. Dissociative responses during a trauma include an altered sense of time (either a slowing down or an acceleration), feelings that the event is not real or that one is outside of one's body, reduced sensations of pain, absence of terror or horror, depersonalization, confusion and bewilderment, and tunnel vision. As discussed earlier, evidence shows that biophysiological and neurohormonal responses during intense stress pose challenges to successfully encoding traumatic experiences and peritraumatic dissociation may reflect an impaired encoding process. Persistent dissociation, in contrast, may suggest ongoing avoidance.

Dissociation and Acute Stress Disorder

Although many symptoms of PTSD have a dissociative flavor (for example, flashbacks, reexperiencing through intrusive recollections, emotional numbing of feelings, stimulus sensitivity with avoidance of environmental cues, and concentration difficulties), dissociation is not listed as a symptom of PTSD. It is, however, acknowledged as a symptom of acute stress disorder (ASD).

The American Psychiatric Association introduced ASD as a new diagnosis in the *DSM-IV* in 1994. There were several goals for the introduction of this new category. Growing recognition of transient and normative stress reactions after trauma paved the way to formulate a new conceptualization that would not pathologize these responses by dictating an early diagnosis of PTSD. On the other hand, there was a desire to capture and describe the significant stress reactions that can occur in the initial month after trauma impact, before an official diagnosis of PTSD can be made. The ASD diagnosis reflected the current scientific thinking that dissociation was a sound predictor of future PTSD. But do initial stress reactions, by and large expected and common and by and large transient, constitute a disorder?

The diagnostic criteria for ASD are similar to PTSD in that they include a stressor and a person's response to it, as well as the core symptoms of hyperarousal, reexperiencing, and avoidance. There is the same emphasis that functioning in key areas is undermined. What is novel about ASD is the emphasis on a person experiencing at least three dissociative symptoms during or immediately after the traumatic event. These include the following:

- Subjective sense of numbing
- Detachment or lack of emotional responsiveness
- Reduction in awareness of surroundings
- Derealization—the perception that one's environment is unreal or dreamlike
- Depersonalization—feeling outside of one's body
- Dissociative amnesia

When ASD was introduced, the belief was strongly held that those who report feelings of dissociation during a traumatic event or immediately afterward become candidates for later PTSD. Theoretically, it was argued that significant dissociative responses, especially those experienced during a traumatic stressor, mediated the link between ASD and PTSD because dissociation was understood to impede integration and resolution of traumatic memories, associated emotions, and splintered images and sensations. Complete memory of an experience requires the integrated recall of the elements of sensation, image, behavior, affect, and meaning (Levine, 1992).

This view resonates with the theories about dissociation proposed by early trauma pioneers, such as Charcot and Janet, who believed that dissociation was the critical factor in determining the eventual adaptation to a trauma. According to Janet, the intensity of emotion behind an event depended both on the emotional state of the victim at the time of the event and on his or her cognitive appraisal of the situation. Unintegrated or split-off memory traces do not become part of one's personal narrative of an event or sense of self. However, having difficult memories remain outside of conscious awareness does not necessarily protect an individual from experiencing the impact of the traumatic event. Instead, traces of what has been blocked out continue to intrude. Fragmented, somatosensory elements of a traumatic event return to consciousness in the form of physical, olfactory, auditory, or kinesthetic sensations; visual images; and intense waves of feelings or behavioral reenactments (Rothschild, 2000).

The actual diagnostic criteria of ASD, with its emphasis on the pivotal importance of dissociation, have been meaningfully challenged. One criticism of the ASD diagnosis was that it was given a place in the *DSM-IV* without enough empirical support. Another is that it had the special role of acting as a predictor disorder for another clinical entity; this relationship exists nowhere else in the *DSM-IV*. Bryant and Harvey (2000; Harvey & Bryant, 2002) have conducted factor analytic studies of ASD in order to ascertain whether the four symptom clusters required—dissociation, hyperarousal, reexperiencing, and avoidance—were supported. Their results suggested that acute stress reactions tended to load on a more generic single construct of distress. They conducted further studies and examined other findings that did validate the appearance of acute stress responses in the aftermath of traumatic experiences; however, it appeared that acute PTSD was more prevalent, suggesting that dissociation is not the significant predictor of further psychological problems as the psychiatric community had hoped.

Harvey and Bryant also discovered in their comprehensive 2002 synthesis and critique of ASD that the existing ASD criteria are too narrow to adequately describe the full range of acute stress responses that subsequently develop into PTSD. Dissociation is not a necessary precursor of chronic PTSD; instead they conclude that there may be multiple pathways to developing PTSD that may or may not include dissociation. Panasetis and Bryant (2003) discovered that persistent dissociation was more strongly associated with ASD severity, leading them to propose that it is persistent dissociation rather than purely peritraumatic dissociation that is linked to posttraumatic psychopathology. PTSD criteria applied in the acute impact phase were also an effective predictor of PTSD at 6 months posttrauma (Brewin, 2003). This implies that work must be done to increase the sensitivity of the ASD diagnostic criteria before it can serve its function of predicting future PTSD. However, it is clear that extreme early distress, no matter what it is called, appears to be a predictor of future adjustment problems.

COMPLICATED GRIEF

PTSD and ASD are not the only clinically significant reactions to disasters. Loss permeates disaster experience in both physical and symbolic ways (Rando, 1993). Although those losses differ in composition and in magnitude, they always bring the task of readjustment. When loss involves the death of a loved one, particularly in a traumatic context, it can sometimes result in **complicated grief.**

After disasters, individuals and a community are expectably heartbroken; but it is equally expectable that their broken hearts will heal and that they will be able to come to terms with their loss and sorrow. Like other forms of posttraumatic stress, grief (the emotional reaction to loss) need not generate special concern until some amount of time has passed and you observe that a bereaved person cannot resume an expected quality of life. Such grief reactions that do not remit over time are described as *complicated grief*. Other terms, such as *traumatic grief, chronic grief,* or *complicated bereavement,* are sometimes used to describe this phenomenon, but there is growing consensus in the field that complicated grief best reflects the understanding that this reaction can occur even when the loss did not occur under traumatic circumstances. Still, due to our focus on DMH, we focus on traumatic loss, which occurs when there is sudden, violent, and shocking death (Raphael & Wooding, 2004), as a possible cause of complicated grief.

Those who experience traumatic loss face greater challenges in terms of negotiating the bereavement process, as described in Chapter 4. Of particular concern are survivors of disastrous events that include mass casualties, especially events of human causation. To be sure, when natural disasters cause extraordinary destruction, disruption, and pandemonium, psychological effects may become quite severe (Norris et al., 2002). In such events, the magnitude of disruptive scope and intensity may impact a person's and a community's coping abilities. But disasters that are the result of human malevolence have the potential for creating even greater negative outcomes. Survivors who have lost their loved ones to a crime are recognized to have more complications in the bereavement process (Office of Victims of Crime, 2005). In addition to coping with the actual death, they may have to negotiate a bureaucratic criminal justice process: There are requirements such as autopsies, trials, and the need for the deceased's family to decide what posture to take toward the perpetrator. There may be issues around release of the body or of remains. Redmond (1989) has reported that homicide cases can take up to 7 years to litigate. All of this can complicate the process of bereavement. The Office of Victims of Crime (2005) recommends providing victims with sufficient support and resources immediately after the trauma and throughout the criminal justice process. Without immediate crisis intervention, they note, the healing and recovery process may be undermined.

Diagnosing Complicated Grief

Complicated grief is a pathological response to loss, a particular syndrome that will require future study for increased understanding, especially in how to guide specific interventions. It is not currently an official diagnostic category in the *DSM-IV*. The American Psychiatric Association has formed a panel of experts to consider including "complicated grief" in its next version of this manual. Complicated grief is prominent and unremitting and interferes with functioning. Clinically, it looks very similar to both PTSD and major depressive disorder, two other consequences that often follow disasters and other traumatic events, but there are also important differences.

Whenever people lose someone they love, especially with no warning, they experience shock and confusion as well as acute emotional and physical discomfort. The finality of the changed reality is almost more than they can bear. Certainly it is more than they can digest quickly, and so it is only through a gradual process of bereavement that they begin to adjust to a world that no longer holds the same comfort, promise, and familiarity as before.

There are no clearly demarcated stages of grief. As Raphael and Wooding (2004) write, "Thoughts, memories, and sadness may return over many years, as may a sense of unfinished business with the deceased." Those who cannot journey through the adjustment process, who, so to speak, reach an impasse, experience what we now call complicated grief. The slow and gradual nature of the "normal" adjustment process makes it difficult to establish a specific cutoff point after which grief should be considered pathological. Prigerson et al. (1999) advocate for a 6-month criterion to establish the confirmed existence of complicated grief, whereas Horowitz, (1997) suggests that 14 months must elapse following a loss to be certain that a complicated grief disorder has ensued.

What defines complicated grief? As Gray, Prigerson, and Litz (2004) write,

> Any three of the following symptoms reported with sufficient intensity to interfere with daily functioning warrants a diagnosis of [complicated grief]: intrusive memories or fantasies related to the lost relationship, strong pangs of severe emotion related to the deceased, strong yearnings for the deceased, feelings of loneliness or emptiness, strong efforts to avoid people, activities or places that remind one of the deceased, disrupted sleep, or loss of interest in social, recreational, or occupational activities.

Although these symptoms are reminiscent of those for PTSD, there are important conceptual and clinical differences that have implications for early intervention. Broadly, in PTSD, the experience is centralized around an event that may or may not include traumatic loss, whereas in complicated grief the lost loved one is central. Both conditions may influence the person on the same spheres— those of cognition, affect, behaviors, and meaning making—but the different stressors lead to variations in how the disrupted experience is expressed. In the following section, we compare complicated grief and PTSD through the core symptom clusters that are the hallmarks of PTSD (an identifiable stressor, reexperiencing, avoidance, hyperarousal, and impairment of functioning) to see how they differ.

Complicated Grief and Posttraumatic Stress Disorder: A Comparison

Stressor: In both PTSD and complicated grief, we can find an identifiable environmental stressor that can be seen as the starting point for subsequent reactions. In PTSD, the stressor is by definition traumatic. In complicated grief, the nature of the loved one's death may or may not be traumatic, though as DMH practitioners we are primarily concerned with that kind of loss.

Reexperiencing occurs in complicated grief in the form of intrusive memories or fantasies about the lost loved one, but there is not the same distress and anxiety that occurs with PTSD reexperiencing of the traumatic event. For those with complicated grief, the recurring thought of the deceased loved one brings with it great sadness, a negative affective state, yet there is a simultaneous pull to remain immersed in this state, which may deliver a sense of solace, of reconnection and sustenance from the attachment. Remembering the lost person allows the survivor to review and become reimmersed in the very special and positive feelings that being together brought. Reexperiencing of the deceased occurs in complicated grief but does not create the fear response diagnostic of PTSD.

Avoidance and numbing also occur both in complicated grief and PTSD. (In fact, avoidance is perhaps the defining feature of PTSD and constitutes much of the basis of treatment strategies for this disorder.) However, although there can be similar behavioral and social withdrawals from investment in the present, in daily social situations, and in others, these occur for very different reasons in the two disorders. In contrast to PTSD's purposeful or unconscious efforts to steer away from cues that will serve as reminders of the traumatic event, the numbing and avoidance in complicated grief, which are expressed as withdrawal from social activity and interpersonal relationships, are a result of wanting to leave the beloved. People with complicated grief avoid that which may disrupt an immersion in the attachment.

There is one other finding that is very significant in distinguishing these pathological responses: Symptoms of hyperarousal and hypervigilance are not common for those with complicated grief. The hypervigilance that emerges in complicated grief reflects the search for those lost or for reminders and clues of their presence. This is very different from the threat scanning of people with PTSD. Thus, the major affective difference between the two groups is that where posttraumatically stressed clients routinely present with heightened anxiety and hyperarousal, the traumatically bereaved instead present with prominent sadness and yearning for those who are gone.

Complicated Grief Risk Factors

It is very important to keep in mind the differences between PTSD and complicated grief, even in working with disaster survivors early on before the trajectory of their responses becomes clear. PTSD and complicated grief can co-occur, but traumatic loss does not guarantee either condition.

Who may be at risk for developing complicated grief? There is some evidence pointing to three characteristics associated with complicated grief:

1. Relationship attachment styles that are marked by dependency and difficulties in separation
2. Adverse early-life experiences such as parental loss and abuse in childhood
3. Being female

It is wise for mental health helpers to remember that grief is a very prevalent reaction to disaster's impact and that complicated grief may also ensue. Additionally, traumatic loss in the context of disasters may increase the complexity of postdisaster reactions. If someone involved directly in a disaster also experiences a traumatic loss, their level of posttraumatic stress may intertwine with their traumatic loss, heightening posttraumatic reactivity in unpredictable ways. As Litz (2004) writes, "There is scant descriptive, epidemiological, or clinical research on the unique psychosocial needs and outcomes of individuals who suffer traumatic loss or those who suffer the dual burden of losing a loved one through trauma while experiencing their own acute trauma."

Also remember that the aftereffects of having been in a disastrous situation may bring additional stressors. Hence, in the initial postimpact weeks, the focus is on surviving and on managing the shock of a suddenly altered reality. As we mentioned in Chapter 4, for those who experience the drastic loss of someone in the context of disaster, it may take the passage of some amount of time after survival is ensured until the bereaved feel they have the emotional stability and fortitude to face the implications of what they have lost.

What does this mean for you as a mental health helper? As Raphael and Wooding (2004) write, "The primary task of those providing assistance is to help without intruding or forcing interventions upon individuals who are neither ready nor able to effectively use them." In contrast to the immediate, unavoidable physical needs for survival, psychological needs postdisaster are much more subtle, and as a result, they require more sensitivity and fewer assumptions on the part of helpers.

Raphael and Wooding (2004) describe a form of early intervention with those suffering from traumatic loss, a therapeutic assessment that they believe is not likely to harm as it explores risk and protective factors and that may facilitate the "normal" grieving process. This therapeutic assessment involves exploring four areas:

1. The death itself
2. The relationship the survivor has had with the deceased
3. The context of the survivor's life in terms of diverse resources
4. What has transpired since the death

They recommend that

Interventions that occur soon after a traumatic event, but not immediately following it, are ideal. In this context, an intervention should not be conducted in the immediate period unless integrated with, but not limited to, initial supportive outreach. Early interventions are more feasible at this stage if they also incorporate practical issues and the needs of the bereaved, alongside a sophisticated and sensitive therapeutic approach. (Raphael & Wooding, 2004)

COMORBID DISORDERS FOLLOWING DISASTER EXPOSURE

To wrap up this chapter on the more severe outcomes that survivors may experience after exposure to a disaster, we expand a bit on the other disorders that often have been found to occur after exposure to a traumatic stressor.

First, PTSD rarely shows up alone; other disorders can be comorbid (occurring at the same time or in some sort of sequential order). These comorbid conditions can complicate both diagnosis and treatment. Such disorders can also exist without a diagnosis of PTSD in response to being involved in a disaster. Eighty percent of those with PTSD will usually meet criteria for at least one other psychiatric diagnosis (Brady, Killeen, & Brewerton, 2000). This may not be surprising given that so many elements of PTSD resemble other disorders. For example, a sense of a foreshortened future and memory problems are also part of depression, and hyperarousal symptoms are consistent with anxiety. Additionally, it is recognized that traumatic events can overwhelm psychological defenses, perhaps leaving survivors more vulnerable to developing other conditions (Horowitz, 1986).

The range of secondary problems that often plague trauma survivors is broad: In an epidemiological study, Brady et al. (2000) found that PTSD can be comorbid with anxiety, affective disorders, somatization, substance abuse, and dissociative disorders. The specific combination of disorders that a particular survivor develops, Brewin (2003) asserts, reflects individual differences in his or her appraisal, emotional reactivity, and coping strategies. In terms of prevalence, Norris et al. (2002) found that the condition most assessed and observed in disaster victims was PTSD (68%), followed by depression, (36%), and generalized anxiety disorders (20%). And in terms of causality, the National Comorbidity Survey (Kessler, 2002) found that depression and substance abuse appeared to be consequences of PTSD, whereas anxiety was a separate disorder, existing independently. As we review these disorders, note that any one of them can be the exclusive diagnosis, without the occurrence of PTSD.

The most common comorbid disorder is depression, or major depressive disorder (MDD). The rate of concurrent MDD and PTSD is very high—from 10 to 60%, depending on the study. There is speculation that MDD and PTSD share some common etiological factors (meaning that they spring from the same underlying cause) in addition to overlapping in diagnostic criteria, suggesting that the experience of MDD may be exacerbated when PTSD is also present. Supporting this belief, Weiss (2001) compared three groups of participants, one with MDD alone, one with both MDD and PTSD, and one with MDD and substance-abuse disorder. Weiss found that the MDD–PTSD group showed significantly more depressive features in terms of number and severity of symptoms than those with MDD alone. The MDD–PTSD participants tended to be more severely and chronically debilitated than those with MDD alone, and they posed a greater suicide risk.

Efforts to quantify the relationship between PTSD and alcohol and substance abuse have so far delivered mixed results. Tassey (2005) reports that an increase in alcohol and substance abuse in a group of emergency service responders after the Oklahoma City bombing of 1995 was limited to groups that already were using these substances habitually before the disaster. Problematic increase in alcohol abuse was found only in those who were already using alcohol problematically; no one reported a decline in alcohol or drug abuse, and no one began to use substances without prior use of them.

Tarrier (2003) found similarly limited results in a study of chronic PTSD sufferers who did not report having a substance-abuse disorder prior to exposure to a traumatic event. Assessment by interview and questionnaires revealed significant comorbidity of mood disorders and anxiety, with depression and generalized anxiety disorders far outranking other entities. However, only a small number of participants had substance-abuse problems, and overall use of alcohol in this PTSD sample did not appear to differ from the general population.

However, other studies do suggest a causal link between trauma and substance abuse (Lisak & Miller, 2003), with drugs or alcohol being used to medicate symptoms of trauma. Ouimette, Read, and Brown (2005) report an underdiagnosed connection between drug use and PTSD. They hypothesized that those with

PTSD often use alcohol and drugs in a problematic manner classifiable as substance use disorder (SUD). By not recognizing the connection between symptoms, providers frequently misdiagnose or do not fully attend to SUD–PTSD comorbidity. In another supporting finding, Karlovic (2004) found that soldiers with combat-related PTSD that was comorbid with MMD had a higher prevalence of alcohol dependence than soldiers with only PTSD. The risk factors for development of alcohol dependence in those with PTSD included prior alcohol-related problems, positive family psychiatric history, and alcohol-related problems in the family.

As this last three-way interaction between PTSD, MDD, and alcohol dependence suggests, coexisting disorders may affect the presentation and clinical course of PTSD. Because of the relative frequency of traumatic events, including disasters, screening for traumatic events and PTSD should be standard in both psychiatric and primary care practice. Also, those with PTSD should be screened for psychiatric comorbidity because accurate assessment of coexisting conditions may be important in determining optimal psychotherapeutic and pharmacotherapeutic treatment options.

A FINAL WORD: EXTREME REACTIONS AND THE DISASTER MENTAL HEALTH PRACTITIONER

As a DMH helper, you may not become directly involved in treating people with clinical PTSD or complicated grief. However, DMH clearly can and will involve the treatment of psychological trauma in its early stages. Given our understanding of what may happen when people are exposed to catastrophic stress, especially knowing that most survivors' reactions tend to evolve and often subside over time, early interventions—based on lowering the general arousal level (both in terms of the individual and the disaster scene); creating safety, warmth, and respite; and meeting basic needs—may be sufficient to enhance most people's ability to process a trauma.

But as we saw in this chapter, some survivors experience more severe reactions and require more assistance to recover from their experiences. Current scientific findings have not been able to pinpoint precisely which early responses to trauma exposure constitute red flags for development of future PTSD or other extreme and lasting reactions, but some research points toward certain survivors who might benefit from extra therapeutic attention in order to head off serious sequelae. As we discussed, dissociative reactions at the time of impact can be meaningful in terms of ascertaining who is at high risk, though they are neither necessary nor sufficient predictors. People who experience both traumatic stress and traumatic loss—those who survive a disaster themselves *and* lose loved ones—may be at higher risk for complicated grief. Those with preexisting alcohol or drug issues may be more likely to escalate their use in an effort to self-medicate their posttrauma stress. However, these paths are not predestined or unchangeable: As a caring and well-trained DMH practitioner, you may be able to influence reactions with an appropriate and well-timed intervention.

References

American Psychiatric Association. (1994). *Diagnostic and statistical manual of mental disorders* (4th ed.). Washington, DC: Author.

Brady, K. T., Killeen, T. K., & Brewerton, T. (2000). Comorbidity of psychiatric disorders and posttraumatic stress disorder. *Journal of Clinical Psychiatry, 61*(Suppl. 7), 22–32.

Bremner, J. D., Randall, P. K., Scott, T. M., Bronen, R. A., Seibyl, J. P., Southwick, S. M., Delaney, R. C., McCarthy, G., Charney, D. S., & Innis, R. B. (1997). Magnetic resonance imaging based measurement of hippocampal volume in posttraumatic stress disorder related to childhood physical and sexual abuse: A preliminary report. *Biological Psychiatry, 41*(1), 23–32.

Breslau, N., Davis, G. C. D., Andreski, P., & Peterson, E. (1991). Traumatic events and posttraumatic stress disorder in an urban population of young adults. *Archives of General Psychiatry, 48,* 218–222.

Brewin, C. (2003). *Posttraumatic stress disorder: Myth or malady?* New Haven, CT: Yale University Press.

Brewin, C. R., Dagleish, T., & Joseph, S. (1996). A dual representation theory of posttraumatic stress disorder. *Psychological Review, 103,* 670–686.

Bryant, R., & Harvey, A. (2000). *Acute stress disorder: A handbook of theory, assessment, and treatment.* Washington, DC: American Psychological Association.

Elbert, T., & Schauer, M. (2002). Burnt into memory. *Nature, 419,* 883.

Foa, E. B., & Rothbaum, B. O. (1998). *Treating the trauma of rape.* New York: Guilford Press.

Gazzaniga, M. S., Ivry, R. B., & Mangun, G. R. (2002). *Cognitive neuroscience: The biology of the mind* (2nd ed.). New York: Norton.

Gray, M. J., Prigerson, H. G., & Litz, B. T. (2004). Conceptual and definitional issues in complicated grief. In B. Litz (Ed.), *Early intervention for trauma and traumatic loss* (pp. 65–85). New York: Guilford Press.

Harvey, A., & Bryant, R. (2002). Acute stress disorder: A synthesis and critique. *Psychological Bulletin, 128*(6), 886–1003.

Horowitz, M. J. (1986). *Stress response syndromes* (2nd ed.). Northvale, NJ: Jason Aronson.

Horowitz, M. J. (1997). Diagnostic criteria for complicated grief disorder. *American Journal of Psychiatry, 154,* 904–910.

Karlovic, D. (2004). Alcohol dependence in soldiers with posttraumatic stress disorder or posttraumatic stress disorder comorbid with major depressive disorder. *Alcoholism: Journal on Alcoholism and Related Addictions, 40*(1), 3–15.

Kessler, R. (2002). National comorbidity survey, 1990–1992. National Institute of Mental Health, National Institute on Drug Abuse, and W. T. Grant Foundation. Conducted by University of Michigan, Survey Research Center.

Kinnunen, M-L., Kaprio, J., & Pulkkinen, L. (2005). Allostatic load of man and women in early middle age. *Journal of Individual Differences, 26*(1), 20–28.

Kolb, L. (1986). Post-traumatic stress disorder in Vietnam veterans. *New England Journal of Medicine, 314*(10), 641–642.

LeDoux, J. (2002). *Synaptic self: How our brains become who we are.* New York: Penguin Books.

Leitch, M. L. (2005). Just like bodies, psyches can drown in disaster. *New York Times, 154*(53231), F5.

Levine, P. (1992). *The body as healer: Transforming trauma and anxiety.* Lyons, CO: Author.

Lisak, D., & Miller, P. M. (2003). Childhood trauma, posttraumatic stress disorder, substance abuse, and violence. In P. Ouimette & P. Brown (Eds.), *Trauma and substance abuse: Causes, consequences, and treatment of comorbid disorders* (pp. 73–88). Washington, DC: APA Press.

Litz, B. T. (1992). Emotional numbing in combat-related posttraumatic stress disorder: A critical review and reformulation. *Clinical Psychology Review, 12*(4), 417–432.

Litz, B.T. (Ed.). (2004) *Early intervention for trauma and traumatic loss*. New York: Guilford Press.

Lowenstein, R. J. (1993). Dissociation, development and the psychobiology of trauma. *Journal of the American Academy of Psychoanalysis, 21*(4), 581–603.

Myers, D., & Wee, D. F. (2005). *Disaster mental health services*. New York: Brunner/Routledge.

Nadel, L., & Jacobs, W. J. (1996). The role of the hippocampus in PTSD, panic, and phobia. In N. Kato (Ed.), *Hippocampus: Functions and relevance* (pp. 455–463). Amsterdam: Elsevier.

Norris, F., Friedman, M. J., Watson, P. J., Byrne, C. M., Diaz, E., & Kaniasty, K. (2002). 60,000 disaster victims speak: Part I. An empirical review of the empirical literature, 1981–2001. *Psychiatry: Interpersonal & Biological Processes, 65*(3), 207–243.

Ouimette, P., Read, J., & Brown, P. (2005). Consistency of retrospective reports of *DSM-IV* Criterion A traumatic stressors among substance use disorder patients. *Journal of Traumatic Stress, 18*(1), 43–51.

Office of Victims of Crime. (2005). Retrieved April 2005 from http://www.ovc.gov/publications.

Panasetis, P., & Bryant, R. (2003). Peritraumatic versus persistent dissociation in acute stress disorder. *Journal of Traumatic Stress, 16*(6), 563–566.

Phillips, K. (1991). The psychophysiology of health. In M. Pitts & K. Phillips (Eds.), *The psychology of health: An introduction* (pp. 15–29). London: Routledge.

Prigerson, H. G., Shear, M. K., Jacobs, S. C., Reynolds, C. F. III, Maciejewski, P. K., Davidson, J. R. T., Rosenhack, R., Pilkonis, P. A., Wortman, C. B., Williams, J. B. W., Widiger, T. A., Frank, E., Kupferl, D. J., & Zisook, S. (1999). Consensus criteria for traumatic grief: A preliminary empirical test. *British Journal of Psychiatry, 174*, 67–73.

Putnam, F. (1989). Pierre Janet and modern views of dissociation. *Journal of Traumatic Stress, 2*(4), 413–429.

Rando, T. (1988). *How to go on living when someone you love dies*. New York: Bantam Books.

Rando, T. (1993). *Treatment of complicated mourning*. Champaign, IL: Research Press.

Raphael, B., Wilson, J. P., Meldrum, L., & Bedosky, C. (2000) Preventing PTSD in trauma survivors. *Bulletin of the Menninger Clinic, 64*(2), 181–197.

Raphael, B., & Wooding, S. (2004). Early mental health interventions for traumatic loss in adults. In B. Litz (Ed.), *Early intervention for trauma and traumatic loss* (pp. 147–178). New York: Guilford Press.

Redmond, L. (1996). Sudden violent death. In K. J. Doka (Ed.), *Living with grief after sudden loss: Suicide, homicide, accident, heart attack, stroke* (pp. 53–71). Philadelphia: Taylor & Francis.

Rothschild, B. (2000). *The body remembers: The psychophysiology of trauma and trauma treatment*. New York: Norton.

Shore, J. H., Tatum, E. L., & Vollmer, W. M. (1986). Evaluation of mental effects of disaster, Mount St. Helen's eruption. *American Journal of Public Health, 76*(3), 76–86.

Tarrier, N. (2003). Alcohol and substance use in civilian chronic PTSD patients seeking psychological treatment. *Journal of Substance Abuse, 8*(4), 197–204.

Tassey, J. R. (2005, May 6). Paper presented at the conference Helping in a Time of Crisis. State University of New York, New Paltz,.

Van der Kolk, B. A., McFarlane, A. C., & Weisaeth, L. (Eds.) (1996). *Traumatic stress: The effects of overwhelming experience on mind, body, and society.* New York: Guilford Press.

Weiss, H. P. (2001). The experience of depression in major depressive disorder alone versus comorbid depression and PTSD. *Dissertation Abstracts International: Section B: The Sciences and Engineering, 62*(3-B), 1605.

Wilson, J. P., Friedman, M. J., & Lindy, J. D. (2001). *Treating psychological trauma and PTSD.* New York: Guilford Press.

Yehuda, R. (2001). Biology of posttraumatic stress disorder. *Journal of Clinical Psychiatry, 62*, 41–66.

Our planet's lack of importance in the universe tells us in no uncertain terms that there is no one segment of humanity that is divinely ordained as being the "privileged" group. There is no one segment of humanity that is "better" than any other segment. . . . No, we are all one people, and we are all on this ride together. Once we realize this, we can understand that the trials and challenges we face, and the solutions we must develop to overcome these, are the collective responsibility of all of us.

Alan Hale

Vulnerable Populations

CHAPTER **6**

In our final chapter on the theoretical background of disaster mental health (DMH), we examine the special issues certain vulnerable populations face in disasters. We explain what is meant by *vulnerable* in this context, and then we focus on the needs of two populations that you are likely to encounter in your DMH work, children and the elderly. In our examination of children, we first look at the difficulties in recognizing posttraumatic stress disorder (PTSD) in this group—difficulties that mean that symptoms are often overlooked, despite ample evidence for the existence of PTSD and other disorders in children. We discuss how children are likely to demonstrate their distress across developmental stages and in a broader environmental context. We look at which children are most at risk for PTSD and other reactions and at what you can do to help them recover.

Our discussion of the elderly in disasters begins with a close look at who this diverse group comprises. We then examine the logistical issues that can cause problems for them during disasters, including their strong resistance to relocating, followed by a look at psychological issues among the elderly, both in general and as a result of trauma. We look at growing evidence for resilience among this vulnerable group and, finally, at how you as a DMH practitioner can best assist the elderly in disasters.

DEFINING *VULNERABILITY*

In the context of DMH, the term *vulnerable populations* describes groups whose disaster-related needs may be more complex or intense than most survivors' needs, exceeding what can be fully addressed by traditional service providers. Vulnerable groups include "those who cannot comfortably or safely access and use the standard resources offered in disaster preparedness, relief and recovery" (PrepareNow, 2005). Sometimes such groups are characterized as having special needs, with an increased susceptibility to a diminished quality of life due to their age, their physical or cognitive disabilities, or various other factors that differentiate them from the general population. Members of vulnerable populations may be considered to be at a higher relative risk during the chaotic time of a disaster, requiring logistical assistance and mental health services that are tailored to their particular attributes in order to mitigate negative outcomes.

These groups may include people with physical disabilities (for example, blindness, hearing impairments, mobility impairments), those who don't speak the predominant language or have other language limitations, the geographically or culturally isolated, people who are medically or chemically dependent due to physical or psychiatric problems, the homeless, the elderly, and children. Even women are sometimes considered a vulnerable group because they tend to have more adverse psychological reactions to disasters than men (Norris, Friedman, Watson, Byrne, Diaz, & Kaniasty, 2002). Because there are so many varied groups that can be considered at higher risk—and very little research on most of them—we focus here on the relatively prevalent groups of children and the elderly, and we also touch briefly upon issues affecting certain other vulnerable populations.

Even our primary two groups of interest, the very young and the very old, exhibit their vulnerabilities in different ways. Children are generally considered vulnerable because of their immaturity and dependency on others for fulfillment of even their basic needs. The picture is more complex when we look at the elderly. Some studies have found that older people actually fare better psychologically than other groups postdisaster (Phifer, 1990). The working hypothesis for this finding is that some older adults may have acquired the ability to cope with traumatic events as a result of exposure to the multiple challenges and difficulties that inevitably arise over a lifetime. However, we do consider this population to be a vulnerable group because many members demonstrate increased needs and physical limitations as a result of the natural aging process. We revisit the meaning of resilience in this group and its limitations later in the chapter.

TRAUMATIC STRESS AND CHILDREN AND ADOLESCENTS

Children are absolutely dependent on adults for security, and the younger they are, the truer this is. Children lack the authority and ability to control their environment, so understanding and responding to their unique needs requires adults to try to adopt a child's perspective. This can be especially challenging because child survivors often find it difficult or impossible to verbalize their trauma experiences and symptoms, which results in underreporting (March, Amaya-Jackson, Murray, & Schulte, 1998). Nonverbal signs of distress in children, such as inappropriate acting out or aggression, can be mistaken for other disorders, such as a conduct disorder. Additionally, accounts of children's reactions often come from parents who either minimize the extent of the child's distress or who fail to interpret signs of upset as manifested by their children (Cook-Cottone, 2004).

Further compounding adults' difficulties in spotting their distress after a disaster, some children may intentionally downplay their feelings. Children are very aware of adults' worries most of the time, and they may be particularly sensitive during the period around a disaster, concealing their symptoms to avoid causing additional stress in the family. Children may be afraid of upsetting their parents or teachers, so they don't always tell their caregivers how they feel, but studies have shown that children are much more affected than initially imagined (La Greca, Silverman, Vernberg, & Roberts, 2002). As a result, children's difficulties are often overlooked as adults in the family respond to the strenuous and consuming demands of disaster stress and loss.

In fact, for many years people assumed that children were either immune to traumatic stress or were so resilient that trauma's impact on them was minimal (Shelby, 1997). Many in the field felt that the category of PTSD was not needed to encapsulate the phenomenology children displayed until studies of children's reactions, including those by Yule, Udwin, and Bolton (2002) began to shift the understanding of PTSD in children and adolescents. Yule and his colleagues conducted a follow-up study tracking the long-term symptoms of 331 adolescent survivors of a fatal ship crash. Of the 111 who developed PTSD after the crash, 34.2% still had this diagnosis 5 to 7 years postdisaster. The researchers conclude that disasters impact adolescents significantly and that PTSD in this group was not a transient phenomenon that was automatically outgrown.

More recently, La Greca, Silverman, and Wasserstein (1998) studied the impact of Hurricane Andrew in Florida in 1992 on younger children. Their work, too, refutes the notion that children do not experience major emotional reactions to disaster. Instead, they found that more than half the children who they studied had moderate to severe PTSD symptoms 3 months after the storm and that these effects continued over time: Ten months after the hurricane, 12% of children still had severe or very severe levels of PTSD symptoms. Other research conducted by Vincent (1998) also shows persistency of effects. In a subsample of children interviewed 3½ years later, 40% of children who had reported high levels of PTSD at 10 months still had significant levels of these symptoms.

Even longer-term effects were revealed by reanalyzing data from the 1972 Buffalo Creek flood, a disaster that occurred well before the diagnosis of PTSD existed. This dam collapse devastated a community, killing 125 people and leaving many children and their families homeless and sometimes separated from each other. Honig, Grace, Lindy, Newman, and Titchener (1993) reviewed earlier research on the disaster's effects on children, including a 1974 interview with 207 local children; a 1988 interview with 99 members of the first group, and a 1990 follow-up with 15 children who were younger than 12 years old at the time of the flood. Their analysis suggests that salient psychopathology, including PTSD, was relatively low and was not different from a control sample. However, they did discover evidence of long-term impact and speculate that the reactions to traumatic stress experienced as children had changed over time as the survivors matured and had shifted into adult "patterns of adaptation."

As these numerous studies demonstrate, children are indeed vulnerable to developing psychological sequelae following traumatic events like disasters. In fact, those effects may be even more potent in children's still-developing minds, just as their growing bodies can be poisoned by exposure to substances that adults can tolerate more safely: "Trauma can be a formative, developmental influence in the ontogenesis of emotional, cognitive, arousal and interpersonal systems" (Cook-Cottone, 2004). In other words, the effects of an early experience of trauma can actually alter the path of a child's development, shaping the ways in which he or she thinks, feels, and relates to other people. And this powerful effect is not limited to a small handful of unfortunates: It is estimated that 25% of all children will experience a traumatic event by the time they are 16 years old (Costello, Erkanli, & Fairbank, 2002).

Diagnosing Posttraumatic Stress Disorder and Other Disorders in Children

Although we have just seen that children can experience significant trauma-related reactions, it is difficult to accurately diagnose PTSD and other disorders in them. The current diagnostic formulation of PTSD may not be operationally sound when applied to children because it lacks age-appropriate sensitivity and specificity (Tierney, 2000). For example, more than one-half of the *DSM-IV* criteria for PTSD require a verbal description of a subjective state (Scheeringa & Gaensauer, 2000), something many children are not developmentally capable of regardless of traumatization. Thus, although PTSD criteria have been validated for adults and older children, they result in a high number of false-negative diagnoses when applied to young children (Scheeringa & Gaensauer, 2000). It is also unclear how acute stress disorder or adjustment disorder is manifested in children (La Greca et al., 2002).

A newer framework for diagnosing younger children is that of *traumatic stress disorder* (TSD) (Evangelista & McLellan, 2004). This nosology, which is not an official *DSM-IV* diagnosis, modifies the standard PTSD criteria by requiring that children display only one symptom in each of the three core symptom areas (reexperiencing, avoidance, and hyperarousal), and it also adds a new cluster observed in younger children: new fears and aggression. The reexperiencing and avoidance symptoms in this framework are more behaviorally based than in the adult PTSD description, so reexperiencing in children can be reflected in nightmares or traumatic play reenactment; avoidance can be noted in constriction in play and exploration or developmental regression.

Comorbid mood disorders such as depression have not been well assessed in children with PTSD, although studies of children after a 1988 Armenian earthquake (Goenjian et al., 1997) found that many had both PTSD and a depressive disorder, with separation anxiety disorder as a third common condition.

The interaction between PTSD and grief is also less clear in children than in adults, with few studies differentiating between symptoms of PTSD and symptoms of grief and bereavement or of childhood traumatic grief.

Children's anxiety levels are often elevated after a disaster, regardless of PTSD symptoms. Yule et al. (2002) found specific phobic reactions, panic disorder, and separation anxiety, in addition to major depression, in child survivors of mass-transportation disasters. Significant anxiety symptoms have been reported in children after a variety of events including earthquakes, hurricanes, and transportation disasters. In fact, following PTSD, anxiety disorders may be the most common diagnosis (American Academy of Child and Adolescent Psychiatry, 2005).

Expression of Symptoms: A Developmental Perspective

In general, children are subject to many of the same clinical conditions as adults following disaster, but diagnosis can be more difficult because they express their distress in ways different than adults. More research is sorely needed to identify signs of disorder in children, and DMH helpers who plan to work with this group need to understand how distress may be manifested at different developmental stages.

People undergo change and growth throughout the course of their lives, but the period from birth to physical maturity is the most malleable and the most subject to being derailed by a disaster or other traumatic event. Maturation takes place in different spheres, including cognitive, psychosocial, and interpersonal, and how people think, their capacity to identify their feelings, their sense of who they are, and how they communicate are partially a reflection of their developmental progress in each sphere.

Development is typically seen as occurring in stages, each with particular agendas or tasks. Thus, in a developmental perspective, the stage in which a disaster occurs can predict (at least to some extent) its impact on an individual child. A DMH textbook is not the place for a complete description of the classic stage theories proposed by developmental experts such as John Bowlby (1973), who examined the unique significance of attachment relationships in humans; Harry Stack Sullivan (1953), who examined the interpersonal sphere of functioning; Jean Piaget (1952), who pioneered a scientific understanding of cognitive development; and Erik Erikson (1964), who studied psychosocial processes. If you plan to focus your work with children, we encourage you to study these theories in detail. Here, we limit ourselves to a few examples of possible disaster disruption within a developmental framework:

- In Bowlby's theory, attachments and bonds formed early in life provide a foundation for survival and security over time. The closeness and presence of a reliable, steady caregiver provides an infant with a secure base in relationships, a place to move out from to explore the world and to return to, especially when feeling frightened or depleted. Separation is the other side of "the coin of attachment" (Farberow & Gordon, 1981). Disasters are times of great disruption to attachments. Family members may become separated, causing distress to babies or young children. Even if a caregiver is physically present, he or she may be emotionally absent due to stress, grief, or other disaster-related problems. Therefore, disasters may be traumatic even for children who seem too young to understand what has happened, as they respond to a loss of attachment.

- Sullivan felt that personality development is determined within the interpersonal context of interactions with others. Until the age of 6 years old, the presence of caring adults is required for having needs met and for organizing activities, but as children transcend these basic needs, they move toward their peer group for acceptance, so it is important for children to have peers or friends in order to develop in socially healthy ways. Thus, an elementary-school-aged child whose access to his or her friends is cut off, perhaps because a disaster destroys the family's home and they need to relocate abruptly, may feel the loss of friendship more acutely than parents recognize, causing distress.

- Piaget's theory reflects a neurodevelopmental framework, with consciousness, judgment, and reasoning dependent on an evolving intellectual capacity to organize and make sense of one's experiences. According to Piaget, by about age 7 years old, children acquire symbolic mental representations and become able to think in terms of the past, present, and future. They then improve their ability to use logic and objectivity, and by around the age of 12, higher-order theoretical thinking and problem solving can begin to take place. As a result, an adolescent may have a markedly different response to a disaster than a slightly younger sibling because the older child is better able to appreciate the enormity of the event and to consider its possible long-term effects personally and for the family.

- Erikson, who emphasized social and environmental factors, contributed the concept of the different life crises at different ages, from birth to death. For example, he gave us the concept of the formation of identity as a key task during adolescence, hence the popular term *identity crisis*. He conceived of adolescence as a time of great change and turmoil as the individual consolidates who he or she truly is. Therefore, a teenager or young adult might experience difficulties in struggling to incorporate the experience of a disaster into a core element of his or her self-image and how he or she anticipates the future.

As these examples suggest, if a disaster causes unacceptably high levels of stress at a critical time in a child's development, the experience may cause a setback, hindering interpersonal trust, elevating anxiety levels, and possibly curtailing the threshold for stress endurance (Klingman, 2002).

Disaster Trauma and Development

However great the pain that children survivors may be in after a disaster, they can only demonstrate what they are thinking and feeling based on their disposition and developed capacities. Therefore, DMH helpers must learn how to interpret signs of posttraumatic issues at all ages. The two most common indicators of distress in children are changes in behavior (for example, an outgoing child becoming shy or withdrawn) and behavioral regression (such as sleep and separation difficulties, renewed thumb-sucking, or reverting to baby talk). Preschool children with PTSD have been found to be at greater risk for developmental delays. School-aged children with PTSD may be at risk for academic problems, possibly because stress can compromise the normal development of activity level, capacity for reflection, and focused attention, all of which are crucial for academic achievement. And it appears that the longer symptoms persist at high levels, the less likely they are to dissipate without intervention. Raphael (1986) reports that children can experience a loss of childhood, displaying a need to act older, essentially becoming "parentified."

Because children are still developing their communication skills, practitioners working with children in the aftermath of disaster must not rely on verbal techniques alone in order to offer support, conduct an assessment, or provide healing. DMH workers must attend to children's nonverbal communication closely, and they need to meet the child where the child is, at whatever level he or she understands the event. Children need to be given permission to do the jobs of children, with opportunities specifically for learning and playing. Interventions should be paced and driven by what the child reports as helpful, good, or fun. Play is the natural medium of expression for children, so play and artwork in particular may have a unique role in diagnosing and treating the stress of traumatic events. Axeline (1969), a pioneer in play therapy, developed the theory that play helps children cope with trauma and change in their lives. Providing opportunities for the stress relief afforded by play should be a priority (Olness, 1999).

Our last general point about common age-dependent responses to disasters concerns grief. Like other reactions, children's understanding of loss and death and their responses are developmentally based. Grief varies with age and the degree to which it has sanctions for release. Disruption of daily patterns of love and care are most likely to affect a young child directly so that it may be easier to cry over lost toys or pets, while grief for a parent is shut away, unrealized. As Raphael (1986) writes, "Children may react to the losses of disaster with typical patterns of grief and mourning. But, often they do not, because their insecurity and the responses of others to them may lead to inhibition of the emotional release and to a blocking of the psychological processes of mourning."

Children may have great difficulty understanding, resolving, and managing their sense of loss and grief. At very young ages, children simply cannot cognitively comprehend the loss of a beloved parent, yet they feel the absence acutely, as Klingman (2002) describes:

> Permanent loss of a parent demands great emotional adjustment, particularly when excessive strain on the remaining parent diminishes the attention and quality of care the child receives. Not talking about the death, for example, may reinforce the child's denial and avoidance of the event, which may undermine the mourning process. A missing parent poses a special challenge because no concrete evidence of

the death, such as a funeral, burial place, or designated period of mourning, is available. Children may fantasize excessively about the missing parent's return, and it is advisable to provide such children with the near certainty of the missing parent's death so that the mourning process can proceed.

In the next three sections, we describe varying stress reactions of children and adolescents as they move through the developmental ranges of preschool, school age, and adolescence. The information in the next few paragraphs is based on the works of several writers including La Greca et al. (2002); Raphael (1986); Young, Ford, Ruzek, Friedman, and Gusman (1998); and Ehrenreich (2001). Table 6.1 summarizes children's reactions to grief, an all too common outcome of disasters, from a developmental perspective.

Preschool Children (0 to 5 Years)   Infants and toddlers cannot comprehend death and often experience a loss in terms of separation or abandonment. Babies and infants as young as 3 months old will react to the loss of their primary caregiver, and infants between 6 and 18 months old are sensitive to separation from their mothers and to their mothers' distress and grief (Raphael, 1986).

For the very young child, symptoms are mostly expressed in nonverbal channels because little ones lack the verbal and conceptual skills to cope effectively with the sudden stress of disaster and loss. They are extremely impacted by their caregivers' behaviors and are still too young to have fully mastered the capacity for self-regulation and organization. Somatic behaviors such as eating more or less, separation anxiety, nightmares, disturbed sleep patterns and fears of the dark, and developmental regressions such as increased clinging or bed-wetting and confusion are often found. Traumatic play is linked to themes of the traumatic events, is compulsive and repetitive in nature, and fails to relieve any of the accompanying anxiety.

Preschoolers display a normative egocentricity, viewing the world entirely in terms of their own needs and actions. As a result, they may view illness, loss, and death as punishment for some wrongdoing (real or imagined) or a deficit in themselves. Young children do not understand where their loved one has gone. In this age group, they shift between reality and fantasy, especially with regard to loss and death. They can sense that the people around them feel sad, worried, or frightened, and they become frightened in turn. Because their understanding is concrete and not conceptual, they struggle with the idea that loss can be permanent. They may see death as a sleep from which one awakens, and they may ask for their deceased family member repetitively. This can be especially heartrending for the adults around them, consumed as they may be in their own grief reactions, and feeling helpless or distraught in the face of their children's confusion and search for understanding.

Because of their cognitive immaturity, preschoolers may misunderstand or misinterpret any complex information they hear discussed, and explanations may be beyond them. Rather, they may be more soothed by a bedtime story, extra attention as they prepare to go to sleep or a comforting bedtime routine, or a night light; caregivers might allow a young child to sleep with them until he or she can comfortably return to his or her own room. Lots of attention and verbal and physical reassurances such as hugs are very comforting and provide the

Table 6.1 | Developmental Considerations Concerning Children's Grief

Age	Developmental Stage/Task	Concept of Death	Grief Response	Signs of Distress	Possible Interventions
2–4	Egocentric. Believes the world centers around them. Narcissistic. No cognitive understanding. Preconceptual— unable to grasp concepts.	Death loss is seen as abandonment. Seen as reversible, not permanent. Common statements: "Did you know my daddy died— when will he be home?"	Intense response but brief. Very present oriented. Most aware of altered patterns of care.	Regression: eating and sleeping disorders, bed-wetting, insecurity.	Short interactions. Frequent repetition. Comforting. Touching. Needs consistency more than anything else.
4–7	Gaining sense of autonomy. Exploring world outside of self. Gaining language. Fantasy thinking/ wishing. Initiative phase: sees self as initiator. Concerns of guilt.	Death still seen as reversible. Great personification of death. Feeling of responsibility because of wishes/thoughts. Common statement: "It's my fault; I was mad at her and wished she'd die."	Verbalization. Great concern with process. How? Why? Repetitive questioning. Wanting the answers to stay the same. May actually play dead or play funeral.	Regression: nightmares, sleeping and eating disturbances. Violent play. Attempts to take on role of person who died.	Symbolic play. Drawings/stories. Allow/encourage expression of energy/feelings of anger. Talk about it.

Continued

Table 6.1 | (Continued)

Age	Developmental Stage/Task	Concept of Death	Grief Response	Signs of Distress	Possible Interventions
7–11	Concrete-operational. Industry vs. inferiority. Beginning of socialization. Development of cognitive ability. Beginning of logical thinking.	Death as punishment. Fear of bodily harm, mutilation. This is a difficult transition period—still want to see death as reversible but beginning to see it as final.	Specific questioning. Desire for complete detail. Concerned with how others are responding. What is the "right" way? How "should" they be responding? Starting to have ability to mourn and understand mourning.	Regression: problems in school, withdrawal from friends. Acting out. Sleeping and eating disturbances. Overwhelming concern with body. Suicidal thoughts (desire to join one who died). Role confusion.	Answer questions. Encourage expression of range of feelings. Encourage/allow control. Be available but allow alone time. Symbolic play. TALK ABOUT IT!
11–18	Formal operational Problem solving. Abstract thinking. Integration of one's own personality.	"ADULT" approach. Ability to abstract. Beginning to truly conceptualize death. Work at making sense of teachings.	Depression. Denial. Repression. More often willing to talk to people outside of family. Traditional mourning.	Depression. Anger. Anger toward parents. Noncompliance. Rejection of former teaching. Role confusion. Acting out.	Encourage verbalization. Do not take control. Encourage self-motivation. Listen. Be available. Do not attempt to take grief away.

security of knowing that a protective other is close. This helps allay abandonment fears. Thus, the consolations provided by explicit, ongoing love, and care are vital for preschoolers.

School-Aged Children (5 to 11 Years)   More discernible PTSD symptoms become evident among school-aged children. Cognitive development picks up speed during this period. Verbal ability and a grasp of time increase, but there is still difficulty in abstract conceptualization. Although children in this age group can speak quite fluently, symptoms typically continue to be expressed behaviorally and may include regression (for example., bed-wetting, clinging behavior, anxious attachment, refusing to go to school), less emotional regulation (for example, a tantrum or emotional "meltdown"), and increases in externalizing or internalizing behavioral expression (for example, fighting with peers, withdrawal from friends, poor attention, declining academic performance).

Chances are that children in this age group may not be able to interpret their somatic–affective states; anxiety may be reflected in a list of concrete physiological complaints such as stomachaches or headaches. They may also be afraid to go to sleep or be alone and experience sleep disturbances. They may cling to others, have event-specific fears, and be worried about their safety. They may perseverate constantly, repeating a detailed verbal review or description that lacks appropriate emotional content. Traumatic play at this age is more complex and sophisticated than that of preschoolers. It can involve specific themes and may include writing, drawing, and pretending.

Young school-aged children, 5 to 9 years old, often feel responsible for a disaster, loss, or death. They still engage in magical thinking and may associate loss and death with witches, monsters, violence, mutilation, or punishment. Older school-aged children (10 to 11 years old) realize that death is permanent and that everyone dies. They are usually curious about the specifics of the event and often ask many questions. The shocking and gory aspects of the tragedy may fascinate them. Feelings of guilt are also common with these older children, and they will often bargain with themselves to become perfect in an effort to make up for the devastating loss. There is a danger that the child will see the loss or disaster as a consequence of his or her own unlovableness or as a rejection.

School-aged children may have increased concerns about safety and security that are demonstrated in high levels of separation fears, sometimes severe enough to meet the criteria for separation anxiety disorder. Increased fears may also be present, often directly related to the kind of trauma experienced: for example, following a hurricane, a child may express more fear of water, thunder, and rainstorms.

At this age and older, caregivers should discuss the disaster or loss with children in order to help them understand at least some of what has happened. Children can be instructed about safety measures and family emergency plans and should be allowed to communicate their concerns and ventilate their fears in a supportive and positive context. Children in this group should be encouraged to express their feelings using whatever level of verbalization they have acquired. Caregiver patience and tolerance is very important, and relaxed expectations around school may be in order for some time after a disaster.

Preadolescents and Adolescents (12 to 18 Years)   The younger adolescent age group typically demonstrates similar behavioral reactions as those listed for the school-aged group, including sleep and appetite disturbances, school problems, and rebelliousness in the home such as a refusal to do chores. They can also manifest their distress physically through headaches, vague pains, and other psychosomatic complaints. Peers are very influential for the preadolescent disaster survivor, and being involved with them in group activities can be helpful.

As children move into adolescence, the tendency to express distress through behavioral symptoms diminishes. The behaviors that do appear are different from the earlier stages, due perhaps to the developing reciprocal relationship between emotions and thoughts. Adolescents are more able to process trauma cognitively, and this leads to the potential for greater integration into the context of their life experiences. At this point, the experience of distress is more similar to that of adults; however, even though adolescents may seem to have an adult view of death, it does not come from an emotionally well-developed perspective. Experiencing a disaster can lead these young adults to begin to acknowledge their own mortality, which can be very frightening. As a result, adolescents' abstract conceptions of identity, future, safety, and connection are extremely vulnerable to the impact of disaster. Many adolescents express a sense of a foreshortened future after experiencing disaster trauma. They may act out their tensions not by regressing but through more risk-taking behaviors. They may present with more self-injurious or aggressive behaviors, suicidal ideation, conduct problems, dissociation, derealization, depersonalization, and substance abuse, which can mask the underlying trauma. They may experience agitation or a decrease in energy level, and they may withdraw and deny the loss.

Disaster stress and grief also may undermine adolescents' natural pull to separate from their families and establish themselves more independently. Their very important peer networks and school relationships can be turned upside down. Their unimpacted friends may be afraid of what has happened to the survivor and find it difficult to offer support. Additionally, fears related to their bodies may be intensified just as they are developing into sexually mature adults. At puberty, most children are uncomfortable with their image. They feel clumsy, shy, and insecure and may not like the way they look even under normal circumstances. Adolescents who are injured in a disaster may be particularly traumatized by their own wounds because at this age even the smallest imperfection is of enormous significance (Klingman, 2002).

It can be helpful to encourage adolescents to participate in community rehabilitative work and to resume their social activities. Because they may be overwhelmed by their emotions, they may not be able to discuss their fears within the family setting, but encouraging open discussions about the subject might be helpful.

Trauma in the Formative Years

It is evident that experiencing a traumatic event during the formative years of childhood and adolescence can impact survivors' development. For children, disaster's effects are magnified because their personalities are still in the process of being formed. "The child has to construct his or her own identity within a framework of the psychological damage done by the disaster" (Ehrenreich, 2001). Each developmental stage presents unique tasks that a child grapples with. For example, attachment serves to organize a child on multiple developing fronts, and young children who suffer a loss of a loved one or primary caretaker are more apt to develop emotional or personality disturbances. This effect may be exacerbated by the environmental instability that often follows disaster. What's more, any disruption of the normal development process can have a ripple effect as one stage builds on another; poorly resolved stages can have implications for adaptation at later points in life.

However, despite disaster's terrible power to cause lasting damage to a child's emotional development, that damage is by no means inevitable. An individual's development does not result from a single factor in a direct cause-and-effect manner: It is affected by multiple simultaneous influences occurring at numerous levels, specific to a child and to an environment. Trauma is just one of those influences, and its effects vary from child to child depending on the collective interaction of multiple factors including but not limited to the stage a child is in at the time of the event. A disaster may raise stage-salient issues, but the caregiver's response and other situational aspects can enhance (or hamper) a child's successful negotiation of those issues.

Which Children Are Most at Risk?

When working with children, it is helpful to consider developmental level within the context of multiple influences. Experts in child life have called this a **developmental ecological framework** (Belsky, 1995), which views maturation as a function of transactions among child, caregiver, and environment. In a model specifically intended to frame a child's reactions after disaster exposure, Korol, Green, and Grace (1999) identified four key variables to consider in predicting posttraumatic reactions: characteristics of the stressor, characteristics of the child, the child's efforts to process and cope with the ensuing distress, and characteristics of the postdisaster environment. The following section summarizes research findings for each of these attributes, with special attention paid to the recovery environment, because that is where DMH workers can play a significant role.

- *Characteristics of the stressor.* An essential criterion for the emergence of PTSD is the perception of a threat to life during the traumatic event. The more that children perceived their lives or the lives of loved ones to be threatened during a disaster, the higher is their report of PTSD symptoms. The actual death of a loved one, especially a violent death, is also strongly linked to PTSD. Physical proximity to a disaster, longer duration, and higher intensity of life-threatening events led to more intense or severe reactions, suggesting a dose–response relationship as is often seen in adults and in the elderly. The loss of possessions and disruption of everyday life, with accompanying stressors lasting for weeks, months, and even years, seriously challenges children's and families' adaptation and coping.
- *Characteristics of the child.* Studies examining demographic characteristics as predictors of a child's reaction to disaster do not yield a very clear picture

of who may be particularly vulnerable within this generally vulnerable population. No clear data on children's disaster reactions by age are available. Gender data is also generally mixed, with boys in the 8- to 11-year age range and teenage girls showing more total PTSD symptoms and intrusion symptoms than boys and girls in other age groups. These findings may be the result of an age by gender interaction, but researchers are not sure why this would be the case. Minority youth reported higher levels of PTSD symptoms, but sociodemographic variables were not well understood and this may reflect economic factors more than cultural or racial ones.

Preexisting psychological or behavioral problems appear to be better predictors of a child's reaction than his or her demographic profile. Preexisting anxiety was a significant risk factor for development of PTSD, and predisaster depression and ruminative coping styles also served as potential risk factors for stress reactions. Children with preexisting academic difficulties and attention problems also exhibited greater postdisaster problems than children without such difficulties. Therefore, caregivers and DMH practitioners should be especially vigilant to watch for signs of posttraumatic trouble in children who were already struggling in some way before the disaster.

- *The child's efforts to cope.* There is scant research regarding which psychological resources serve to buffer more negative outcomes among children. At least average intelligence, good communication skills, strong beliefs in self-efficacy, an internal locus of control, and positive and adequate ways of coping were found to be helpful. Negative coping strategies for dealing with stress, like anger or blaming others, resulted in higher levels of PTSD after a natural disaster than positive coping strategies. Negative coping strategies were also associated with greater persistence of symptoms.

- *Characteristics of the postdisaster environment.* One of the major predictors of a child's reaction to disaster, the postdisaster environment, can often be made more conducive to recovery by strengthening social support and providing appropriate resources. Children's perceived social support from significant others such as parents, friends, and teachers can have a powerful protective effect. Good social support was found to be an important protective factor associated with a reduction in distress (Green, 1998), mitigating the impact of natural disasters on children and adolescents and predicting fewer PTSD symptoms in high school students in reaction to crime and violence.

Schools can play an important role in assisting children in postdisaster adjustment. The classroom can be a valuable resource because it is generally the environment that the child is most familiar with outside of the family and immediate community, so it can be a safe haven of structure and routine and help in stabilization. Trained school personnel can lead classroom exercises to help identify children who might benefit from professional counseling (Young et al., 1998). Discussion of disaster-related events, promotion of positive coping and problem-solving skills, and strengthening of friendships and peer support are types of interventions that have been identified as promising (La Greca et al., 2002) though not empirically validated. Schools can also provide a forum where parents can meet to share information regarding their children, as well as exchange ways to enhance and assess coping.

Part of providing a secure environment means protecting children from inappropriate reminders of their disaster experience. Adults must guard against expressing vivid descriptions of their own fears in front of their children. Events seen in the media should be discussed and explained calmly and reassuringly. It is best to monitor children's television viewing or to watch television reports of a disaster with them.

For children experiencing long-term separation from both parents, the mobilization of community resources appears crucial. Studies of children exposed to war in England in World War II showed that the level of emotional upset displayed by the adults in a child's life was the best predictor of a child's response, but children appeared more distressed by separation from their parents than by exposure to bombings or witnessing destruction, injury, or death. Remaining with parents or parent substitutes and maintaining a familiar routine has a buffering effect for preschool and school-aged children (Bat-Zion & Levy-Shiff, 1993). Children will show more resilience if their parents are close by; when children feel that grown-ups cannot be depended on to assume full responsibility for their security, they can become anxious and insecure.

Parental Psychology and the Recovery Environment

Although parents may try to ensure a secure recovery environment for their children, they may not be able to control one very significant factor: their own emotional states. Several studies have found that parents' psychosocial functioning, including levels of psychopathology and reactions to the disaster, plays a significant role in how children recover. Green et al. (1991) found that parental psychopathology predicted higher PTSD in children and adolescents following the Buffalo Creek dam collapse. In the case of a nuclear waste disaster, the psychological health of the parents was found to be a strong predictor of children's disaster reactions (Korol et al., 1999). Cornely and Bromet (1986) and Handford et al. (1986) found that current parental psychiatric symptoms or distress were related to stronger children's responses to the event and mothers' distress was associated with persistence of children's postdisaster emotional and behavioral difficulties after Hurricane Hugo (Swenson, Saylor, & Powell, 1996).

Research indicates that children do better after a fire or other disaster when their parents are calm and supportive; otherwise, the parent's anxiety appears to be contagious. In fact, McFarlane (1987) found that a parent's reaction to disaster is a better predictor of a child developing symptoms than the child's level of exposure to the disastrous event. This suggests that effective family counseling should emphasize supporting and calming parents, who should also be educated about the importance of attending to and calming their own children. However, although a definite linkage exists between children's symptoms and parents' trauma-related symptoms (Foy, Madvig, Pynoos, & Camilleri, 1996), this correlation needs to be clarified.

Common sense may suggest that if parents are having adjustment difficulties themselves, they may be less able to provide needed support and comfort to their children. On a practical level, they may not be able to provide a normal routine and sense of control so that children can feel safe and contain their worries. Still, care must be taken in drawing an absolute conclusion that all children's reactions are mediated by the parents' reactions (McFarlane, 1987). In one study of Bosnian children, direct exposure to war trauma accounted for more variance in child distress than the mother's stress reactions. This suggests that there may be a more complicated interactional effect in how parents and their children respond to disasters. For example, it is possible that the relationship between parent's and child's distress runs in the other direction, with a parent's reaction worsened by concerns about a symptomatic child.

In some cases, the child may contribute directly to the disastrous situation: The majority of residential arson fires are actually caused by children and adolescents. In fact, children playing with fire cause 2 out of every 5 fires that kill children. It seems apparent that it must be more difficult for a parent to calmly comfort and support a child who started a fire that results in serious loss and hardship for the family. Thus, the responsible child could be in much more distress, with less support from family and community; he or she could also become a target for rage. Given the number of fires that are started by children, it would seem important to develop an empirically supported approach to assist families when a child starts a fire, but at the present time we know of no research that has been done to address this problem.

Clearly, the issue requires further exploration, but whatever the cause of the correlation, it is evident that DMH practitioners should consider the parents' state as well as the child's in trying to ensure recovery. As Raphael (1986) notes, "If parents are so distraught from their own grief or psychological traumatization or from the burdens of the relocation and recovery, then they may require support so as to meet the child's needs."

Key Principles in Helping Children

There is general consensus in the literature about guiding principles for helping children and adolescents across all developmental ranges. Some of these principles have received empirical support, and others rely more on good common sense. Some are practices that DMH practitioners can apply directly, and others should be suggested to parents (we expand on the ways that DMH practitioners can help parents to help their children in Chapter 9). These include the following:

- Children and adolescents are profoundly affected by how the adults closest to them conduct themselves, absorbing fear and anxiety as well as composure and proactiveness.
- Children thrive on consistency, so restoring a "normal" childhood as soon as possible through the resumption of routines and rituals and the security of familiar activities is very helpful.

- Encouraging but not forcing expression of thoughts and feelings provides children with an opportunity to sort things out. Talk about and explain what has happened (even about death) and see where the conversation can go.
- Protect children from overexposure to graphic and disturbing images and from further harm. However, provide children with factual information about what has happened in simple and direct language.
- Postdisaster social support is essential. Parents should be encouraged to provide a verbal and physical presence and attention; disaster workers should keep families united, if possible.
- Include children in recovery activities as is age appropriate.
- Create (and practice) a family disaster preparedness plan for the future.

In summary, the long-term prognosis for child disaster survivors hinges on the ability of the adult community to be psychologically available to children, to reassure them, to protect them, and to clarify and interpret the experience (Garbarino & Kostelny, 1996). Although experiencing helplessness and exposure to catastrophe is likely to cause regression in youngsters' development (for example, delays in attaining independence, identity formation, establishing trust and intimacy), such patterns can be minimized by the availability of a highly cohesive support system (Caplan, 1964; Garmezy, 1985; Klingman, 2002).

THE ELDERLY IN DISASTERS

Let's now move to the other end of the age spectrum and consider disaster's effects on the elderly. A review of the literature on how the elderly respond in disasters suggests different patterns of vulnerability in social, psychological, and physiological dimensions. In general, this group's needs often seem to be strongest before, during, and immediately after a disaster, and they are often more practical or logistical in nature than psychological; longer-term adverse reactions appear to be less prevalent than we might expect.

Who Are the Elderly?

Mitigating the vulnerability of older disaster survivors requires an understanding of the specific needs and traits of this diverse population as well as identification of the risk factors that lead to their vulnerability, so we begin with a look at what we mean when we discuss the elderly in the context of DMH.

As in our discussion of children, there are significant differences within this group in terms of age and abilities, and these differences are reflected in their range of responses to disaster. Generally the label "elderly" encompasses anyone age 65 years or older. People aged 65 through 74 are the "young old," those 75 to 84 are the "aged," and those over 85 are the "oldest old" (Hobbs, 1996). The National Institute on Aging (1990) stresses the heterogeneity of the elderly—that is, they are more dissimilar than similar; those born in 1910 have grown old in a very different context than those born in 1940. The size of the elderly population is growing due to demographic trends and better health care. By 2030 older adults will account for 20% of the U.S. population, which is a significant rise from the estimated 13% in 2001 (The National Institute on Aging, 1990). Between 1960 and 1994, the "oldest old" grew in numbers by 274% (Oriol, 1999).

It is important to recognize that aging does not inherently make an individual vulnerable to disaster effects. Only those people whose faculties, senses, or physical or mental capabilities are diminishing should be seen as more likely to require assistance from others in preparing for a traumatic event or in maintaining equilibrium in its aftermath. Therefore, it may be more useful for the DMH practitioner to categorize the older population in terms of functional capacity rather than chronological age, thinking of them as the "frail elderly" and the "well elderly."

The frail elderly are those who are over 65 years old and have physical, cognitive, social, psychological, and/or economic conditions that limit their ability to perform one or more activities of daily living (such as bathing, grooming or moving from bed to chair) or instrumental activities of daily life (including shopping, using public transportation, and managing their finances). These limitations undermine their independence and increase reliance upon others. The frail elderly may have to use their entire functional reserve for basic survival and so may have minimal resources available for managing added stress (Oriol, 1999).

Logistical Issues Faced by the Elderly

Older people demonstrate their own set of vulnerabilities that can serve to increase their level of stress during disasters, but for the frail elderly many of these vulnerabilities are logistical in nature rather than emotional. Issues such as impaired physical mobility, diminished sensory awareness, cognitive limitations, preexisting health conditions, and social and economic restraints can all make it difficult for people to take protective action before a disaster or to adapt to altered living conditions in its aftermath. These areas may seem outside of the scope of DMH, but failure to address them effectively can ultimately lead to more significant problems for elderly survivors. Therefore, it is well worth learning how a properly timed logistical intervention can help prevent more serious outcomes in this population. Problems affecting the frail elderly in disasters may include the following:

- *Mobility problems.* As part of the natural aging process, many older people experience impaired balance, decreased motor strength, and poorer exercise tolerance. As a result, they may find fleeing from a disaster very difficult. Many elderly people no longer drive or do not have access to transportation, limiting their capacity to escape or even to obtain needed supplies before or after an event. They may be unable to evacuate or to prepare their homes for an approaching storm, particularly those without nearby family or other social supports to help out, leaving them more vulnerable to personal and/or property damage (Langer, 2004). Mobility problems can continue to play a role during the recovery phase; for example, someone with a chronic debilitating illness like arthritis may find it nearly impossible to stand in a lengthy line for assistance.

- *Preexisting medical condition.* Preexisting medical conditions can inhibit people's ability to function during disasters, and they may be aggravated by loss of medications, health-care venues, and electricity needed to power medical equipment. Even if frail elderly people have an adequate supply of needed medications during a disaster, stress and confusion may cause them to take inappropriate doses, sometimes leading to physical or cognitive problems. In general, older people are more vulnerable to the effects of heat or cold and more likely to become ill as a result of extreme temperatures. This was demonstrated in the European heat wave of 2003 in which more than 13,000 elderly people died.

- *Sensory limitations.* Sensory acuity naturally deteriorates as people age. As a result, the frail elderly may be less able to hear danger signals and alarms, and they may have a harder time locating avenues of escape. Sensory limitations may make it challenging for the elderly to truly appreciate the extent of a threat; hence, a delayed response syndrome has been noted in this group (Young et al., 1998). They may have difficulty detecting the taste or smell of spoiled food, leaving them vulnerable to food poisoning if power remains out for a long time after a disaster.

- *Cognitive limitations.* It can be difficult for frail elderly people to fully understand the significance of what is taking place before or after a disaster. Some can become easily confused or disoriented and may not be able to recall emergency instructions accurately. Limitations may be exacerbated by memory disorders, but even in elderly people without preexisting dementia, disruptions in medication schedules can increase confusion.

- *Other logistical issues.* Older people are frequently the victims of crimes; they are the most likely to be taken in by fraudulent contractors and other recovery-related scams following a disaster (Davila, Marquart, & Mullings, 2005). They appear to be particularly vulnerable to fraud because they are susceptible to high-pressure sales tactics; they are willing to help those who claim they are in need; and they often have cash reserves on hand. Additionally, elderly survivors whose homes are damaged may be especially anxious to get back to normal and regain their independence, so they may take a calculated risk by hiring a contractor without fully vetting his or her credentials, sometimes leading to shoddy work, overcharges, or outright theft (Davila et al., 2005).

Finally, but not insignificantly, it should be noted that many elderly people must face disasters with few financial or social resources to cushion the experience. Social support decreases with age as spouses, siblings, and peers pass away and children move away. Of those over the age of 85, 50% live alone. The elderly are disproportionately afflicted by a lack of insurance, a smaller financial cushion, and existence on a fixed income.

Relocation Trauma

Having to relocate during a disaster is a terribly difficult experience for anyone, but older adults appear especially prone to debilitating adjustment stress that has been called *transfer trauma* (Oriol, 1999). As a result, many elderly people do not want to evacuate even when ordered to do so. They would rather "ride it out" at the home they know and feel comfortable in. Sudden and unexpected uprooting is especially hard for those who have impaired mobility, special medication needs, or cherished possessions or pets that they must leave behind. In fact, pets may be key points in decision making for the elderly: Many will not go to a public shelter because their pet cannot accompany them.

If the frail elderly do agree to be evacuated, the process of moving them can be slower and more complicated than for most other groups due to the various limitations described above. Relocating the elderly requires more planning and preparation to make sure that all essential medications and equipment are packed, and extra time needs to be allowed to accommodate slower movements and the need for more rest stops. Older people may require medical attention in transit, and some may need to go to a special-needs shelter where they can receive appropriate assistance. After the Kobe earthquake in Japan, many previously healthy elderly survivors developed dementia, disorientation, and incontinence, apparently in response to the stress of life in a shelter (Shinfuku, 2005).

After a relocation is accomplished, the psychological task of adjustment to a new surrounding can lead to depression, irritability, serious illness, and even death in the frail elderly (Young et al., 1998). Oriol (1999) describes a tragic incident in which 15 of 47 residents of a nursing home were dead 7 months after they were evacuated during a flood. The nursing home director believes that the stress of being moved in the middle of the night and placed in unfamiliar and distant settings was simply "too much" for many of his elderly patients. In another example (Sanders, 2003), older public housing residents who were forcibly relocated from their homes when Hurricane Andrew struck Miami–Dade County in 1992 suffered from an array of physical and mental health maladies that were exacerbated when they were uprooted from key support systems they depended on, including families, social services, and health-care facilities. A variety of complaints surfaced about their new living arrangements and almost 70% expressed a desire to return to their previous homes after long-term structural repairs were complete.

Psychological Issues Among the Elderly

The American Psychiatric Association (Estes, 1995) estimates that at any given time, 15 to 25% of the elderly have symptoms of mental illness such as dementia and depression. In nursing homes, approximately two-thirds manifest such symptoms. But these findings are considered suspect due to underreporting by the elderly, who demonstrate a consistent and pervasive resistance to accessing and using mental health services. Older people, especially the current cohort of elderly who lived through the Depression and place a high value on self-sufficiency, may resist accepting mental and other social services, perceiving the need for assistance as a sign of failure (Langer, 2004). Many feel a stigma regarding perceived "handouts." This may be especially true among minority groups, who have been taught by past experience not to trust authorities (Langer, 2004). Young et al. (1998) point out another possible motivation for that self-sufficiency: Older people may fear that they will lose their independence if they ask for help.

The later years bring with them a number of poignant losses of varying magnitude. There are changes in one's physical hardiness, increased likelihood of disability, and often the experience of being widowed and having friends and older family members pass away as well. Over time, the support systems of the elderly may be quite fragile and small in scope. Isolation can be increased. The effects of intense stressors like those that characterize disasters may compound these more normative losses and changes. Additionally, emergencies may stimulate dormant emotions related to difficulties encountered at other points in one's life. In the most extreme cases, new disasters can even reactivate chronic PTSD resulting from severe trauma experienced decades earlier, as in some Holocaust or war survivors. In this context of multiple losses, a striking attachment to specific items of property and routine can be found (Young et al., 1998), perhaps explaining this group's strong resistance to relocation. Disasters may become a "final blow," making recovery even harder for the elderly.

Developmental considerations can play a role in disaster reactions for adults as well as children. Erik Erikson described the last stage of life (from age 65 until death, in his categorization) as a time when people reflect upon their lives and try to come to terms with their eventual death. The goal is to accept one's life and feel as if one has come into one's own. If older people can achieve a sense of fulfillment about life and a sense of unity within themselves and with others, death will not be feared. But disaster may significantly undermine this developmental task: "One particular issue that may appear is feelings that [the elderly] have lost their entire life (loss of children, homes, memorabilia) and, that due to their age, there is not enough time left in their life to rebuild and recreate" (Ehrenreich, 2001).

Strengths of Older Disaster Survivors

To be sure, not all of the facts about older people are so dire. The elderly are by definition survivors (U.S. Department of Health and Human Services, 1999), and there has been a recent pendulum swing within the mental health field to increasingly recognize the resiliency and competency of older adults. This change in attitude toward the elderly may be in response to the fact that early gerontological studies focused on those who were institutionalized, perhaps leading to an impression of older people as generally ill or frail. But recent evidence supports the recognition that physical capacity, outlook, and achievement can all be sustained and even improved throughout the lifespan (Inglish, 1991). "Successful aging is multidimensional, encompassing three distinct domains: avoidance of disease and disability, maintenance of high physical and cognitive functioning, and sustained engagement in social and productive activities" (Rowe & Kahn, 1997).

Despite growing interest in mental health issues and the elderly, specific research examining their reactions to disasters is minimal (Norris, 1994). In the next few paragraphs, we review current research findings regarding the impact of disasters on the elderly. From a broad psychological perspective, none of these studies found a significantly worse long-term outcome among the elderly after disaster exposure in comparison with survivors in other age groups. In fact, some studies have found milder effects in older adults. However, even though the few studies available indicate limited postdisaster psychopathology among the elderly, more refined research is needed with greater controls, better definition of variables, and a richer and more complex developmental perspective. For example, some studies have included people as young as 55 years old in their definition of elderly, and some have excluded participants who are in long-term care or other medical/nursing settings (Fernandez, Byard., Chien-Chih, Benson, & Barbera, 2002). Both of these filters would presumably dilute the prevalence or severity of symptoms found.

With that caveat, let's look now at some relevant studies of elderly survivors. We present most of them briefly in order to demonstrate the range and prevalence of postdisaster symptoms before discussing three more revealing studies in detail.

STUDIES SUGGESTING VULNERABILITY AMONG THE ELDERLY

- Of a sample of elderly residents of Lockerbie, Scotland, 84% met criteria for PTSD, and 51% had coexisting major depression 1 year after the crash of Pan Am 103; but after 3 years, only 16% were diagnosable with PTSD (Jenike, 1995). Younger residents (aged 18 to 65 years) had similar initial responses but with less frequent coexisting depression (Livingston, Livingston, & Fell, 1994).

- Elderly earthquake survivors in Taiwan reported a diminished quality of life in terms of physical capacity, psychological well-being, and environment 12 months after the event, regardless of the level of damage to their residences (Lin, Huang, & Huang, 2000).

- Australian earthquake survivors over age 65 years old used fewer general and disaster-related support services than younger survivors, despite reporting higher overall levels of PTSD symptoms. Within the older group, those who had high levels of symptoms were more likely to be female, to report higher levels of exposure, and to use behavioral and avoidant coping styles (Ticehurst, Webster, Carr, & Lewin, 1996).

STUDIES SUGGESTING RESILIENCE AMONG THE ELDERLY

- Eighteen months after exposure to a Kentucky flood, survivors aged 55 years and older demonstrated increases in anxiety, depressive, and somatic symptoms, but generally these symptoms were mild to moderate and not at clinically diagnosable levels. Interestingly, depressive symptoms were most prevalent among the youngest subgroup studied, those aged 55 to 64, and less significant in the 65 to 74 or 75 and older groups, perhaps because members of the youngest group were dealing with other life stressors (Phifer, 1990).

- Three weeks after a Japanese earthquake, evacuees of all ages experienced similar sleep disturbances, depression, hypersensitivity, and irritability. Eight weeks later, the percentage of the younger group experiencing symptoms did not decrease, while the elderly showed a significant decrease in most symptoms.

The study's author suggests that this may have been due to such factors as decreased psychological stress, extensive social networks, and previous disaster experiences among the elderly (Kato, Asukai, & Miyake, 1996).

Thus, it appears that elderly survivors may suffer short-term effects after a disaster (though these are generally no more severe than those seen among younger survivors when a comparison was included), but most posttraumatic symptoms resolve over time. Additionally, older adults who have survived previous disasters may fare better psychologically in subsequent disasters than inexperienced counterparts. Some researchers believe that prior experience may effectively "inoculate" elders against the depression and anxiety that can result from natural disaster. As Phifer (1990) suggests, "Several factors may account for the relative resiliency of the older old. Although older adults may endure more severe exposure to disaster, have poorer health, and have less social and economic resources, they also possess two advantages that may promote the process of adaptation to disasters: a higher incidence of past resolved stressful experiences and a lower incidence of current unresolved stressful experiences."

Let's now look more closely at a few studies that provide a more nuanced picture of how the elderly react to disasters.

First, in keeping with the stress inoculation theory, a study looking at several generations of earthquake survivors in California concluded that an individual's degree of prior disaster experience was a better predictor of postearthquake psychological functioning than chronological age and that elderly earthquake survivors may be more psychologically resilient than younger adults in the wake of natural disasters (Knight & Gatz, 2000). Although this study—which interviewed 166 adults ranging in age from 30 to 102 years old following the 1994 Northridge, California, earthquake—found general support for a protective effect of prior experience, there were exceptions. Experience level did not prevent two postdisaster symptoms, ruminative thoughts about the earthquake and a heightened startle response to normal vibrations, which were more closely associated with the degree of personal damage experienced by disaster survivors. Nor was prior disaster experience the best predictor of depressive reactions: In analyzing longitudinal depression data for the same adults, which were available from before the earthquake through a nondisaster-related survey of multigenerational families, the authors found that "the level of depressive symptoms in people after Northridge was almost entirely predicted by their level [of depression] before the earthquake" (Knight & Gatz, 2000).

On a practical note, the same longitudinal study yielded a second report looking specifically at cross-generational differences in disaster preparedness. Heller, Alexander, Gatz, Knight, and Rose (2005) found that elderly individuals took far fewer steps to increase their level of preparedness than did younger family members in the aftermath of an earthquake. The authors suggest that the significant disparity between generations may reflect a certain fatalism among elderly quake survivors, indicating a need to make preparedness more relevant to elders.

Second, in thorough research that aimed to elucidate posttraumatic responses of young, middle-aged, and elderly subjects as well as to differentiate coping strategies, Chung, Werrett, Easthope, and Farmer (2004) examined differences in reactions to two types of technological disasters, an airplane crash that killed those on board and endangered hundreds of community residents and a freight train collision resulting in the evacuation of community members. From the two affected communities, 148 participants were divided into three age groups, young (18 to 39), middle-aged (40 to 64), and elderly (65 and older) to evaluate reactions across ages. They were further divided into low-, medium-, and high-exposure groups depending on proximity to the crashes. Six to seven months after each disaster, participants were given the Impact of Event Scale to measure intrusive thoughts and avoidant behavior related to the crash; the General Health Questionnaire to detect psychiatric symptoms; and the Ways of Coping Checklist to determine whether individuals used "problem-focused" coping methods (that is, "confrontive coping, accepting responsibility, and planful problem solving") or "emotion-focused coping" (that is, "distancing, self-controlling, seeking social support, escape-avoidance, and positive reappraisal").

Chung et al. (2004) found that those with the highest level of exposure experienced the most symptoms, repeating the dose–response pattern that has been seen in many disaster studies. Most notably, there was no significant effect of age group for either impact or general health symptoms, nor was age correlated with differences in coping strategies. Escape–avoidance coping correlated with more negative item endorsement across all three age groups. Instead, responses tended to correlate with event type and exposure level rather than age group, further supporting the theory that adults of different ages react to traumatic events in similar fashion.

Finally, Norris (1994) conducted an epidemiological study examining the frequency and impact of several potentially traumatic events among 1000 residents of four cities in the southeastern United States. Half of the participants were African American, and half were female; they were evenly divided among younger (18 to 39), middle-aged (40 to 59), and older (60 and older) adults. Sixty-nine percent of the sample had experienced one or more traumatic events. Older adults did not report more events over the course of their lifetime or in the year prior to the survey. Rates of PTSD symptoms in response to the traumatic events were determined. Whereas rates of 9 to 10% were found in the younger and middle-aged groups, the elderly showed markedly lower rates of 3% with PTSD. As a result, Norris concludes that older adults cannot be described as a group that is more prone to trauma exposure or the development of PTSD. But the elderly rates of traumatic exposure (14% alone for the previous year) and prevalence of PTSD (3%) should not be overlooked. Based on a 1990 census, those rates would translate into 6 million older adults experiencing a traumatic event in any given year and at least 1 million currently suffering from PTSD. Norris (1994) explains, "These numbers clearly justify professional concern regarding the prevention and treatment of trauma among older adults."

In general, although the studies we have reviewed suggest that the elderly are no more vulnerable to lasting psychological effects following disasters, they are still largely affected by the same factors that influence reactions in the general population. For example, a dose–response relationship has been seen in both older and younger adults, with more intense exposure to a disaster resulting in more postevent symptoms. On the protective side, availability of resources and positive coping styles have been linked with better recovery for all adults.

But the elderly are clearly vulnerable in the logistical areas that we identified earlier, and they are at risk for negative emotional responses as well as heightened morbidity and mortality if they do not get appropriate practical assistance before, during, and immediately after disasters. Too often, those simple needs may go unmet, lost between this group's recognized resistance to asking for help and the bustle of other activity around a disaster: "In the context of increased stress on the family and community, meeting the special needs [of the elderly] may take on a lowered priority" (Ehrenreich, 2001).

Key Principles in Helping the Elderly

As we have just seen, research findings regarding the mental health functioning of the elderly during disasters are in many ways contrary to expectations commonly held. Perhaps, as Raphael wrote in 1986, "The old may be slow to accept the realities of disaster threat and may be injured or killed as a consequence. As survivors, they may suffer many dislocations and considerable economic difficulty. But, they seem to 'make the best' of the situation and they do not complain. Their emotional hurt may go deep, but they tend to suffer it quietly, often failing to use resources that might be available to help with their economic and emotional needs."

As a DMH worker, how can you work in this dynamic to deliver the help that elderly survivors most need? Disaster mental health sets a high priority on pragmatic consideration; practitioners understand the significance of restoring depleted basic resources including safety, shelter and food. Similarly, working with the elderly in the aftermath of a catastrophe will require a practical, hands-on, and proactive approach. For example, in looking for signs of distress in clients, it may be advisable to use multiple assessment methods because problems in this group may be underreported.

In the process of recovery, it is important to help the elderly reestablish a sense of control, predictability, and comforting routine and to help them feel connected to others through outreach and opportunities for increased contact. Internal feelings of connectedness need to be established as well in order to mitigate the potential sense of fragmentation, which is the hallmark of trauma. Young et al. (1998) note: "Activities as simple as remembering and talking about their life can be seen as a starting point that helps them reconnect with their unique perspective as a part of the history of mankind." Talking about past successes can enhance self-worth and confidence.

The National Institute of Mental Health (1983) recommends the following as guiding principles for working with the elderly after a disaster:

- Provide strong and persistent verbal assurance and attention.
- Assist with recovery of physical possessions, make frequent home visits, and arrange for companions. Outreach to elders is often the most effective way

to help. In the early days of a disaster, it may be the only way to help isolated individuals.

- Give special attention to suitable residential relocation, ideally in familiar surroundings with family or friends.
- Help reestablish familial and social contacts.
- Assist in obtaining medical and financial assistance; help reduce the barriers to accessing resources.
- Help reestablish medication regimens.
- Provide escort service.

As a result of the expected increase in the elderly population, emergency management strategies for helping the elderly are increasingly important and not always sufficient: In a report on emergency preparedness for older people, O'Brien (2003) observed that "within 24 hours following the 9/11 terrorist attacks, animal advocates were on the scene rescuing pets, yet abandoned older and disabled people waited for up to seven days for an ad hoc medical team to rescue them." Plans of action for vulnerable populations should include:

- Appropriate emergency management for older and disabled persons so that interdependent emergency and relief organizations have a formal plan for assisting special-needs populations.
- Creation of a coordinated community-wide emergency plan so that respond-ing agencies can pool their resources.
- Development of a system to identify and locate older and disabled people; this can include developing maps highlighting neighborhoods with a high concentration of older people.
- Dissemination of pertinent public information before and after emergencies, with information on public services and emergency planning, several times a year.
- Development and enhancement of geriatric mental health services such as the development of a universal system of providing medication or prescription refills on an emergency basis.

Finally, Fernandez et al. (2002) recommend community acknowledgment to help address the special recovery needs of the frail elderly. They suggest that emergency management strategies should include personal involvement so that the elderly, their families and their neighbors will have increased awareness and be more self-prepared. Specifically, they recommend utilizing the well elderly as volunteers to help their peers. Because evidence shows that previous experience with disaster can make some older adults more resilient in the face of new dis-asters, such a peer group may be invaluable during a time of crisis; indeed, the federal Administration on Aging is proposing a project called EAGLES (Elder Action Global Logistical Emergency System) that involves training elders to respond to their peers with special needs. The kind of strength and resilience seen among many older people is well illustrated in this quote from an elderly disaster survivor, which we use to conclude this section:

It was terrible, awful, and we lost everything we had. I'll never get over it in some ways. But it was worse for the young ones —it was such a shock—they're just starting in life and everything. Bill and me—we've had our lives and gone through bad times before—we'll make it. And we don't want to be no trouble to anyone. Not our kids or anyone else. We'll manage. (Raphael, 1986)

PEOPLE WITH SERIOUS MENTAL ILLNESS

As we learned from our discussion of the elderly, some populations that one might assume to be particularly vulnerable to strong posttraumatic responses may not in fact demonstrate any more lasting effects after a disaster than the general population. People with serious mental illness (SMI) appear to fit this description, though they remain vulnerable in other ways. Hamblen, Jankowski, and Rosenberg (2004) note that it is a commonly held belief that people who are hospitalized or in outpatient treatment with severe psychiatric disorders are less able to cope with the stress of disasters. This does not appear to be true.

Of course, this leaves open the question of how people with SMI who are *not* in treatment fare after disasters, as McMurray and Steiner (2000) point out, particularly those with schizophrenia or other psychotic disorders: "Although pre-existing psychopathology is sometimes mentioned as a predictor of psychiatric disorder following a disaster, the illnesses described were nonpsychotic. The SMI population has been neglected in the disaster literature—surprisingly, since stressful life events are known to be associated with relapse, and these patients often have poor social support networks, a predictor of poor adjustment following disasters." Clearly, more research is needed on how members of this population respond to disasters.

The few studies that do exist suggest that people with SMI (or at least those receiving professional treatment) may be less fragile than expected, with psychiatric inpatients showing no increase in symptoms and outpatient members of a treatment group showing no increase in hospitalizations after a disaster. However, although this group seems fairly resilient to the effects of disaster, they are by no means immune to PTSD. In fact, studies assessing the prevalence of PTSD in people with SMI show that approximately 30 to 40% have PTSD at any given time, which is 20 to 30 times the rate for people without SMI. Unfortunately, exposure to marginal and sometimes violent circumstances is often part of life for those with SMI: They are more vulnerable to risky situations and victimization and may be more prone to stress reactions as a result of their mental illnesses. And yet, screening for PTSD is not routinely conducted in those with SMI even after a traumatic event, but it should be even if presenting symptoms suggest an exacerbation of the original mental illness rather than the development of comorbid PTSD. Underdetection of PTSD in SMI patients could compromise treatment of the primary disorder and possibly make this group even more vulnerable after being exposed to a new trauma like a disaster (Hamblen et al., 2004).

Like the elderly, the disaster-related needs of people with SMI seem to be strongest before, during, and immediately after a disaster and are largely logistical in nature. Many people with SMI depend on medications to keep their illness in check, so an unpredictable disaster that disrupts access to necessary medications can lead to a reemergence of symptoms. Providing adequate care in shelters for the mentally ill and for elderly people with dementia can be very difficult because these populations may not adapt well to an unfamiliar and overstimulating environment. This can result in a worsening of preexisting symptoms or the development of new ones: The busy environment of public emergency shelters caused some mentally ill survivors to begin decompensating following a major Canadian ice storm in 1998. These individuals were moved to a hospital where an in-house shelter was set up specifically to provide a more appropriate environment and where case management teams could monitor their psychological states (McMurray & Steiner, 2000).

Just as disruptions in access to medications can cause problems for people with SMI, so can disruptions in access to their usual treatment routines. As McMurray and Steiner (2000) observe, "In the postdisaster period, the usual model of patient attendance at the outpatient clinic may be severely disrupted. Therefore, to ensure that the mental health needs of SMI patients are met, outreach work . . . may be required. Once the immediate crisis has passed, attention can be directed toward longer-term issues, such as finding alternate housing for patients and rebuilding the service delivery system." Mental health professionals may need to perform outreach to members of an outpatient group or others with SMI who are known to be at risk in order to make sure they are physically safe and not experiencing a psychological crisis. They also might need to help patients make alternate arrangements for receiving medications, such as obtaining them through a hospital pharmacy if their usual commercial pharmacy has been shut down by the disaster (McMurray & Steiner, 2000).

Describing an extreme but highly successful effort to prevent a disaster from reawakening mental illness in a group of clients, Lachance, Santos, and Burns (1994) recount some actions taken by the staff of an Assertive Community Treatment (ACT) Program, a new model treatment program for adults with SMI who were strongly affected by Hurricane Hugo in South Carolina in 1989. Preparations that the staff took for the approaching storm included helping patients shop for essentials like candles, flashlights, bottled water, and canned goods; providing a weekly pill-minder to encourage medication compliance; and distributing information on every patient, including medication needs, to all staff members so that anyone who came in contact with a particular patient would be able to help appropriately. As prestorm evacuations began, staff either assisted patients in reaching appropriate shelters or they spoke to patients' family members to make sure that they were being taken care of.

After the storm, the staff worked out of a tiny temporary office because the main facility had been damaged. They initially focused on basic needs like obtaining shelter and food for patients and then worked to teach them coping skills like preparing meals without electricity (which took weeks to be restored in some areas) and decontaminating drinking water. Lachance et al. (1994) note, "Medication remained a priority but daily deliveries for a large number of patients became impossible. Instead, a transition to weekly pill-minders was made with more aggressive teaching about the importance of compliance. Daily medication deliveries were made only for patients most in danger of relapse." In some cases, family members or neighbors were recruited to assist with compliance.

Despite staff concerns, there were no patient hospitalizations for 3 months after the hurricane, though Lachance et al. (1994) acknowledge that they could not evaluate other outcomes such as increased perceived family burden or law enforcement episodes. They also did not have information on how SMI patients functioned in the social environment of the emergency shelters. They do comment that most patients did not complain about issues with housing or medication; instead, for some, the biggest complaints were about boredom because the loss of electricity meant their televisions did not work and concern about receiving their program-distributed cigarettes and spending money. Some also seemed to enjoy having the opportunity to help others with recovery tasks rather than being "helpees" as usual.

If we can extrapolate from the sparse research on people with SMI in disasters, it appears that this group is no more likely than others to suffer from long-term reactions to disaster. However, members of this population do appear to be particularly sensitive to disruptions in medication and treatment routines. The most helpful DMH interventions may be those aimed at returning this group to their usual habits as quickly as possible and helping them with immediate coping actions.

PEOPLE WITH PHYSICAL DISABILITIES

There is even scanter literature on people with disabilities in disasters than on the other vulnerable population, which we have discussed. One study (Gignac, Cott, & Badley, 2003) examined a group of adults over age 55 with musculoskeletal disorders (osteoarthritis and osteoporosis) who had been exposed to a severe Canadian ice storm in 1998, comparing them with a similarly disabled group that had not been exposed to the storm. Both exposed and comparison groups had been surveyed 2 weeks before the storm about health, arthritic helplessness, perceived independence, and depression and then at postdisaster intervals spanning nearly 2 years. Exposed participants who had reported higher levels of helplessness in managing their disability before the storm were significantly more likely to report that the storm was stressful, that it impacted their physical condition, and that they continued to ruminate about it almost 2 years later. In contrast, those who reported a better self-appraisal of their condition before the storm were less likely to report that it affected them physically. Comparing the two groups, those exposed to the storm were more likely to report increased disability and less likely to report decreased musculoskeletal pain over time than those in the unexposed comparison group. However, there were no significant differences in psychological measures between the two groups, suggesting that even if the storm did have an immediate psychological impact on survivors, it faded over time. Still, the authors note, "Perceptions of lost control and autonomy may leave people especially vulnerable when faced with additional stressors" (Gignac et al., 2003).

Those who are physically disabled or mentally ill have distinct presentations and different needs from one another. What they have in common is that disasters can disrupt their own ways of adaptation as well as the normal patterns of care or assistance that they receive in order to maintain acceptable levels of functioning (Ehrenreich, 2001). As a result, direct effects are accompanied by increases in anxiety and stress. Interestingly, Ehrenreich (2001) describes what may be called reactions to those with disabilities during times of disasters: "The ongoing problems of the disabled may seem to the other victims of the disaster to be of only minor importance in comparison to their own acute and unaccustomed suffering. Their disabilities may even seem like an obstacle to dealing with the disaster itself. The disabled are especially vulnerable to marginalization, isolation, and to 'secondary victimization.'"

CONCLUSIONS ABOUT VULNERABLE POPULATIONS

As we discussed in the beginning of this chapter and in the introduction to this book, there are different ways to define groups as vulnerable or at risk for psychological problems after exposure to a disaster. We have reviewed four populations that are commonly considered to require at least special consideration or understanding during times of disaster. As we discovered, there is a general consensus in portraying children as at risk for psychological problems. The elderly are appropriately viewed as being at risk but in very specific ways that appear more logistical rather than psychological in nature. The frail elderly are especially vulnerable because they may have multiple physical limitations and medical needs, and logistical or practical concerns that are not addressed or mitigated can lead to psychological distress and can heighten the potential for a range of events to occur from increased exposure to dangerous elements to death. The seriously mentally ill and those with disabilities are groups requiring further examination, but they, too, can suffer in ways that may destabilize their adjustment, leading to possible difficulties after an event has passed. These groups also do not consistently demonstrate poorer psychological outcome after disasters, though the research literature is scant.

This chapter concludes our first part devoted to theory in DMH. In the second part, our emphasis shifts to practice issues, ranging from what to expect to how to intervene, to prepare you to become an effective DMH practitioner.

References

Axeline, V. (1969). *Play therapy.* New York: Ballantine Books.

Bat-Zion, N., & Levy-Shiff, R. (1993). Children in war: Stress and coping reactions under the threat of Scud missile attacks and the effect of proximity. In L. Leavitt & N. A. Fox (Eds.), *Psychological effects of war and violence on children* (pp. 143–161). London: Erlbaum.

Belsky, J. (1995). Expanding the ecology of human development: An evolutionary perspective. In P. Moen & G. H. Elder Jr. (Eds.), *Examining lives in context: Perspectives on the ecology of human development* (pp. 545–561). Washington, DC: American Psychological Association.

Bowlby, J. (1973). *Attachment and loss* (Vol. 2). New York: Basic Books.

Caplan, G. (1964). *Principles of preventive psychiatry*. New York: Basic Books.

Chung, M. C., Werrett, J., Easthope, Y., & Farmer, S. (2004). Coping with post-traumatic stress: young, middle-aged and elderly comparisons. *International Journal of Geriatric Psychiatry, 19*, 333–343.

Cook-Cottone, C. (2004). Childhood posttraumatic stress disorder: Diagnosis, treatment, and school reintegration. *School Psychology Review, 33*(1), 127–139.

Cornely, P., & Bromet, E. (1986). Prevalence of behavior problems in three-year-old children living near Three Mile Island: A comparative analysis. *Journal of Child Psychology and Psychiatry, 27*, 489–498.

Costello, E. J., Erkanli, A., & Fairbank, J. A. (2002). The prevalence of potentially traumatic events in childhood and adolescence. *Journal of Traumatic Stress, 15*, 99–112.

Davila, M., Marquart, J. W., & Mullings, J. L. (2005). Beyond Mother Nature: Contractor fraud in the wake of natural disasters. *Deviant Behavior, 26*, 271–293.

Ehrenreich, J. (2001). *Coping with disasters: A guidebook to psychosocial intervention*. Old Westbury: Center for Psychology and Society, State University of New York. Retrieved January 18, 2003, from http://www.mhwwb.org

Erikson, E. H. (1964). *Childhood and society* (2nd ed.). New York: Norton.

Estes, C. L. (1995). Mental health services for the elderly: Key policy elements. In M. Gatz (Ed.), *Emerging issues in mental health and aging*. Washington, DC: American Psychological Association.

Evangelista, N., & McLellan, M. J. (2004). The zero to three diagnostic system: A framework for considering emotional and behavioral problems in young children. *School Psychology Review, 33*(1), 159–173.

Farberow, N. L., & Gordon, N. S. (1981). *Manual for child health workers in major disasters* (DHHS Publication No. ADM 81-1070). Rockville, MD: Center for Mental Health Services.

Fernandez, L. S., Byard., D., Chien-Chih, L., Benson, S., & Barbera, J. A. (2002). Frail elderly as disaster victims: Emergency management strategies. *Prehospital and Disaster Medicine, 17*(2), 67–74.

Foy, D. W., Madvig, B. T., Pynoos, R. S., & Camilleri, A. J. (1996). Etiologic factors in the development of post traumatic stress disorder in children and adolescents. *Journal of School Psychology, 34*, 133–145.

Garbarino, J., & Kostelny, K. (1996). The effects of political violence on Palestinian children's behavior problems: A risk accumulation model. *Child Development, 67*, 33–45.

Garmezy, N. (1985). Stress resilient children: The search for protective factors. In J. Stevenson (Ed.), *Recent research in developmental psychopathology*. Oxford, England: Pergamon Press.

Gignac, M. A. M., Cott, C. A., & Badley, E. M. (2003). Living with a chronic disabling illness and then some: Data from the 1998 ice storm. *Canadian Journal on Aging, 22*, 249–259.

Goenjian, A. K., Karayan, I., Pynoos, R. S., Minassian, D., Najarian, L. M., Steinberg, A. M., & Fairbanks, L. A. (1997). Outcome of psychotherapy among early adolescents after trauma. *American Journal of Psychiatry, 154*, 536–542.

Green, A. H., & Kocijan-Hercigonja, D. (1998). Stress and coping in children traumatized by war. *Journal of the American Academy of Psychoanalysis & Dynamic Psychiatry, 26*(4), 585–597.

Green, B. L., Korol, M. S., Grace, M. C., Vary, M. G., Leonard, A. C., Gleser, G. C., & Smith-Cohen, S. (1991). Children and disaster: Gender and parental effects of PTSD symptoms. *Journal of the American Academy of Child and Adolescent Psychiatry, 30*, 945–951.

Hamblen, J. L, Jankowski, M. K., & Rosenberg, S. D. (2004). Cognitive–behavioral treatment for PTSD in people with severe mental illness: Three case studies. *American Journal of Psychiatric Rehabilitation, 7*(2), 147–170.

Handford, H. A., Mayes, S. D., Mattison, R. E., Humphrey, F. J., Bagnato, S., Bixler, E. O., & Kales, J. D. (1986). Child and parent reaction to the Three Mile Island nuclear accident. *Journal of the American Academy of Child Psychiatry, 25,* 346–356.

Heller, K., Alexander, D. B., Gatz, M., Knight, B. G., & Rose, T. (2005). Social and personal factors as predictors of earthquake preparation: The role of support provision, network discussion, negative affect, age, and education. *Journal of Applied Social Psychology, 35*(2), 399–424.

Hobbs, F. B. (1996). *65+ in the United States.* U.S. Bureau of the Census. Current Population Reports, Special Studies, P23-190, Washington, DC: Government Printing Office.

Honig, R. G., Grace, M. C., Lindy, J., Newman, C. J., & Titchener, J. L. (1993). Portraits of survival: A twenty-year follow-up of the children of Buffalo Creek. *Psychoanalytic Study of the Child, 48,* 327–335.

Inglish, H. (Ed.). (1991). Tornado: Terror and survival. Kansas City, KS: The Counseling Center, Butler County.

Jenike, M. A. (1995). Posttraumatic stress disorder in the elderly: A 3-year follow-up of the Lockerbie disaster. *Journal of Geriatric Psychiatry & Neurology, 8*(2), 137.

Kato, H., Asukai, N., & Miyake, Y. (1996). Posttraumatic symptoms among younger and elederly evacuess in the early stages following the 1995 Hanshin-Awaji earthquake in Japan. *Acta Psychiatrica Scandinavica, 93*(6), 477–481.

Klingman, A. (2002). Children under stress of war. In A. M. La Greca, W. K. Silverman, E. M. Vernberg, & M. C. Roberts (Eds.), *Helping children cope with disasters and terrorism* (pp.359–380). Washington, DC: American Psychological Association.

Knight, B. G., & Gatz, M. (2000). Age and emotional response to the Northridge earthquake: A longitudinal analysis. *Psychology & Aging, 15*(4), 627–635.

Korol, M. S., Green, B. L., & Grace, M. C. (1999). Developmental analysis of the psychosocial impact of disaster on children: A review. *Journal of the American Academy of Child and Adolescent Psychiatry, 38,* 368–375.

Lachance, K. R., Santos, A. B., & Burns, B. J. (1994). The response of an assertive community treatment program following a natural disaster. *Community Mental Health Journal, 30,* 505–515.

La Greca, A. M., Silverman, W. K., Vernberg, E. M., & Roberts, M. C. (Eds.). (2002). *Helping children cope with disasters and terrorism.* Washington, DC: American Psychological Association.

La Greca, A. M., Silverman, W. K., & Wasserstein, S. B. (1998). Children's predisaster functioning as a predictor of posttraumatic stress following Hurricane Andrew. *Journal of Consulting and Clinical Psychology, 66,* 883–892.

Langer, N. (2004). Natural disasters that reveal cracks in our social foundation. *Educational Gerontology, 30,* 275–285.

Lin, M-R., Huang, W., & Huang, C. (2002). The impact of the Chi-Chi earthquake on quality of life among elderly survivors in Taiwan: A before and after study. *Quality of Life Research: An International Journal of Quality of Life Aspects of Treatment, Care & Rehabilitation, 11*(4), 379–388.

Livingston, H. M., Livingston, M. G., & Fell, S. (1994). The Lockerbie disaster: A 3-year follow-up of elderly victims. *International Journal of Geriatric Psychiatry, 9*(12), 989–994.

March, J. S., Amaya-Jackson, L., Murray, M. C., & Schulte, A. (1998). Cognitive–behavioral psychotherapy for children and adolescent with posttraumatic stress disorder after a single incident stressor. *Journal of the American Academy of Child and Adolescent Psychiatry, 37,* 585–593.

McFarlane, A. C. (1987). Posttraumatic functioning in a longitudinal study of children following a natural disaster. *Journal of the American Academy of Child and Adolescent Psychiatry, 26,* 764–769.

McMurray, L., & Steiner, W. (2000). Natural disasters and service delivery to individuals with severe mental illness—ice storm 1998. *Canadian Journal of Psychiatry, 45*(4). Retrieved July 18, 2005, from EBSCO/Host.

National Institute on Aging (1990). *The Behavioral and Social Research Program at the National Institute on Aging: History of a Decade.* Bethesda, MD: National Institute on Aging.

Norris, F. (1994). Frequency and impact of traumatic life events in the older population. *National Center for PTSD Clinical Quarterly, 4*(1), 8–9.

Norris, F., Friedman, M. J., Watson, P. J., Byrne, C. M., Diaz, E., & Kaniasty, K. (2002). 60,000 disaster victims speak: Part I. An empirical review of the empirical literature, 1981–2001. *Psychiatry: Interpersonal & Biological Processes, 65*(3), 207–243.

O'Brien, N. (2003). Emergency preparedness for older people. *International Longevity Center (USA): Issue Brief,* 1–5.

Olness, K. (1999). New handbook offers advice on aiding children. *The Kansas City Star.*

Oriol, W. (1999). *Psychosocial issues for older adults in disasters* (DHHS Publication No. ESDRB SMA 99-3323). Emergency Services and Disaster Relief Branch, Center for Mental Health Services (CMHS), Substance Abuse and Mental Health Services Administration. Washington, DC: Department of Health and Human Services.

Phifer, J. E. (1990). Psychological distress and somatic symptoms after natural disaster: Differential vulnerability among older adults. *Psychology and Aging, 5,* 412–420.

Piaget, J. (1952). *The origin of intelligence in children.* New York: International Universities Press.

Practice Parameter for Psychiatric Consultation to Schools (2005). *Journal of the American Academy of Child & Adolescent Psychiatry, Vol 44(10),* pp. 1068–1084.

PrepareNow.Org. (2005). Supporting special needs and vulnerable populations in disaster. Retrieved March 19, 2006 from www.preparenow.org/prepare

Raphael, B. (1986). *When disaster strikes: How individuals and communities cope with catastrophe.* New York: Basic Books.

Rowe, J. W., & Kahn, R. L. (1997). Successful aging. *Gerontologist, 37*(4), 433–440.

Sanders, S., Boy, S. L., & Bowie, Y. D. (2003). Lessons learned on forced relocation of older adults: The impact of Hurricane Andrew on health, mental health, and social support of public housing residents. *Journal of Gerontological Social Work, 40*(4), 23–35.

Scheeringa, M. S., & Gaensauer, T. J. (2000). Posttraumatic stress disorder. In C. H. Zeanah Jr. (Ed.), *Handbook of infant mental health* (2nd ed.) (pp. 369–381). New York: Guilford Press.

Shelby, J. S. (1997). Rubble, disruption, and tears: Helping young survivors of natural disaster. In H. G. Kaduson, D. M. Cangelosi, & C. E. Schaefer (Eds.), *The playing cure: Individualized play therapy for specific childhood problems* (pp. 143–169). Lanham, MS: Jason Aronson.

Shinfuku, N. (2005). The experience of the Kobe earthquake. In J. J. López-Ibor, G. Christodoulou, M. Maj, N. Sartorius, & A. Okasha (Eds.), *Disasters and mental health* (pp. 127–136). Chichester, England: Wiley.

Sullivan, H. S. (1953). *Interpersonal theory of psychiatry.* New York: Norton.

Swenson, C. C., Saylor, C. F., & Powell, M. P. (1996). Impact of a natural disaster on preschool children: Adjustment 14 months after a hurricane. *American Journal of Orthopsychiatry, 66,* 122–130.

Tierny, J. (2000). Post-traumatic stress disorder in children: Controversies and unresolved issues. *Journal of Child & Adolescent Psychiatric Nursing, 13*(4), 147–159.

Ticehurst, S., Webster, R., Carr, V., & Lewin, T. (1996). Psychological impact of an earthquake on the elderly. *International Journal of Geriatric Psychiatry, 2*(11), 943–951.

U.S. Department of Health and Human Services. (1996). *Responding to the needs of people with serious and persistent mental illness in times of major disaster* (DHHS Publication No. SMA 96-3077). Emergency Services and Disaster Relief Branch, Center for Mental Health Services (CMHS), Substance Abuse and Mental Health Services Administration. Washington, DC: Department of Health and Human Services.

Vincent, N. (1998). Children's reactions to Hurricane Andrew: A forty-one month follow-up. *Dissertation Abstracts International: Section B: The Sciences & Engineering, 59*(2-B), 0891.

Young, B. H., Ford, J. D., Ruzek, J. I., Friedman, M. J. & Gusman, F. D. (1998). *Disaster mental health services: A guidebook for clinicians and administrators* (pp. 1–158). White River Junction, VT: National Center for PTSD.

Yule, W. (1989). The effects of disasters on children. *Association of Child Psychology and Psychiatry Newsletter, 11*(6), 3–6.

Yule, W., Udwin, O., & Bolton, D. (2002). Mass transportation disasters. In A. M. La Greca, W. K. Silverman, E. M. Vernberg, & M. C. Roberts (Eds.), *Helping children cope with disasters and terrorism* (pp. 223–240). Washington, DC: American Psychological Association.

We are threatened with suffering from three directions: from our own body which is doomed to decay and dissolution and which cannot even do without pain and anxiety as warning signals; from the external world, which may rage against us with overwhelming and merciless forces of destruction; and finally from our relations to other men.

Sigmund Freud

The Challenges of Counseling in Chaos

CHAPTER **7**

We begin the part on disaster mental health (DMH) practice with a chapter describing unique aspects of the field. The practice of DMH is different from traditional types of clinical work. No one comes to an office. In fact, there is no office and no waiting room. There are no scheduled appointments. There are no insurance forms. Counseling can last for a few minutes or for a few hours. If there is one thing that is predictable, it is that the practice of DMH is unpredictable. You can never be sure what you are likely to see, smell, or hear. You might have little to do one day and find yourself inundated with many clients the next. You often need to make on-the-spot decisions about how to best make use of your time with clients and the community. Typically, you are assigned to go wherever you are most needed, and at large disasters, some of the settings where you might work can be most unusual. The ability to be flexible and have an open mind is essential.

In this chapter, we describe how one prepares to be active in DMH, including determining whether this is the right time in your life to become involved in the field, preevent self-care, and how to get the proper training and credentials. We describe the settings and also the players and stakeholders—those individuals and organizations who are likely to be a part of a disaster response. We also describe the practitioners—those mental health professionals who are at the scene. We review some of the many practical considerations such as what you should pack and what you should wear when you go on an assignment. Finally, we discuss the occupational hazards of burnout, compassion fatigue, and vicarious traumatization, and we revisit the importance of self-care in preventing those responses.

IS DISASTER MENTAL HEALTH RIGHT FOR YOU NOW?

DMH workers should not, under any circumstances within personal control, be exposed to physical danger. You should not see yourself as a first responder or hero pulling people from a burning building. In fact, you should make efforts to be nowhere near a burning or collapsing building where you might get in the way of trained emergency services personnel. To be sure, given the chaotic nature of disasters, DMH helpers may sometimes inadvertently be placed in danger, if, for example, aftershocks shake an earthquake recovery scene or a second bombing follows a first attack. In general, DMH workers do not reach the disaster scene until the immediate danger of the impact period has safely passed. However, although DMH workers should not be exposed to physical danger in the course of disaster work, they can and often are exposed to devastating sights and to extreme emotional pain and trauma among the survivors they are trying to aid. It is therefore particularly important to monitor self-care at every stage of the response and to be certain that this is a field that suits you.

Most mental health professionals have experience working with people in pain, but DMH fieldwork brings counselors into regular contact with victims who are experiencing trauma. You might also find yourself in a room filled with people in acute states of grief: Survivors may appear numb or may be frighteningly expressive, wailing or throwing things. In traditional clinical work, the soothing environment of a serene office can help provide a comfortable container for difficult and painful feelings, but in DMH there are no such props or buffers. DMH practitioners come into contact with many organizations and work in a constantly changing "playing field." There is often little that is orderly about the experience of DMH. If order, structure, and calm are prerequisites for you to practice successfully, DMH may not be the best fit for you. If most of your experience is in administration or psychological testing, DMH may not be the best place to learn or rehearse your clinical skills.

Therefore, self-care should begin with self-reflection before the event. Imagine yourself at a disaster: What do you feel? Feeling some nervousness or fear does not in any way disqualify you from disaster work; in fact, it is a normal response. If you imagine that you would not be able to hold back tears if you heard someone describe a missing loved one, this, too, is natural and healthy. However, if you imagine that you would not be able to function if you heard a tragic story or you realize that you cannot tolerate being near intense pain, it would be a sign that this type of work may not be for you at this time. Sometimes disaster work is not a good fit for someone at a particular point in his or her life. Perhaps you have young children or an elderly parent who needs care, or you may have a particularly demanding work schedule. Perhaps you don't feel seasoned enough as a clinician. It is entirely permissible to postpone doing this work to a time best suited to you. Unfortunately, disasters are an inevitable aspect of human existence, so you need not worry that the opportunity to do this work might pass you by. There will always be ample opportunities to get involved at a later time.

To be certain that your circumstances will permit you to be an effective DMH worker, you should not only engage in self-reflection but also have a conversation with friends, family, and work associates well before you go on an assignment. Can you leave work or your family if there is a community emergency? How much time can you commit to being available or on-call in the event of a disaster without overextending yourself? You will be a more effective DMH worker if you feel supported by family, friends, and colleagues while on assignment. These conversations should be attended to considerably in advance of accepting an assignment because desperate calls from work or an overburdened spouse can interfere with or undermine your effectiveness while on the job.

Even veteran DMH workers should continue to practice self-reflection throughout their careers to be sure that changing circumstances—including changes resulting directly from their disaster experiences—have not compromised their ability to help. In a general discussion about training counselors to concentrate on the therapeutic relationship as a core determinant of patient improvement, Lambert and Barley (2001) suggest that "clinicians are advised to watch for a reduction in their ability to empathize and relate to clients that can indicate professional stress or burn out. For therapists to be effective, it is essential that they take care of themselves so that they are better able to care for clients." This can be a challenge for DMH workers who are commonly subject to vicarious traumatization due to the often-devastated plights of their clients (James & Gilliland, 2005), a reaction we discuss in more detail at the end of this chapter. And contributing even more strain, as the National Institute of Mental Health report (NIMH, 2002) points out, in responding to episodes of mass violence and disaster, "early interventions are usually provided with limited resources in an atmosphere of chaos, environmental pollution, and the possibility of continued threats. To be effective, training should incorporate content that addresses the organizational, procedural, emotional, and environmental aspects of this operational reality." DMH workers must be trained not only in efforts to bring order to chaos but also in how to retain their empathy in the face of great suffering.

TRAINING TO RESPOND

Should you decide that the time is right to become involved in DMH, how do you prepare for the realities of disaster response? The American Red Cross conducts the longest-established training. With its mission of humanitarian relief, the American Red Cross has the recognized authority to be present at domestic disasters. It is usually among the very first agencies to provide help, and mental health assistance is incorporated in service delivery. The Red Cross pioneered the development of Disaster Mental Health Services training, currently referred to as Mental Health Services. (Thus, when we refer to MHS helpers throughout this chapter, we specifically mean practitioners working under the auspices of the Red Cross, and references to DMH mean disaster mental health in general.) American Red Cross MHS have four primary functions (ARC, 1995):

1. To monitor the level of stress among workers and clients
2. To reduce high levels of stress
3. To prevent serious short- and long-term emotional trauma
4. To provide opportunities for healthy emotional response

To be eligible for American Red Cross training, you must be a licensed mental health provider, and you must take the Red Cross course "Foundations of Disaster Mental Health." This 1-day course covers the emotional impact of disaster and teaches how MHS supports American Red Cross paid and volunteer staff as well as those impacted by disaster. The Red Cross recommends that MHS workers take other Red Cross courses, most especially the course on working with diverse populations. All American Red Cross courses are made available at no cost to paid and volunteer MHS workers. Successful completion of these courses allows the licensed practitioner to participate in local disaster responses as a member of and under the direction of the American Red Cross. With experience, further course work, and recommendations, MHS volunteers can participate in national disasters as part of the American Red Cross's Disaster Services Human Resources system. Virtually all MHS workers are volunteers, though travel expenses and a daily allowance are paid on national assignments.

Some mental health professionals would like to serve as American Red Cross volunteers without the American Red Cross training, but no matter how skilled you might be as a practitioner and no matter how well trained you are in crisis counseling or as a trauma expert, the American Red Cross training is necessary in order to participate under the auspices of this agency. We very much support this policy because even the most experienced clinician needs to learn the scope of MHS interventions and how to work within the policies and structure of the organization. The "Foundations of Disaster Mental Health" course can also serve as an excellent review for the most veteran clinician.

Although the American Red Cross training and credentialing may be the best entry into disaster work, there are also other routes. Other relief agencies, such as the Green Cross and the National Organization of Victims Assistance, also provide disaster mental health training and, through their response efforts, offer opportunities for DMH practice. At the present time, there are not many programs or universities offering training in DMH. However, some professional organizations, such as state psychological associations, offer DMH training opportunities to their members, making them eligible to be part of a disaster response network. Most of these professional organizations, including the National Association of Social Workers and the American Psychiatric Association, have statements of understanding (SOUs) with the American Red Cross. SOUs serve to define a particular group's role in relation to the delivery of relief assistance by the American Red Cross.

State and local government mental health organizations are also beginning to offer DMH trainings to their employees. The Office of Victims Services, discussed later, offers some instruction to those who may deliver assistance at a disaster. We also see the beginning of DMH trainings at colleges and universities. The Disaster Mental Health Institute at the University of South Dakota established the first doctoral program with a specialty track in Clinical/Disaster Psychology. They also offer a graduate certificate in DMH whereby students from a variety of mental health fields can do some course work in residence over the summer; other coursework is done from home. In the private sector, institutions and groups such as the International Critical Incident Stress Foundation also offer trainings on how to provide mental health interventions after a disaster. (For a general overview of trainings offered by this organization, see http://www.icisf.org/.)

Training Drills

Of course, training in DMH must go beyond courses taught in a classroom. To become proficient in DMH, you first need to become a regular and active participant in a disaster response setting where you can be mentored and supervised. If you become an American Red Cross volunteer, this could mean responding frequently when the local American Red Cross chapter needs help. Or it could mean going to a large disaster where you will spend a concentrated period of time focusing exclusively on disaster work.

In addition to learning by doing, **drills** are conducted for disaster workers to practice their skills. These exercises are another unique aspect of disaster services. They provide an opportunity for responders to role-play various emergency scenarios and are intended to increase the responders' familiarity with not only the circumstances surrounding a disaster but also the personnel active in disaster response. Preparing for effective mental health interventions involves developing relationships with other mental health staff, other disaster workers, and other organizations such as fire and police departments. It is desirable to meet and develop a connection to the people you will be working with at a disaster scene, before the disaster. Knowing the participants, their names, titles, functions, and styles or personalities is an important aspect of predisaster planning and preparation.

There are essentially two types of drills: **tabletop drills** in which a scenario is described and those around the table have an opportunity to discuss practical and clinical issues and **live drills** in which volunteers act out prearranged roles as survivors/clients, providing mental health workers with the opportunity to role-play their response.

In the spring of 2001, American Red Cross Disaster Services in Greater New York held a tabletop exercise where we planned for our response should a commercial plane crash into a large populated area in New York City. Most participants around the table were MHS workers because, in the aftermath of this worst case–scenario event, there is typically more need for mental health services than for food and shelter. Much of the attention of the group was focused on practical considerations: how we would get to the site and which organizations we could expect to find at the scene. We discussed the responsibilities of the alphabet soup of organizations—for example, the National Transportation Safety Board (NTSB) and the Federal Bureau of Investigation (FBI)—that would be involved. What can be unnerving about these drills is the sense that we are not planning for what might happen *if* there is a plane crash, but rather how we will respond *when* there is one. At the end of this exercise, many participants remarked that this was a particularly horrific scenario. We were grateful that nothing like this had ever happened in New York City. It was painfully ironic that a few short months later what occurred on September 11th was so much more tragic than the worst-case scenario that we had imagined.

With an increased awareness of the possibility of a terrorism/weapons of mass destruction attack in the United States, there has been a need for more elaborate drills. For example, "Operation Recovery," the largest human services table-top drill in New York City history, was developed by the Department of Homeland Security and carried out with the participation of more than 80 agencies in December 2003. The featured scenario presented three near-simultaneous explosions in three boroughs of New York City, including the release of potentially hazardous material. Representatives from many organizations (American Red Cross, State Mental Health, and Disaster Psychiatry Outreach, for example) formed one group tasked with the following:

- Identify the mental health needs of a community after a large-scale disaster.
- Make decisions regarding how many, where, and when to deploy mental health workers.
- Identify and address coordination issues with hospitals and human services providers.
- Identify health, safety, and self-care issues for mental health workers, public health workers, health-care providers, and other social service providers.
- Address the needs of vulnerable populations.

Drills like this are useful because they raise awareness of likely needs that various agencies can prepare for in advance of an actual disaster. For example, in thinking about the issues that they would face in the scenario just described, mental health participants were eager to obtain information on the language and cultural issues likely to arise in such a diverse city. They especially wanted to know if language barriers would create obstacles for mental heath providers. As part of the drill, the NYC Office of Emergency Management (OEM) was able to provide requested demographic information: Of the population impacted in the scenario, 40% were composed of immigrants, and many households did not have an English-speaking person in the household. Instead they spoke languages such as Urdu, Chinese, Tagalog, Hindi, Gujarathi, Italian, Hebrew, or Persian. In one "affected" neighborhood in Queens, 7.5% of residents were children under age 5 years, 12% were disabled and had difficulty going outside the home, and 14% were considered linguistically isolated (meaning that no household member age 14 years or older speaks English well). This cultural and language diversity suggests some of the challenges faced by DMH workers. Fortunately, some human services groups specializing in immigrant affairs and language services are able to help. There is also increasing acknowledgment in emergency management that adequate disaster response globally requires even more enhanced predisaster planning and preparedness to ensure that the services of these agencies are coordinated effectively.

Although tabletop drills are useful for raising awareness of logistical needs, live drills provide the opportunity for responders to become desensitized to chaotic and disturbing disaster scenes. They also offer a chance to interact with the multiple stakeholders who are summoned to disasters. Participants in live drills are immersed in efforts to coordinate and communicate in a scripted yet unpredictable rehearsal where one can end up "dead" by accidentally walking into a "hot zone."

Live drills are staged at a range of possible disaster sites such as major transportation hubs. Drills vary in their verisimilitude to actual disasters. Aviation drills are often among the most compelling because the expectation is that the carnage would be high after an airplane crash. These exercises can be held on the tarmacs of local airports, with plumes of smoke rising from the ground, fake debris from the "wreckage" strewn about, and dozens of role players realistically made up to simulate various injuries. Mental health workers provide support to the victims as they are carried into ambulances as well as to the uninjured and first responders. The most important part of these drills is to expose workers to the sights, sounds, and commotion of such events so that they can function optimally under actual stimulation overload.

RESPONDING TO DISASTERS

In addition to the Red Cross, mental health departments at the city, county, or state levels can all deploy mental health workers to disasters. As mentioned above, professional associations such as the American Psychological Association, the National Association of Social Workers, the American Counseling Association, and the American Association of Marriage and Family Therapy also have agreements with the Red Cross and can deploy their own trained volunteers to a disaster. If you are asked to respond to a disaster, what are you likely to encounter? To some extent, it depends on the size of the disaster and on whether it occurs in your local region or if you are part of a national response effort. We describe each situation, with the assumption that you are likely to be deployed via the American Red Cross.

Small or Local Disasters

Across the country, each local Red Cross chapter has a Disaster Action Team (DAT) made up of volunteers who are ready to respond any hour of the day to breaking disasters. If the disaster is "small"—a residential fire, for example—a DAT sent by the local Red Cross chapter is first on the scene and makes the decision about whether to request the involvement of MHS. All staff and volunteer responders are instructed to consult with MHS under the following circumstances (ARC, 2002):

- When a death or serious injury has occurred
- When children are involved

- When pets have been lost
- When the person affected by the disaster is clearly in deep distress or grief
- When people have major negative reaction to being displaced, such as refusing to leave a damaged home
- When an incident involves several families
- When people act very confused and are not making sense

MHS workers can provide support to clients and also to Red Cross workers on the scene, as well as to emergency services personnel as needed. In large urban areas such as New York City, the fire and police departments have their own mental health services and are less likely to rely on Red Cross MHS, but rural communities around the country may depend on volunteer firefighters, who are more likely to be supported by MHS. Disaster survivors in hospitals are not likely to be assisted by MHS because hospitals typically have their own social workers or other mental health providers. It should also be noted that it is not unusual for clients to reject the offer of mental health services and to specifically request help from family, friends, or clergy.

In large urban areas, responding to a local disaster can present the volunteer with extraordinary challenges, beginning with how to reach the client or scene by driving through city traffic or navigating bus and subway lines. There is also the challenge of diversity. As discussed previously, the populations of most urban areas contain a wide range of ethnicities, religions, cultures, and classes, often with large immigrant and non–English speaking populations. On occasion, a translator must be sought and deployed.

Providing services to clients in rural areas presents different but equally difficult challenges. Clients can live in isolated regions and are sometimes without transportation, so helpers must arrange transportation to shelters and service agencies if necessary. Deploying available volunteers in a timely manner can also be a problem because it can be a very long drive from a volunteer's home to the disaster site. As well as in cities, cultural and linguistic diversity are not uncommon in certain rural areas in the United States.

Although large national disasters tend to get most of the attention and headlines, local disasters can expose DMH workers to extraordinary trauma. Most local assignments involve assisting families who have lost their homes and possessions to fires or floods. This "routine" disaster typically overwhelms survivors. When there is injury or death due to a local residential fire or any other disaster, the grief and trauma experienced by family members can result in as difficult an assignment for a DMH worker as can any larger-scale disaster, like in the following example:

In the winter of 2000, there was a residential fire in the rural northeast. The fire, the result of a malfunctioning coffee maker, occurred in the middle of the night. Both parents and two children were rescued, but the youngest child perished, despite the extraordinary efforts of emergency services personnel. Everyone on the scene was traumatized as they heard the trapped child call for help. Dozens of people who attempted to help this family in the moments, weeks, and months that passed after the event were also traumatized by their story. Mental health workers also requested help for themselves as a result of their own vicarious traumatization.

As this case demonstrates, local disasters may be small in scope but they can be extreme in intensity and provide daunting challenges to DMH workers.

Large or National Disasters

If a disaster is too large to be effectively responded to by a local chapter of the Red Cross, a regional office is contacted, and MHS workers can be deployed from throughout the state and/or nearby states. If the disaster is also beyond the scope of the region to cope with, the nationwide network of Red Cross people and resources is called upon. This national network, the Disaster Services Human Resources (DSHR) system, is automatically called when the president of the United States declares a national disaster. American Red Cross DSHR reaches out to Red Cross mental health workers and other Red Cross volunteers from all over the country to determine if they can give 3 weeks of service to assist in disaster relief. Volunteers may be asked if they can be ready to leave their homes, families, and work to go to another part of the country within 24 hours. MHS workers usually commit to somewhat less time, from 10 days to 2 weeks, with the understanding that they have heavy professional obligations.

National disasters are likely to involve not only local and national Red Cross mental health workers but also many other groups and organizations, including the disaster response networks of psychologists, social workers, counselors, and marriage and family therapists. When there is a large disaster, state, county, and local mental health organizations, both public and private, enter the scene. Psychiatrists can become involved. There may also be mental health personnel from clinics, psychotherapy and counseling institutes, hospitals, and universities, as well as private practitioners who want to lend a hand. That is not the end of the list of people and groups who may become involved when a disaster is large and well publicized. There can be massage therapists, creative arts therapists, and pet therapists. There can be federal agencies, victims' services, school systems, universities, hospitals, and community- and faith-based organizations. There will be press, police with sirens and lights, and sometimes heavy equipment and construction workers.

On-Scene Hierarchies

Given all of these different players involved in disaster response, how do you know who is in command? If it is a suspected or known crime scene, the police or a federal law enforcement agency such as the FBI is in charge. If there is fire or an explosion that is not the result of a criminal act, the fire department takes the lead. For plane crashes, the NTSB is in charge. If the cause of a plane crash or fire is unclear, there may be ambiguity about which agency is in command. The changing hierarchy can be confusing.

Mental health organizations are in the process of developing their own order and hierarchy to ensure efficiency in their disaster response efforts, drawing up memorandums of understanding between groups to stipulate who is in command under different circumstances. But although there are agreements and understandings, there is not yet a comprehensive structure to the mental health response to a disaster. Everyone involved in disaster response discusses issues of coordination and cooperation frequently. In contrast to any other type of mental health response, in DMH there can be hundreds of professionals involved with the same event. Counselors should be forewarned that in the aftermath of a large disaster, confusion and problems with coordination can become significant issues and a major cause of stress. The following is a list of some of the potential stressors that you might anticipate working with the many other mental health providers at a large disaster

- If you are part of a local response to a national disaster, you can feel displaced when large numbers of counselors arrive from out of town. You might also feel proprietary because this is *your* hometown and you know the practical and clinical issues better than these outsiders. It is important for out-of-town practitioners to be sensitive to these feelings. It is equally important that local helpers be hospitable to volunteers who have left their homes, work, and families to be of assistance.
- If you arrive at a central disaster location, you may find yourself waiting to be deployed with many other mental health professionals. You may have to wait for hours to be assigned to a specific location. In large-scale operations, this experience is not unusual and should be expected.
- Similarly, it is difficult for administrators to predict precisely how many counselors to deploy to a particular setting. Based on the number of clients served on one day, a decision could be made to deploy a certain number of mental health workers the next, but the situation is always fluid; so although the estimate is often appropriate, sometimes it is not. It is not unusual for too few or too many counselors to be at a scene. If there are too few counselors, this needs to be communicated to supervisors so that additional resources can be deployed. If there are too many, this also needs to be communicated, and counselors need to be careful to not inundate clients or compete with other mental health workers for clients in order to feel useful.

Just as local DMH helpers may experience issues when out-of-town volunteers enter their home territory, the visiting volunteers also face difficulties in adapting to a new setting, as in the following case:

In spring 2001, in the aftermath of Tropical Storm Allison, volunteers in rural Louisiana were warned to watch out for cottonmouths and water moccasins, poisonous and extremely aggressive snakes that, the volunteers were told, would attack people if they saw them. Relief workers were also told that the recent 20 inches of rainfall had caused alligators and fire ants to seek higher ground. One local volunteer said it was unlikely that anyone would see alligators or snakes, but that fire ants were a much more realistic problem. Fire ants sting like bees, and their stingers can get lodged under the skin and need to be scraped out one by one. After floods these ants usually manage to assemble on sticks or pieces of wood and float along until they find dry land so, the local volunteer advised, "If you see a stick or an object that appears to be moving, don't touch it."

It seems almost surreal to have to consider details like the fire ant factor in counseling victims of disaster, but this illustrates the kind of strange conditions and unnerving warnings about unfamiliar threats that sometimes provide a backdrop for the real work of DMH. In this particular case, that work involved helping thousands of families, many of whom had lost everything in the storm. Mental health helpers who volunteer at disaster sites outside of their own home territory are often called on to adapt almost instantaneously to regional or cultural variations. Indeed, volunteers who come from out of town to assist with urban disasters can experience the same kind of confusion and dislocation that urban residents experience when they assist in rural areas.

SPIRITUAL CARE IN DISASTER RESPONSE

Pastoral counselors and other members of the clergy, such as chaplains, rabbis, priests and imams, often work alongside mental health helpers in disaster operations. Interdisciplinary, collaborative work can be challenging. Some mental health workers will try to maintain distance from religious and spiritual care workers, preferring to be more closely identified with the secular and scientific traditions. Spiritual care workers can be aware of and sensitive to this perspective. Similarly, some spiritual care workers feel that the exclusively secular approach of some mental health counselors is incomplete.

Both mental health care and spiritual care are important in tending to disaster victims. Americans are very religious; 96% believe in God, 90% report that they pray regularly, and 60% say they pray every day (Brawer, Handal, Fabricatore, Roberts, & Wajda-Johnston, 2002). According to a national poll conducted less than a month after the attacks of September 11, 2001, 59% of Americans said they would be likely or very likely to seek help from a spiritual counselor, whereas only 40% reported they would be likely or very likely to seek help from a mental health professional (Jacobs & Quevillon, 2001). These findings make clear that an effective response necessitates an integrated joining of forces between mental health and spiritual care workers.

The American Red Cross September 11 response included more than 900 religious leaders volunteering at various sites throughout the greater New York area (Roberts, 2002). The following case, based on an article by one of the authors (Halpern, 2001), illustrates the potential value of collaboration between MHS and Spiritual Care Services, as well as one of the more unusual settings where MHS can be conducted:

In the weeks following September 11, 2001, the New York City Fire Department arranged boat trips to ground zero for the families of lost firefighters so that they could see in person where their loved ones perished. Firefighters and Red Cross Mental Health and Spiritual Care workers were assigned to the Marine Boat Fire Station in the Brooklyn Navy yard to meet family members and escort them by boat to lower Manhattan. MHS and Spiritual Care workers, present to support the surviving firefighters and grieving families, joined the firefighters in the station before the family members arrived.

Every firefighter in New York City lost friends and colleagues. The relationships were close, with loyalty built from depending on one another for their lives. These survivors were exhausted from helping the grieving families while grieving themselves. One man said, "I haven't slept in my own bed for days. We don't want to leave a widow or parent alone, so we tell them we are too tired to go home and ask if we can sleep on the couch. This way they are not alone, and they don't think we are doing them a favor." MHS and Spiritual Care Services volunteers listened to their stories of stress and loss, offered bolstering and gratitude, praised their loyalty, and explored and strengthened constructive coping efforts.

When family members arrived, counselors initially offered them basic sustenance in the form of coffee and snacks. We sat and talked about the missing cousin, brother, husband, or son. There were identifiable mood changes from the beginning to the end of the trip. As people boarded the boat, settled down, and chatted, there was a social phase. On the boat, MHS provided family members with food and water, handouts ("Helping Children after Disaster," "When Bad Things Happen"), and teddy bears. Almost everyone gratefully accepted a stuffed animal, and many held onto them for the rest of the day. As the boat rounded the tip of Manhattan and the skyscrapers with gaping wounds came into view, the mood changed to shock and disbelief. National Guard, police, construction workers, and officials all stood silently at attention and often saluted as our group of family members, firefighters, and Red Cross volunteers walked solemnly from the boat to the site.

At ground zero, family members held maps to help them locate where their loved one was last seen and was probably buried. In this context of being with those who were experiencing traumatic loss, the World Trade Center site was a mass grave, unimaginable and indescribable. This view of utter destruction with few identifiable objects made it achingly clear to all that no one would be found alive. It was time for a blessing, and a chaplain offered a beautiful and simple prayer, asking for God's help to provide strength and praising the fallen firefighters for saving the lives of thousands of civilians. An informal procession began to a nearby wall that had been converted into a shrine for all the uniformed personnel who perished in this disaster. Here, there were mementoes of those who had died: photos, patches, poetry, flowers, and teddy bears to accompany the tears and prayers. The mood on the boat ride home was quiet and reflective. No one sobbed. Most of the time it didn't seem enough, but all we could provide was kindness.

The Spiritual Care workers who we have collaborated with on this and other scenes have expertise in bringing together members of the community, in assisting survivors with rituals, and in offering solace to the bereaved. They may be more accustomed to being with people in anguish than are most mental health providers and many understand the importance of offering a "ministry of presence." It is inevitable that mental health and spiritual care workers will see one another at the scene of a disaster, and it is therefore important for these groups to work well together.

OTHER ORGANIZATIONS ACTIVE IN DISASTER

In addition to the mental health practitioners and spiritual care workers involved in disaster response, a range of government agencies and volunteer groups are active in response and recovery. At a large disaster operation, you may come into contact with some or many of these organizations. We first describe the public and then the private organizations; be advised that there are also businesses active in disaster response.

Government Agencies

A number of government agencies are involved in different aspects of disaster relief, most notably the following.

Federal Emergency Management Agency   When local and state governments believe that responding to a disaster is beyond their capabilities, the governor of the state can request that the president declare that a major disaster or emergency exists. This declaration activates an array of federal programs to assist in the response and recovery effort. The Federal Emergency Management Agency (FEMA), now part of the Department of Homeland Security, has the responsibility of coordinating that response. Individual assistance from FEMA can include temporary housing or grants to repair damage from the disaster, funds to replace a disaster-damaged home, and direct assistance or grants for the construction of a new home. Grants can also be supplied for medical, dental, funeral, personal property, transportation, moving and storage, and other expenses.

FEMA also coordinates Small Business Administration Disaster Loans to repair or replace homes, personal property, or businesses that sustained damages. Also available are disaster unemployment assistance benefits as well as reemployment services to those who have become unemployed because of major disasters. Through an agreement with FEMA, the Young Lawyers Division of the American Bar Association provides free legal assistance to disaster victims. This assistance can include help with insurance claims, consultations on landlord/tenant problems, assisting in consumer protection matters, and replacement of wills and other important legal documents that may have been destroyed. FEMA can also help survivors obtain special tax considerations.

Another FEMA program, the Crisis Counseling Assistance and Training Program, is designed to provide supplemental funding to states for short-term crisis counseling services for people affected by disasters declared by the president. A state may request either or both of two types of funding: The **immediate services** program is intended to enable the state or local agency to respond to immediate mental health needs with screening, diagnostic, and counseling techniques, as well as outreach services such as public information and community networking. The **regular services** program is designed to provide up to 9 months of crisis counseling, community outreach, and consultation and education services. (For a general overview of FEMA disaster programs for individuals, see http://www.fema.gov/rrr/inassist.shtm.)

State Emergency Management Office   Each state has a State Emergency Management Office (SEMO) These offices are responsible for coordinating all activities necessary to protect communities from natural, technological, and human-made disasters as well as other emergencies that threaten the residents of the state. SEMO coordinates the response of various state agencies, attempting to ensure that the most appropriate resources reach the areas impacted by disaster. SEMO also works with local governments, volunteer organizations, and the private sector across the state to develop disaster-preparedness plans and mitigation projects and to provide training and exercise activities. (For a listing of all SEMOs, see http://www.fema.gov/fema/statedr.shtm.)

Office for Victims of Crime   When a disaster is the result of a criminal act, the Office for Victims of Crime (OVC), established by the 1984 Victims of Crime Act, is involved in overseeing a number of programs that benefit victims, including providing funding to states so that they can provide services to help victims recover. One of the units within OVC that is most relevant to disaster work is the Terrorism and International Victims Unit (TIVU). TIVU staff is responsible for coordinating OVC resources and funding for victims of terrorism and for administering the new International Terrorism Victims Compensation Program. OVC notes that as countries and their citizens become more linked through tourism, Internet usage, and international trade, issues of violent crime and victimization increasingly become an international concern. TIVU attempts to improve awareness of and responsiveness to the needs of terrorism victims and individuals who are victimized outside the borders of their own country. (For information, see http://www.ojp.usdoj.gov/ovc.)

Volunteer Organizations

As long as there have been natural and human-caused disasters bringing tragedy and despair, there have been people willing to supply victims with food and clothing and even to rebuild damaged or destroyed homes. Many of these groups did not and do not see themselves as providing mental health support, but one can see that their actions not only address material needs but also inspire trust and restore faith. As we will explore more fully in the next chapter, these actions can be seen as part of psychological first aid.

The American Red Cross   Each year, the American Red Cross responds to more than 60,000 disasters. Red Cross disaster relief focuses on meeting people's immediate, emergency, disaster-caused needs. When a disaster threatens or strikes, the Red Cross provides shelter, food, and health and mental health services to address basic human needs.

Red Cross volunteers and staff are divided into divisions that focus on specific needs. Community Services workers provide individuals, families, and emergency workers with shelter, food, and water, mobile and fixed feeding, and bulk distribution of items like cleanup supplies or bottled water. Health Services workers ensure that clients' postdisaster health needs are met by providing or helping clients to obtain items such as lost medication, eyeglasses, dentures, and health equipment. Welfare Information workers assist family members outside the affected community to establish contact with their loved ones who have been impacted by a disaster.

Client Caseworkers provide information, make referrals to other agencies, and deliver financial assistance so that clients can find temporary housing and buy clothing, food, toiletries, and household items. The goal of Client Caseworkers is to help clients bridge the gap between what they are able to do on their own and what more is needed to allow them to resume a normal life. Because all American Red Cross assistance is funded by donations, Client Caseworkers strive to satisfy immediate needs, but they also make certain that clients have proper identification and that the damage being compensated is a result of the disaster and not a preexisting condition. Ultimately, these workers want to assist clients so that they have something to wear; something to eat, drink, and cook with; a safe place to stay with something to sleep on; a place to store food, clothing, and other possessions; and a plan to return to work.

The core of Red Cross disaster relief is the assistance given to affected individuals and families to enable them to resume their normal daily activities independently, to come close to reestablishing their predisaster functioning. The Red Cross also feeds emergency workers, handles inquiries from concerned family members outside the disaster area, provides blood and blood products to disaster victims, and helps those affected by disaster to access other available resources. MHS workers assist not only clients but also other staff and volunteers.

National Voluntary Organizations Active in Disaster   National Voluntary Organizations Active in Disaster (NVOAD) is not a direct service delivery organization. Instead, it attempts to coordinate planning efforts by many voluntary organizations responding to disaster. There are regular meetings between members of NVOAD so that when a disaster occurs members from the various organizations have trained and prepared together. NVOAD began by serving as a hub of communication among voluntary organizations engaged in disaster response, in order to bring them together to promote more effective service to disaster victims. The guiding principles through which NVOAD serves member organizations include the following:

- *Communication.* Disseminate information through electronic mechanisms, a newsletter, a directory, research and demonstration, case studies, and critique.
- *Cooperation.* Create a climate for cooperation at all levels (including grassroots) and provide information.

- *Coordination.* Coordinate policy among member organizations and serve as a liaison, advocate, and national voice.
- *Education.* Provide training and increase awareness and preparedness in each organization.
- *Leadership development.* Give volunteer leaders training and support so as to build effective state VOAD organizations.
- *Mitigation.* Support the efforts of federal, state, and local agencies and governments and support appropriate legislation.
- *Convening mechanisms.* Put on seminars, meetings, board meetings, regional conferences, training programs, and local conferences.
- *Outreach.* Encourage the formation of and give guidance to state and regional voluntary organizations active in disaster relief.

As can be seen in the list of member organizations shown in Table 7.1, most of the groups represented in NVOAD are religious organizations. Many of these

Table 7.1 | National Voluntary Organizations Active in Disaster Member Organizations

- Adventist Community Services
- American Baptist Men
- American Radio Relay League, Inc.
- Ananda Marga Universal Relief Team
- Christian Disaster Response
- Church of the Brethren Disaster Response
- Disaster Psychiatry Outreach
- Friends Disaster Service
- International Aid
- International Relief Friendship Foundation
- Mennonite Disaster Service
- National Emergency Response Team
- Nazarene Disaster Response
- Presbyterian Church (USA)
- Society of St. Vincent de Paul
- The Phoenix Society for Burn Survivors, Inc.
- The Salvation Army
- United Methodist Committee on Relief and the General Board of Global Ministries
- Volunteers of America
- World Vision

- America's Second Harvest
- American Disaster Reserve
- American Red Cross
- Catholic Charities USA
- Christian Reformed World Relief Committee
- Church World Service
- Episcopal Relief and Development (formerly The Presiding Bishop's Fund for World Relief)
- Humane Society of the United States
- Best Friends Animal Society
- International Critical Incident Stress Foundation
- Lutheran Disaster Response
- Mercy Medical Airlift: National Patient Travel Center
- National Organization for Victim Assistance
- Northwest Medical Teams International
- REACT International, Inc.
- Southern Baptist Convention
- The Points of Light Foundation
- United Jewish Communities
- Volunteers in Technical Assistance
- Wider Church Ministries, United Church of Christ

groups have long histories of involvement in disaster relief. Our experience in working at disasters with many members of these groups is that, although individuals may be affiliated with a specific religion and set of beliefs, their work is nondenominational and is almost always filled with charity, generosity, and kindness. We describe a few of these many organizations; to learn more about NVOAD itself, see http://www.nvoad.org/about.php.

The Southern Baptist Convention describes their disaster relief program as "Christian love in action, meeting urgent needs of hurting humanity in crisis situations." Local churches can be involved in feeding, child care, elder care, clothing banks, shelter, communication center or as a collection, distribution, or information center. Churches can also be used as Service Centers for the American Red Cross. The Southern Baptists Disaster Response has built 335 mobile mass-feeding, recovery, child-care, command, and other units.

The Mennonite Disaster Service includes various constituencies of the Anabaptist church who respond to those affected by disasters in North America. While their main focus is on cleanup, repair, and rebuilding homes, they understand that this activity becomes a means of touching lives.

The Salvation Army describes itself as an "international movement, sharing in the mission of Christ for the salvation and transformation of the world. Its members are at worship and at work in over a hundred countries. Its mission is to preach the gospel of Jesus Christ and to meet human needs in His name without discrimination." The Salvation Army provides emergency assistance in the form of mobile feeding units and the distribution of donated goods including food, clothing, and household goods.

The Church of the Brethren Disaster Response provides volunteers to clean up debris and to repair or rebuild homes for disaster survivors. Caring for children after disasters has also been a significant ministry of the Church of the Brethren since 1980 when a team of volunteers first set up temporary Child Care Centers in Kalamazoo, Michigan, after a devastating tornado. Since then, over 2000 volunteers have cared for more than 67,000 children in the wake of floods, earthquakes, hurricanes, fires, ice storms, tornadoes, terrorist attacks, and air incidents.

There are many other paid and volunteer groups that are not a part of NVOAD that you might find at a disaster. For example, we have worked with members of Americorps and groups of Mormon youth who are encouraged to do community service, as well as veterinarian groups attending to the needs of pets and pet owners.

SETTINGS FOR DISASTER MENTAL HEALTH WORK

As we mentioned at the start of this chapter, DMH services are rarely delivered in an office. Unlike most clinical interactions in which the client comes to the practitioner, in DMH the helper goes to the survivors, wherever they may be. We now discuss the various settings where DMH work may be performed and the particular challenges and stressors that each kind of condition can produce.

General Settings

At the Gathering Place of a Mass-Casualty Disaster   Working at a mass-casualty disaster exposes the DMH worker to death, grief, and chaos. When there is a plane crash, family members and friends are usually told to come to a location close to the airport, such as a nearby hotel. This scene can be filled with confusion and turmoil. There are hundreds of friends, family members, emergency service and airline workers, police and other law enforcement personnel, and television and radio crews as well as print journalists. DMH begins in a scene filled with the racket and hubbub of pandemonium.

After a crash, the airline involved provides travel arrangements and escorts for the families of the victims. These escorts help take care of practical matters such as making hotel and car reservations for the families. DMH volunteers often work cooperatively with the escorts. It may seem that there is an overlap in services, but help with small tasks by mental health workers is not always an end in itself. This kind of assistance can serve as a platform for building the trusting relationship that is a prerequisite to addressing the emotional needs of the grieving survivors.

> One hotel in the New York area, the Ramada Plaza near John F. Kennedy Airport, has served as a central meeting place where family members and assorted responding agencies have gathered to obtain information, to seek consolation, to plan interventions, and to hear briefings after several air disasters. It was here that the American Red Cross and other mental health workers went to counsel survivors and support airline and hotel personnel following the crashes of TWA 800 in 1996 (230 dead), Swissair 111 in 1998 (229 dead), Egypt Air 990 in 1999 (217 dead), and American Airlines 587 in 2001 (265 dead). With each successive tragic incident, this location became more and more familiar. To emergency service personnel, the site became known as "Heartbreak Hotel."

There are many experienced counselors, competent in a wide range of situations, who find they cannot work effectively in a mass-casualty disaster. These events affect, frighten, and upset everyone at the scene, but when exposed to so much loss, some DMH workers become so distraught that they cannot be available for another. Self-monitoring and self-care become extremely important in these types of situations.

At the Site of the Disaster   DMH helpers do not usually arrive at a disaster site until after the period of impact has passed and the site has been made physically safe, but they do often go directly to the affected area in order to reach clients. This is more than just a matter of convenience for survivors: DMH workers who witness the devastation caused by a disaster can better appreciate the chaos that the client is faced with. This often means that counseling takes place in or around homes that have been damaged by natural disasters such as floods, hurricanes, or tornadoes. DMH workers sometimes arrive on the scene when families are first returning to their homes, and they may see together for the first time the devastation caused by the disaster.

The scene surrounding a disaster can be sensational and distracting, and counseling at the scene can mean experiencing unpleasant or rotten odors and seeing bizarre or horrific sights. It is the responsibility of counselors to be attentive to clients, but this can be more of a challenge if the sights and sounds of catastrophe surround them. In the same way that an individual therapist needs to expand the focus when working with a family or group, so too does a DMH worker need to be able to adjust his or her lens at a disaster site, taking in the event but concentrating on the clients. Although it may be important to see that a flood rearranged the appliances or that a tornado threw automobiles into bizarre places, this must stay in the background for the counselor, who needs to stay focused on how the client is experiencing the disaster.

Shelters   When there is an impending disaster and an evacuation is necessary or if victims cannot return to their homes because they were destroyed or damaged, shelters provide a safe haven for those who cannot stay with family or friends or stay in a hotel. These shelters, typically staffed by American Red Cross or city housing services personnel, are likely to be in churches or schools where arrangements have been made previously. The atmosphere in a shelter is often bustling and stressful as residents worry about possible damage in the case of impending disaster or contemplate their known losses in the aftermath of one. The conditions in a shelter are more crowded than most residents are used to. There is much less privacy, often with row upon row of cots placed in huge space to accommodate as many displaced people as possible. There are more people sharing a bathroom or TV than most are accustomed to. To ensure safety and maximize the comfort of all, there are rules that can be upsetting and stressful for some residents: no tobacco, alcohol, or illegal drugs; no pets; lights out at a specific time. All of the DMH interventions discussed in the next chapters are likely to be used if you assist in a shelter.

Schools and Hospitals   Every school district has its own plan to respond to the mental health needs of its students. Many school psychologists are trained to respond to emergencies and disaster. These psychologists are likely to be the first line of response to an incident in a school requiring a mental health intervention following a disaster. If a school district lacks resources or trained personnel to respond, they can call on the National Emergency Assistance Team (NEAT), which is part of the National Association of School Psychologists (NASP). These teams have specific expertise in crisis intervention and are available to help schools, families, and communities cope with crisis situations. NEAT is composed of nine nationally certified school psychologists who have had formal training and direct crisis experience involving human-caused and natural disasters. Counselors can contact the NASP website to obtain psychoeducational material related to children's postdisaster needs (http://www.nasponline.org). Materials are available in many languages.

In the same way that schools utilize their own mental health personnel to respond to a local disaster, hospitals usually rely on their own mental health staff. Hospital social workers and psychologists have to address the mental health needs of the injured and the bereaved in the hospital setting. As we discussed in Chapter 2, these mental health professionals may have to contend with the anxiety and trauma associated with epidemics.

Memorials   DMH workers can play an understated but significant role at memorials following disasters. On these occasions, counselors escort grieving friends and family as they board buses to go to the memorial locations, help them with small tasks, find restrooms, and provide a basic orientation. Counselors might let survivors know where they are going, how long the trip will be, and what to expect at the site of the memorial. Counselors might also distribute programs. DMH workers need to be prepared to witness varied grief reactions, which depend on many factors including the nature of the person grieving, the nature of the relationship with the deceased, the nature of the death, and so on. With mass-casualty disasters, commemorations can be held for many years, and survivors' reactions over the years can be wide ranging. Virtually every culture recognizes that it is helpful for those in mourning to have people present and available. Therefore, the primary role of DMH workers at memorials is to be a visible supportive presence—to simply be with those who are suffering.

Just About Anywhere   DMH helpers can be assigned to hotel lobbies to be available to the bereaved friends and relatives of those lost in a disaster. Counselors can be deployed at morgues to assist family members who are identifying bodies. In protracted recovery efforts, DMH assists construction workers and others involved in the recovery process in designated respite centers. Red Cross MHS also can assist with Welfare Information, as concerned friends and relatives try to locate their loved ones who may have been impacted by catastrophe.

DMH workers, who are carefully chosen and trained spokespersons, can put a public face on disaster. They provide psychoeducation through the media, recording TV and radio interviews in an attempt to educate the public about DMH and, hopefully, mitigate worries about what to expect psychologically. Additionally, people are frequently curious about how those impacted by disasters are faring. The confidentiality of survivors who are helped must be preserved at all costs, but counselors can provide an anxious public with broad information about expectable reactions and remind them of the need for some privacy and space during the healing process. DMH practitioners can also address groups to provide information about coping with disaster-related stress.

Red Cross–Specific Response Settings

There are a number of settings where DMH services may be provided within the larger American Red Cross response operation, including the following.

Family Service Centers or Family Assistance Centers   A service center, set up by the American Red Cross or other agencies, is where clients come for support and to apply for aid. In the aftermath of large disasters, state or local governments may establish Family Assistance Centers so that clients can come to one centralized place to receive the services from all the public and private organizations active in disaster recovery. This may be the setting where the most mental health services occur. In Red Cross service centers, MHS workers have an assigned area, usually adjacent to Health Services, where they can meet with clients. The area is not private or closed off and is not a typical counseling setting. MHS workers can also "float." The staff in the main service area, usually Client Caseworkers, interviews clients to determine their eligibility for aid. MHS workers keep a close watch on these interviews to monitor stress and distress.

The staff knows to refer clients to MHS if the client is highly distressed or agitated. Sometimes a staff member signals that he or she needs help from a MHS worker during the interview. Sometimes it is clear without such a signal that a staff member or client could benefit from a mental health intervention. If the service center is crowded, lines of clients could be waiting for services both inside and outside the center. MHS practitioners "work the crowd," making supportive contact with clients, engaging in conversations with clients who are waiting, providing brochures to adults, and giving toys, coloring books, and crayons to children. The role of MHS workers in these circumstances is to maintain the calm by lowering the arousal level through these simple actions and through outreach that offers modest but cumulatively helpful stress relief.

In service centers, MHS workers also provide assistance to stressed staff and volunteers. To accomplish this, counselors spend time with workers "schmoozing" in the kitchen, having lunch together, and lending a hand with all the tasks and chores that need to be done to keep a service center operating. MHS workers may make sure that there is toilet paper in the bathrooms and replace light bulbs. This is helpful for the obvious reasons of keeping the bathrooms usable and the lights on, but it also builds a sense of trust and camaraderie with the workers who MHS is there to support, should they need assistance. Counselors monitor the staff for stress, encourage them to take breaks and time off, and advocate for an environment that is conducive to mental health.

Emergency Response Vehicles   MHS workers with the American Red Cross sometimes ride with the large Red Cross vehicles that carry food, water, and other supplies. These emergency response vehicles (ERVs) are often first to the scene of a disaster. MHS workers riding with an ERV should ask clients if they have utilities (especially heat and water) and if they have medications. They should also inquire if the client's family members are safe and if they have been to a Family Service Center. MHS workers riding with ERVs also supply toys, snacks, and brochures for impacted families.

Outreach Teams   These teams could be composed of a Client Caseworker, Health Care, and Mental Health worker who go door to door to assess and respond to the needs of families in the impacted community. Mental health helpers can support both clients and workers. Client Caseworkers sometimes specifically request the assistance of MHS if a client refuses to leave an uninhabitable structure or seems especially distraught. MHS workers bring boxes or duffle bags with toys, coloring books, and crayons for children as well as brochures with psychoeducational material for adults.

Headquarters   Distraught clients can come to an American Red Cross head-quarters seeking support or MHS, but it is more likely that a MHS worker assigned to headquarters will provide assistance to staff. This is where disaster services staffing decisions, including those for MHS, are made and where volunteers wait to be deployed. At large disasters, many of these staff members are far from home and have to deal with many frustrations. Another important function of MHS at headquarters is to have conversations with volunteers as they prepare to leave the disaster, to prepare them for their reentry back to their normal lives.

For MHS workers assigned to headquarters in the role of leadership or administration, this center of operations can be both hectic and nerve wracking. Phone calls come in from the field requesting more or less staff, volunteers arrive and want to be deployed as soon as possible, emergencies and crises need to be managed and every manner of problem appears. Administrators must deal with issues such as a general sense of urgency to get responders out, objections to certain assignments by volunteers, and endless documentation and friction caused by competing needs between functions. Frequently, updates about what is required at a disaster site come in piecemeal, making it unclear whom to deploy where. The stress level can be unexpectedly exorbitant in the eye of the planning storm.

SOME PRACTICAL CONSIDERATIONS

Because many disasters arise without warnings, DMH workers need to be ready to respond with little advance notice. Most of us doing work for the local Red Cross chapter keep our Red Cross IDs handy because people without proper identification will not have access to the disaster site and will not be able to provide assistance. At some disasters, which may also be considered crime scenes or are sensitive due to their high-profile nature, event-specific IDs can expire within weeks and need to be renewed regularly. When arriving at any disaster site or when meeting clients, it is important to introduce yourself and let people know what agency you represent and the role you are playing in the relief operation.

DMH workers have to think seriously about how to dress when we go to a local disaster. To work effectively, you will need comfortable, presentable clothes and sturdy footgear. At a fire scene or in the aftermath of a flood, it is a good idea to have waterproof shoes. Give consideration to the weather and be prepared for extremes of heat and cold. The proper clothing, sunscreen, rain gear, and even an umbrella can become a crucial part of the response. Many of us have "go" bags with enough clothes and supplies to last several days in case we need to spend that much time on an assignment.

If you accept an assignment to assist in a national disaster, many more factors need to be considered as you pack. Think about where you are going, how long you are likely to be gone, what kind of a disaster it is, and whether or not it is a hardship assignment. There are settings where there is no electricity or water and DMH workers may have to sleep on the floors of churches or schools, which often serve as shelters. In a situation like this, it is important to arrive during the day so that you can see any potential hazards. When traveling to any national disaster, you must bring a copy of your professional registration or license. If possible you should bring enough clothes so that you do not have to do laundry. Volunteers on their way to the Gulf Coast to assist survivors of Hurricane Katrina needed to consider what the appropriate attire was for counseling during home visits in the bayou country. Plenty of insect repellent, sturdy shoes, and rain gear were all good recommendations.

What can be daunting and yet exhilarating is that you cannot be sure what you will be getting into when you agree to assist in the aftermath of a disaster. At any particular disaster, all aspects of the response can be fundamentally different from one day to the next. This lack of predictability can be foreign when you begin to do disaster work, but over time most of us have come to find this uncertainty more routine and even stimulating.

DISASTERS' IMPACT ON COUNSELORS

Everyone who responds to a disaster is impacted. Mental health workers need to be alert for signs of vicarious trauma, burnout, and compassion fatigue in themselves and their colleagues (Myers & Wee, 2005; Raphael, 1986; Weaver 1995). These terms have sometimes been used interchangeably, but there are important differences between them (Trippany, White Kress, & Wilcoxon, 2004).

Vicarious trauma typically refers to a counselor who experiences a trauma reaction due to exposure to their client's traumatic experiences. Vicarious trauma is rooted in counselors' empathy for their clients. By listening to the intimate or explicit details of a client's story, counselors can come to feel as though they witnessed these events personally. Vicarious trauma is specific to those assisting trauma victims (for example, trauma therapists, rescue workers, hospital and emergency medical staff), and it can lead to "profound changes in the core aspects of the therapist's self" (Pearlman & Saakvitne, 1995).

Observing and working with trauma victims and listening to their stories can lead to reactions generally associated with primary trauma—namely, changes in needs related to trust, esteem, control, intimacy, and safety (Trippany et al., 2004). Counselors can also develop intrusive imagery specific to the vicarious trauma (Rosenbloom, Pratt, & Pearlman, 1995). (We discuss in Chapter 11 how long-term involvement with disaster survivors or traumatized clients can lead therapists to manifest the same pathologies as their patients.) When working in the acute phases of a disaster, counselors need to be most careful to control and monitor their level of exposure to trauma to prevent or limit their own vicarious trauma.

Burnout is the gradual exhaustion and depletion of emotional energy that comes from being overworked, without sufficient rest, reward, or recovery. Burnout is common among DMH workers but not specific to them; in the aftermath of disaster, there can be so much client need that all helpers and workers are vulnerable to it. There are four stages of burnout: loss of enthusiasm, stagnation, frustration, and apathy (Edelwich & Brodsky, 1982). In the final stage, there is a significant decrease in the quality of care because a counselor's concern and esteem for clients are diminished.

Compassion fatigue (Figley, 2002) is similar to burnout but applies more specifically to mental health or spiritual care workers. It is a symptom caused by overextending one's capacity for selflessness. After a period of time spent extending oneself, caring for clients can come to seem like a chore. When compassion fatigue manifests itself, counselors become angry, sarcastic, or bored with clients; change or avoid subjects that clients wish to talk about; wish or suggest clients just "get over it"; feel numb or avoidant; aren't able to pay attention; hope the client won't show up; or become frustrated over a lack of progress (Baronowsky, 2002).

Vicarious trauma, burnout, and compassion fatigue are all related and are not mutually exclusive. At the site of a disaster, counselors can find themselves exposed to horrific experiences and overwhelmed clients, called upon to be constantly caring, and working long hours. In the immediate aftermath of a disaster, it is unusual for helpers to *not* be overworked, making all helpers vulnerable to vicarious traumatization *and* burnout *and* compassion fatigue. Relief organizations that do not seriously attempt to mitigate these problems in their workers are likely to have a high rate of turnover. Agencies that deploy workers to disasters have a responsibility to decrease the likelihood of vicarious traumatization and burnout by monitoring workload and providing supervision and opportunities for peer supervision and continuing education (Trippany et al., 2004).

Most mental health workers will experience some degree of vicarious traumatization, compassion fatigue, and burnout over the course of their work responding to disaster. The same model for risk factors among survivors holds for counselors as well; for example, if the disaster is small, damage is minor, and if there is no death or serious injury, it is not likely to lead to vicarious traumatization. However, with mass-casualty or human-caused disasters or disasters with many injuries or grotesque sights and sounds, vicarious traumatization is more likely. Counselors who spend days or weeks working with survivors of plane crashes or talking with grieving parents will certainly be vulnerable to any and all of these problems. Although agencies have some responsibility to decrease the likelihood of compassion fatigue, vicarious trauma, and burnout, each disaster worker should take active responsibility for his or her own well-being.

Self-Care During the Event

Good self-care begins before a disaster, continues during a disaster, and is essential afterwards. At the beginning of this chapter, we discussed the importance of self-care before the event; now we discuss the need for it during and after the disaster.

During a disaster response, all helpers should take care of their own basic needs and do periodic self-checks. Helpers should be alert to signs of vicarious trauma in themselves and in colleagues as well as in disaster victims, so steps can be taken to alleviate stress and/or seek out the services of other mental

Table 7.2 | Effective Ways to Manage Stress During a Disaster Relief Operation

1. *Take breaks.* A reasonable time frame is a 10- to 15- minute break every 2 hours. More time may be needed. Get away from the scene for a few moments. Find a quiet spot where you can relax or step outside for a change of scene.

2. *Eat and drink well and exercise.* A healthy and balanced diet along with a short walk can significantly improve your ability to cope with high levels of stress. Beware of caffeine and alcohol. Both can significantly impair your ability to function. If you need caffeine to continue to function in this supercharged environment, you are probably not getting enough sleep. Beware of too much junk food. Too much sugar can cause sugar lows in addition to the famous sugar highs. Feeling good physically goes a long way to feeling good mentally.

3. *Get support from colleagues and family.* Talk about things other than the relief operation with colleagues on your team. Talk with your family back home. Call colleagues who understand what you're going through. Recognition and positive reinforcement make it easier to stay enthusiastic about the work you're doing.

4. *Stick to your shifts.* With the exception of the first day or two when schedules may be less clearly established, be certain that you stick to the shift to which you are assigned and leave at the end of that shift. You will be more effective if you are not overworked.

5. *Take time off.* If you are on a long-term relief operation, talk with your supervisor about taking appropriate time off. The high intensity and stress of larger disasters may create a need for more frequent time off or shorter shifts to avoid burnout or compassion fatigue.

6. *Breathe deeply.* People often hold their breath when they are tense. Breathing deeply helps your body relax.

Source: American Red Cross (2002).

health professionals as needed. Everyone has his or her own methods for reducing stress. It is important to think about what works for you personally and to have a plan in place *before* an incident occurs. This way you will know what strategy to rely on when the pressure is building. Some general principles should be adhered to, which are listed in Table 7.2. Remember that self-care cannot be overemphasized. It benefits not only you but also the clients you work with and the loved ones you will return to after the event.

Consider what you do to relieve stress in your everyday life. Counselors should be sure to bring to the disaster location the things that they need to relax and unwind. For example, if you find it calming to listen to music, bring your iPod or CD player. If you like to read, bring a book. If you always play solitaire before you go to bed, don't forget a deck of cards. Counselors may also benefit from calling on whatever spiritual resources they can utilize—for example, speaking with a member of the clergy, attending a religious service, prayer, or meditation (Trippany et al., 2004).

Always remember that people under stress can make unhealthy choices such as drinking too much alcohol, gambling, or being overcontrolling. One common danger for relief workers is the tendency to relieve stress by working too hard, increasing the likelihood of burnout. For a number of reasons including unrelenting client need, pressure by the organization to continuously give more, and the inherent adrenaline pull of disaster work, workers can begin to feel irreplaceable. They lose the capacity to step back and emotionally separate from the work. This behavior is potentially dangerous to the counselor and to clients. You must be sure to pace yourself, and you should be assertive with colleagues who can't step back or take time away.

Transitioning Home From a Disaster Assignment

As you leave a disaster, take advantage of the opportunity to do an exit interview with a mental health counselor. Exit interviews are voluntary but can prove useful and are recommended for all American Red Cross volunteers, including mental health workers, when they leave a national disaster. At such an interview, you have the opportunity to talk about the meaning of the event, how you handled challenges, and what you learned from the experience. Some workers may not want to have an exit interview, preferring to get home and speak with a trusted family member, friend, or professional, but talking about the experience with an experienced disaster worker afterwards is something that many find beneficial. American Red Cross chapters often have mental health staff or volunteers available to responders coming back from national disasters. For some responders, writing about their experience when they return from an assignment can be helpful. It is important to process or attempt to make meaning of the event in a manner that feels comfortable to you.

The transition from disaster to home can be difficult. Volunteers can come home thinking that coworkers, friends, and family will want to hear all of the details of the experience. This is not always the case. Coworkers may expect you to pick up more of the load at work since you were away; family members, too, might expect you to do more chores because you were at what they may perceive to be an exotic and exciting adventure. Everyone you return home to still has their own very real problems and may not want to hear about all of your trials and tribulations at the disaster site, your larger-than-life experience. If you have friends or family who are interested, be grateful but do not expect it. This lack of recognition can be very troublesome for some and is another important reason to take advantage of the exit interview when you complete your disaster assignment. By doing so, you will certainly have some opportunity to talk about your experience at the disaster. If you do an exit interview and it is not satisfying or if your organization does not provide one, consider taking the initiative to talk with a trusted friend, clergy member, or therapist.

Do not come home from a disaster and go to work the next day; it takes time to decompress from the intensity of such involvement. Also remember that self-care should continue when you return home and is important for months afterwards. Research suggests that lifestyle factors over a long period of time after assisting at a disaster response can determine how well individuals recover from the experience. For example, a recent study of 1500 American Red Cross volunteers who volunteered in the aftermath of September 11, 2001, suggested that negative life events over a period of a year after the response weakened their resilience and led to increased distress and a greater susceptibility to PTSD (McCaslin, Jacobs, Meyer, Johnson-Jiminez, Metzler, & Marmar, 2005).

AFTERTHOUGHTS

When considering all the intricacies of DMH work, the essential, rewarding essence of the work may be overlooked. DMH workers have the opportunity to be with and help people during what may well be the most important and difficult moment of their lives. It is an opportunity to have the satisfaction of giving of oneself that feels pure, unimpeded by the layers of bureaucracy and professionalism in current health-care systems. The core spirit of altruism is very real.

One American Red Cross mental health worker, Jeanne Parr Lemkau, described her experience responding to the Xenia, Ohio, tornado in September 2000:

> What I was able to give, I freely gave without thought of either the economic status of the recipient or the economic ramifications for me of providing care. "Payment" was in the form of good feelings, as my sense of helplessness in the face of natural forces was transformed through the act of helping. To a greater degree than in my office practice, my behavior matched my espoused personal politics of providing service in proportion to need rather than ability to pay, and I felt an immediate and direct connection between my own actions and satisfactory outcomes, a tremendous antidote for the burnout I carry from doing longer term psychotherapy and writing grants and manuscripts with uncertain futures. . . . Give me a disaster anytime. (Lemkau, 2001)

Loss from disaster shakes us out of the notion that our lives are predictable, controllable, and reasonably safe. Disasters can also reawaken other painful experiences from our past. This is true for helpers as well as survivors. However, the positive aspects of this work should not be lost in the equation. Disaster work can dramatically alter the comfort zone of helpers. We cherish our routine days and weeks. But when we take on the challenge of counseling in disaster chaos, we face straight on the fragility of the structures of our lives and the effects of sudden changes of fortune. It can truly deepen our appreciation for both the vulnerability and resilience of the human spirit and the power of collective action.

References

ARC (American Red Cross). (1995). Disaster mental health services I. Washington, DC: Author.

ARC (American Red Cross). (2000). Family services: Providing emergency assistance (ARC 3072-1). Washington, DC: Author.

ARC (American Red Cross). (2002). Disaster mental health services: An overview, instructors manual (ARC 3077-2), 1–5. Washington, DC: Author.

Baranowsky, A. B. (2002). The silencing response in clinical practice: On the road to dialogue. In C. R. Figley (Ed.), *Treating compassion fatigue* (pp. 155–170). New York: Brunner/Routledge.

Brawer, P. A., Handal, P. J., Fabricatore, A. N., Roberts, R., & Wajda-Johnston, V. A. (2002). Training and education in religion/spirituality within APA-accredited clinical psychology programs. *Professional Psychology: Theory and Practice, 33*(2), 203–206.

Edelwich, J., & Brodsky, A. (1982). Training guide-lines: Linking the workshop experience to need on and off the job. In W. S. Paine (Ed.), *Job stress and burnout* (pp. 133–154). Newbury Park, CA: Sage.

Figley, C. R. (Ed.). (2002). *Treating compassion fatigue.* New York: Brunner/Routledge.

Halpern, J. (2001). Red Cross crisis counseling after the World Trade Center disaster. *Academy of Clinical Psychology Bulletin, 7*, 7–11.

Jacobs, J. A., & Quevillon, R. P (2001). *Outreach strategies in the recovery process.* Paper presented in The Ripple Effect From Ground Zero: Coping with Mental Health Needs in Time of Tragedy and Terror, New York.

James, R. K., & Gilliland, B. E. (2005). *Crisis intervention strategies.* Belmont, CA: Thomson Brooks/Cole.

Lambert, M. J., & Barley, D. E. (2001). Research summary on the therapeutic relationship and psychotherapy outcome. *Psychotherapy: Theory, Research, Practice, Training, 38*, 357–361.

Lemkau, J. P. (2001). Give me a disaster. *Professional Psychology: Research and Practice, 32*(3), 333.

McCaslin, S. E., Jacobs, G. A., Meyer, D. L., Johnson-Jiminez, E., Metzler, T. J., & Marmar, C. R. (2005). How does negative life change following disaster response impact distress among Red Cross responders? *Professional Psychology: Research and Practice, 36*(3), 246–253.

Myers, D., & Wee, D. F. (2005). *Disaster mental health services.* New York: Brunner/Routledge.

NIMH (National Institute of Mental Health). (2002). *Mental health and mass violence: Evidence-based early psychological intervention for victims/survivors of mass violence. A workshop to reach consensus on best practices.* (NIH Publication No. 02-5138). Washington DC: Government Printing Office.

Pearlman, L. A., & Saakvitne, K. W. (1995). *Trauma and the therapist: Countertransference and vicarious traumatization in psychotherapy with incest survivors.* New York: Norton.

Raphael, B. (1986). *When disaster strikes: How individuals and communities cope with catastrophe.* New York: Basic Books

Roberts, S. (2002). *Why the need for this conference?* Paper presented at the conference The Lifecycle of a Disaster: Ritual and Practice, New York.

Rosenbloom, D. J., Pratt, A. C., & Pearlman, L. A. (1995). Helpers' responses to trauma work: Understanding and intervening in an organization. In B. H. Stamm (Ed.), *Secondary traumatic stress: Self-care issues for clinicians, researchers, and educators* (pp. 65–79). Baltimore: Sidran Press.

Trippany, R. L., White Kress, V. E., & Wilcoxon, S. A. (2004). Preventing vicarious trauma: What counselors should know when working with trauma survivors. *Journal of Counseling & Development, 82*, 31–37.

Weaver, J. (1995). *Disasters: Mental health interventions.* Sarasota, FL: Professional Resource Press/Professional Resource Exchange.

Three things in human life are important: the first is to be kind; the second is to be kind; and the third is to be kind.

Henry James

Psychological First Aid

8

In this chapter, we examine the theory and practice of psychological first aid (PFA). Although PFA can be used throughout a disaster response, it is generally considered to be the early intervention of choice in the period immediately following a disaster (Litz, 2004; NIMH, 2002; Watson, 2004). We review the definitions, history, and theoretical underpinnings of PFA, but our main focus is to describe its more frequently cited components or elements. We also examine the questions of who should practice PFA and whether there is evidence for its effectiveness.

A VISIBLE SUPPORTIVE PRESENCE

As we discussed in Chapters 4 and 5, surviving a disaster or experiencing the sudden loss of a loved one to disaster frequently traumatizes survivors, sometimes leaving them frenzied, sometimes numb. Survivors experience a shattering of meanings, constructions, and expectations of how the world should be. The feeling that the universe is orderly and predictable that usually allows people to carry on with their lives is deeply shaken, engendering confusion, fear, and helplessness. Survivors' broken trust must be restored before recovery can begin. Therefore, the fundamental purpose of PFA is to provide comfort and support.

Disaster services personnel responded immediately when an airplane crashed into the Atlantic Ocean. An American Red Cross Disaster Mental Health Services worker, one of the team of mental health counselors, entered the hotel near John F. Kennedy Airport in New York City that served as a disaster response center, just as some of the first family members were arriving. The worker saw a distraught woman crying and quietly approached her. The client looked up, embraced her, and began sobbing. The woman was South American and spoke only Spanish. The worker spoke only English. While the woman cried, the volunteer remained quietly attentive and held her hands. Eventually, friends arrived to be with the grieving woman. Shaken by the interaction, the disaster worker moved on to help others. She felt enormous compassion for the client but was upset about being able to do so little to help. Later an English-speaking friend of the survivor told the volunteer that the woman was enormously grateful for the help she had received. She said that she would be forever grateful to the counselor and would not have made it through the day without her support.

Grief and loss are intensely human experiences that transcend culture and language; it is possible to comfort another person without words. In this example, the stricken survivor felt understood by the volunteer without a single word exchanged between them. Presence and compassion are the underpinnings of disaster mental health (DMH) work, and experienced disaster counselors we have spoken to agree that the most important aspects of this type of PFA are deceptively simple: Be physically available and emotionally present for the survivor. Less experienced counselors might try to do or to say too much; in trying to mitigate the emotional impact of the pain and suffering in front of them, they might ask too many questions and make too many suggestions when all the survivor really needs or wants is a supportive presence.

Psychological first aid is not counseling, and it is not "treatment." The fundamental nature of PFA is to provide soothing, basic, practical, and emotional support. In many traditional therapies and psychological interventions, the counselor helps the client explore the emotions and thoughts that lie below conscious experience in order to expand awareness and to change dysfunctional patterns of thinking and behavior. In the immediate aftermath of a catastrophe, a DMH counselor is not interested in challenging or changing the client. Counselors recognize that the survivor's world has been dramatically broken apart. To promote healing rather than opening up and exploring thoughts and feelings, the counselor attempts the opposite. The goals are stabilization and containment. Counselors "hold" or "embrace" their clients—sometimes physically and always emotionally—so that the client does not fall apart. Psychological first aid focuses on the here and now.

DEFINING PSYCHOLOGICAL FIRST AID

Consider these two descriptions of PFA:

> Pragmatically oriented interventions with survivors or emergency responders targeting acute stress reaction and immediate needs. The goals of psychological first

aid include the establishment of safety (objective and subjective), stress-related symptom reduction, restoration of rest and sleep, linkage to critical resources and connection to social support. (NIMH, 2002)

Basic strategies to reduce psychological distress include orientation to disaster and recovery efforts, reduction of physiological arousal, mobilization of support for those who are most distressed, facilitation of reunion with loved ones and keeping families together, providing education about available resources and coping strategies, and using effective risk communication techniques. (Watson, 2004)

Both definitions suggest that PFA interventions are designed to address simultaneously the interrelated practical, physical, and psychological needs of survivors. In the following case, we can see how an effective PFA intervention addresses these multiple needs.

In the aftermath of Hurricane Ivan in 2004, an older woman returned to her home and found it uninhabitable. Mold and water damage had made it unsafe. But she refused to leave the vicinity of her home and insisted on sleeping in her car so that no one would loot her house. Her car was neither a safe nor a comfortable place for her to stay. She had back problems, and sleeping in the car made them even worse. Emergency responders thought the woman was anxious, exhausted, and "paranoid." They asked that a mental health counselor intervene and convince her to stay in a motel room. But the counselor, who understood the principles of PFA, determined that the woman was not paranoid. In fact, there were reports of looters in the neighborhood. The counselor knew that to provide effective DMH services, one must consider the practical, physical, and psychological aspects of a disaster situation. With the woman's permission, the counselor asked her trusted neighbors to help secure her valuables. Only then did the woman consent to stay in a nearby motel while cleanup of the area was underway.

Psychological first aid involves attending to the biopsychosocial needs of clients impacted by disasters. It is often proactive, holistic, and practical and always meant to be a "down to earth" model. Psychological first aid is a human way to help people in anguish. It is a minimalist approach based on an understanding of what is happening to those struck by disasters. Sometimes such assistance can appear to be a commonsense approach akin to problem solving. And much problem solving is involved in PFA, but there is nothing at all common about common sense in the aftermath of a disaster. In the chaos of disaster, counselors can overlook many obvious and practical considerations such as the possibility of a client's home being looted, the possibility that the home is not safe to return to, or the possibility that the client is physically injured or lacking prescription medication lost in the disaster.

PFA interventions generally are seen as most appropriate in the earliest period after a disaster strikes, when survivors are still experiencing the aftereffects of the fight-or-flight response and are not yet fully capable of taking in much information or seeing beyond their own immediate needs. The length of that period can vary depending on the individual survivor and the event. At the very least it probably encompasses what Litz and Gray (2004) call the "immediate impact phase," a period of approximately 48 hours after the individual regains safety following exposure to trauma. In many cases, it can extend through the postincident phase, or about 1 week after the event (NIMH, 2002). During this period, physiological and psychological arousal may limit the survivor's thinking and coping capacities. The counselor therefore provides support for the needs of survivors until they are better able to absorb new information and are more able and likely to articulate their experiences. Thus, PFA is most appropriately applied in the early stages of a disaster, but it also could be a component of other interventions throughout a disaster response.

HISTORY AND RATIONALE

Beverly Raphael is generally credited with first using the term *psychological first aid* in her 1977 discussion of the treatment of the bereaved and injured in a railway disaster. On January 18, 1977, a train jumped the tracks at the Granville station in Sydney, Australia, crashed into the supports of a bridge, and brought down more than 100 tons of concrete and steel directly onto the third and fourth carriages of the train. There were 213 injuries and 83 deaths. Raphael (1977) wrote that "distressed victims and their relatives have passed through the early days of horror and uncertainty, and for the most part they received the very best in comforting support, in *psychological first aid* for their distress." She described this assistance as demonstrating concerned caring and empathy and allowing victims and relatives to express all feelings, including helplessness, anxiety, and rage. She emphasized hands-on, concrete assistance and the importance of reuniting victims with significant others as important components of this first aid. Other writers have subsequently summarized core features of PFA with the catch phrase of "protect, direct, and connect."

As we have discussed in earlier chapters, the great majority of survivors recover from trauma and disaster without professional help (for example, Bonnano, 2004; Litz & Grey, 2004; NIMH, 2002; Norris et al., 2002; Watson, 2004). Early interventions should therefore "first do no harm" and not interfere with natural recovery. Psychological first aid may be seen as an approach that sets the stage for and promotes this recovery (Brewin, 2003) and removes obstacles to its natural progression. In the case of the woman with the hurricane-damaged home discussed earlier, for example, the counselor determined that the survivor could recover from the loss of her house without extensive counseling. She needed to rest and to sleep in a safe environment in order to begin emotional healing, but that was not possible as long as she thought her home and possessions were under siege. By recruiting her neighbors to help protect her valuables and by reassuring her that her response to the damage to her house was understandable and normal, the counselor assisted the women in recovering on her own.

Theoretical Roots: Carl Rogers and Abraham Maslow

The theoretical underpinnings of PFA appear to be derived from the work of two eminent humanistic psychologists: Carl Rogers and Abraham Maslow. The core attitudes and actions of disaster responders using this intervention can be traced back to Rogers's and Maslow's seminal frameworks for working with and understanding others.

Rogers labeled his approach to helping as "non-directive" and "client- or person-centered" (1951, 1970). He emphasized unconditional positive regard, empathy, and genuineness and is generally credited with describing a therapeutic stance that is helpful and effective, irrespective of the theoretical orientation of the counselor (that is, psychoanalytic, cognitive–behavioral, interpersonal). For Rogers, it was not the theory that determined the effectiveness of the therapy but rather the helper's attitude. In this view, a context of caring sets the stage, allowing a client to grow and change.

Textbooks on counseling and psychological interventions rarely make reference to Maslow, perhaps because he developed a theory of personality and motivation rather than an approach to conducting counseling or psychotherapy (Maslow, 1999). Yet we believe there are few figures in psychology of more importance to DMH work than Maslow. He suggested that our motivations are tied to a hierarchy of needs. Basic needs take priority over more complex ones: If you lack self-esteem and are caught in a blizzard, you will be more likely to attend to the basic physical need of getting warm than to questioning your need for self-worth (Maslow, 1954).

Applied to DMH, Maslow's hierarchy emphasizes the importance of attending to survivors' physical and safety issues before anything else. Indeed, DMH counseling involves "working the Maslow hierarchy" from the bottom up. According to the National Institute of Mental Health report (NIMH, 2002) on early interventions after mass-casualty events, "Optimal efforts to conduct early mental health assessment and intervention should recognize and be conducted within a hierarchy of needs." Counselors focus first on assisting clients with their very most basic concerns (food, water, shelter) and gradually attend to the more complex ones (self-esteem or belongingness). Although this hierarchical model involves a more direct approach to helping than is usually seen in mental health interventions, PFA can vary in the need for directness. The counselor needs to be flexible—at times very indirect, calling on the Rogerian skills of being present and calm and listening supportively and, at other times, being more forceful to address essential needs such as in helping a survivor to safety or encouraging a survivor to leave a dangerous situation.

GOALS AND COMPONENTS OF PSYCHOLOGICAL FIRST AID

Psychological first aid includes four broad goals, which are important to keep in mind:

- *To relieve suffering, both physical and emotional.* When disaster strikes, suffering is abundant. People are in pain as a result of the horror they witness, the losses they experience, and the disruption they must endure. They may experience both emotional and physical afflictions in response.
- *To improve survivors' short-term functioning.* Right after a crisis, people may need to make decisions with serious and long-term implications at a

Table 8.1 | PFA Attitudes and Actions

Attitudes	Actions
Being calm	Attending to physiological needs
Providing warmth	Attending to safety needs
Providing acknowledgment and recognition	Obtaining information
Expressing empathy	Providing information
Showing genuineness	Helping clients access social supports
Empowering the survivor	Assisting with traumatic grief

time while they are experiencing strong reactions. Helping survivors function well in the short term can help mitigate future problems.

- *To help survivors' course of recovery.* Early psychological and practical support that encourages and enhances coping may help reduce or relieve stress. This starts the road of recovering from a disaster in an optimal way, and it may mitigate a poorer outcome.
- *To provide linkage to critical resources.* Resources can either be material or psychological. People impacted by disasters may be too overwhelmed to obtain for themselves the information, forms, or a host of other things they may need. Additionally, providing basic support early on may facilitate help seeking at a later point should the need arise.

Now that we have explained when and why PFA is appropriate after disasters, let's discuss in more detail what it actually involves. The essentials of PFA are listed in Table 8.1 and described more fully in the following section. These elements were identified from a review of the discussions and models of PFA proposed by a range of experts including the American Red Cross (ARC, 2002); the NIMH (2002), Litz and Grey (2004); Raphael (1986); Weaver, (1995); Brewin, (2003); James and Gilliland (2005); Slaikeu (1990) and Pynoos and Nader (1988). Remember, components of PFA are a blend of attitudes and actions on the part of the helper. These elements are not presented in any order of importance, nor are they meant to dictate a chronology of how they should be utilized because the postdisaster situation and the client's specific needs will determine the order.

Psychological First Aid Attitudes

Being Calm   In the aftermath of disaster, all responders must attempt to remain calm in order to function effectively. For mental health workers, *maintaining a calm presence, without being emotionally distant* in the face of emotional trauma, is the basis for any assistance. Disasters induce tremendous physical and emotional arousal levels, and anxiety is contagious (Sullivan, 1940). One core aim of PFA is to reduce this globally heightened arousal level (NIMH, 2002), and being calm serves this aim. A DMH worker who is frightened, unnerved, or overstimulated, either by an overwhelming event or an overwhelmed client, will not be helpful. Survivors may be shaken or in shock, and the helper needs to remain steady in order to help them master or regulate their experiences. It is important not to allow the client or the stressful situation to make you "lose your cool" (Weaver, 1995).

On a practical note, evacuations and other circumstances can make follow-up work with survivors difficult, so obtaining their contact information as soon as possible is important so that they can be reached even if they travel far from the disaster area. A helper who remains calm and focused is more likely to obtain demographic information even in a chaotic situation (Raphael, 1986; Weaver, 1995).

Providing Warmth   Carl Rogers defined *unconditional positive regard* as valuing the client and offering him or her a warm, prizing acceptance. Perhaps because mental health professionals strive for objectivity and appropriate neutrality, there is not much attention in the psychotherapy literature emphasizing the importance of warmth. But Rogers pointed out that caring and kindness are essential in the helping process, giving permission to counselors to feel compassion and even nonpossessive warmth for clients. For person-centered counselors, this compassion and kindness is expressed in attentiveness and open posture, a soothing tone of voice and acceptance of anything the client says. Offering your heart to the survivor of a disaster does not need to be done in a sugarcoated or overdemonstrative manner, but it does mean conveying a warm and caring attitude.

We should point out that warmth is expressed differently in DMH than in other counseling settings in at least one aspect: the judicious use of physical contact, which is strictly avoided in other settings but is sometimes appropriate in DMH as a way to demonstrate compassion and warmth to survivors. It has been noted (Litz, 2004) that if someone we cared about were traumatized we would want our loved one to receive solace such as *respectful and well-timed physical touch as in handholding or a hug*. Raphael (1986) points out that PFA includes consoling victims by *holding and touching them* or sitting beside them in a caring manner. Weaver (1995) notes that *physical touch* such as a hug might be appropriate in some disaster situations. During times of such intense arousal as in disasters, a reassuring hand on the shoulder can be grounding for the survivor. When emotions are running high and chaos abounds, words may not suffice, and an embrace may be shorthand for conveying warmth and empathy. We must also point out that some survivors might react negatively to touch. Counselors need to be attuned to the specific needs and sensibilities of their clients and attend to signals indicating their receptivity to touch.

Providing Acknowledgment and Recognition   Survivors require acknowledgment and validation that they have experienced a trauma. "The first and most general level of psychosocial care for disaster-affected people and communities lies in the recognition, by statements or actions, that they have suffered from the disaster" (Raphael, 1986). If the helper or others downplay the significance of the trauma, survivors may not take the necessary time to rest and recover (Brewin, 2003); they may minimize their needs. But if an impacted community is encouraged to acknowledge the reality of what they have experienced, they may feel less stigma in accepting needed resources and aid. Disempowerment and strong feelings of helplessness are common postdisaster reactions, but validation of a survivor's ordeal counters these reactions.

Acknowledgment needs to be offered by not only the helper but also "natural support systems," such as friends and relatives, and other entities. The media can be helpful in this regard: By reporting stories about what occurred, the press can increase awareness of the plight and of the suffering of those impacted. Headlines or articles in the press and other media coverage can allow survivors to feel that their suffering is being taken seriously. Survivors also feel recognized when either a state or federal emergency is declared.

Although the inherent emotional strength of the survivors needs to be recognized, their suffering needs to be validated as well. Acknowledgment and validation help normalize the stress reactions that people commonly undergo after exposure to the intensity and shock of a disaster.

Expressing Empathy   Empathy refers to listening to clients, entering into their worlds, seeing their point of view, and communicating this point of view to the satisfaction of the client (Rogers, 1970). Often clients who experience a disaster want to share their horror. They want someone to know what they are feeling and what they have been through. Survivors of natural disasters may want you to see what is left of their flooded or burned-out homes and will invite you in to see the ruins. They are looking for more than support or consolation; they want to be sure that you can understand the magnitude of their loss (empathy) before they can accept your support (unconditional positive regard). They may need you to bear witness to their pain so that they, too, can absorb the extent of their injury.

The American Red Cross's model of PFA (ARC, 2002) suggests that all responders to a disaster listen to and accept the thoughts and feelings of their clients. Responders should be prepared to listen to survivors describe what happened to them; they should concentrate and attend to all aspects of the client's communication at both the emotional and cognitive levels. Following a disaster, survivors might feel anxiety, grief, and guilt, and they might express anger toward almost anyone. They can experience great joy and relief at escaping injury or guilt or shame about their survival. They also can experience anger toward a friend or relative who was injured or killed. Several models of PFA (Raphael, 1986; Weaver, 1995) note that the helper should allow the victim to express the range of such possible feelings as anguish, fear, anger, futility, or helplessness. Helpers need to accept these feelings, however strange or extreme they may seem at the time.

The helper needs not only to *feel* compassionate empathy with the client but also to *communicate* this supportive understanding effectively. It is not enough to think that you are being empathic; it is most important that the client experiences your empathy. The following empathic responses can assist counselors dealing with clients:

- "So you feel . . . "
- "I hear you saying . . . "
- "I sense you are feeling . . . "
- "You appear . . . "
- "It seems to you that . . . "
- "You place a high value on . . . "
- "So tell me if I am getting this right? You seem to be feeling that . . . "

Given a climate of empathy and warmth, most survivors want to share their stories. These might be detailed accounts of the day of the disaster or how the event raised memories of other earlier events in their lives. Or the stories might lead survivors to other thoughts, feelings, or connections. By telling their stories, survivors create order and meaning from their fragmented memories and from their feelings, thoughts, and impulses. Having a conversation about the unimaginable can make it seem less chaotic and more manageable and perhaps make the memories less intrusive (Brewin, 2003).

> In the days following September 11, 2001, a mother asked a DMH worker to look at the pictures of her murdered daughter. She wanted him to affirm that she had lost a beautiful and lively young woman. She talked about her grief and sadness, her memories of her daughter, and the hopes she had had for the future. While they talked about her daughter, the mother needed the counselor to hold her daughter's picture in order to be assured that he was not distanced or detached from her painful loss and grief.

Immediately after the disaster, clients may not be ready to talk about the experience while PFA is being offered. Empathy would then involve respecting and supporting clients who for a variety of reasons are not self-disclosing. Some in the mental health field worry that a helper might pressure clients to speak about a traumatic event before they are ready to do so (Bonnano, 2004; Litz, 2004). However, helpers can also make mistakes in their efforts to be empathic if they have a need to distance themselves from survivors' pain. Counselors may discourage survivors from telling their stories in an effort to avoid hearing their pain (Herman, 1992). The following examples are what an inexperienced or unsure helper might say, thereby discouraging a client from speaking about the trauma:

- "Don't feel bad."
- "You're strong" or "You'll get through this."
- "Don't cry."
- "It's God's will."
- "It could be worse."
- "At least you still have . . ."
- "They are in a better place."
- "I know how you feel."
- "Try not to think about it."
- "Let's talk about something other than the disaster."

Such statements can minimize the trauma for the helper but might lead to a similar tendency on the part of the survivor to avoid painful memories, only to be haunted by them later on (Herman, 1992).

Much counseling involves the ability to offer empathic understanding. Working with survivors of disaster or other trauma can be especially challenging because to be empathic means that the helper must be willing to enter the client's world of pain, loss, anguish, hopelessness, rage, shock, and despair. Weaver (1995) notes that as survivors tell their stories, helpers should not try to stop them from crying. It is also acceptable for DMH workers to shed a few tears with survivors.

As a final point on empathy, it is important to note that, although acceptance of the survivor's feelings is central, clients should not be left with unmanageable or uncontrollable feelings. If a survivor is experiencing overwhelming feelings, the helper should remain with him or her until friends and family can provide a supportive environment and the counselor is reasonably certain that the client is stable (Raphael, 1986).

Showing Genuineness   Rogers (1970) is emphatic that only *genuine* empathy and warmth are helpful for clients. Clients can sense when a counselor is offering false compassion, and this is likely to be not only not helpful but also harmful. The counselor must be very open to his or her own feelings and aware of his or her own experience. Support must be heartfelt for it to be of value.

This is not always easy, for many reasons. The reactions of victims following disaster can be so intense and so irrational that genuine empathy can be difficult to offer. In the aftermath of a mass-casualty disaster or mass violence, a counselor can speak with many clients who are in shock and grieving. The counselor can be pushed to the limits of his or her capacity to be empathic in a short period of time. *Knowing your limits so that you can stay genuinely empathically engaged may be one of the most important aspects of DMH.* Helpers should be aware of their vulnerabilities. Some counselors can find it difficult to remain genuinely engaged with traumatized children, whereas other counselors have a more difficult time with grieving parents. Knowing your own strengths and weaknesses is a key to effectiveness.

Feeling empathy may not be difficult for trained counselors or other helpers in the immediate aftermath of disaster. In fact, many people want to be of service when the need is so obvious and compelling (Litz, 2004). However, sustaining genuine warmth and compassion can become difficult for mental health workers for a variety of reasons:

1. If disaster mental health workers have been working long hours or for many weeks, they can become tired or numb and may experience compassion fatigue.
2. In the aftermath of a disaster, clients may express rage, making helper warmth difficult. One survivor who lost a relative in the World Trade Center attacks said, "The only way this will be fixed is to take a nuclear bomb to the whole [*expletive*] Middle East." Even in a case like this, acceptance of the client's anguish is important. Arguing about the wisdom or effectiveness of a nuclear attack is inappropriate.

3. Survivors can experience considerable loss and pain for a long time after a disaster. Some counselors who show compassion in the acute phase of the disaster can become disengaged or desensitized over the long haul.

Like traditional therapists, DMH workers need to be "grounded"—that is, confident that they are in touch with reality as well as their own personal feelings. The counselor's wishes or desires may be submerged or put on hold (Winnicott, 1958) during the relief operation; at the same time, there should be ongoing self-monitoring for compassion fatigue.

Remember, being genuine does not mean being blunt or indiscreet. Although honesty is vital, using common sense and respecting the client's emotional defenses also need to be considered. If you saw a victim's charred body and a relative asks you what it looked like, there may be no need to discuss the gruesome details. In fact, you might say you didn't get a very good look or that you don't think that it would be helpful to the client to discuss these details. In the aftermath of September 11, some grieving relatives wanted to know if their loved ones died a painful death. Some mental health professionals suggested, without real knowledge, that the heat from the fires and the sudden building collapse probably made the deaths quick and painless. Other counselors were more direct and observed that it was impossible to know about the death experience. It would seem hard to fault counselors who attempted to soften the blow to survivors by allowing them to embrace a possibility that provided comfort. A survivor who asks "Do you think my spouse died a painful death?" may be pleading "Please tell me my spouse did not suffer." The experienced counselor needs to rely on instincts, intuition, and listening skills to determine what information the survivor can tolerate.

Empowering the Survivor   Herman (1992) notes that trauma robs the victim of a sense of control. Acknowledging and supporting a survivor's strength, competence, courage, and power—his or her resilience—can begin restoring that control. Empowering survivors means letting them determine the kind of assistance they receive, the pace of any kind of self-disclosure, and as many other aspects of the DMH process as possible. As Litz (2004) observes, if someone we loved were traumatized, we would want the person to be asked what he or she needed and wanted. We would not want the helper to be intrusive, nor would we want the helper to pressure the person to disclose what happened.

To be empowering, counselors should offer respect and admiration and not "infantilize" the client. Counselors should acknowledge survivors' courage in dealing with the disaster and communicate that, although the clients may be suffering or feel fragile at that moment, they are strong, competent, confident, and independent. (Once again, genuineness and common sense should not be overlooked. A client who appears to be numb, crying hysterically, or decompensating should not be told that he or she is showing great strength.)

To help survivors recognize their own strengths, it may be useful to ask them questions like "How have you gotten through tough times before?" or "What skills do you have that will allow you to get through this?" In response to their answers, helpers may say that given what survivors have been through they seem to have accomplished a lot. Helpers might emphasize what the client did well. They also might offer suggestions for problem solving and give the client credit.

As another source of empowerment, survivors can be encouraged to contribute to the relief operation. On the scene, they can be enlisted to make phone calls or to obtain food and water for others. In shelters, clients can be asked to help distribute food and blankets. Both adults and children often find strength, control, and competence in being useful.

Psychological First Aid Actions

Attending to Physiological Needs   Physiological needs include requirements for air, water, food, sleep, proper body temperature, and so on. As we discussed earlier, people need to first focus on their physical and material states. When their needs in these areas are not fulfilled, they may feel sickness, irritation, and pain, unpleasant sensations that provide the motivation to attend to unmet needs as soon as possible in order to establish some kind of homeostasis. Only after these immediate needs are satisfied can people think about other things (Maslow, 1954). Therefore, several models of PFA (for example, ARC, 2002; Raphael, 1986) include attending to physical needs and obtaining treatment for physical injuries.

In the aftermath of disaster, people can lose their homes and their clothes; they can be without food and water. They may also be injured. DMH counselors must first assess whether basic needs are being met. Clients can be taken to receive medical attention or offered water, hot drinks, or blankets. Helpers may need to assist clients in finding shelter. It is not unusual for disasters to leave communities without power, so counselors can help clients obtain "hot meals" that can be warmed without power.

Counselors can ask the following kinds of questions to determine if basic needs are being met:

- "Do you need something to eat or drink? Can I help you to collect your belongings?"
- "Can I help you with any tasks—finding newspapers, making phone calls, finding services, directions, car rentals?"
- "Are you warm enough? Do you need a sweater or blanket?"
- "Do you need anything for yourself or your children?"
- "Do you need help locating a place to rest if you are tired?"
- "Can you stay with relatives or friends?"
- "Can your family stay with these folks while repairs are being done to the home?"
- "If there isn't enough room for the whole family, are there homes close enough to each other where the family could stay?"
- "The Red Cross can arrange for your family to stay in a hotel for a certain period of time, but you need to speak with a Client Services worker."

Experienced DMH counselors carry backpacks with bottles of water, snacks, tissues, and other supplies that are part of comprehensive mental health intervention. They also carry stuffed animals and toys. The loss of toys in a fire or a flood can evoke strong emotion in a young child, and it is much more helpful to give a new toy to the child than to ask how he or she is feeling about the loss. These services may seem outside the realm of mental health practice, but helpers are engaged in PFA when they assist clients in finding shelter or help them decide which friend or relative to stay with because unresolved problems in these areas will prevent the beginning of emotional recovery from disaster.

Attending to Safety Needs   A core component of PFA involves supplying safety and security and protecting survivors from danger and further harm (NIMH, 2002). It cannot be overemphasized that people need to feel that they and their loved ones are safe after a disaster in order to begin their recovery. Brewin (2003) suggests that any psychological intervention focusing on the traumatic experience will be ineffective if the victim is feeling threatened.

Safety needs can be both physical and psychological and center on establishing stability and consistency in a chaotic environment. Responders should make efforts to reduce survivors' physiological arousal (Fullerton, Ursano, Norwood, & Holloway, 2003) and to provide as secure an environment as possible, as soon as possible, where victims do not need to fear a return of the original trauma, be it another bomb, an aftershock to an earthquake, or other repetition (Holloway & Fullerton, 1994). Raphael (1986) notes that helpers should protect survivors from any threat or danger from the ongoing disaster, especially those who may be so disoriented that they cannot care for themselves.

Once safety has been established, the helper needs to demonstrate this to the survivor. Even after the disaster has passed and the physical threat is over, fear and insecurity may remain, so counselors may need to actively convince a family that the danger has passed, and they should encourage parents to reassure their children that this is the case. Counselors can further support client safety and stability by encouraging families to maintain their routines. When the immediate danger has passed, families should try to eat their meals together at regular times. Children should have regular bedtimes and waking times even if schools are closed due to the disaster. Children should return to school as soon as they are able to.

On September 17, 2004, the remnants of Hurricane Ivan caused massive flooding in Pennsylvania, resulting in damage and destruction to more than 30,000 homes and businesses. One man was swept away and drowned in the Chartiers Creek in Carnagie, Pennsylvania. Bacteria from raw sewage entered the floodwaters, making the water and everything it touched dangerous. A firefighter who assisted during the flood died from infection in an open wound from the contaminated floodwaters (Conti & Reynolds, 2004). Area residents were urged to get tetanus shots for themselves and their families. A woman with two children appeared at a Service Center visibly upset and covered with mud as a result of her cleanup efforts. The woman explained that she had been unable to get tetanus shots for her family. She said, "I went to the health department, but they were closed. I am afraid the little one is not feeling well, and I am terrified she will die." The mental health counselor tried to calm the mother, an appropriate intervention. But then she explained that in the aftermath of a disaster we sometimes don't think clearly and might "catastrophize." This response may not have been helpful; instead the counselor would have been more effective had she simply helped the mother find out where and how to get tetanus shots.

It is not always easy to assess the threat or danger level in the aftermath of a disaster. However, one always needs to be aware of the real possibility of danger and assist clients to obtain the resources and information they require to be and to feel safe.

Providing Information and Orientation to Services   Helpers should use effective risk-communication techniques to provide survivors with information about the postdisaster situation, as well as education about what they might experience in the future (Fullerton et al., 2003). This means paying close attention to how and when and to whom you give information, as the following quote from the NIMH explains:

> It is often assumed that mental health workers who have an understanding of disasters and their consequences can pass on this information to survivors and their closest relatives. Because of the physical and psychological state of survivors in the early aftermath of mass violence and disasters, some survivors may find it difficult to learn and remember the content of such information. It is, therefore, important to train workers to appreciate the importance of both the content and manner of communicating effectively and systematically, as well as to encourage the distribution of written material. (NIMH, 2002)

Victims sometimes are in shock immediately after a disaster, so it is a good idea to be sure that they are paying attention to and comprehending any information you provide. One suggestion is to provide this information to more than one member of the family (Weaver, 1995). Some studies have indicated that using simple language is best, so framing important communications in language that even a 12-year-old can understand is recommended.

Survivors will need a number of different kinds of information, which are discussed next.

Information About Loved Ones   It is an appropriate PFA intervention to help a client to be certain that loved ones are unharmed, so survivors should be provided with information about the safety of family and friends, especially if those loved ones were also in danger from the same threat (Holloway & Fullerton, 1994). Clients can become very distressed if they are not sure that other family members or loved ones are also safe. Fear about the fate of loved ones, especially partners or children, can not only cause intense emotional distress but also may lead individuals to search for the missing, possibly exposing them to further harm (Raphael, 2003). However, panicked survivors should not be falsely reassured that everyone and everything is under control. Instead, helpers can assist them in locating family or friends who might be missing, either directly or by connecting them with the appropriate organization or system for assistance (Raphael, 1986). If phone service is disrupted, the counselor may need to offer use of a cell phone or strive to find a working phone.

Table 8.2 | Sample Resource List

1. American Red Cross
2. Area agency on aging
3. Appliance, furniture, and household items (organizations and churches offering free or reduced-rate appliances)
4. American Bar Association for insurance issues
5. Bedding and linen sources
6. Carpets and tiles (merchants who supply items at cost)
7. Cleaning supplies (what was available through American Red Cross or Salvation Army)
8. Clothing (merchants accepting vouchers, churches providing donated clothes)
9. County offices
10. Crisis hotlines (for example, mobile units, phone assistance)
11. Crisis centers for the American Red Cross
12. Federal Emergency Management Agency
13. Food (government and nongovernment organizations with locations)
14. Food replacement assistance and information on food stamps
15. Health department
16. Housing (American Red Cross for short-term housing needs; county and city agencies for long-term housing)
17. Hotels (many offer reduced rate for disaster victims)
18. Water heaters
19. Laundry services
20. Phone service, where to find public phones
21. Plumbing issues
22. Salvation Army
23. Shower facilities
24. Transportation/coordination
25. Unemployment relief
26. Veterinary care and shelter (for example, animal friends societies, animal rescue leagues)

Information About Resources   In the immediate aftermath of a disaster, helpers should provide clients with as much factual information as possible about specific resources that are available to help them in their cleanup and recovery efforts (ARC, 2002). DMH workers should create an up-to-date list of available resources for victims. Table 8.2 shows a sample list of resources from a recent national disaster. (Each resource included a phone number and address.)

This example is not comprehensive, nor is it intended to be a model for all situations and disasters, but it illustrates the sort of list that could be assembled by disaster workers as soon as possible and distributed to survivors. Lists should be updated frequently and distributed throughout the relief operation.

Information About the Future   Providing good information about what is happening is reassuring. Clients may ask for help in assessing danger and risk.

- "What is the risk of another storm coming, creating another flood, and destroying my house again?"
- "Could this toxic accident have effects that I won't notice until later on?"
- "Are we in danger of another attack?"

Counselors may not have the facts required to answer these critically important questions, but they must try to assist clients as they attempt to obtain the accurate answers needed to assess risk and danger realistically (NIMH, 2002; Fullerton et al., 2003).

Helping Clients Access Social Support   According to Maslow, love and belongingness follow physical and safety needs in the hierarchy of needs. Humans have a desire to belong to groups: clubs, work groups, religious groups, family, gangs, and so on. We strive to feel loved, needed, and accepted by others (Maslow, 1954). The support we receive from family and friends (Cohen, Frank, Doyle, Skoner, Rabin, & Gwaltney, 1998), the quality and quantity of our social relationships, and our experiences of loneliness and isolation can influence not only our emotional well-being but also our physical health (Cacioppo et. al. 2002; Cohen, Gottlieb, & Underwood, 2000). Therefore, whenever possible, survivors should be physically reunited with loved ones who can provide emotional support and security. Counselors should make every effort to keep families together (Fullerton et al., 2003), for example, during subsequent evacuations or in temporary housing.

Social support can be expressed in different ways, but all can help an individual cope with stress. Cohen (2004) and others describe three kinds of social support: instrumental, emotional and informational. **Instrumental support** is practical in nature, taking the form of money or help with tasks and chores. **Emotional support** provides an individual with warmth, caring, and a trusting relationship (House & Kahn, 1985). **Informational support** includes advice or guidance that is intended to help someone cope with difficult circumstances. A supportive helper (friend, relative, or professional) can suggest a solution to a problem or help the survivor see that the problem is manageable, or the helper can temporarily distract survivors from their problem. Such interventions need to be carefully and artfully facilitated in the aftermath of a disaster. Attempting to put a problem in perspective or distracting the client needs to be done in such a way as to provide comfort while simultaneously acknowledging the magnitude of the event and the survivor's suffering. Distracting clients by talking about less painful or neutral topics should be timed to provide respite or rest for them, not to encourage them to avoid their problems.

Substantial evidence shows that perceived social support can be a significant buffer to stress, even if the support comes exclusively from one reliable person.

Friends and family can offer money, food, clothes, help with chores, affection, perspective, comfort advice, and information—a sense that survivors are not isolated or alone. The cognition that a caring other or others will be available to help shoulder a burden can significantly lower the amount of distress a survivor experiences, thereby mitigating anxiety and depression and lowering maladaptive coping behaviors such as drinking alcohol or taking drugs (Cohen, 2004). In fact, simply having contact with others can be beneficial to health and well-being.

Social integration, defined as participation in a broad range of social relationships, promotes self-esteem, stability, self-regulation, a sense of purpose, and positive feelings. By staying connected to and interacting with others an individual can strengthen his or her sense of identity, belonging, security and purpose. Social relationships also provide opportunities for advice and suggestions. People with a large network of relationships even live longer. The benefit of social integration may be especially salient for men (House, Landis, & Umberson, 1988). Therefore, DMH workers should encourage and assist their clients to stay connected to their clubs, neighbors, associations, and places of worship as a source of support and connection as they recover from their disaster experience. Of all of the components of PFA, there appears to be unanimity on the importance of DMH workers helping clients access their natural support systems (ARC, 2002; Brewin, 2003; NIMH, 2002; Raphael, 1986; Weaver, 1995).

However, despite the well-established research findings on the importance of social support postdisaster, we also should recognize that relationships can be sources of stress and misery. In one experiment, researchers (Cohen et. al., 1998) exposed subjects to the common cold virus by placing the virus directly in their noses. All subjects tested positively for the presence of the virus, but those who were involved in conflict with family members, spouses, and friends were more than twice as likely to become ill as compared to those without such conflicts. So, when you encourage clients to contact their natural support system, first try to be sure that these contacts will not strain the client with additional stress. There is a well-recognized tendency for people to blame the victim in order for the world to appear orderly or predictable (Brewin, 2003). Even when it seems obvious that survivors were blameless, some might persist in questioning why they were at the disaster scene, or if they did all they could have to avoid the disaster, or whether they could have reacted better or more quickly. Exposure to this kind of misplaced blame can have serious consequences: Negative reactions from family and friends are a strong predictor of not recovering from PTSD (Brewin, 2003), and a recovery environment that is impoverished, punitive, blaming, demanding, anxiety filled, and invalidating is one that creates a risk for chronic PTSD (Bolton, Litz, Glenn, Orsillo, & Roemer, 2002).

Thus, counselors should be cognizant that some "friends and family" can be invalidating, stressful, depressing, or punishing and must not assume that an individual's social support network invariably will be helpful. Counselors should help clients sort out whom they should seek out in the aftermath of a disaster:

- "It is important that you contact people who care about you at a time like this. Who would be a supportive person for you?"
- "Could we talk about who you would like to contact?"

- "Is there someone you would like to talk with about what is going on?"
- "Is there a close friend or family member I could call for you?"
- "When will you make the call?"
- "How will you contact this person?"
- "Is there a rabbi, minister or priest who you would like to talk to?"
- "Are there religious services you could attend that might comfort you?"

The counselor, too, can be a source of social support and can offer instrumental, informational, and emotional support.

Assisting Victims With Traumatic Grief   When disaster results in loss of life and traumatic grief, the quality and type of aid required may be less pragmatic and more psychological in nature. Later, there may be practical problems such as identifying remains or arranging funerals, but in the immediate or postincident phase, often there are no problems to solve. As was discussed at the beginning of this chapter, the role of the helper in this situation is to supply a visible supportive presence. The helper attempts to be present for someone in grief and shock. A bereaved client may also benefit from receiving support and companionship during potentially wrenching tasks. Psychological first aid may involve accompanying someone to a hospital, providing emotional support while a dead body is being identified, or helping someone dispose of a dead pet.

After September 11, 2001, DMH workers accompanied surviving family members to ground zero and attended memorials with them. This show of support and solidarity has its roots in the many religious and cultural rituals surrounding loss, where a community pays its respect by attending a memorial or funeral. Through these actions, helpers offer consolation and demonstrate that they care about the survivor. In most circumstances, the role of the counselor is similar to the role of family and friends—to be available and to share the loss with those in grief. In unusual circumstances (for example, relatives fighting, someone decompensating, someone asking for help), the counselor is also available to provide assistance.

The following are interventions to consider when there is a death due to disaster or when attending a memorial or funeral:

- Be there.
- Be aware that there are individual and cultural differences in how people experience and express grief. At a commemoration, you may see mourners who show little or no emotion and others who appear on the verge of emotional collapse.
- If there are friends and family present, counselors should stay in the background.
- Say "I am so sorry for your loss."
- If the person is crying, offer him or her a tissue.
- Be careful not to hug someone who may not want to be touched.
- Be low key.

For the most part, volunteers should follow the opposite of the dictum "Don't just stand there, do something." There is value to being a supportive presence: *"Don't just do something, stand there."*

A Case Study: Psychological First Aid on the Phone

Perhaps the largest telephone counseling operations ever established was the New York City Missing Persons Hotline that was created very soon after the September 11, 2001, terror attacks. The operation had two goals: to provide crisis counseling (PFA) and to develop a database of missing persons. This operation was set up by volunteers from the New York Public Broadcasting Station (Channel 13 in New York), which had telephone banks in place from their pledge drives.

Mental health volunteers answered calls from those seeking information about when they might be able to get to their homes, about pets left in apartments they could not reach, and many other matters. Counselors were given daily updated resource lists. Large signs with frequently asked questions and answers were pasted all over the room. Counselors attempted to find answers to a broad range of practical questions. However, most of the calls were from panicked, depressed, and grieving relatives trying to find missing loved ones.

Information about the person being sought was matched with a Consolidated Hospital List to establish the status of the person: "Found," "Possibly Found" (names were slightly different perhaps due to a misspelling), and "Still Missing." Mental health workers called back family members to inform them of their loved one's status. If the person was still missing ("Hello Mrs. Smith, I am calling from the City Hotline. We have not yet located Mr. Smith, have you heard from him?"), more information would be gathered. Family members went into heartbreaking details in response to questions, "Aside from height, weight, eye and hair color, are there any identifiable markings on Mr. Smith?" (They were very careful to ask such questions in the present tense.) On the other end of the phone, there would be sighs and tears and stories such as "John always wore his wedding ring. It had a little scratch from the time he fell down playing basketball on a cement court. I gave him such a hard time about that. I guess I shouldn't have, should I? I am pregnant and I know he will be all right."

The central theme in the training sessions was "to meet the client where the client was." This meant supporting and accepting the client's view of the status of his/her loved one. Some callers knew that since their loved one worked on a high floor of the Towers, it was unlikely that they had survived. Others were more optimistic, and some were in denial. One caller talked about the many food courts in the basement of the World Trade Center and how his/her loved one probably was having a swell time eating gourmet foods while we all worried needlessly. Family members often seemed to move between denial and overwhelming pain. Volunteers' job was not to convince clients to be more hopeful or to be more realistic but to listen and to try to help them cope. Psychological first aid on the phone meant "being there for the other person." Volunteers were willing to share clients' losses and to help them express their feelings, not only to the workers but also to others close to them. They helped clients to better access their support systems. They asked, "Who knows how you are feeling? Who are you talking with about this experience? Who can you confide in? Who are you willing to talk with about your distress?" These versions of the same questions about the client's support systems helped clients feel less alone.

WHO CAN PROVIDE PSYCHOLOGICAL FIRST AID?

At the present time, no studies have addressed whether mental health professionals, paraprofessionals, or others are best equipped to provide PFA. Litz and Gray (2004) argue that it is best for mental health professionals to be the providers of PFA because victims might be unable to access their natural support systems if friends and family also have been impacted by the disaster. Or a survivor might be too traumatized to take advantage of the support systems that are available. In either case, professionals not only can offer effective PFA but also can provide information and education on stress and recovery. According to Litz (2004), professionals are also "guaranteed to know what *not* to do (not be intrusive and demanding of self-disclosure)—some bystanders, or untrained emergency medical professionals may inadvertently be intrusive or demanding, which may be destructive." Trained professionals are also more likely to be accustomed to hearing trauma stories and would not react negatively if a survivor feels the need to describe a painful or shocking experience.

Another point of view suggests that paraprofessionals and others may be equally proficient at providing PFA. Much early postcrisis intervention involves a type of emotional and practical support that, in this view, could be offered by most helpers and responders who will be present at the scene of a disaster, including almost anyone who has had some orientation to being with people in need or crisis and who has a functioning role at the time a disaster occurs. Taking a stance somewhere in the middle, the NIMH wrote that, although mental health personnel should provide some of the components of early intervention, other components can be provided by non-mental health personnel (NIMH, 2002). These individuals could include the following:

- Paraprofessionals
- Community volunteers
- Medical professionals including primary care practitioners, pediatricians, and family practice doctors
- Disaster responders
- Clergy
- School personnel
- Staff of paraprofessional helping organizations such as Alcoholics Anonymous
- Firefighters
- Police officers
- Hospital trauma center personnel
- Coroners

Gerard Jacobs (2003), the director of the Disaster Mental Health Institute at the University of South Dakota, maintains that PFA should be a community-based and culturally sensitive intervention and that it should be administered by trained members of the community because, in the event of a large-scale disaster, there would not be enough mental health professionals to offer assistance. Jacobs posits that, by teaching people PFA, communities can be better prepared for disasters so that the population's stress can be reduced. He characterizes such first aid as accomplishing the following:

- Providing low-cost, easily sustainable, culturally appropriate strategies for responding to the need for psychological support following disaster and other traumatic events
- Providing effective strategies for coping with difficulties and frustrations of daily life (not only disasters)
- Contributing to a community and civic involvement
- Stimulating interest in volunteerism
- Reducing alienation in minority populations

The American Red Cross also teaches PFA to all responders and expects all staff and volunteers to provide basic psychological assistance (ARC, 2002). As was discussed in Chapter 7, the American Red Cross also deploys mental health professionals when interventions based on first aid alone may not be sufficient.

We believe that all disaster workers should be offered training in PFA so that they know what to do and, perhaps just as importantly, know what *not* to do. As Litz (2004) observes, "Because individuals' decisions about seeking care in the weeks and months after trauma may be influenced by the way they were treated and the things they learned immediately after the trauma occurred, it is important for all [those] in the response chain to appreciate how they might be constructive and not inadvertently destructive."

IS PSYCHOLOGICAL FIRST AID EFFECTIVE?

The debate about who is best equipped to administer PFA aside, few DMH practitioners question the appropriateness of PFA. Given how much controversy surrounds other interventions in the field, PFA may qualify as DMH's current "best practice." And yet there are no solid empirical studies documenting its impact. Does PFA work? That depends on what you think it should accomplish.

At present, there is little empirical support for PFA's effectiveness in preventing long-term problems in the aftermath of trauma or disaster (Litz & Gray, 2004; Neria, Suh, & Marshall, 2004; Raphael & Dobson, 2001). However, as we noted earlier, PFA is not intended to be secondary prevention. Other mental health interventions that will be discussed in future chapters, such as debriefing and cognitive–behavioral, are specifically meant to prevent PTSD and other problems after exposure to disasters, and a small but growing body of literature examines their efficacy (for example, Litz & Gray, 2004; Neria et al., 2004; Shalev, 1994; Raphael, 2003). But good data are lacking even here, as Litz (2004) observes: "The early intervention field is dominated by non-evidence-based practices, poorly defined and anachronistic notions about recovery from trauma and risk for trauma-linked disorders, and an apparent unresponsiveness to scientific inquiry."

When we consider the methodological difficulties that DMH presents, the lack of data is understandable. A daunting combination of practical and ethical barriers makes study of even secondary interventions that take place days or weeks after a disaster difficult, and these difficulties are multiplied in the earliest period when PFA occurs. For example, dividing trauma victims into experimental and control conditions and collecting pretreatment data is the last thing on responders' minds in the immediate aftermath of a disaster. It would not be ethical to deny some survivors water or kindness or accurate information to determine if such deprivation had long-term effects (not that anyone has proposed doing this). Even asking vulnerable victims who are still in the immediate throes of a traumatic experience to provide valid informed consent is ethically questionable (Gray, Litz, & Olson, 2004). At a more elemental level, the goals of PFA are in need of more precise definition before researchers can even decide just what to evaluate in gauging effectiveness. And there are different models of PFA involving different components, raising the question of which models and which components should be studied.

Determined and creative DMH researchers are working to develop solutions to some of the methodological problems that have thus far limited study of secondary interventions. For example, Gray et al. (2004) have detailed an argument in support of developing ethical and practically feasible randomized clinical trials to evaluate the efficacy of secondary interventions specifically comparing various methods of psychological debriefing to alternative treatments. However, they suggest that these trials begin *after* the immediate impact phase of approximately 48 hours following a traumatic event. Of course, PFA typically begins to be administered during that first 48 hours period, so a feasible and ethical way to collect data remains undiscovered.

Because of this general lack of evidence regarding effective early intervention in the aftermath of a disaster, PFA is intentionally geared to be a broader, less specific and less narrowly defined intervention. It is now really an umbrella term for many components and processes that researchers will need to explore further in order to ascertain what elements actually help a person at a particular time. Psychological first aid is understood to be an early disaster response intervention that does not appear to be harmful. It contains no hard and fast mandates and has the attributes of kindness, comfort, and practical and emotional support at its core. These are features that have always guided humanitarian relief.

Still, despite its apparent benignity, is there any evidence to support the continued use of PFA? A review of the psychological literature suggests indirect findings that could be relevant. In 2001 the American Psychological Association Division 29 Task Force on Empirically Supported Therapy Relationships attempted to identify the most significant components of therapeutic relationships (Norcross, 2001). They concluded that four elements were empirically supported as being "demonstrably effective": the therapeutic alliance, cohesion in group therapy, empathy, and goal consensus and collaboration. Another seven elements were deemed "promising and probably effective": positive regard, congruence/genuineness, feedback, repair of alliance ruptures, self-disclosure, management of countertransference, and quality of relational interpretations (Ackerman et al.,

2001). In other words, according to the task force's analysis, the core principles of Rogerian person-centered therapy, which are also core principles of PFA, provide the backbone of the most successful therapeutic relationships, regardless of the specific counseling technique used (Cornelius-White, 2002).

Some of these empirically supported relationship principles involve a longer-term relationship than the mental health early responder and disaster victim are likely to establish, but several of them clearly are incorporated into PFA that is provided during the immediate impact phase. In particular, the "demonstrably effective" (Ackerman et al., 2001) elements of *empathy*, *goal consensus*, and *collaboration* fit into the disaster treatment guidelines supported by the NIHM (2002) and American Red Cross (Hamilton, 2004). All models of PFA suggest that helpers should maintain a consistently empathetic tone as they offer practical assistance to survivors in the aftermath of a disaster because that early support may lay the groundwork for later more intensive interventions as survivors move past the immediate impact and begin the recovery phase. As DeWolfe (2000) observes, "When disaster mental health workers are visible and perceived as helpful during [the earliest] phase, they are more readily accepted and have a foundation from which to provide assistance in the difficult phases ahead."

Regarding the demonstrated elements of goal consensus and collaboration, Egan (2002) suggests that helpers should not view clients as being overly fragile but rather as individuals capable of taking an active role in what they want from the therapeutic relationship. Although he is referring to clients in general and not specifically to disaster survivors, the point is consistent with a principle of PFA: Providers should support survivor autonomy and empowerment.

We conclude this review of PFA by pointing out that in PFA, as in any other psychological intervention, one size does not fit all. Survivors of a disaster should not be treated identically; individual needs and cultural differences must be respected when providing PFA or any other mental health service. Some survivors may prefer the comfort and support of peers, whereas others may prefer to work out their problems alone or only want support from family members. Clients might also have very different needs that develop over the days or weeks that they are working with a DMH counselor. The range of PFA interventions—from being a visible presence, to supplying food or information, to escorting a client to safety, to listening to a client's story—suggests that effective counseling necessitates considerable flexibility on the part of the practitioner. Even as researchers attempt to establish evidence-based best practices in DMH, we should not overlook our clinical experience and common sense (McCabe, 2004).

References

Ackerman, S. J., et al. (2001). Empirically supported therapy relationships: Conclusions and recommendations of the Division 29 Task Force. *Psychotherapy: Theory, Research, Practice, Training, 38,* 495–497.

ARC (American Red Cross). (2002). *Disaster mental health services: An overview* (ARC 3077-2A). Washington, DC: Author.

Bolton, E. E., Litz, B. T., Glenn, D. M., Orsillo, S., & Roemer, L. (2002). The impact of homecoming reception on the adaptation of peacekeepers following deployment. *Military Psychology. 14,* 241–251.

Bonanno, G. A. (2004). Loss, trauma and human resilience: Have we underestimated the human capacity to thrive after extremely aversive events? *American Psychologist, 59,* 20–28.

Brewin, C. R. (2003). *Posttraumatic stress disorder: Malady or myth?* New Haven, CT: Yale University Press.

Cacioppo, J. T., et al. (2002). Loneliness and health: Potential mechanisms. *Psychosomatic Medicine, 63,* 407–417.

Cohen, S. (2004). Social relationships and health. *American Psychologist, 59,* 676–684.

Cohen, S., Frank, E., Doyle, W. J., Skoner, D. P., Rabin, B. S., & Gwaltney Jr., L. M. (1998). Types of stressors that increase the susceptibility to the common cold in adults. *Health Psychology, 17,* 214–223.

Cohen, S., Gottlieb, B., & Underwood, L. (2000). Social relationships and health. In S. Cohen, L. Underwood, & B. Gottlieb (Eds.), *Measurement and intervening in social support* (pp. 3–25). New York: Oxford University Press.

Conti, D., & Reynolds, D. (2004, September 29). Flood link eyed in fire policeman death. *Pittsburgh Tribune Review,* 8.

Cornelius-White, J. H. D. (2002). The phoenix of empirically supported therapy relationships: The overlooked person-centered basis. *Psychotherapy: Theory, Research, Practice, Training, 39,* 219–222.

DeWolfe, D. J. (2000). *Training manual for mental health and human service workers in major disasters* (2nd ed.). U.S. Department of Health and Human Services: Center for Mental Health Services (Publication No. ADM 90-538). Retrieved February 14, 2005, from http://www.mentalhealth.org/publications/allpubs/ADM90-538/index.htm.

Egan, G. (2002). *The skilled helper: A problem-management and opportunity-development approach to helping* (7th ed.). Pacific Grove, CA: Brooks/Cole.

Fullerton, C. S., Ursano, R. J., Norwood, A. E., & Holloway, H. H. (2003). Trauma, terrorism, and disaster. In R. J. Ursano, C. S. Fullerton, & A. E. Norwood (Eds.), *Terrorism and disaster: Individual and community mental health interventions* (pp. 1–20). Cambridge, England, and New York: Cambridge University Press.

Gray, M. J., Litz, B. T., & Olson, A. R. (2004). Methodological and ethical issues in early intervention research. In B. T. Litz (Ed.), *Early intervention for trauma and traumatic loss* (pp. 179–198). New York: Guilford Press.

Hamilton, S. E. (2004). Where are we now? A view from the Red Cross. *Families, Systems, & Health, 22,* 58–60.

Herman, J. L. (1992). *Trauma and recovery.* New York: Basic Books.

Holloway, H. C., & Fullerton, C. S. (1994). The psychology of terror and its aftermath. In R. J. Ursano, B. G. McCaughey, & C. S. Fullerton (Eds.), *Individual and community responses to disaster: The structure of human chaos* (pp. 31–45). Cambridge, England, and New York: Cambridge University Press.

House, J. S., & Kahn, R. L. (1985). Measures and concepts of social support. In S. Cohen & S. L. Syme (Eds.), *Social support and health* (pp. 83–108). New York: Academic Press.

House, J. S., Landis, K. R., & Umberson, D. (1988). Social relationships and health. *Science, 241,* 540–545.

Jacobs, G. (2003, April 11). *Current developments in disaster mental health.* Paper presented at Lessons From Disaster: A Conference and Conversation, State University of New York, New Paltz.

James, R. K., & Gilliland, B. E. (2005). *Crisis intervention strategies* (5th ed.). Belmont, CA: Thomson Brooks/Cole.

Litz, B. T. (2004). Introduction. In B. T. Litz (Ed.), *Early intervention for trauma and traumatic loss* (pp. 1–12). New York: Guilford Press.

Litz, B. T., & Gray, M. J. (2004). Early intervention for trauma in adults: A framework for first aid and secondary prevention. In B. T. Litz (Ed.), *Early intervention for trauma and traumatic loss* (pp. 87–111). New York: Guilford Press.

Maslow, A. H. (1954). *Motivation and personality.* New York: Harper & Row.

Maslow, A. H. (1999). *Toward a psychology of being* (3rd ed.). New York: Wiley.

McCabe, O. L. (2004). Crossing the quality chasm in behavioral health care: The role of evidence-based practice. *Professional Psychology: Theory and Practice, 35,* 571–579.

NIMH (National Institute of Mental Health). (2002). *Mental health and mass violence: Evidence-based early psychological intervention for victims/survivors of mass violence. A workshop to reach consensus on best practices* (NIH Publication No. 02-5138). Washington DC: Government Printing Office.

Neria, Y., Suh, E. J., & Marshall, R. D. (2004). The professional response to the aftermath of September 11, 2001, in New York City. In B. T. Litz (Ed.), *Early intervention for trauma and traumatic loss* (pp. 201–215). New York: Guilford Press.

Norcross, J. C. (2001). Purposes, processes, and products of the Task Force on Empirically Supported Therapy Relationships. *Psychotherapy, 38,* 345–356.

Norris, F., Friedman, M. J., Watson, P. J., Byrne, C. M., Diaz, E., & Kaniasty, K. (2002). 60,000 disaster victims speak: Part I. An empirical review of the empirical literature, 1981–2001. *Psychiatry: Interpersonal & Biological Processes, 65,* 207–239.

Pynoos, R. S., & Nader, K. (1988). Psychological first aid and treatment approach to children exposed to community violence: research implications. *Journal of Traumatic Stress, 1,* 445–473.

Raphael, B. (1977). The Granville train disaster: Psychological needs and their management. *Medical Journal of Australia, 1,* 303–305.

Raphael, B. (1986). *When disaster strikes: How individuals and communities cope with catastrophe.* New York: Basic Books.

Raphael, B. (2003). Early intervention and the debriefing debate. In R. J. Ursano, C. S. Fullerton, & A. E. Norwood (Eds.), *Terrorism and disaster: Individual and community mental health interventions* (pp. 146–161). Cambridge, England, and New York: Cambridge University Press.

Raphael, B., & Dobson, M. (2001). Acute posttraumatic intervention. In J. P. Wilson, M. J. Friedman, & J. D. Lindy (Eds.), *Treating psychological trauma and PTSD* (pp. 139–158). New York: Guilford Press.

Rogers, C. (1951). *Client-centered therapy.* Boston: Houghton Mifflin.

Rogers, C. (1970). *On becoming a person: A therapist's view of psychotherapy.* Boston: Houghton Mifflin.

Shalev, A. Y. (1994). Debriefing following traumatic exposure. In R. J. Ursano, B. G. McCaughey, & C. S. Fullerton (Eds.), *Individual and community responses to disaster: the structure of human chaos* (pp. 201–219). Cambridge, England, and New York: Cambridge University Press.

Slaikeu, K. A. (1990). *Crisis intervention: A handbook for practice and research* (2nd ed.). Boston: Allyn & Bacon.

Sullivan, H. S. (1940). *Conceptions of modern psychiatry.* New York: Norton.

Watson P. (2004). *Behavioral health interventions following mass violence.* Retrieved July 2005 from the National Center for PTSD at www.istss.org/publications/TS/Winter04/behavioral.htm.

Weaver, J. D. (1995). *Disasters: Mental health interventions.* Sarasota, FL: Professional Resources Press.

Winnicott, D. W. (1958). *Through paediatrics to psychoanalysis.* London: Hogath.

Make a habit of two things—to help, or at least to do no harm.

Hippocrates

9 CHAPTER | Early Interventions Beyond Psychological First Aid

In this chapter, we examine the early interventions that go beyond psychological first aid (PFA). We do not mean to suggest that these interventions are necessarily more sophisticated, nor do they necessarily occur at some time after PFA is applied, though we do believe that the interventions are more likely to be utilized by mental health providers, whereas many volunteers and disaster workers could supply the interventions that we discussed in Chapter 8. Just as PFA can be used throughout a disaster response, so too can assessment, triage, screening, psychoeducation, rumor control, conflict mediation, cognitive restructuring, and referral for continued care. Note that the skilled and experienced disaster mental health (DMH) worker does not first build rapport, then assess, and finally intervene. The skilled worker is likely to be engaged in all of these activities throughout the response.

ASSESSMENT

In traditional mental health practice, **assessment** usually refers to evaluating a client according to a *DSM* nosology. In the practice of DMH, workers are continually involved in observation and assessment at multiple levels. The scene and scope of a disaster are larger than what is involved in most clinical work, so the task of assessment is therefore more complex but essential, according to the National Institute for Mental Health (NIMH): "Screening and needs assessments for individuals, groups and populations are important for the provision of informed early interventions following mass violence and disasters" (NIMH, 2002).

At the most basic level, there is an ongoing *needs assessment,* which is a systematic appraisal of the current status of individuals, groups, and the overall affected community. Included in the needs assessment should be an evaluation of whether survivors' needs are being adequately addressed, the characteristics of the recovery environment, and what additional interventions and resources are required (Watson, 2004). Mental health workers should not have to assess whether the site is physically safe or secure because first responders should do this. At the same time DMH workers should keep physical safety issues in mind, especially if they are deployed on-scene in the early impact stage. But they will need to ask themselves if the environment is suitable for psychological recovery. Helpers should continually assess whether more workers are needed and ask for such resources, if necessary.

As the relief operation proceeds, there is ongoing evaluation of the needs of each survivor as well as recovery workers. Assessment can involve a multitude of observations and judgments. It can involve counselors deciding to make a follow-up visit to the home of a survivor who appears to need further assistance or recommending that the survivor seek additional help from community mental health services. Mental health workers might assess whether spiritual support is needed, if more information should be made more accessible to more members of the community, if the community is by and large angry or disappointed, and if disaster workers need to take breaks. The stress level of the affected population as well as those working on recovery needs to be monitored at all times. The discussions that follow focus on assisting survivors. However, all these interventions can and should be applied to relief workers, including other mental health workers.

Triage

Triage is a specific type of assessment. It derives from the medical practice of deciding who is most in need of care and delivering services first to these clients. Triage has been defined as "the process of evaluating and sorting victims by immediacy of treatment needed and directing them to immediate or delayed treatment. The goal of triage is to do the greatest good for the greatest number of people" (NIMH, 2002).

As was noted in Chapter 4, the emotional reactions of those impacted by disaster can be intense but normal and transient. A victim might cry or scream, but this may be a normal reaction in someone who is simply expressive by nature. On the other hand, a victim who appears to be unemotional may in fact be dazed, emotionally shut down, or in shock. Helpers attempting to assess who is in most need of mental health assistance may have a difficult time sorting out who is showing the most distress from who needs the most help—not always the same thing. This being said, an extreme reaction can be one indication for the survivor being triaged. Victims showing signs of significant impairment such as severe depression, panic, or psychosis should be directed to psychiatric care if available. Such victims might benefit from psychotropic medication and certainly from rest (Raphael, 1986). Physical injuries such as concussions or some toxic exposure can sometimes mimic psychological symptoms, so they should be looked for as well. Mental health workers should err on the side of caution and refer any such cases to medical personnel or a hospital.

Mental health workers who need to make decisions about who to treat first may be guided by the recommendations of the NIMH (2002). Although the recommendations listed below are for survivors who should be targeted for follow-up interventions, they also offer guidance in terms of prioritizing treatment. The NIMH report proposes that survivors of mass violence who should be targeted for follow-up interventions to prevent adjustment difficulties include those

- Who have acute stress disorder (ASD) or other clinically significant symptoms stemming from the trauma.
- Who are bereaved.
- Who have a preexisting psychiatric disorder.
- Who require medical or surgical attention.
- Whose exposure to the incident is particularly intense and of long duration.

These guidelines suggest that mental health workers should give special attention to those who are injured or hospitalized, those who have lost a loved one, those whose exposure to the event was long or grotesque, and those with a history of mental illness. Through a process of conversation, a worker might discover the level of exposure of a survivor. It may be more difficult to ask probing questions about psychiatric history. A worker might ask the survivor if he or she is taking any medications. If the medication is psychotropic, the worker might give more attention to such a survivor.

Additionally, research makes clear that children are the most vulnerable population to trauma (Norris, Friedman, Watson, Byrne, Diaz, & Kaniasty, 2002). Therefore, workers might consider offering assistance to children or families with small children first.

Screening

Screening involves attempting to identify those who are at risk for developing symptoms but may not have yet shown signs of this outcome. Screening survivors of disaster usually refers to the act of monitoring a large population in order to determine which individuals need or will need treatment, a practice that raises both logistical and ethical concerns. "Specific screening methodologies used for individuals or groups considered to be at high risk for chronic PTSD and other serious mental health outcomes following mass violence and disasters should be evaluated to ensure that their use is both safe and effective" (NIMH, 2002).

Much PFA involves supporting natural recovery processes. Taking a more active or intrusive mental health approach to *all* victims of disaster may not be helpful and could be harmful (Bonnano, 2004; Brewin, 2003; Litz, 2004;

Raphael, 2003). Brewin suggests that "an alternative, and perhaps more rational, strategy is called *Screen and Treat,* which involves careful monitoring of survivors' symptoms and referral for treatment only when symptoms are failing to subside naturally." This seems like a reasonable way to treat victims of disaster: allowing most to recover on their own and screening out only those most vulnerable who will need treatment. Unfortunately, there is not yet much evidence to support this approach as helpful or efficient. It is also not without peril, as the NIMH report (2002) points out: "Can screening harm some individuals exposed to trauma? If so, what is the nature and extent of such harm (i.e., the risk of the screening being used for purposes not intended by the investigators)? Is the risk of such harm offset by the risk of failing to use screening instruments to identify those at high risk for negative outcomes?"

According to the National Screening Committee (1998), screening should only be done if

1. The condition is an important health problem.
2. There is evidence that early intervention would lead to better outcomes than later intervention.
3. Over time those identified would not recover on their own.
4. There is an effective treatment for the disorder.
5. Vulnerable people would not come forward to be treated if there were no screening.
6. The test is simple, safe, precise, valid, and acceptable to the population being screened. Is the test predictive of who will and who will not develop a disorder?

Let's consider these points in order.

1. *Is the condition serious?* As was discussed in Chapter 5, posttraumatic stress disorder (PTSD) is a very serious and important health problem. If vulnerable disaster survivors can be screened and effectively treated, thereby preventing PTSD, a significant service would be provided.
2. *Is there evidence that early intervention would lead to better outcomes?* There is some controversy about this point. Some advocate treating people with ASD as soon as possible after the trauma (Bryant & Harvey, 2000; Spiegel & Classen, 1995), arguing that early treatment may prevent survivors from developing a chronic style of avoidance. Others have suggested that treatment should begin only after the normal peritraumatic stress reactions have subsided, many weeks after the event (Brewin, 2003; Litz & Grey, 2004).
3. *Do people recover on their own?* Most survivors of disaster who are symptomatic do recover over time (Bonnano, 2004; Norris et al., 2002). However, as was discussed in Chapter 5, depending on the nature of the event, the particular person, the level of exposure, and other variables, a significant percentage of survivors can develop PTSD or other disorders. PTSD, for example, can be chronic and the recovery quite difficult. Further underscoring the risk for chronicity, Kessler, Sonnega, Bromet, Hughes, and Nelson (1995) found that one-third of people with PTSD fail to recover after many years.

4. *Are there effective treatments?* There are a number of treatments, which we discuss in Chapter 11, that have been shown to be effective with people suffering with ASD, PTSD, depression, and anxiety disorders caused by disaster. Psychotherapy helps most people most of the time (Smith, Glass, & Miller, 1980). However, if such care is not available or acceptable to a population, there is no point in screening. The NIMH report (2002) asks whether it is "acceptable to screen for conditions if care is not provided or readily acceptable." We think the answer is clearly no. Fortunately, most urban and many rural communities in the United States do have some resources to supply counseling and therapy.

5. *Do people come forward?* Some evidence indicates that large numbers of people with PTSD do not come forward on their own to be treated. This is the sort of finding that would appear to make screening useful. Certainly, everyone has the right to refuse treatment, but why do people not seek help? Perhaps they want to tough it out, or they want to avoid the shame of being labeled with a psychiatric diagnosis, or they are concerned that others will see them as weak. For others, the thought of treatment may produce reminders and triggers of the event, so it may be that their avoidance of treatment could be seen as part of the disorder. According to Wessely (2003), these people could be educated and sensitively encouraged to seek treatment with effective screening.

6. *Does it work?* Can screening predict who will develop a disorder such as PTSD following a disaster? Is there an effective and precise test? Unfortunately, at this time we don't know the answer to this most basic question. Mental health screening excluded hundreds of thousands of men from the war effort during World War II. It was believed that such screening could "select out" those who could not tolerate the experience of combat (Castro, Engel, & Adler, 2004). That attempt is now considered a failure because selecting for vulnerability is a blunt instrument. Many competent potential members of a group (for example, police officers and soldiers) could be rejected whereas those who would break down in the face of adversity are missed. Screening programs are currently being used with soldiers in Afghanistan and Iraq to determine who will need help in the aftermath of combat. However, this screening has not been systematically evaluated (Castro et al., 2004).

Brewin (2003) proposes a simple test that could be administered to predict the development of PTSD postdisaster. In the aftermath of a train crash that occurred just outside of London, resulting in deaths and injuries, Brewin and his colleagues (2002) administered the questionnaire shown in Figure 9.1. The questions tap the hyperarousal and reexperiencing associated with PTSD. They found that of the survivors who answered yes to six or more questions, 86% were then found to have PTSD based on extensive clinical interviews, whereas only 7% were similarly diagnosed if they answered yes to five or fewer questions.

Problems With Screening   Although these results suggest the potential value of a simple screening instrument for PTSD postdisaster, there needs to be replication

Figure 9.1 | Trauma Screening Questionnaire

Please consider the following reactions that sometimes occur after a traumatic event. This questionnaire is concerned with your personal reactions to the traumatic event that happened a few weeks ago. Please indicate whether or not you have experienced any of the following AT LEAST TWICE IN THE PAST WEEK:

Your Own Reactions Now to the Traumatic Event	Yes, at Least Twice in the Last Week	No
1. Upsetting thoughts or memories about the event that have come into your mind against your will		
2. Upsetting dreams about the event		
3. Acting or feeling as though the event were happening again		
4. Feeling upset by reminders of the event		
5. Bodily reactions (such as fast heartbeat, stomach churning, sweatiness, dizziness) when reminded of the event		
6. Difficulty falling or staying asleep		
7. Irritability or outbursts of anger		
8. Difficulty concentrating		
9. Heightened awareness of potential dangers to yourself and others		
10. Being jumpy or being startled at something unexpected		

Source: Brewin (2003).

of this type of study to determine if there is the same level of predictability in other disaster situations, with different populations. Brewin (2003) notes that, for a screen and treat strategy to be effective, "it will almost certainly be important to have some initial contact with survivors postincident, providing them with reassurance, information, and a point of contact for them to seek further advice and support if required." It would appear that PFA would then be the first level of intervention and would contribute to establishing the rapport necessary for survivors to allow themselves to be screened. After a period of time, such a screening could lead to possible referral for follow-up treatment.

Who should be screened and under what circumstances should a screening take place? In the aftermath of a disaster that is not particularly intense but wide in scope, such as the blackout in the northeastern United States in 2003, an attempt at screening millions of victims is probably not cost effective or worthwhile. However, when people have been exposed to major or prolonged trauma or particular hardship (for example, intense combat, exposure to gruesome sights, identifying body parts, severe injury, rape), rates of developing a disorder may be high enough to justify a screening program (Wessely, 2003). Another question arises as to when a screening should take place. Many experts (for example, Shalev, 2001) note that following trauma a large proportion of patients who exhibit symptoms recover within a short time. Therefore, screening that is too early can overestimate the numbers of people who need help. But if it is done too late, it could result in unnecessary suffering. There is only speculation about the optimal time to do a screening following a disaster (Wessely, 2003).

Screening can be costly in terms of money and resources, and all screening carries a risk of harm (NIMH, 2002; Wessely, 2003). If it is communicated to survivors of disaster through screening that they have been identified as vulnerable to symptoms and may break down, we may be inadvertently changing their view of themselves from healthy to unhealthy. There are also practical obstacles to screening. It is not simple, easy, or cost effective to get an instrument distributed to a large population of people impacted by disaster. The likelihood of large numbers of false positives also raises ethical issues (NIMH, 2002) because people who are incorrectly identified as being at risk could feel labeled and stigmatized despite not having any disorder.

Wessely (2003) points out that "with the best of intentions in the world, mental health programs based on screening for existing disorders has not been a success." He concludes that

> I am skeptical that routine screening for psychological disorders after trauma is justified, and am inclined to think that the resources could be better spent on better treatment facilities for those who do come forward. Likewise, I am also inclined to think that in our present knowledge we are better advised to make efforts to ensure that the population at risk is aware of the availability of services and what they can offer, and allow those affected to make up their own minds. (Wessely, 2003)

Assessment, screening, and triage should all be considered by mental health workers and administrators before disaster strikes, as part of planning and preparation. Community mental health workers should, as part of their planning, know the locations of vulnerable populations—the nursing homes, assisted-living residences, preschools and schools, and residences for the disabled or mentally ill. This could be viewed as a type of *prescreening*. It is most effective to target resources where they are most likely to be needed when disaster strikes, so in this way DMH workers could be deployed in the early stages of a disaster to these most vulnerable sites.

PSYCHOEDUCATION

Trauma robs survivors of a sense of control and power. If survivors are educated about their condition and the recovery process, they may regain understanding and a sense of control and mastery over the chaotic situation and their own chaotic feelings, thereby mitigating the impact of trauma. In psychoeducation, helpers tell receptive individuals about the typical reactions and symptoms experienced by many trauma survivors and inform them about treatment resources. The goal should be to let survivors know what they might experience, without alarming them or causing them to anticipate future distress (Miller, 2002). More specifically, **psychoeducation** in the aftermath of a disaster involves providing information about a range of biopsychosocial processes including common reactions to disaster, stages of reactions to disaster, symptoms, resilience, treatment, effective and ineffective coping strategies, the stages of loss and other information about grief, and ways that parents can help children. These topics are examined more fully in the discussions that follow.

Psychoeducation appears to be one of the least controversial and most recommended early interventions in DMH (ARC, 2002; Litz & Gray, 2004; Miller, 2002; Raphael & Wooding, 2004). It is a component of traditional supportive interventions (Raphael, 1986), Critical Incident Stress Management/ Debriefing (Mitchell, 1983), and cognitive–behavioral therapies (Rothbaum, Meadows, Resick, & Foy, 2000). The NIMH (2002) report on early intervention notes that it is "widely accepted" that members of any early intervention workforce should be trained to educate trauma survivors. According to the NIMH, most survivors do not actively seek out psychoeducation or other mental health services after a disaster, so as a key component of early intervention efforts it is important that mental health workers perform *outreach,* defined as an "array of disaster mental health services extended to survivors wherever they congregate, designed to increase understanding of common reactions, coping, and when and where to receive more in-depth help" (NIMH, 2002). They suggest that psychoeducation provided through outreach can be accomplished through a variety of channels by helpers who may

- Offer information/education and "therapy by walking around."
- Use established community structures such as places of worship, schools, or community centers.
- Distribute flyers.
- Host websites.
- Conduct media interviews and programs and distribute media releases.

Counselors should keep in mind that survivors may be fragile, confused, disoriented, distracted, or even in shock and may therefore find it difficult to concentrate and to learn or remember the psychoeducational material that is being offered. Because of this, the manner of communicating the information may be as important as the content that is being presented (NIMH, 2002). Helpers should not sound condescending, and the information should be presented in a clear and simple manner without jargon. Counselors should not assume because they presented information that it was heard and understood. George Bernard Shaw once said, "The single biggest problem with communication is the illusion that it has taken place."

Psychoeducation on Normal Reactions to Stress

One regularly cited element of psychoeducation is to provide information on stress and stress management and to let victims know that they are experiencing a normal reaction (Weaver, 1995). In fact, one of the most common interventions in DMH is simply to assure survivors that they are not going crazy, that the strange uncomfortable feelings or responses they are having are not a sign of psychosis. Through conversations and written material, survivors should be educated that they are *experiencing a normal reaction to an abnormal situation*. There are other versions of this central intervention in DMH: "You are experiencing an ordinary (usual, typical, common) reaction to an extraordinary (unusual, atypical, uncommon) circumstance." This intervention is intended to normalize the survivors' reaction so that the survivor does not feel odd or weak or as if he or she is suffering from some character flaw. It is intended to prevent the survivor from feeling different, tainted, or mentally ill; to provide information; and to be reassuring. It also suggests that these very distressing symptoms will dissipate over time.

Counselors may not be very good at predicting how long the distress following a disaster will last. A review of the research (Norris et al., 2002) does show that symptoms decline over time for the great majority of samples studied, with most symptoms occurring in the first year. Therefore, it would seem appropriate for a counselor to offer reassurance to a client who asks, "I am afraid I will always feel this way. Will I?" A counselor would be honest in saying that the great majority of survivors do recover emotionally from disaster and trauma. The information provided in Chapter 4 details the expected traumatic reactions following disaster. This information can be easily used to develop a handout. We provide a sample handout in Appendix A.

There are potential problems with providing this kind of psychoeducational material. There is the possibility that the extreme reactions of a survivor may *not* be normal and that the individual needs professional help. Assuring every survivor that they are experiencing a normal reaction to an abnormal situation may discourage someone who needs expert help from seeking it. On the other hand, a DMH worker might assume and communicate to survivors that they *must* experience stress reactions and if they do not, there is something wrong with them. It is possible that such a survivor, who is resilient and not impaired, may come to feel that he or she is being defensive or closed.

> In the aftermath of September 11, 2001, a DMH worker was talking with a young police officer in the big white tent that was set up as a respite center near ground zero. The officer, who was at ground zero on the day of the attacks, described the sound of bodies hitting the ground that morning. The worker said to the officer, "Honey, you're going to have nightmares, certain. I have some handouts you might read, and you need to think about how to best handle all this stress." The policewoman reported that she was put off by the arrogance of the counselor's insistence that she would experience symptoms.

Although this example may appear extreme, it illustrates how discussing normal reactions with a survivor can be mishandled and can have an unintended effect.

This was clearly a misguided attempt at providing psychoeducation, perhaps because the counselor was so upset from listening to the story that she was projecting her own sense of being overwhelmed onto the officer. A counselor should not predict symptoms in a client or try to convince survivors that they must go through a certain set of experiences following disaster. Such a heavy-handed approach undermines rapport and possibly the future utilization of mental health services. Instead, the psychoeducational material on normal responses to disaster is intended to communicate that it is not unusual for survivors to experience certain typical reactions.

Providing Stress Management Skills

Sometimes it is helpful to explain that, in times of great upheaval, people can make poor decisions about coping with stress. Counselors can ask, "How have you coped with adversity or other stressors in your life?" "What will you do this evening after cleaning the debris out of your house?" Survivors can be alerted to the dangers of *ineffective coping mechanisms* such as overworking, not getting enough rest or sleep, binge eating, chronic television addiction, drinking alcohol, and smoking. One ineffective coping mechanism that has not received sufficient attention, but is common after disaster, is attempting to regain a sense of control by acting in an overaggressive manner. Survivors (or stressed-out disaster workers) may try to overcome feelings of helplessness by becoming overcontrolling of others—bullying those around them.

When counselors suggest positive or effective coping mechanisms, they need to ensure that their admonitions do not sound like platitudes or boilerplate advice. Counselors can explain that experienced first responders understand the importance of healthy habits in times of great stress. There is considerable research that demonstrates the effectiveness of stress-reducing strategies such as obtaining social support (Cohen, 2004; Wortman & Dunkel-Schetter, 1987), emotional disclosure (Pennebaker, 1995, 1997), exercise (McCann & Holmes, 1984; Rostad & Long, 1996), writing in a journal (Pennebaker & Beale, 1986), relaxation and meditation (Sanderson, 2004), humor (Martin & Lefcourt, 1983), and religion or spiritual practice (Sanderson, 2004). These strategies need to be suggested with care and sensitivity. It would not be a good idea to suggest that survivors go for a bicycle ride or go jogging shortly after a disaster or when they were exhausted from trying to clean and get the mold out of their house following a flood. Similarly, humor should be used carefully and judiciously. In lower Manhattan, hours after the twin towers fell, one of us helped evacuate an assisted-living facility. As volunteers escorted the residents onto buses that would take them out of Manhattan, we joked about whether they thought the Yankees would play that night, and we joked about being able to ride the city buses without a token. These residents did not suffer any immediate personal losses, so humor about the situation seemed friendly, helpful, and appropriate.

Some stress management techniques that could be suggested to survivors include the following. (Many of these are similar to the self-care tips we suggested for DMH professionals in Chapter 7 because survivors and workers face many of the same pressures and can benefit from the same practices.)

- Try to take care of yourself; recognize that you have experienced great stress and try to be gentle and patient with yourself.
- Try to keep as normal a schedule as possible; take frequent breaks, alternating times of activity with times for rest and relaxation.
- Prioritize; make "to do" lists of things that must be done; put other tasks on a "wait" list.
- Set realistic short-term goals and, when possible, delegate duties and responsibilities to others.
- Set limits for yourself; you may want to learn/use some relaxation/stress reduction techniques.
- Eat well-balanced meals even if you don't feel like it; increase fluid intake; decrease the use of caffeine and do not abuse alcohol or drugs.
- Try to be aware of your feelings; don't be afraid to experience them and talk about them.
- Try to get plenty of rest; there may be temporary changes in your sleep patterns.
- Use your support systems—family, friends, colleagues, and clergy.
- Be willing to ask for and accept the concern and help of others.
- Try to decrease environmental stress such as noise and clutter.
- Avoid overexposing yourself with media images that could be flooding TV sets and newspapers. These images can be quite provocative. Take a break from the coverage of the event.
- Think about your own preferred ways to manage stress. Get a massage; soak in a long bath; listen to music; watch a ball game or a movie.
- Pray.
- Exercise.
- Breathe deeply. People often hold their breath when they are tense. Breathing can help your whole body relax.

Providing Coping Skills Training

In our previous section, our focus was on stress management skills, techniques, and strategies; now let's look more at "styles" of coping. For the most part, it has been shown that *active* or *problem-focused coping* is beneficial (Folkman & Lazarus, 1980). This coping style may involve doing something about the problem, making a plan of action, taking direct action, working at keeping from getting distracted, or seeking support and assistance (Carver, Scheier, & Weintraub, 1989). A more emotional style of coping may involve not thinking about the problem through avoidance or denial or venting emotionally (Folkman & Lazarus, 1980). This type of coping is not as helpful or as useful, but when little can be done to change a negative situation, acceptance or even avoidance can be a more useful approach to stress than problem solving (Roth & Cohen, 1986). However, sometimes avoidance and denial are used when in fact there is a problem that can be tackled or solved, and this can be dangerous. Avoiders may not seek medical or psychological assistance when it could be advantageous.

Different types of situations may call for different types of coping styles. Since not everyone is flexible enough to shift styles when necessary, a counselor could educate a survivor about the importance of matching the best coping style with the situation. A more active style may be useful if, for example, there are financial and other material benefits for disaster victims that need to be investigated. In this case, a counselor may encourage a more active style. In contrast, if a loved one is injured or hospitalized and one has no real capacity to improve the situation, a more problem-focused style could increase frustration, and the survivor may need to be encouraged to pray or simply be more accepting.

Psychoeducation on Loss and Grief

Psychoeducation is recommended not only for trauma survivors but also for those experiencing grief as a result of losing a loved one in a disaster. Gray, Prigerson, and Litz (2004) point out that in the aftermath of a mass-casualty disaster, such as a plane crash, survivors should be educated about normal and complicated grief reactions, common maladaptive coping strategies, and utilizing natural support systems and mental health resources if needed.

Understanding Grief and the Myth of Closure   As discussed in previous chapters, *grief* is a normal reaction to the loss of a loved one, and most people manage to learn to live with loss through the passage of time. But learning to live with a loss is not the same thing as closure, which suggests some sort of final resolution. The notion of closure or resolution is not only a myth but can also be a destructive one. Family members are sometimes led to believe that within months they will be back to normal. When the media is no longer interested in a disaster or in grieving survivors, some friends, relatives, or employers may tell grieving survivors that it is time to move on. This advice is not helpful.

Instead, family members could be counseled that it may take a year or more to *learn to live with a loss* and that coping with the loss is not the same thing as no longer feeling any pain or "getting over the loss" or "closure." Learning to live with the loss means that gradually one will feel less acute pain, be better able to function, and be able to enjoy life, although perhaps always with a sense of sadness about the loss (Raphael, 1983).

Providing Information on Stages of Loss   Survivors may be helped to understand the stages of response to a disaster or the stages of loss or mourning. Some counselors confuse the Kübler-Ross (1969) stages of *dying* (preparing for one's own death) (1969) with the stages of grieving for a lost loved one. One influential approach to stages of grieving was developed by Worden (1991). He suggests there are four stages for adults in mourning:

1. Moving beyond denial and accepting the reality of the loss
2. Experiencing the pain or the emotional aspects of the loss
3. Adjusting to an environment in which the deceased is missing with every detail of life altered
4. Emotionally relocating the deceased as a psychological presence or memory and moving on with life

Educating Parents to Help Children

Parents are often more concerned about their children's reactions to disaster than any other issue. For the most part, we believe this is appropriate and is not a distraction from the parent's own distress because research makes it clear that children are the most vulnerable population (Norris et al., 2002). It is regularly noted in the family therapy literature (for example, Haley, 1987; Minuchin, 1974) that parents are the best helpers for their children. It empowers parents to help their children, and it maintains a healthy hierarchy when counselors consult and advise parents on how to help their children.

The NIMH report (2002) describes the need to develop educational materials on "teaching parents how to talk with their children about the event and its consequences." As a starting point, Table 9.1 offers a list of tips that DMH helpers can use in trying to help parents and caregivers help their children following a disaster, some of which are also reviewed in Chapter 6. Also, see Appendix B for a listing of Internet resources that provide more information about helping children recover from experiencing a disaster.

What to Tell Children About Loss and Death   One of the most common questions survivors ask is what to tell their children about loss and death resulting from a disaster. There is usually not a clear answer to many of the questions that parents ask counselors. So much depends on the age and maturity of the child. In the aftermath of sudden and traumatic death, questions about death are fraught with emotion. Some of the things adults need to do for children who have lost a loved one are obvious and commonsensical whereas others are not. For children, the research indicates that grief counseling is helpful (Shut, Stroebe, van den Bout, & Terheggen, 2001). Much of the advice offered by counselors and educators depends on the culture, religious faith and beliefs of the survivors. Table 9.2 offers some suggestions that a counselor might offer parents to consider when talking to their children.

Helping Survivors Cope With the Media

As a final aspect of psychoeducation, counselors can also help survivors contend with the media. It appears to us that members of the media have become more sensitive in dealing with victims of disaster. On occasion, however, reporters have been known to falsify credentials in order to get closer to the story, closer to the disaster, and closer to the victims.

It is not unusual for family members to feel obligated to speak to the media. Sometimes when people do, they may regret it later. Sometimes a reporter is looking for a story and may ask questions intended to provoke tears for the camera. The deceased can be referred to as "the person who crashed into the World Trade Center" or "the person who died in the Oklahoma City bombing." For family members, the deceased was a lot more than the way he or she died. Family members want the person to be remembered for the loving and complicated person he or she was.

Table 9.1 | Advice for Working With Parents After a Disaster

- Assist parents in understanding behaviors and developing ways to help their children deal with the disaster.
- Remind parents that children often mirror the parents' responses to disaster.
- Recognize the differences in the intellectual, developmental, and emotional growth of children and develop response plans accordingly.
- Talk with children and offer accurate information in terms they can understand.
- Talk to children about feelings (yours and theirs). Let them know it's all right to feel those feelings.
- Try to keep families together.
- Offer reassurance that they are safe and cared for, especially if in a shelter. Explain that safety and care are the purposes of a shelter.
- Listen when children talk about their fears.
- Try to have coloring books and other resources available.
- Let the children tell you their feelings and what they think has happened.
- Encourage caregivers to spend extra time with the children, especially at bedtime.
- Encourage caregivers to give children extra physical comfort like hugging and holding.
- Provide opportunities for expression through play activities such as drawing, finger painting, or even physical reenactments of the disaster.
- Counsel caregivers to temporarily lower expectations for performance, both at school and at home.
- Monitor children's media exposure. Too much time watching graphic images of the disaster can be harmful.
- Include older children in discussions about preparing and planning for the future.
- Encourage older children to be involved in the recovery effort.
- Understand that teenagers may find security and companionship with their friends and may need to spend more time with them.

Source: ARC (1995).

The fame and sensationalism associated with talking with the media can be harmful to the survivors and the grieving process. However, sometimes the visibility provided by the media can be useful to survivors. With help from media exposure, they can further their efforts to apply pressure for extending the recovery processes or for increasing benefits. Counselors experienced with disaster can have conversations with survivors about the advantages and disadvantages of dealing with the media, clarifying their expectations, and can inform family members that they don't have to speak to the press unless they wish to.

Table 9.2 | Thirty-Five Ways to Help a Grieving Child

1. Listen.
2. Listen some more.
3. Be honest. Never lie to a child.
4. Answer the questions they ask, even the hard ones.
5. Give the child choices whenever possible.
6. Encourage consistency and routines.
7. Make a child's world safe for grieving.
8. Talk about and remember the person who died.
9. Expect and allow all kinds of emotions.
10. Forget about the "grief stages."
11. Respect differences in grieving styles.
12. Get out the crayons, pens, pencils, paint, and chalk.
13. Run! Jump! Play! (Or find other ways to release energy and emotions.)
14. Be a model of good grief.
15. Hug with permission.
16. Practice patience.
17. Support children, even when they are in a bad mood.
18. Expect some kids to act younger than their age.
19. Expect some kids to become little adults.
20. Encourage kids to eat right and drink lots of water.
21. Help the child at bedtimes. Sleep may come hard for grieving children.
22. Inform the child's teacher and school about what has happened.
23. Resist being overprotective.
24. Don't force kids to talk.
25. Take a break.
26. Remember: "Playing" is "Grieving."
27. Seek additional help for the child if needed.
28. Attend to the physical aspects of grief.
29. Help children know that they are not alone in their grief.
30. Understand that grief looks different at different ages.
31. Set limits and rules and enforce them.
32. Remember special days that impact the child.
33. Plan family times together.
34. Be available for children when they need you.
35. TAKE CARE OF YOURSELF AND DO YOUR OWN GRIEVING.

Source: The Dougy Center for Grieving Children. (2004). 35 Ways to Help a Grieving Child. Portland, OR: Author.

Is Psychoeducation Effective?

All the preceding guidelines are based on the assumption that providing psychoeducation has a protective effect on disaster survivors, but little evidence supports this general hypothesis, let alone research on the most effective timing and delivery method. Currently, there are no clear answers to the following questions regarding psychoeducation:

- Is psychoeducation a useful intervention postdisaster?
- Do populations most in need of psychoeducation get the information needed?
- Do survivors read the psychoeducational material that they are given?
- If material is presented through the mass media, do survivors pay attention or learn from what they see?
- Are certain types of psychoeducation more useful than others?
- Is psychoeducation more useful with different populations, different disasters, or different mental health conditions?
- Is there a most effective means of delivering psychoeducation: mass media, written materials, or personal communication?
- Is there an optimal time postdisaster to deliver psychoeducation?
- For psychoeducation to be effective, should it be delivered more than one time?
- Do certain people benefit more than others, and can some be harmed by psychoeducation?

Much psychoeducation can be provided in direct conversations with victims as well as with written material or through the media. However, distributing handouts or pamphlets does not guarantee that they will be read. In fact, considering the stress that survivors are under, it may be hard for them to concentrate or carefully read anything, let alone materials that are associated with the disaster. It is therefore advisable to check with survivors to be sure that information is not only being distributed but is also being heard or read. The issue of timing for this as well as other early interventions has not been adequately researched.

Litz & Grey (2004) point out that if a disaster is large in scope, it may be difficult to treat a large population. Novel approaches to treatment that incorporate psychoeducation, such as websites or telemedicine-type technology, could be used to provide psychoeducation by teaching and promoting stress management skills. However, no research points to the usefulness of such approaches, and risks are associated with providing education on mental health and disaster.

The NIMH report (2002) lists these potential risks:

- Dispensing erroneous information, current fad, or uninformed opinion as proven fact
- Compounding the social stigmatization of those with more symptoms
- Causing *reverse stigmatization* and guilt (for example, "If you don't have these symptoms, then there is something bad and unfeeling about you")

- Using vocabulary and concepts unfamiliar to the specific audience, especially technical terms and jargon that have unintended negative effects (one script does not suit all audiences)
- Overpathologizing and focusing on therapy and disability compensation rather than facilitating natural supports and resilience

Despite these risks and despite the lack of specific research on psychoeducation's effectiveness as a post-DMH intervention, findings from the field of health care support the idea that timely information can help individuals cope with traumatic events. For example, Dunkel-Schetter and Wortman (1982) found that newly diagnosed cancer patients expressed many of the precise concerns typically seen among disaster survivors, concerns that were best addressed through a combination of empathetic listening and psychoeducation:

> The intensity of their fears and uncomfortable feelings may lead many cancer patients to worry that they are coping poorly or are losing their grip on reality. They experience a need to understand the meaning of their responses. Are their reactions to the crisis reasonable or "normal"? How *should* they be responding? How long will their fears and anxieties last? (Dunkel-Schetter & Wortman, 1982)

In addition to benefiting from discussing their fears and feelings with friends, relatives, or health-care workers, many cancer patients found reassurance through *social comparison*. This involved exposure to the responses of other patients grappling with the same illness, either in person or through brochures, films, or other prepared materials (Dunkel-Schetter & Wortman, 1982) and is clearly a form of psychoeducation.

Timely information has also been demonstrated to help prevent psychological distress in patients undergoing a variety of medical procedures: "When people know what to expect in terms of what will happen to them, their fear is reduced" (Blackman, 1982). This protective effect not only helps minimize physical pain (Blackman, 1982) but also impacts how patients interpret symptoms and reactions. For example, cancer patients who were informed in advance about possible side effects of radiation treatment did not demonstrate any increased likelihood of developing those symptoms as their doctors sometimes feared; in contrast, those who were not warned in advance tended to interpret their side-effect symptoms as signs that the disease had metastasized, and they were less likely to accept their doctors' subsequent reassurances that they were simply experiencing typical reaction to treatment (Dunkel-Schetter & Wortman, 1982). This is consistent with Rauch, Hembree, and Foa's (2001) finding that psychoeducation interventions tend to benefit survivors of rape, other types of assault, and motor vehicle accidents by normalizing posttrauma reactions. For example, the authors suggest, education may help a survivor recognize a flashback as a typical PTSD symptom rather than as an indication that he or she is going crazy, making it less frightening.

Extrapolating from health education also suggests some specific ways to maximize the timing and delivery of disaster psychoeducation. For example, Rodin and Janis (1982) found that immediately after receiving a cancer diagnosis, a patient's anxiety about the future tends to distract his or her attention from any information being delivered. Important facts were absorbed better if given in small doses, which helped prevent informational overload, a finding that seems likely to apply to survivors struggling to absorb a recently experienced disaster. Rodin and Janis (1982) also observe that an unfamiliar and busy environment is likely to distract a listener's attention and impede information processing; although the authors are referring to patients newly admitted to a hospital, the same effect could be expected in the noisy and alien environment of an emergency shelter or other disaster recovery setting. This suggests that mental health workers should try to hold psychoeducation discussions in a quiet, distraction-free area, if possible. Indeed, the following guidelines (after Hunt & MacLeod, 1979) for communicating with patients whose cognitive abilities are somewhat impaired may be helpful for mental health workers trying to provide psychoeducation to disaster survivors who may feel overwhelmed by their recent experiences and who are not absorbing new information as fully as they would in calmer circumstances:

- Be certain that you have the survivor's attention and they are not being distracted by competing noise.
- Choose your words carefully to be as clear and precise as possible and avoid sentence structures that could be misinterpreted. Tell the patient what to do or expect rather than what not to do, because negatives can be confusing.
- Reiterate important points using different wording to increase the chances the information will be absorbed.
- Ask survivors to paraphrase information to make sure they understood it.

Finally, additional health-care research suggests that mental health helpers should not force information on survivors who are not receptive because some individuals may have a repressive coping style that functions best by avoiding stressful thoughts. For this group, information about potential unpleasant symptoms may produce more anxiety than it allays (Kaplan, 1982).

MONITORING AND CONTROLLING RUMOR

In Chapter 2, we touched on the frequent emergence of rumors following disasters. These rumors can be more than just another factor in the hectic environment following disasters; in fact, they often produce additional stress or anxiety for survivors, so early interventions for **rumor control,** to prevent their spread, can be an important part of the mental health response. Many rumors begin with a kernel of truth, but as they are passed from person to person they evolve as members of the chain focus and elaborate on the elements that concern them personally (Allport & Postman, 1947). It is essential to act quickly to address rumors because the longer that they circulate, the more entrenched they become and the more they are likely to diverge from the truth.

Therefore, authorities should not simply wait for rumors to come to their attention but should actively seek them out. DMH workers might routinely ask in the course of other interactions whether survivors have heard any rumors about the disaster or recovery efforts. In a shelter or other environment where rumors are likely to spread quickly, authorities should consider enlisting people who are likely to be exposed to hearsay in its early stages as "rumor reporters" who will communicate any questionable information that they hear to appropriate staff members or volunteers (Maiese & Burgess, 2003). DMH workers may be well placed to serve as the recipients of rumor reports. Additionally, survivors may view helpers as independent or neutral third parties rather than as representatives of the authorities who they feel are misleading the public and therefore may be more likely to cooperate with DMH workers than with shelter staff or other professionals.

In the case of large-scale disasters that affect an entire community, information hotlines and/or websites can be established for citizens to report rumors that they hear and to learn the truth about the situation, like the rumor control centers many American cities operated during the cold war to collect, evaluate, and dispel misinformation that could otherwise lead to civil disorder (Rosnow & Fine, 1976).

As the flurry of rumors that circulated after September 11, 2001 demonstrated, following a disaster people often seem to accept information as valid that they would, in calmer times, dismiss as improbable or absurd. Hovland, Janis, and Kelley (1953) attribute this increased credulity to the emotional arousal that typically follows exposure to trauma: People are so desperate for information about their situation that they believe reports they would usually recognize as false or at least questionable. This lack of critical judgment is compounded by the *sleeper effect,* which suggests that the credibility of the source of an opinion becomes less important over time (Hovland et al., 1953). In other words, the longer that a survivor can dwell on an unchallenged rumor, the more it is likely to be accepted, regardless of the initial source. This is yet another reason why swift detection and action are important.

Survivors are most likely to be vulnerable to hearsay about the postdisaster situation when they do not feel they are receiving complete and reliable facts from the government or other sources in command. Therefore, the best way to control rumors is to make them unnecessary by disseminating enough accurate information to reduce the cognitive and affective uncertainty that motivates the initial quest for alternative sources of news. If prevention fails and rumors do start to spread, the only effective way to stop them is to provide prompt, unequivocal evidence of their falsity. Simply dismissing a rumor as untrue after it has gained public acceptance is likely to be perceived as a cover-up and to increase distrust of authorities (Rosnow & Fine, 1976), as was seen after the anthrax mailings of 2001 when an unconvincing government response to initial concerns led to an escalation of rumors, fear, and false alarms (Brachman, 2003). Efforts to prohibit rumor mongering through censorship and legal sanctions rarely succeed and in fact may backfire by increasing the perceived value of the illicit information (Rosnow & Fine, 1976). Instead, authorities need to confront rumors head on by using good information to counter bad information. As former U.S. Supreme Court Justice Louis Brandeis observed, "Sunshine is the best disinfectant."

Finally, the media can play a valuable role in dispelling rumors, but authorities should not assume that reporters will simply pass along the message that the authorities would like communicated. If media members feel that they are being used, misled, or kept in the dark, they may report information that conflicts with the "official" version, thereby fueling the rumor mill rather than restraining it. In contrast, if the message being received through the media is consistent with that provided through other official channels, survivors will put more faith in the information and will be less inclined to accept rumors.

CONFLICT MEDIATION AND RESOLUTION

Like rumor control, **conflict mediation** is another important postdisaster intervention that is not likely to be found in other kinds of mental health practice. In every social situation, there will be differences of opinion, arguments, and conflicts (Ting-Toomey, 1994). As defined by Folger, Poole, and Stutman (2001), conflict is the "interaction of interdependent people who perceive incompatible goals and interference from each other in achieving those goals." Conflict is especially likely in situations where parties feel they are in competition for finite resources, so that one person's gain is perceived as another's loss. This perception of scarcity is typical in the aftermath of a disaster if survivors feel they need to compete for shelter space, cleanup supplies, recovery funds, and so on.

Additionally, disasters increase stress, which can in turn increase conflict (Halpern, 1994). Therefore discord may be more pronounced in a postdisaster setting than in a normal situation. One cause of this increased conflict is the frustration and anger that accompanies most disasters. The relationship between frustration, anger, and aggression is well established (Dollard, Doob, Miller, Mowrer, & Sears, 1939). Survivors often feel that assistance does not come at the right time, not quickly enough, or in the wrong form, and they may express their emotions through conflict directed at workers or at other survivors. Disaster workers face their own conflict-escalating issues, most notably the burnout that can occur when they become emotionally, psychologically, and physically exhausted from coping with cleanup, recovery, long hours, fear and worry, and a lack of resources. Some workers are more prone to burnout if they are overconscientious, anxious, and susceptible to identifying with their clients (Piedmont, 1994). Workers may also be prone to burnout if it is a difficult and traumatic job, have been on the job a long time, have had few breaks, and are not getting enough support from their supervisors. The resulting stress may lead to friction among workers or between workers and clients.

For example, in the aftermath of the floods caused by Tropical Storm Ivan in 2004, one client raged, "Why does the government have $87 billion to spend in the Middle East, and all I can get is some kind of loan?" Another said, "Why is the government offering lower-interest loans to business than to home owners?" One aid worker muttered, "Some of these clients expect the darn world and whatever assistance we offer is just not good enough for them." This kind of frustration and anger can lead to conflicts between aid workers and clients.

In short, conflicts can occur

- Between workers and clients.
- Among workers who are offering assistance.

- Between family members impacted by the disaster.
- Among survivors who feel they are competing for limited resources like shelter space or funds.

Preventing Conflict

The ideal way to handle conflict is to keep it from occurring in the first place. This is best accomplished by monitoring stress levels, encouraging workers to take breaks or take time off, and encouraging survivors to take breaks and get enough rest and sleep. Preventing burnout or trying to limit frustration before they result in arguments is preferable to mitigating conflict after it occurs. Workers need to be nurtured, praised, and supported whenever possible so that they can feel positive about themselves despite the difficult conditions and long hours.

Despite these and other preventive efforts, is it highly likely that mental health workers will come upon workers and clients who show an inability to cope with minor interpersonal problems or who show an increased expression of anger and mistrust. Counselors may have some training and familiarity with helping couples and other family members resolve conflicts in their regular practice, but they may be less experienced in conflict resolution between workers or between workers and clients, so the following is an overview of what is involved in mediation.

Working With and Mediating Conflict

Mental health workers should not intervene at the first sign of argument, disagreement, or conflict. Most often the open airing of differences can be helpful, and people will resolve their issues on their own. However, intervention may be appropriate if the disagreement is intense or has been keeping workers from doing an optimal job. In this case, a DMH worker may step in as a neutral third party to help break through the self-perpetuating cycle that characterizes many conflicts and to alter the nature of the interaction (Folger et al., 2001).

Folger et al. (2001) describe the role of the third-party mediator as involving two essential phases, "sharpening conflicts" and "inducing integration." Sharpening conflicts means clarifying the precise nature of the problem without inspiring either avoidance (so that one or both parties walk away or refuse to address the issue) or escalation to the point where resolution is impossible. To accomplish this, the mediator works to refocus the participants on the original conflict rather than on current emotions, helps refine what a solution will need to accomplish, and breaks down the problem into smaller, more manageable parts than the larger issue may seem to be to the parties. After the issue has been clarified, the mediator next helps lead the parties through developing solutions in the integration phase. At this point, the mediator should suggest common goals and draw attention to similarities rather than differences, focus the participants on the process they will use to reach a resolution rather than on the outcome, and work to create cooperation and to overcome mistrust between the parties by obtaining a promise of concessions from each side.

Throughout the conflict mediation process, it is important to remember that it is the *perceptions* of the involved parties that matter more than the reality of the situation: If one side perceives that another is getting preferential treatment or somehow thwarting his or her desires, conflict may arise regardless of whether an imbalance actually exists. Differences in participants' communication styles may compound the problem by producing misunderstandings and placing people in an unnecessarily defensive position. Saving face or avoiding threats to one's self-image can also play a role in conflict escalation.

The following guidelines will help workers become effective mediators in shelters or other postdisaster situations:

- *Enter the system.* Ask participants if you can help them to problem-solve the conflict, using an opening remark such as "I see you folks are having a hard time with one another. Can I help you to talk about this and find a way to resolve this?" As Bowen notes (Kerr & Bowen, 1988), when a calm person enters an emotional dyad, it becomes less emotional.
- *Remain impartial.* To be an effective mediator, you must be perceived by both sides as being neutral and not representing or favoring one party.
- *Keep calm.* Ask the participants to tell you their view of the conflict. If someone interrupts, asks that person to wait until his or her turn. Say you want to hear each of their points of view.
- *Be accurate.* After a joint meeting to determine the basic conflict, it may be helpful to meet privately with each party because each may be willing to discuss their concerns more openly when alone than in the presence of the other. If separate discussions are held, be extremely careful to transmit any messages from one side to the other accurately and respect requests to keep any information confidential if asked to.
- *Break it down.* If there is more than one topic being disputed, it may be productive to tackle the smaller, more easily solved ones first in order to create a sense of progress and cooperation (Kheel, 1999).
- *Inform and educate.* Don't hesitate to fill in gaps in information that one or both parties are contributing to the conflict. Correcting misperceptions about shelter rules or clarifying worker responsibilities may sometimes be enough to dispel an argument.
- *Respect the outcome.* You can make every effort to help the participants reach agreement, but the final decision should still belong to those involved (Kheel, 1999).

CORRECTING DISTORTED SELF-COGNITIONS

In Chapters 4 and 5, we pointed out that in the aftermath of trauma, survivors may think in ways that are distorted and or not helpful. The NIMH report (2002) states that "two of the best validated treatment elements for PTSD and depression are direct therapeutic exposure and *cognitive restructuring*." These approaches will be more fully explicated in Chapter 11 because they tend to be longer-term interventions. Still, although it may be difficult to engage in exposure therapy with survivors until they are involved in ongoing counseling or therapy, it may be possible to provide some **cognitive restructuring** at an earlier stage.

Survivors of disaster may think a number of unhelpful and distorted negative cognitions (Beck, 1995; Elhlers & Clark 2000; Shapiro, 1995; Steil & Ehlers, 2000; Wilson, Friedman, & Lindy, 2001). Any of the following thoughts or beliefs could be detected or uncovered when speaking with a victim of disaster:

1. "It is my fault."
2. "I am shameful."
3. "I am terrible."
4. "I am stupid."
5. "I am weak."
6. "I cannot protect myself or my family."
7. "I did something wrong."
8. "I should have done something."
9. "I might go crazy."
10. "I am inferior to other people."
11. "I will never get over this."
12. "It will happen again."
13. "I am in danger."
14. "This is unjust."
15. "My life is ruined."
16. "Something is seriously wrong with me."
17. "I cannot trust anybody."
18. "I want to have revenge."
19. "I want to make it undone"
20. "I am not myself anymore."

Counselors should be careful not to attempt to correct cognitions that are valid. If a survivor comments that he or she has few supports and friends, it would be unwise to say, "Oh, I am sure you have more friends than you think." Perhaps the survivor actually *does* have few friends. Similarly, a survivor might think, "I know I could have done more to protect my property." A counselor might point out that we can usually think of ways to improve our performance in most situations and might challenge the usefulness or fairness of the thought— yet the thought might still be correct. A helper who tells someone during a blizzard that it is not snowing too hard or tells a survivor of a terrorist attack that there will not be another one is misusing cognitive restructuring. Counselors should attempt to assist a survivor to find a more helpful perspective, but it must be consistent with reality.

The following case study occurred in the aftermath of Tropical Storm Allison in June 2001, during outreach with an integrated care team of the American Red Cross. It is meant to illustrate an early intervention involving rapport building and cognitive restructuring.

Like many of the other victims of the flood in Louisiana, Mr. Green, a slight African American man, had dark rings around his eyes. Outside his home, under a carport, were piles of books with damp wrinkled pages—all beyond repair. There were also piles of ruined clothes, an ironing board, lamps, pillows, and other furnishings. There was the stench of his now molding ruined carpet. Mr. Green told a visiting DMH helper that he and his wife were struggling to support their children, two sons in college. He explained that he was at work as a salesman, a job he had had most of his life, when the heavy rains came. He thought about trying to get home, but the store was busy. When he went outside, he faced almost ankle-deep water. He thought the trip home would be difficult, so he continued to work. He worried all night. Around midnight when he tried to go home, he couldn't get to his house. There were already several feet of water covering his neighborhood. Two days later, when he was finally able to survey the damage, he cried.

Mr. Green took the DMH worker to his renovated garage. This was a special place for him, his sons, and his friends—a place for the guys to hang out. There had been a big-screen TV, card table, and refrigerator in this space. He and his friends played cards and watched sports there. The counselor asked him what their favorite types of games were to watch. He said they watched baseball and football, but he was a very big basketball fan. The two talked about the recent NBA finals between the LA Lakers and the Philadelphia 76ers. He had rooted for the underdog 76ers. They talked about basketball for a while as a way of getting to know each other. Then the DMH worker asked Mr. Green how he was feeling about what had just happened to him and his family. He said, "At first the insurance company promised that someone would be out to the house within days. No one has come, and they are not even answering my calls." The insurance agent sold him a type of policy that was factored to a European company. He wasn't sure what was going to happen. He was angry at the insurance company but angrier with himself for not looking more carefully into the fine print of the policy. He also blamed himself for not getting home sooner. He believed he could have saved a lot of what was lost if he had put valuables up in closets, or in the crawl space of the attic, or taken some things out of the house into his car to safety. He was now finding it hard to do his job. Mr. Green said that for 25 years he had been a successful salesman. He explained that you need to be positive in order to make any money. Regular customers knew him, enjoyed being served by him, and always did right by him. Over the years, he always managed to put on a positive attitude for his customers, no matter what trouble he might be going through. Now, for the first time, he said, he just couldn't fake it.

Self-blame is often a significant issue for disasters survivors, and it was the focus of the counseling. Mr. Green and the DMH worker talked about how the refrigerator had floated to the other side of his garage, in a powerful demonstration of the incredible force and power of the floodwaters. They talked about how dangerous it could have been for him to be there at the height of the flood. The electricity could have been popping. He could have lost his car in the high water, and he could have drowned. Rather than talk about the misery that comes with self-blame and self-recrimination, they talked about the hazards and silliness of second-guessing—the foolhardy practice of Monday morning quarter-backing. He was a knowledgeable sports fan and knew how easy and lame it was to criticize a coach after the fact. The counselor also told Mr. Green that following disaster people often blame themselves and tend to make a bad situation worse in the process. They spent a few hours together, and by the end the DMH worker thought that the conversation had been helpful. Mr. Green said he was grateful.

It is not possible to know if this conversation had long-lasting effects or whether any one-time intervention, however helpful it may have been, is generalizable to other survivors. A survivor who experiences self-blame and self-recrimination may be able to come to understand "I did the best I could." In different situations after a disaster has passed, a survivor may think "I am still in danger." A counselor might help a survivor to restructure the cognition to "The danger has passed" or "It is over, I am safe now." Although such cognitive restructuring has been shown to be effective (Beck, 1995), Shapiro (1995) points out that reprocessing traumatic events such as an earthquake, too soon after the event, may not be helpful because the memory does not have time to be consolidated into an integrated whole. Although Bryant and Harvey (2000) do not advocate a one-session approach, they do suggest that cognitive therapy is helpful as an early intervention. They maintain that such cognitive restructuring should be done in the context of a larger treatment plan, as discussed in Chapter 11.

MAKING REFERRALS FOR FOLLOW-UP TREATMENT

Referral is the "process of recommendation and linkage to other service providers" (NIMH, 2002). Although most survivors may not need a **referral for continued care** for such additional services as evaluation and therapy, the American Red Cross (ARC, 1995) advises that mental health workers should immediately refer a survivor to a local mental health professional if they exhibit the following behaviors:

- Significant disturbance of memory
- Inability to perform necessary everyday functions
- An inability to care for one's personal needs
- Inability to begin cleanup or to apply for necessary assistance
- Inability to make simple decisions
- Preoccupation with a single thought
- Repetition of ritualistic acts
- Abuse (rather than "misuse") of alcohol or drugs
- Talk that "overflows"—shows extreme pressure of speech
- Suicidal or homicidal talk or actions
- Psychotic symptoms
- Excessively "flat" emotions, inability to be aroused to action, and serious withdrawal

- Frequent and disturbing occurrences of flashbacks, excessive nightmares, and excessive crying
- Regression to an earlier stage of development
- Inappropriate anger and/or abuse of others
- Episodes of dissociation
- Inappropriate reaction to triggering events

As part of preparedness and planning, a DMH worker should know before a disaster strikes where and how to make a referral for follow-up care. There should be a clear liaison with local and neighborhood agencies and organizations to ensure continuity of care. DMH personnel should have a list of phone numbers and addresses before being deployed so that referrals could be made for individual, family, and group psychotherapy; pharmacotherapy; spiritual/existential support; or short-term or long-term hospitalization. This is one reason why local practitioners should provide the mental health response to disaster, if possible. "Interventions are most likely to be helpful when they are tailored to address individual, community, and cultural needs and characteristics" (NIMH, 2002). An out-of-town helper to a disaster in New York City may not realize that referring a client from Brooklyn to a clinic in the Bronx (this is another borough in New York City) may be contributing to noncompliance because the trip can take several hours.

As part of referral planning, workers should be able to let survivors know if there will be a fee and, if so, how much it is or if there is a waiting list for receiving services and, if so, how long. Mental health counselors should also be prepared to provide resource information that is closely allied with traditional mental health services, such as:

- Domestic violence hotline
- Children's services
- Crime victim's help line
- Where and how to refer seeing or hearing-impaired clients
- Burial assistance
- Services for the elderly
- Social services
- Interpreters or translators
- People locators

As part of coordination and collaboration before a disaster strikes, DMH workers should have established relationships with local mental health associations and county or government mental health organizations so that follow-up treatment can be seamless. A more difficult assignment for disaster workers is to ensure that such referrals are made to competent and experienced providers and organizations with expertise in treating disaster victims. Not all therapists, though licensed, may be experts in treating victims of trauma. Not all experts in treating adult victims of trauma may be experienced or competent treating traumatized children. Some survivors may need treatment with a focus on substance abuse and others on assistance with grief. The most effective referrals for continued care are likely to be made if disaster workers have the most detailed information concerning the expertise and competence of their various referral sources.

The same individuals who may be comfortable receiving immediate services from mental health professionals under emergency conditions may view additional assistance from a mental health agency as indicative of weakness. They may fear stigmatization from coworkers, family, or community members if they are not able to recover immediately. Corrigan (2004) points out that many people who would benefit from mental health services do not pursue them because they fear that doing so would lead to stigmatizing responses from others. The fear is well founded. It is quite clear that to be labeled "mentally ill" can result in significant harm from others. There may also be a "self-stigma" associated with seeking mental health treatment. This is the process of internalizing the public stigma and viewing oneself as incompetent. It is therefore important to be particularly sensitive to these issues when making a referral (Corrigan, 2004).

Generally, a matter-of-fact or direct approach works best. You can discuss available mental health follow-up services in the community. You can also normalize the process by explaining how many survivors of disaster have been helped by further assistance. Quite frequently this information is received with gratitude and an indication that the survivor will contact and utilize the referral. However, you may encounter the strongest resistance from the individuals who you deem to have the strongest need for continued help. If the survivor needing more assistance is a parent, treatment can be recommended to help the family. Parents are often open to anything that may be beneficial to their children or the family. Encouraging survivors to continue a commitment to self-care not only for themselves but also for their family may provide the permission they need to seek help.

SOME CAUTIONS ABOUT EARLY INTERVENTION

In the last two chapters, we have reviewed a range of attitudes and techniques suitable for early intervention in the aftermath of disaster. We would like to point out a few cautions for those working with victims in the aftermath of disaster.

- Trauma experts (for example, Wilson, 2001) refer to a *trauma membrane*, which refers to the adaptive process of sealing off the traumatic experience. This suggests that in some circumstances and for some survivors "putting the material aside" and not remembering the event may be the best option. People need to be allowed to deal with extremely traumatic events in their own way at their own pace, so DMH must be careful not to pressure survivors to confront their experience before they are ready.

- It has been pointed out (Lindy, 1996) that people need to deal with the discussion and processing of disaster in small doses. Counselors should not equate catharsis and expressiveness with progress. Intense and overwhelming feelings may best be handled in small doses.

- As was discussed in Chapters 4 and 5, trauma and grief are not the same thing, and if survivors are affected by both, they may need to be treated separately—trauma first (Raphael, 1986).
- When there is a major catastrophe, it is easy to assume that the survivor is suffering primarily due to the disaster. This is not always the case. There may be other traumas, illnesses, family conflicts, or financial distress that is the primary cause of the symptoms that are observed. Counselors should be careful not to treat the wrong trauma (Raphael & Dobson, 2001).

With all of this in mind, in Chapter 10 we discuss a commonly used but controversial, early intervention technique before moving on to longer-term treatments for postdisaster distress.

References

Allport, G. W., & Postman, L. (1947). *The psychology of rumor.* New York: Holt, Rinehart & Winston.

ARC (American Red Cross). (1995). *Disaster mental health services I participant's workbook* (pp. 9, 21). Washington, DC: Author.

ARC (American Red Cross). (2002). *Disaster mental health services: An overview.* (ARC 3077-2A). Washington, DC: Author.

Beck, J. S. (1995). *Cognitive therapy: Basics and beyond.* New York: Guilford Press.

Blackman, S. (1982). Social psychological perspectives on pain. In H. S. Friedman & M. R. DiMatteo (Eds.), *Interpersonal issues in health care* (pp. 169–186). New York: Academic Press.

Bonanno, G. A. (2004). Loss, trauma and human resilience: Have we underestimated the human capacity to thrive after extremely aversive events? *American Psychologist, 59,* 20–28.

Brachman, P. S. (2003). The public health response to the anthrax epidemic. In B. S. Levy & V. W. Sidel (Eds.), *Terrorism and public health: A balanced approach to strengthening systems and protecting people* (pp. 101–117). New York: Oxford University Press.

Brewin, C. R. (2003). *Posttraumatic stress disorder: Malady or myth?* New Haven, CT: Yale University Press.

Brewin, C. R., Rose, S. Andrews, B., Green, J., Tata, P., McEvedy, C., Turner, S. W., & Foa, E. B. (2002). A brief screening instrument for posttraumatic stress disorder. *British Journal of Psychiatry, 181,* 158–162.

Bryant, R. A., & Harvey, A. G. (2000). *Acute stress disorder: A handbook of theory, assessment and treatment.* Washington, DC: American Psychological Association.

Carver, C. S., Scheier, M. F., & Weintraub, J. K. (1989). Assessing coping strategies: A theoretically based approach. *Journal of Personality and Social Psychology, 56,* 267–283.

Castro, C. A., Engel, C. C., & Adler, A. B. (2004). The challenge of providing mental health prevention and early intervention in the U.S. military. In B. T. Litz (Ed.), *Early intervention for trauma and traumatic loss* (pp. 301–318). New York: Guilford Press.

Cohen, S. (2004). Social relationships and health. *American Psychologist, 59,* 676–684.

Corrigan, P. (2004). How stigma interferes with mental health care. *American Psychologist, 59,* 614–625.

Dollard, M., Doob, L., Miller, N., Mowrer, O., & Sears, R. (1939). *Frustration and aggression.* New Haven, CT: Yale University Press.

Dunkel-Schetter, C., & Wortman, C. B. (1982). The interpersonal dynamics of cancer: Problems in social relationships and their impact on the patient. In H. S. Friedman & M. R. DiMatteo (Eds.), *Interpersonal issues in health care* (pp. 69–100). New York: Academic Press.

Ehlers, A., & Clark, D. M. (2000). A cognitive model of posttraumatic stress disorder. *Behavior Research and Therapy, 38,* 319–345.

Folger, J. P., Poole, M. S., & Stutman, R. K. (2001). *Working through conflict: Strategies for relationships, groups, and organizations* (4th ed.). New York: Addison Wesley Longman.

Folkman, S., & Lazarus, R. S. (1980). An analysis of coping in a middle-aged community sample. *Journal of Health and Social Behavior, 21,* 219–239.

Gray, M. J., Prigerson, H. G., & Litz, B. T. (2004). Conceptual and definitional issues in complicated grief. In B. T. Litz (Ed.), *Early intervention for trauma and traumatic loss* (pp. 65–84). New York: Guilford Press.

Haley, J. (1987). *Problem solving therapy* (2nd ed.). San Francisco: Jossey-Bass.

Halpern, J. (1994) The sandwich generation: Conflicts between adult children and their aging parents. In D. D. Cahn (Ed.), *Conflict in personal relationships* (pp. 143–162). Hillsdale, NJ: Erlbaum.

Hovland, C. I., Janis, I. L., & Kelley, H. H. (1953). *Communication and persuasion: Psychological studies of opinion change.* New Haven, CT, and London: Yale University Press.

Hunt, E. B., & MacLeod, C. M. (1979). Cognition and information processing in patient and physician. In G. C. Stone, F. Cohen, N. E. Adler, & Associates (Eds.), *Health psychology—a handbook: Theories, applications, and challenges of a psychological approach to the health care system* (pp. 303–332). San Francisco: Jossey-Bass.

Kaplan, R. M. (1982). Coping with stressful medical examinations. In H. S. Friedman & M. R. DiMatteo (Eds.), *Interpersonal issues in health care* (pp. 187–208). New York: Academic Press.

Kerr, M. E., & Bowen, M. (1988). *Family evaluation.* New York: Norton.

Kessler, R. C., Sonnega, A., Bromet, E., Hughes, M., and Nelson, C. B. (1995). Posttraumatic stress disorder in the National Comorbidity Survey. *Archives of General Psychiatry, 52,* 1048–1060.

Kheel, T. W. (1999). *The keys to conflict resolution: Proven methods of settling disputes voluntarily.* New York: Four Walls Eight Windows.

Kübler-Ross, E, (1969). *On death and dying.* London: Macmillan.

Lindy, J. (1996). Psychoanalytic psychotherapy of posttraumatic stress disorder: The nature of the therapeutic relationship. In B. van der Kolk. A. McFarlane, & L. Weisaeth (Eds.), *Traumatic stress: The effects of overwhelming experience on mind, body, and society* (pp. 525–536). New York: Guilford Press.

Litz, B. T. (2004). Introduction. In B. T. Litz (Ed.), *Early intervention for trauma and traumatic loss* (pp. 1–12). New York: Guilford Press.

Litz, B. T., & Gray, M. J. (2004). Early intervention for trauma in adults: A framework for first aid and secondary prevention. In B. T. Litz (Ed), *Early intervention for trauma and traumatic loss* (pp. 87–111). New York: Guilford Press.

Maiese, M., & Burgess, H. (2003). *Rumor control.* Intractable Conflict Knowledge Base Project Conflict Research Consortium, University of Colorado. Retrieved June 24, 2005, from http://www.beyondintractability.org/m/rumor_control.jsp.

Martin, R. A., & Lefcourt, H. M. (1983). Sense of humor as a moderator of the relation between stressors and moods. *Journal of Personality and Social Psychology, 47,* 145–155.

McCann, I. L., & Holmes, D. S. (1984). Influence of aerobics on depression. *Journal of Personality and Social Psychology, 46*, 1142–1147.

Miller, L. (2002). Psychological interventions for terroristic trauma: Symptoms, syndromes, and treatment strategies. *Psychotherapy: Theory/Research/Practice/Training, 39*, 283–296.

Minuchin, S. (1974). *Families and family therapy.* Cambridge, MA: Harvard University Press.

Mitchell, J. T. (1983). When disaster strikes: The critical incident stress debriefing process. *Journal of Emergency Medical Services, 1*, 36–39.

National Screening Committee. (1998). *First report of the National Screening Committee.* London: Health Department of the United Kingdom.

NIMH (National Institute of Mental Health). (2002). *Mental health and mass violence: Evidence-based early psychological intervention for victims/survivors of mass violence. A workshop to reach consensus on best practices* (NIH Publication No. 02-5138). Washington, DC: Government Printing Office.

Norris, F., Friedman, M. J., Watson, P. J., Byrne, C. M., Diaz, E., & Kaniasty, K. (2002). 60,000 disaster victims speak: Part I. An empirical review of the empirical literature, 1981–2001. *Psychiatry: Interpersonal & Biological Processes, 65*, 207–239.

Pennebaker, J. W. (1995). *Emotional discloser and health.* Washington, DC: American Psychological Association.

Pennebaker, J. W. (1997). *Opening up: The healing power of expressing emotions* (Rev. ed.). New York: Guilford Press.

Pennebaker, J. W., & Beale, S. K. (1986). Confronting a traumatic event: Toward an understanding of inhibition and disease. *Journal of Abnormal Psychology, 52*, 781–793.

Piedmont, R. L. (1994). A longitudinal analysis of burnout in the health care setting: The role of personal dispositions. *Journal of Personality Assessment, 61*, 457–473.

Raphael, B. (1983). *The anatomy of bereavement.* New York: Basic Books.

Raphael, B. (1986). *When disaster strikes: How individuals and communities cope with catastrophe.* New York: Basic Books.

Raphael, B. (2003). Early intervention and the debriefing debate. In R. J. Ursano, C. S. Fullerton, & A. E. Norwood (Eds.), *Terrorism and disaster: Individual and community mental health interventions* (pp. 146–161). Cambridge, England: Cambridge University Press.

Raphael, B., & Dobson, M. (2001) Acute posttraumatic interventions. In J. P Wilson, M. J. Friedman, & J. D. Lindy (Eds.), *Treating psychological trauma and PTSD* (pp. 139–158). New York: Guilford Press.

Raphael, B., & Wooding, S. (2004). Early mental health interventions for traumatic loss in adults. In B. T. Litz (Ed.), *Early intervention for trauma and traumatic loss* (pp. 147–178). New York: Guilford Press.

Rauch, S. A. M., Hembree, E. A., & Foa, E. B. (2001). Acute psychosocial preventive interventions for posttraumatic stress disorder. *Advances in Mind–Body Medicine, 17*, 187–192.

Rodin, J., & Janis, I. L. (1982). The social influence of physicians and other health care practitioners as agents of change. In H. S. Friedman & M. R. DiMatteo (Eds.), *Interpersonal issues in health care* (pp. 33–49). New York: Academic Press.

Rosnow, R. L., & Fine, G. A. (1976) *Rumor and gossip: The social psychology of hearsay.* New York: Elsevier.

Rostad, F. G., & Long, B. C. (1996). Exercise as a coping strategy for stress: A review. *International Journal of Sports Psychology, 27*, 197–222.

Roth, S., & Cohen, L. J. (1986). Approach, avoidance and coping with stress. *American Psychologist, 41,* 813–819.

Rothbaum, B. O., Meadows, E. A., Resick, P., & Foy, D. W. (2000). Cognitive behavior therapy. In E. B. Foa, T. M. Keane, & M. J. Friedman (Eds.), *Effective treatments of PTSD* (pp. 60–83). New York: Guilford Press.

Sanderson, C. A. (2004). *Health psychology.* Hoboken, NJ: Wiley.

Shalev, A. (2001). What is posttraumatic stress disorder? *Journal of Clinical Psychiatry, 62*(Suppl. 17), 4–10.

Shapiro, F. (1995). *Eye movement and reprocessing: Basic principles protocols and procedures.* New York: Guilford Press.

Shut, H., Stroebe, M. S., van den Bout, J., & Terheggen, M. (2001). The efficacy of bereavement interventions: Determining who benefits. In M. S. Stroebe, R. O. Hansson, W. Stroebe, & H. Schut (Eds.), *Handbook of bereavement research* (pp. 705–737). Washington, DC: American Psychological Association.

Smith, M. L., Glass, G. V., & Miller, T. I. (1980). *The benefits of psychotherapy.* Baltimore: Johns Hopkins University Press.

Spiegel, D., & Classen, C. (1995). Acute stress disorder. In G. O. Gabbard (Ed.), *Treatment of psychiatric disorders* (Vol. 2) (pp. 1521–1535). Washington, DC: American Psychiatric Association.

Steil, R., & Ehlers, A. (2000). Dysfunctional meaning of posttraumatic intrusions in chronic PTSD. *Behavior Research and Therapy, 38,* 537–558.

Ting-Toomey, S. (1994). Managing conflict in intimate intercultural relationships. In D. D. Cahn (Ed.), *Conflict in Personal Relationships* (pp. 47–78). Hillsdale, NJ: Erlbaum.

Watson, P. (2004). *Behavioral health interventions following mass violence.* Retrieved January 6, 2005, from the National Center for PTSD at www.istss.org/publications/TS/Winter04/behavioral.htm.

Weaver, J. D. (1995). *Disasters: Mental health interventions.* Sarasota, FL: Professional Resources Press.

Wessely, S. (2003). The role of screening in the prevention of psychological disorders arising after major traumas: pros and cons. In R. J. Ursano, C. S. Fullerton, & A. E. Norwood (Eds.), *Terrorism and disaster: Individual and community mental health interventions* (pp. 121–145). Cambridge, England, and New York: Cambridge University Press.

Wilson, J. P. (2001). An overview of clinical considerations and principles in the treatment of PTSD. In J. P. Wilson, M. J. Friedman, & J. D. Lindy (Eds.), *Treating psychological trauma and PTSD* (pp. 59–93). New York: Guilford Press.

Wilson, J. P., Friedman, M. J., & Lindy, J. D. (2001). Treatment goals for PTSD. In J. P. Wilson, M. J. Friedman, & J. D. Lindy (Eds.), *Treating psychological trauma and PTSD* (pp. 3–27). New York: Guilford Press.

Worden, J. W. (1991). Grief counseling and grief therapy. From *A handbook for the mental health practitioner* (2nd ed.). New York: Springer.

Wortman, C. B., & Dunkel-Schetter, C. (1987). Conceptual and methodological issues in the study of social support. In A. Baum & J. E. Singer (Eds.), *Handbook of psychology and health* (pp. 329–344). Hillsdale, NJ: Erlbaum.

Give sorrow words. The grief that does not speak whispers the o'er-fraught heart, and bids it break.

William Shakespeare

Debriefing and the Impact of Disaster Trauma on First Responders

In our final chapter on early interventions, we discuss a process that is currently widely used in response to disasters and other traumatic events, despite growing doubts about its appropriateness in certain situations. Debriefing, particularly the "Mitchell model" of critical incident stress debriefing, has come under scrutiny over the last few years because questions have arisen about whether it truly helps—or possibly harms—the populations to which its use has been expanded. We discuss both the procedure and the current debate about it, to enable you to judge for yourself whether it is an appropriate intervention following disaster. The remainder of the chapter is dedicated to examining the effects of chronic exposure to terrible, shocking, and dangerous events on the group that debriefing was originally intended to help, emergency professionals including police officers, firefighters, and other first responders. We will describe specific issues relevant to understanding and supporting this population, who represent our very first line of aid in times of disasters.

BACKGROUND OF THE DEBRIEFING DEBATE

The quote that opens this chapter reflects an almost universally held sentiment: Talking about painful experiences is beneficial and soothing. Yet what seems to be obviously helpful may not always be so in the immediate aftermath of a disaster when survivors may have other more urgent psychological and practical needs.

After a shocking event, trauma scholars suggest that a *trauma membrane* forms around survivors. This self-protective cocooning (which can also be provided by friends and family who strive to protect the disaster victim; Lindy, 1985) is considered an adaptive process, a way of sealing off distressing experiences during the initial response phase. Any premature early intervention that intrudes through the membrane may inhibit this protective distancing. As such, there is growing recognition that it is important to respect psychological defenses in relation to trauma containment and mastery. How much talking through an experience can help an individual resolve what has happened versus how much it may reinforce helplessness is a critical question in disaster mental health (DMH) (Raphael & Wilson, 2000).

Yet at the very core of psychological debriefing is an emphasis on discussing the details of a distressing event, as well as one's accompanying cognitive and emotional reactions, shortly after the incident occurs. The process was often found to be beneficial among military and paramilitary groups including emergency responders, but it is not now and has never been a recommended intervention for primary victims following a disaster. Yet over the last 20 years, the technique has become widely used as an early intervention tool following exposure to a traumatic event in diverse settings where adverse events sometimes occur, such as businesses, schools, and hospitals (McNally, 2005).

However, in light of the growing recognition that sharing is not automatically helpful, mental health professionals are reevaluating the technique's nature, its use, and the value of its very existence. Scholars and practitioners alike have entered a very heated fray on the subject. Strong opinions are volleyed back and forth between polarized camps that either endorse psychological debriefing or deny its potential benefits and advocate that its employment be ceased. It is beyond the scope of this book to attempt to sort out this debate or to train you to use an intervention that is (as you will see) generally not recommended for our main population, disaster survivors. We merely hope to present the relevant facts and to clarify issues central to the debate so that you may have some basic reference points to use in filtering the controversy about an intervention that you are likely to encounter in DMH practice, even if you do not participate in it yourself.

We return to the debate in more detail later in the chapter to examine evidence on both sides, following a description of how debriefing evolved and how it is currently administered.

A HISTORY OF DEBRIEFING

What does the term *debriefing* mean? If a friend told you that he or she had been debriefed today, what would that imply? A one-on-one meeting or a group session? Would it suggest that your friend had been involved directly in some sort of terrible, potentially traumatic event? What would you assume?

A *debriefing* in its broadest definition refers to a recounting of what transpired during a specific event. Additionally, Raphael and Wilson (2000) point out that a debriefing often includes a sense of reviewing an experience and the actions involved in order to obtain clarity and meaning. The original context came from the **operational debriefing,** sometimes called an **instrumental** or **after-action debriefing,** a method used in organizations that are routinely called upon to deliver a prepared or carefully planned immediate intervention during a critical event. Such organizations are characteristically military or paramilitary in mission and structure, including national armed forces as well as civilian groups whose mission is to address the daily battles of local crime and disasters and their victims.

On its website, the National Institute of Mental Health (NIMH) defines an operational debriefing as "a routine individual or group review of the details of an event from a factual perspective, for the purposes of: learning what actually happened for the historical record or planning process, improving future results in similar missions, and increasing the readiness of those being debriefed for further action. Operational debriefings are conducted by leaders or specialized debriefers according to the organization's standard operating procedure." Operational debriefings offer the opportunity to learn from an event and to develop ways to improve performance in future related occurrences.

A **preevent briefing** is a key component in the operational debriefing model. *Briefing* and *debriefing* go hand in hand; these are linked processes. A briefing before an event fills responders in about what they might expect to encounter, preparation that offers a chance for individuals to ready themselves. This way, although the actual circumstances may be quite different from the best-laid plans, responders will at least go into an event with a sense of purpose and unity of goal, equipped with the skills that have been identified as necessary for the task at hand. This advance preparation may buffer the stressful aspects of the experience and diminish subsequent negative reactions (Raphael & Wilson, 2000). Similarly, although positive psychological benefits are not a stated goal of the postevent operational debriefing, such procedures can provide members of responder groups with accurate information about what took place, helping them clarify their impressions and form a shared sense of meaning about the event. These debriefings also offer an opportunity for team building and can increase morale and purpose by affirming each participant's individual role (Raphael & Wilson, 2000).

In contrast to the well-defined and formalized operational debriefing process, the meaning of psychological debriefing has become less precise over time. This has been a primary concern. According to the NIMH, debriefing is now used to describe a "variety of structured events, led by a person or team, which include education and review processes with a positive focus on resilience and coping strategies and sometimes detailed review of emotional reactions." The NIMH recommends that although the term *debriefing* has been applied in popular use to describe a variety of psychological interventions, this word alone should only be used to describe operational debriefing; other forms should be qualified with a more descriptive label.

How did this overuse of the term begin? In 1983 Jeffrey Mitchell published a paper in the *Journal of Emergency Services* entitled, "When Disaster Strikes: The Critical Incident Stress Debriefing Process." This landmark article introduced the concept of offering emergency service workers a clearly delineated technique designed to help this specific population manage work-related stress. Mitchell discovered during his own experiences as an emergency service provider that discussing gruesome and painful events with colleagues ameliorated their stressful effects. He used this observation as the basis for the technique that he developed, which he initially called critical incident stress debriefing (CISD). Mitchell's model of CISD describes a group intervention with an extremely structured format that is conducted by a trained team, as part of a larger response effort he calls critical incident stress management (CISM). We describe CISD and CISM in detail in our next section; for the moment, it is mostly important to note that Mitchell originally intended this form of debriefing to be used for emergency response professionals only.

In 1986 in a remarkably comprehensive book on disasters entitled *When Disaster Strikes: How Individuals and Communities Cope With Catastrophe*, Beverly Raphael also described the specific use of psychological debriefing to support emergency service workers and helpers as a way of alleviating disaster stress. Like Mitchell, Raphael wrote about a formal group process with several steps. She stressed the importance of having a leader who is skilled in understanding individual and group dynamics as well as disaster stressors and behavior.

Following these early references, in which psychological debriefing was proposed to be of use *in a specific way, for specific groups,* the concept took on momentum. Psychological debriefing arrived during a time of increasing awareness of the impact of trauma on individuals and communities. People earnestly wanted to help others during the worst of times, but a vacuum seemed to exist in terms of possible interventions. To fill that vacuum, psychological debriefing was embraced and transformed into an early intervention tool used with ordinary individuals and groups, not just emergency responders. It also became a handy way for organizations to provide assistance to their employees in the aftermath of workplace violence, disastrous accidents, and unexpected fatalities in any form—a great leap beyond the original intent.

CRITICAL INCIDENT STRESS DEBRIEFING: THE "MITCHELL MODEL"

Before we expand further on the controversy around debriefing, let's describe the most widely used version of it, sometimes referred to as the "Mitchell model." As we have mentioned, Mitchell's CISD process is only one portion of a larger system, critical incident stress management. Critical incident stress management is composed of a comprehensive series of interventions that are designed to prepare individuals prior to critical incidents, to provide support during and after these events to additionally offer services to family members, and to assist individuals in locating referrals and follow-up interventions.

Mitchell developed this comprehensive model in 1983 based on his own first-responder experience with on-the-job trauma. According to Mitchell's theoretical conceptualization, CISD should be used after traumatic events that initiate a crisis response and that are outside of the usual range of experiences that an individual encounters at work or in life; in other words, events must be significant enough to merit such a structured and formal intervention. Mitchell himself considers CISD and CISM to be a form of crisis intervention; he does not conceptualize them as psychotherapy. Instead, CISM attempts to provide psychological immunization through prevention, intervention, and recovery (Pulley, 2005).

Quite importantly, Mitchell and Everly (1998) assert that a CISD should only be conducted as part of the holistic approach of CISM; they emphasize that using CISD out of that context, as is often the case today, is not recommended. Mitchell admits that some of the lack of clarity around this crucial point arose from his initial terminology: Originally, he himself used CISD as a generic term to denote the overarching CISM program, while he used "formal CISD" to describe the specific seven-phase group discussion process that he now calls CISD (Everly & Mitchell, 1999). Critics assert that Mitchell has only recently emphasized CISM and that this change in emphasis reflects an expansion of his vision, but he counters that he has been writing about the need for integrated crisis management services since the early 1980s, which is reflected in his writings.

Mitchell writes that although the roots of CISM are in the emergency services profession it has become a "standard of care" in many schools, communities, and organizations well outside of the emergency professional domain. Even so, he believes it is most appropriately used at the organization level, not the exclusively individual one. In a document defending crisis intervention and CISM, Mitchell described appropriate and inappropriate recipients:

> The primary focus in the field of CISM is to support staff members of organizations or members of communities which have experienced a traumatic event. What CISM does not share with the field of crisis intervention is the range of the populations served. For example, CISM does not focus on primary victims such as auto accident victims, dog bite victims, women suffering post-partum depression, women who have lost a child in a miscarriage, child abuse victims, substance abusers, victims of elder abuse or sexual assault victims all of whom are typically served through various other crisis intervention programs. Should primary victims with those concerns come into contact with CISM trained personnel, the best course of action is a referral to appropriate crisis intervention or psychotherapy resources which are beyond the central focus and capabilities of most CISM teams. (www.icisf.org)

Components of Critical Incident Stress Management

Critical incident stress management includes seven distinct activities that are intended to be used in combination:

1. Precrisis education and preparedness training
2. One-on-one interventions and psychological support sessions throughout the crisis spectrum
3. Disaster or large-scale event interventions such as demobilization and community support programs
4. Small group defusings
5. Family and significant other support programs and organizational support programs

6. Critical incident stress debriefings (structured group discussions of a highly stressful event)
7. Follow-up and referral mechanisms for further assessment and therapy

None of these components, including debriefings, are meant to exist as stand-alone interventions. The next few paragraphs describe some of these components as defined by Mitchell and his colleagues.

Preincident traumatic stress education is considered essential for preventing and reducing critical incident stress. Stress education is held to have many benefits. Preevent information may inoculate responders, protecting them from adverse reactions. Forewarned personnel may recognize any symptoms they do develop early on. Advance warning may allow for the development of coping strategies. Responders can learn how to deal with routine stress as well as critical stress. And, at the very least, creating awareness about the reality of stressors within highly demanding, high-risk occupations may reduce the stigma of admitting their existence or impact.

Critical incident stress management providers offer **on-scene support and staff advisement** including emotional first aid, allowing for the ventilation of feelings. Suggestions about how to decrease high-intensity stress may be made. Staff physical needs are also monitored.

A **demobilization** is defined as a "decompression" mechanism for responders as they leave a large-scale event. It is conducted in an exit staging area that can include food and psychoeducation on stress management. **Defusings** occur either at the individual or small-group level. They involve a neutralizing intervention between a CISM provider and the concerned individual(s). A defusing may substitute for a debriefing, or it may identify the need for one. It is a short-term tool used soon after stress has escalated.

Additional CISM activities can include a **crisis management briefing** such as a town hall meeting for a large group, a community, or a neighborhood. In such gatherings, an authority figure can work in conjunction with the CISM leadership to provide information about the event as well as information about typical reactions and stress management. **Family support** assists families, friends, and colleagues with understanding what is happening to a loved one who was involved in a critical incident and how they can best support him or her. Emergency responders often do not like to discuss the details of their occupations because they may seem socially unacceptable, grotesque, or distressing to a lay public. CISM family support helps family members obtain information on the unique stressors, circumstances, and culture of emergency service work. They can also be validated for their own stress reactions and learn ways to take care of themselves.

Assessment/consultation can provide support in areas that fall within the purview of CISM. For those that don't, appropriate options are suggested or **referrals** are made. Critical incident stress management is strictly short-term assistance; brief follow-up meetings can be held. However, if it appears that individuals may need more formal counseling, they may be referred to professionals. Finally, **mutual aid** is relied upon when a CISM team may have to respond to an event that is too close for their own comfort, resources cannot be mustered, or events are too large for one team to handle. A system of mutual assistance with other CISM teams should be in place to help in these situations.

Components of Critical Incident Stress Debriefing

A CISD is the most intense and complex component of CISM. Although it used to be the Mitchell model's main focus, it now is considered to be only a part of the total management process. If needed, a debriefing is offered 2 to 14 days after an event and lasts about 2 to 3 hours. It is a peer-driven process focusing on the psychological and emotional aspects of an incident. It is not an operational critique of professional performance during the event, nor is it group therapy. Its highly structured, one-shot format and emphasis on peer leaders remove it from the realm of standard group therapy, which is most often led by a mental health professional with a focus on a group's process dynamics and subsequent sessions. Trained CISM team members are selected to complement the particular group being debriefed so that group members can discuss their feelings with people who have shared similar experiences.

The debriefing process includes seven highly delineated phases:

1. Introduction
2. Fact
3. Thought
4. Reactions
5. Symptoms
6. Teaching
7. Reentry

In moving through these phases, the leader guides participants from the cognitive realm, where they focus on what actually happened and what they thought about it at the time, to the emotional realm, where they examine their affective responses. The final phases return them to the cognitive realm and include psychoeducation about typical reactions and constructive coping mechanisms.

Trained teams conduct CISD interventions. For example, a CISD is a structured group meeting that includes a trained mental health professional, trained peer counselors, and often a trained member of the clergy. Critical incident stress debriefing teams are often voluntary and composed of local volunteers from these separate disciplines in a defined region. They may provide debriefing services for local emergency responder groups who experience a line-of-duty event that is particularly disturbing or of a type that is recognized as especially troubling for responders. These include line-of-duty deaths or serious injury to operations personnel, child deaths, and gruesome or mass-casualty events.

Attending a debriefing should be a voluntary process, although some agencies have made them mandatory as a way to reduce the possible stigma attached to mental health assistance. Actual participation (that is, talking) during the meeting is voluntary, though participants are encouraged to speak because their experiences may be helpful to others group members. The only verbal requirement on the part of attendees is introducing themselves by name; otherwise they are free to remain silent and simply listen throughout the session. Finally, a low-keyed, informal postdebriefing gathering is suggested where group members and leaders can mingle together. This informal closeout allows the leaders to identify troubled group members and to provide linkage and referral and follow-up information.

OTHER PSYCHOLOGICAL DEBRIEFING MODELS

Although it is the most widely recognized, the Mitchell model is not the only formalized psychological debriefing approach being used today. There are at least two other articulated models in use: historical group debriefing and process debriefing.

Historical group debriefing (HGD) was established during World War II by Brigadier General Marshall. Macdonald (2003) describes this model as intended to reconstruct complex historical data about military events through a group narrative. She writes,

> HGDs were conducted immediately after the engagement with no focus on military rank structure. Each soldier's testimony, whether complementary or contradictory, was accepted unconditionally. Soldiers were directed to reconstruct combat events chronologically in detail, including thoughts, feelings, assumptions, and subsequent decisions. Such personal factors were considered important contributors to individual actions during the engagement. HGDs, although not intended for stress reduction, appeared to result in a feeling of relief, which General Marshall termed, "a spiritual purge."

Shalev (2000) tested this group debriefing model with Israeli infantry units using a pre/posttest design; results suggested that HGD positively affected anxiety and self-efficacy in military personnel after combat trauma. Shalev (2000) and Raphael and Wilson (2000) note that an HGD is similar to an operational debriefing since it focuses on fact-finding rather than on emotional reactions. From Shalev's theoretical perspective, this is an extremely important point since he believes that reducing distress and arousal is the key to preventing post-trauma morbidity. A significant concern about psychological debriefing is that it may open up the expression of emotion in a manner that heightens a responder's arousal level rather than calming it, thereby increasing distress and interfering negatively with natural, spontaneous recovery. Shalev reflects that digging for emotions when a stressor or danger is ongoing and response duty is still in order may also serve to disturb and disrupt a responder's functioning. Given this concern, HGD's factual focus may make it a better debriefing model than psychological debriefing in situations where stressors are chronic.

The other model, process debriefing, is a type of psychological debriefing developed within a European context by Dryegrov (1997, 2003). It is an adaptation of Mitchell's CISD with a nearly identical structure. However, Dryegrov emphasizes the process elements of debriefings in a more overtly clinical and psychodynamic manner, with a special emphasis on leadership. Dryegrov believes that a process debriefing group leader must be extremely skillful, possessing a solid understanding of group processes, fostering safety and trust within the group, and utilizing effective verbal and nonverbal communication and educational skills.

He also writes that a group leader should receive thorough predebriefing preparation so that he or she can focus more on the group members' needs as well as the group process and less on the details of the traumatic event itself. Dryegrov is emphatic about the importance of the training and competency of the facilitator, so much so that he states that it is not a viable option to conduct a process debriefing unless a trained leader is available.

Critical incident stress management, HGD, and process debriefing are all designed to be used with groups of participants. Although debriefing has been used with individuals, there are no well-described protocols for individual debriefings. At best, some studies of debriefings conducted with individuals suggest loose adherence to the CISD model so that the thoughts and feelings are explored and education on symptoms and symptom management is provided.

DEBRIEFING'S THEORETICAL CONTEXT

Even as the use of psychological debriefing has grown, professional differences remain concerning its proper theoretical home. Psychological debriefing has been framed as a form of emotional or psychological first aid (Mitchell, 2003), as a part of crisis intervention (Devilly & Cotton, 2003; Macy, Behar, & Paulson, 2004; Mitchell, 2003), and as a form of psychoeducation. It is fairly clear that debriefing does not fall under a current definition of psychological first aid (PFA). As we have discussed, PFA is not structured or formal; it is a nonintrusive way of being present for disaster victims that centers on meeting basic needs first, restoring a sense of safety, providing comfort, and offering a listening ear as needed. Unlike debriefing, PFA does not advocate urging people to speak about their experiences, though it does involve listening to survivors who choose to share their experiences.

Crisis Intervention

Whether debriefing should be considered a form of crisis intervention depends as much on how one defines crisis intervention as how one defines psychological debriefing. In Mitchell's view, crisis intervention is emergency psychological care provided with the goals of "stabilizing the current situation, assisting people in mobilizing their resources, and restoring people to an adaptive level of independent functioning that approximates the pre-crisis level of adaptation" (Mitchell & Everly, 1998). Mitchell describes the three principles of crisis intervention as proximity, immediacy, and expectancy. This definition of crisis intervention could encompass a debriefing conducted in the context of the multitactic CISM because Mitchell's model considers a critical incident to be a precursor to a potential crisis (Flannery & Everly, 2000). Thus, a debriefing could be used to prevent a critical incident from turning into a crisis.

Raphael and Wilson (2000), on the other hand, largely disagree that psychological debriefing is part of crisis intervention because of differences in timing and target audience. Regarding timing, they write that a crisis arises when one's normal coping mechanisms are insufficient to deal with particular life events, yet debriefings are usually offered just days after the event, well before any such inability may be evident. Instead, crisis intervention usually takes place weeks after a traumatic event, often in the form of a number of individual sessions. Raphael and Wilson also point out two significant differences in the groups psychological debriefing and crisis interventions are aimed at. First, a crisis intervention model holds that most people will prevail through a crisis with minimal assistance but that it is possible to identify those who are coping worse, who are overwhelmed, and who have failing social networks; interventions should therefore focus on these at-risk groups. In contrast, debriefings are often offered to everyone who has experienced a particular stressful event, regardless of indications of resilience. Perhaps most critically, they also point out that debriefings conducted with primary victims, meaning ordinary citizens rather than emergency professionals, have not shown to be effective. For example, in one study, burn unit victims who had been individually debriefed reported *more* symptoms when tested 13 months after the intervention (Bisson, Jenkins, Alexander & Bannister, 1997). Crisis intervention, in contrast, has been proven effective with primary victims.

Raphael and Wilson (2000) acknowledge that debriefing could be seen within a crisis intervention framework if it were embedded as part of a comprehensive CISM program, as Mitchell recommends. However, they conclude,

> What both procedures have in common is that both conceptually deal with disruptions to coping in normal persons who have experienced some degree of disequilibrium caused by a stressful life event. But the mantle of crisis intervention does not help the cause of debriefing, or its ubiquity. The formats are different, the focus and timing frequently differ, and where randomized controlled trials of crisis intervention exist, debriefing has been shown to be ineffective and possibly harmful to some.

Psychoeducation

Different models of debriefing vary in their emphasis on education, so debriefing could be viewed as a form of psychoeducation (Raphael & Wilson, 2000). Education prior to a traumatic event has been noted as an important determinant of successful mastery (Ursano, McCaughey, & Fullerton, 1994). Dunning (1988) discusses the potential effects of educating workers about possible reactions to severe experience and ways of coping. However, Raphael and Wilson (2000) express concern as to what participants are actually learning during a debriefing—do they learn how to identify pathological symptoms within themselves, or do they learn that everyone needs assistance to recover? How does the learning in debriefing intersect with someone's previous training or experience of having managed a stressful and difficult event? Raphael urges further research and examination in this area, especially in terms of understanding how principles of adult educational theory that emphasize active learning and problem solving may be applied, in contrast to the passive learning typically used in debriefing.

Somewhat akin to psychoeducation, Shalev (2000) views debriefing as belonging within a stress management framework. As Raphael and Wilson (2000) point out, this view fits with Mitchell's CISM model, which encompasses a whole spectrum of workplace-related responses to stressful incidents. As these differing theoretical views demonstrate, the controversies surrounding debriefing are significant.

CRITICAL QUESTIONS ABOUT DEBRIEFING

Currently, psychological debriefing broadly connotes talking with distressed individuals after a possibly traumatic episode in their lives. Just as the term *debriefing* lacks conceptual clarity, the practice of debriefing has invited a sweeping and heated backlash as well as confusion about what the technique's future should be.

A primary source of confusion is that psychological debriefing approaches in general often appear to be incorrectly equated with the specific protocols of CISD. Even published studies citing the use of debriefing do not always specify precisely what technique is meant. For example, in a 2002 NIMH review of 76 studies regarding early psychological intervention for victims/survivors of mass violence, 17 of the studies were self-described as using psychological debriefing, and 15 included self-described debriefings delivered within a month of a traumatic event. Of these, four clearly indicated that they used a CISD model; two used a modified CISD approach; one used a debriefing model "loosely" based on CISD, and seven did not specifically define what they meant by psychological debriefing. The remaining study was a 3-year follow-up of an intervention described as a "one hour individual psychological debriefing . . . a review of the traumatic experience, encouragement of emotional expression, promotion of cognitive processing of the experience" (NIMH, 2002) Out of these 15 studies, it appears that only one included a preincident component of an "Operational Stress Training Package" and assessment.

And the variability cited by the NIMH (2002) review extended to the recipients of the intervention and to the kinds of traumatic events that it was meant to address. Participants in seven studies received individual debriefing sessions of varying quantities and lengths and ranging in timing of delivery from 10 hours to 21 days postevent. Of the eight studies conducted to treat a collective trauma, seven used group interventions, and one used both individual and group interventions. Two of these studies involved civilians, one a group of noninjured women who had survived a terrorist attack in Israel and the other adult employees who had been in bank robberies. Of the remaining six, one involved police officers, one involved emergency medical responders, and four involved assorted military personnel. The traumatic events included a terrorist attack, severe burns, bank robberies, recovery efforts after a plane crash and severe car accident, a mass shooting, motor vehicle accidents, handling and identification of bodies, miscarriages, and attempted physical or sexual assault or bag snatching.

The term *psychological debriefing* is ill defined even in the professional literature, and, more disturbingly, the intervention is applied far more broadly than Mitchell (1983) or Raphael (1986) originally intended. As we have described, these processes were originally designed to help workers quickly begin to integrate their thoughts and feelings about traumatic events so that the experiences would lose their potential to be frightening or disturbing. As Weaver (1995) commented over a decade ago, "Done well, it helps keep good people physically and emotionally healthy and it keeps them on the job. . . . Most mental health professionals have not been taught about defusing or debriefing and report being amazed at how helpful these simple but powerful tools can become in their day-to-day practices, in helping clients cope with various life crises."

But that success led to an overextension that is the source of much of the controversy around the practice today. Understandably, an apparently effective model appealed to managers of workplaces and environments that were increasingly exposed to violence and unexpectedly distressing and shocking events, including disasters. In a time of increasing awareness of the consequences of traumatic stress, psychological debriefing provided a ready tool of on-scene crisis intervention, and in recent years it has been widely applied after traumatic events, despite there being little empirical evidence of its efficacy in stabilizing acute trauma (Macy et al., 2004). Yet debriefing has become a powerful social movement (Gist & Woodall, 1998). Part of its appeal has rested on its face validity (it just seems like it should be helpful), on survivor appreciation, and on the popular belief in the value of talking through traumatic experiences. Additionally, its use seems to have accelerated in the context of a society that made trauma ubiquitous. Unlike in past decades when the impact of painful events was often ignored or denied, today many of life's challenges and losses are seen as requiring outside intervention.

McNally (2005) reflects that although psychological debriefing was originally developed for firefighters, law enforcement officers, and other emergency service personnel, it has become a standard practice in diverse settings where adverse events sometimes occur, such as businesses, schools, and hospitals. As a result, a veritable debriefing industry has been created. Gist and Woodall (1998) criticize this development vividly:

> A simple technique took on the proportion of a movement. . . . The CIS movement was spawned and nourished far outside the critical and conservative waters of scientific psychology, espoused instead through trade magazines, proprietary conferences and workshops. . . These point to one ethically defensible position regarding the debriefing movement: apply the brakes to the runaway train this popularized movement has become, and explore instead the enhancement of essential resiliency, informal and instrumental support, invisible interventions, similar quiet but effective approaches to organizational and community response to individual and collective challenge.

Is this criticism fair? The answer is not completely clear, but the balance of current evidence does suggest that natural resilience outweighs any benefits debriefing might provide. The NIMH (2002) has stated that normal recovery should be expected in the immediate postincident phase and that presuming clinically significant disorder in the early postincident phase is inappropriate. They also recommended that participation by survivors of mass violence in early intervention sessions, whether administered to a group or individually, should be voluntary. And after conducting a meta-analysis of randomized, controlled trials, Rose, Bisson, and Wessely (2001) report that single-session individual debriefings did not prevent the onset of posttraumatic stress disorder (PTSD), nor did they reduce psychological distress. There was also no evidence that debriefing reduced general psychological morbidity, depression, or anxiety or that it was superior to an educational intervention. As a result of such evidence, they recommended an end to compulsory debriefings.

However, methodological issues cloud the evidence. Bisson and Deahl (1994) note that most published data studying debriefing suffers from serious methodological problems including small sample size and sampling bias, absence of control groups, lack of baseline data, comparison of single versus multiple debriefing, lack of uniformity in psychological debriefing, timing variance, and varying degrees of trauma exposure experienced by participants. Better methodology, intervention assessment, and measures of trauma are needed, beginning with a refined definition of what is actually being studied, as Shalev (2000) observes: "The term debriefing refers to a heterogeneous array of interventions, which may include various degrees of abreaction, cognitive restructuring, suggestion, self diagnosis, and education. Hence, a conceptual basis for debriefing as such is very elusive, as each component of this ensemble may have a rationale for itself . . . the core of the argument for or against debriefing can not be theoretical and must remain empirical."

Mitchell and his supporters have done much to advance debriefing within the CISM format and have been vocal in its defense. They frame the debriefing controversy as a matter of method, noting that many psychological debriefing practitioners tried to adapt the standard CISD group protocol for use in one-on-one individual debriefings; researchers then inappropriately generalized those results to CISD. As such, Mitchell (2004) suggests that CISD has been wrongly targeted, blamed for failing to help a type of client for whom it was never intended. McNally, Bryant, and Ehlers (2003) counter this defense by stating that it is "devoid of merit. . . . These advocates must first demonstrate that their method actually works. Then their complaints about protocol departures may be warranted—only after they have furnished convincing evidence of the efficacy of their method." Indeed, there are currently no controlled studies of CISM in its entirety.

Possible Drawbacks, Possible Benefits

The debate about debriefing is important because not only continuing use of an unsupported intervention may waste valuable resources in the aftermath of disaster but also, for some people, psychological debriefing may actually *increase* psychological distress. As we mentioned earlier in discussing Shalev's (2000) examination of the HGD model, one major criticism of psychological debriefing is concern that emotional processing that is premature will lead to an increase in arousal, stress, and anxiety, which are acknowledged to be pathogenic in those exposed to severe, traumatic stressors. Also, because debriefing calls attention to symptoms, debriefing participants may report increased symptoms that they would otherwise have ignored. Many complex factors determine whether a person recovers naturally from trauma or develops serious psychopathology, yet individual personality variables or personal coping mechanisms are not considered in this "one-size-fits-all" approach. A debriefing may feel like invasive surgery to someone who might be better off working through an event with a close friend or family member. Different group members may have had different levels of trauma exposure so that hearing about others' experiences may result in secondary traumatization. As a result of these factors, psychological debriefing may have an iatrogenic effect, inadvertently causing harm rather than reducing it.

So why are debriefings still in use at all? They do appear to offer some benefits to some people, under certain circumstances. Debriefings share six admirable objectives: ventilation of impressions, reactions, and feelings; promotion of cognitive organization through clear understanding of both the events and reactions; a decrease in the sense of uniqueness or abnormality of reactions; achieving normalization through sharing, leading to mobilization of resources within and outside the group; increasing group support, solidarity, and cohesion; and identification of avenues of further assistance if needed (Snelgrove, 2005).

That emphasis on shared experience can be comforting for some survivors. As Busuttil and Busuttil (1997) describe CISD, the aim is to "diminish the impact of catastrophic events by promoting support and encouraging processing of traumatic experiences in a group setting; to facilitate the piecing together of traumatic information while personal experiences are normalized and participants are helped to look into the future and to attempt to accelerate recovery before harmful stress reactions have the chance to damage the performance, careers, health and families of victims." At their best, debriefings acknowledge and validate feelings and deliver an ultimate message of empowerment; they can increase morale and cohesion in responder groups in the face of a catastrophe. As this implies, meaningful bonding and social support can occur as a by-product of debriefings, which can serve as a health-promoting, structured, sociocultural ritual that can help a work community to individually and interpersonally process a shocking event (Snelgrove, 2005). However, where individuals already have adequate support networks, debriefings may be redundant (Deahl, 2000).

The CISM model does include several positive factors. It is not described as therapy, so those who see mental health interventions as stigmatizing may better receive it. The incorporation of peer leaders lends credibility within organizations. A debriefing can be a useful screening tool, providing team leaders with a sense of whom may be in need of further mental health support. Debriefings may meet many needs: "the needs of survivors to articulate what has happened, understand it and gain control; the symbolic needs of workers and management to aid those who suffer and to show concern; and the needs of those not directly involved to master vicariously the traumatic encounter, overcome their sense of helplessness and survivor guilt, and to make restitution" (Rick & Briner, 2004).

Based on self-reports, CISD is generally well received. Many recipients positively rate their experiences of this procedure—even if later assessment measures indicate that they are symptomatic, suggesting that the debriefing failed as a primary prevention method. It appears that people feel they have been given something they need. Workers may feel that their organizations have acknowledged what has happened to them. Trauma survivors need affirmation for their experience, and debriefings can apparently fill that short-term need, regardless of their longer-term protective effects.

Although psychological debriefing is contraindicated for direct survivors of disaster, where the more comprehensive CISM is virtually impossible, debriefing may be appropriate for emergency services personnel following their involvement in disaster response—with the notable caveats about efficacy and possible iatrogenic effects that we have discussed. In the next section, we review findings regarding the potential impact of the combination of unique stressors and traumas that first responders experience. When CISM emerged as a seemingly appropriate intervention, many first-responder groups embraced it as a way to address on-the-job events. But is it appropriate for this population in response to disaster experiences? How do disasters affect emergency professionals in comparison to the rest of the population?

FIRST RESPONDERS AND DISASTER TRAUMA

Numerous studies suggest that emergency workers, including firefighters, police officers, paramedics, and other professionals who are likely to be first responders to various disasters, are less likely to develop PTSD or other lasting psychological responses to trauma than are members of the general public. For example, North et al. (2002) examined postdisaster psychopathology among male firefighters who participated in the rescue effort after the Oklahoma City bombing of 1995 and compared their responses with those of male survivors who were in the building at the time of the blast. They found a significantly lower rate of PTSD related to the bombing in the rescue workers than in the survivors, 13% and 23%, respectively. One percent of rescue workers developed postdisaster panic disorder, compared with 6% of survivors. According to North et al. (2002), the lower prevalence of PTSD among firefighters than among direct bomb blast survivors "may reflect firefighters' lower injury rates and reduced vulnerability from selection and self-selection for work entailing trauma exposure, preparedness, experience with routine job-related trauma exposure, and attention to mental health needs through education and debriefing pre- and post-bombing."

Although that list of characteristics describes possible reasons for first responders' relative resilience, they are certainly not immune to lasting reactions from disaster recovery work, as Fullerton, Ursano, and Wang (2004) found in a comparison between emergency workers with and without exposure to a disaster. The 207 exposed workers had participated in the recovery effort after a major plane crash; the 421 members of the comparison group worked in a community about 90 miles from the crash site and were not involved in the recovery efforts but were otherwise similar in demographic characteristics and experience levels. Examining levels of depression, acute stress disorder (ASD) and PTSD at 1 month, 7 months, and 13 months after the crash, the authors found that the exposed disaster workers had significantly higher rates of ASD than the comparison subjects (25.6% versus 2.4%), of PTSD at 13 months (16.7% versus 1.9%), and of depression at 7 months (16.4% versus 10.0%) and at 13 months (21.7% versus 12.6%). Clearly, some portion of the responder population remains vulnerable to distress after exposure to trauma, if perhaps at a lower rate than the general population.

Fullerton et al. (2004) then examined demographic characteristics and the nature of exposure within the group that had responded to the plane crash and found the following patterns of responses:

- Younger workers were at greater risk for ASD.
- Unmarried workers were 2.26 times more likely to develop ASD than those who were married.

- Workers who were depressed at 7 months were 9.5 times more likely to have PTSD at 13 months than those who were not depressed.
- Workers with ASD were 7.33 times more likely to develop PTSD.
- ASD was not related to previous disaster experience or to the nature of the exposure during the crash recovery.
- However, workers with previous disaster experience were 6.34 times more likely to develop PTSD than those without, even after controlling for level of exposure.

These findings suggest that two distinct groups of emergency workers may be at higher risk for developing PTSD: those whose early psychological response includes ASD or depression and those who have experienced disasters in the past. The negative impact of previous disaster experience is especially troubling because the nature of their jobs dictates that emergency workers are likely to be exposed to disasters repeatedly. As Fullerton et al. (2004) write, "Whether previous disaster experience sensitizes or inoculates against future risk is a complex issue that has implications for training. In addition, sensitization versus inoculation may be important to unsuccessful versus successful coping after trauma and to the possible development of PTSD." One could also speculate that at an early stage in their careers, younger, less-resilient workers select themselves out of emergency services, leaving the hardiest to have the least symptoms postdisaster.

Another subset of disaster workers who appear to be subject to significant emotional distress are people who work with human remains, both those recovering remains from the disaster site and those working in a lab or forensic setting identifying them. In a survey (Tucker, Pfefferbaum, Nixon, & Foy, 1999) of 51 professionals and volunteers who had worked with remains after the Oklahoma City bombing, participants reported 2 years later that handling the bodies of children was especially traumatic, as was the knowledge for some helpers who knew that they were potentially working on the remains of acquaintances, creating a troubling sense of identification with the victims. This disturbing feeling of identification was even stronger among firefighters and other emergency personnel working to recover remains from the World Trade Center after 9/11 because so many of the fatalities were colleagues (Cable & Martin, 2003). Tucker et al. (1999) also found higher levels of distress among workers with less experience handling remains, such as dentists or medical students who volunteer after a disaster. Of the body handlers surveyed by Tucker et al. (1999), 14% reported seeking mental health treatment, and 10% increased alcohol use in the first 2 months after the Oklahoma City bombing to cope with their distress, but scores of both depression and PTSD symptoms decreased from the end of the body-recovery period to the 1-year anniversary of the bombing.

Regehr and Bober (2005) suggest that the traumatic impact of handling remains may be reduced to some degree by appropriate preparation and training (that is, preevent briefings), including education about the recovery and identification process and "highlighting the meaning and value of this work for surviving family and friends. Focusing not only on the technical aspects of the job, but also on the benefits to others helps reduce the sense of futility associated with work when there is no one left to save." Advance briefings about recovery work conditions, including information about the likely state of the remains workers will encounter, allows helpers to prepare themselves mentally. Briefings also provide the opportunity to suggest coping skills that workers can use to manage their emotions both on the scene and afterward (Regehr & Bober, 2005). Long-term psychological support should also be made available and palatable to members of this group, given the recognized impact of the terrible but necessary task they perform.

Many studies point to the importance of social support from spouses, family, and friends for first responders (Fullerton et al., 2004; Regehr & Bober, 2005). However, the demands of disaster rescue and recovery work in terms of both time commitment and emotional intensity may put a strain on family relationships just when the workers need them most (Regehr & Bober, 2005). Responders may feel compelled to work long shifts, especially immediately after a disaster, and may rest near the disaster site rather than returning home so that they can get back to work more quickly. Families may be highly supportive of this dedication during the early stages of the recovery, but as time passes and their own needs go unmet, they may become less understanding, placing additional strain on the worker as well as on other family members.

And the trauma experienced by emergency workers can impact family members in turn. For example, Pfefferbaum, Bunch, Wilson, Tucker, and Schorr (2002) interviewed 27 partners of Oklahoma City firefighters who had participated in the 1995 bombing rescue effort. They found that 42 to 44 months after the bombing more than one-third reported permanent changes in their marital relationship and 15 percent reported that their health had worsened.

Emergency Workers as Public Figures

By definition, disasters are public tragedies, and therefore they capture attention of people well beyond those directly affected. This can bring welcome recognition of the difficult work that emergency responders perform, but it may also attract a degree of media scrutiny that can impede natural recovery from trauma (Rando, 2003). Firefighters, police, and other first responders play extraordinary roles during such high-profile events as the attacks of September 11, 2001 or the Oklahoma City bombing. Emergency workers are often perceived as heroes; but as those involved in the World Trade Center response discovered, the admiration carries a price. As workers struggled to rescue the few survivors and then to recover the many victims, they did so in the spotlight, their despair and exhaustion broadcast to the world:

> At the World Trade Center, where so many rescue workers were buried in the rubble, first responders had to deal with their own sense of personal disaster at the loss of colleagues and friends. They were torn between the macro and the micro impacts of the tragedy, between public and personal evaluations of their efforts. This conflict was especially powerful as rescue became recovery. In the eyes of the world, the 9/11 first responders performed magnificently. In their own eyes, however, they fell short, haunted by what they wanted to find and could not. (Cable & Martin, 2003)

Thus, while first responders were being elevated to hero status by the public and glorified by the press, privately many workers experienced survivor guilt for being alive while so many colleagues had died (Cable & Martin, 2003), sometimes compounded by performance guilt for their inability to have saved more victims (Regehr & Bober, 2005). This conflict between external perceptions and internal feelings may have complicated recovery for many 9/11 first-responder survivors.

Mourning in Public

We must also note that the very public aspect of disaster extends beyond first responders to affect all survivors and victims' families. In a disaster, especially one of broad impact, the public nature of the victims' deaths may overwhelm their loved ones' power to experience their grief and other emotions privately (Cable & Martin, 2003). However well meant the community's recognition of the loss may be, it can leave survivors feeling burdened by the expectations of strangers and robbed of control over postdeath rituals by the demand for public ceremonies, which may be attended by outsiders and by the media rather than being a gathering of intimates (Rando, 2003). This effect can be seen among emergency responders whose colleagues have been killed and among widows and other bereaved when a "hero" has been killed in the line of duty. The public admiration for the deceased may "inhibit the survivor's ability to address issues such as ambivalence or anger. It is not socially appropriate to resent the times your spouse let you down when everyone else is calling him a hero" (Rando, 2003).

Even if the victim isn't perceived as heroic, losing a loved one in a public tragedy like a disaster may lead to "complicated grief" that is not resolved with the passage of time like more typical losses, discussed in Chapters 4 and 5. As we noted, some of the factors (Rando, 2003) that can make a death traumatic include

1. Suddenness and lack of anticipation.
2. Violence, mutilation, and destruction.
3. Preventability and/or randomness.
4. Loss of one's child (including adult children).
5. Multiple deaths.
6. The mourner's personal encounter with death secondary to a significant threat to survival or a massive and/or shocking confrontation with the death and mutilation of others.

If one or more of these factors characterize a death due to disaster, survivors are more likely to suffer from traumatic stress, which may interfere with their ability to mourn. In addition to grief, these mourners experience anxiety, vulnerability, anger and guilt, and psychic numbing. They are likely to feel a strong need to find meaning in the death, to assign responsibility for it, and to punish the responsible party (Rando, 2003). Mental health helpers should be aware that mourners may need to address the trauma and anxiety about the manner of death before they are fully able to grieve and adapt to the loss.

Those whose loved ones die in high-profile disasters may yet face another factor that complicates recovery: constant reminders in the media. Early media attention can have a beneficial effect if it validates the significance of the death and reassures the bereaved that others in the community care about their loss, but when ongoing coverage provides a constant reminder of the death, it can retraumatize the mourner (Rando, 2003). This effect was movingly described by Evelyn Husband, the widow of Col. Rick D. Husband, one of the seven astronauts who were killed when the space shuttle *Columbia* broke apart upon reentry to the earth's atmosphere in 2003. Mrs. Husband told the *New York Times* about visiting a pizza place with her son and daughter in 2005, shortly before the first scheduled launch following the disaster, only to be confronted yet again by a television showing the *Columbia* crew walking toward the shuttle and then the shuttle breaking up in the sky. Her comment describes the situation of many family members of first responders who lose loved ones in disasters: "We just cannot escape it. Has anybody else had to watch their husband die on television over and over? I know that it's public and I know that it's national, but it's so private for me" (Kershaw, 2005).

CRITICAL INCIDENT STRESS MANAGEMENT AND FIRST RESPONDERS

First responders are traditionally understood to be groups that form tight bonds; having the support of colleagues who are loyal and competent is vital, both in terms of response during times of danger and around the other circumstances in responders' lives. This reliance on each other, the esprit de corps formed, is considered the most mitigating, protective psychological factor during difficult times and a hallmark of what makes such dangerous and trying work possible to accomplish.

David Halberstam (2002) describes this bond in *Firehouse*, a book he wrote after 9/11, about the firehouse nearest his New York City home:

A firehouse . . . is like a vast extended family—rich, warm, joyous and supportive, but, on occasion quite edgy as well, with all the inevitable tensions brought on by so many forceful men living so closely together over so long a period of time. What gradually emerges is surprisingly nuanced; the cumulative human texture has slowly evolved over time and is often delicate. It is created out of hundreds of unseen, unknown, and often unidentified tiny adjustments that these strong, willful men make to accommodate one another . . . how the men live with one another day in and day out, and surprisingly the degree to which, whether they realize it or not, they come to love one another (sometimes even as they dislike one another)— because love is a critical ingredient in the fireman's code, which demands that you are willing to risk your life for your firehouse brothers. . . . The men not only live and eat with one another, they play sports together, go off to drink together, help repair one another's houses, and, most important, share terrifying risks; their loyalties to one another, by the demands of the dangers they face, must be instinctive and absolute. Thus are firehouse codes fashioned. When a probie—a probationary firefighter—joins a firehouse, he must adjust to the firehouse culture, rather than the firehouse adjusting to him. It is like the military in that respect: Idiosyncrasy can come later; adherence to rules and traditions come first.

First responders go through life-and-death situations together, often on a daily basis. Stress can range on a continuum from paperwork, administration, rotating schedules, and family interference, to problematic professional relationships and critical incidents such as rarer line-of-duty events, and on to huge traumatic events that involve mass fatalities, especially those of first responders themselves. In terms of disasters, emergency service personnel play critical on-scene roles from rescue to recovery. Pulley (2005) suggests that during critical incidents a responder has to both react and deny at the same time, to remain calm and do the job at hand. If emotions were allowed to surface, it would be impossible to accomplish the work that has to be done. To accomplish this split, first responders cope by distancing themselves, often using gallows or dark humor. Those not in their rank and file may find this shocking, but there are benefits to humor's use because it can free responders from negative emotional states while also creating another source of bonding together. The downside to such intimacy is that it may be a challenge for those in cohesive groups to feel understood or to trust outsiders: How could someone from the outside possibly understand what they undergo and what they share?

Compounding this resistance to trusting outsiders, there has been a historic reluctance among first-responder cultures to admit problems. Such an admission could raise questions regarding fitness for duty, which could lead to significant consequences in terms of promotability or even in terms of being able to work sufficient hours to make ends meet. Additionally, these organizations remain largely male dominated, and men typically have a harder time seeking psychological and emotional assistance than women. In recognition of that pattern, NIMH has recently created a special outreach initiative to encourage men to seek mental health help if they need it. This "Real Men, Real Depression" campaign features New York City firefighter Jimmy Brown as one of its spokespersons, urging other men to obtain help for depression as he did.

Debriefing may also provide an acceptable forum for first responders to confront traumatic events; after all, emergency service workers represent the original client group that Mitchell developed CISD to serve. As Raphael and Wilson (2000) write, "The debriefing movement has contributed to 'making it alright' for men to talk about their traumatic wartime or other experiences, and this in itself may have contributed positively towards lessening the negative sanctions in all-male environments against emotional expression and recognition of personal distress." But debriefing alone may be insufficient for all of the reasons we discussed earlier in this chapter. In a detailed book, *In the Line of Fire: Trauma in the Emergency Services,* authors Cheryl Regehr and Ted Bober (2005) assert that assistance to emergency responders must be comprehensive and take into account multiple levels of influence. They recommend that components should include prevention, early intervention after a traumatic event, and long-term follow-up. Interventions should not only include individual responders but also their families, the organizations in which they work, and the community as a whole in a holistic, multilevel systems approach.

Regehr and Bober (2005) discuss both positive and negative aspects to CISD in the emergency service culture. Because organizational stressors and supports have been found to intensify or mitigate traumatic stress reactions, a debriefing may demonstrate management support and concern to the worker. The time and economic resources offered to provide the space for such an event can be an additional buffer to responders. Debriefings often take place during workers' regular tours so that they are not additionally burdened by having to attend during time off.

The normalization of PTSD symptoms may be viewed as a considerable strength of the CISM model. Such "normalization" may reassure an emergency service responder who may be experiencing intrusive imagery or increased arousal for the first time after a particularly traumatic event (Regehr & Bober, 2005). Without knowledge that such symptoms generally pass and are common, self-doubt may begin to percolate as they wonder if they have "the right stuff" for the job. However, a crisis debriefing not only encourages discussion about symptoms but also may help initiate further discussion among group members about the traumatic experience and their reactions. The psychoeducational component of a CISD not only teaches members about possible reactions to traumatic events but also usually includes cognitive–behavioral strategies for symptom management as an alternative to self-medication through alcohol.

The limitations to debriefings include the drawbacks cited earlier: Debriefings have not been consistently proven to reduce symptoms of PTSD, and individual group members may experience secondary traumatization as they listen to the painful and horrific details of others' narratives. "The inability to assess and screen out individuals who may have vulnerabilities such as difficult life histories, concurrent life crises, and co-morbid substance abuse or mental health problems may further increase the risk for some people" (Regehr & Bober, 2005). These writers recommend that detailed descriptions of traumatic experiences should not be encouraged during the CISD reaction stage, echoing Shalev's (2000) concern cited earlier that such emotional recounting may only serve to increase unhealthy hyperarousal.

Finally, Regehr and Bober (2005) identify key elements from the research literature that can be added to any intervention in order to support emergency workers:

- Properly timed and accurate information lowers arousal levels and distress in workers.
- An organizational climate that supports workers reduces the risk of more severe reactions after a traumatic event.
- Teaching workers skills for how to cope with distressing symptoms helps them attain a sense of mastery and restores a sense of control.
- Those workers who are most distressed following a traumatic event should have access to individual services, which may include empirically tested cognitive–behavioral approaches and possibly medication. Those making referrals should screen providers to make certain that these practitioners understand the first-responder culture.
- Families and friends are a worker's most important assets; relationships that are positive and affirming may help deter the alienation that can develop due to daily strain in the aftermath of a traumatic event.

DISASTERS AND DEBRIEFING

As we have seen, there is little agreement about the appropriate use of debriefing. However, there is a general consensus that psychological debriefing should not be used with primary victims or survivors of trauma, that it should not be used in the immediate aftermath of a disaster, that it should not be a stand-alone intervention, and that it should not be mandatory. Debriefing is also contraindicated when an individual must continue to function and deal with ongoing episodes of violence or horror, so it is not recommended for those in chronic stressor situations or those subjected to chronic traumatization.

A disaster is a shared traumatic event, composed of multiple pressures that impact a community. "The complex aftermath of disasters is characterized by newly arising stressors. In addition to the stress of trauma exposure and the initial losses incurred (e.g., loss of loved ones, friends, and/or property), the stress response of a survivor may be influenced by resulting problems with unemployment, financial resources, substance abuse, marital and family discord, or mental health problems, as well as disaster related organizational politics involving safety, rebuilding and relocating" (Hilley-Young & Gerrity, 1994). Given all of these contraindications, survivors in the wake of disaster chaos are clearly not candidates for debriefing, yet the CISD protocol continues to be used in times of community-wide disasters (Hilley-Young & Gerrity, 1994).

But if psychological debriefing is not appropriate for disaster survivors, what is? Shalev (2000) writes,

> The main reason for conducting early interventions after traumatic events is a moral one. Army commanders may also wish to conduct such interventions to reduce loss of personnel. State economists may expect them to reduce the burden of financial compensation to victims. The medical profession would be pleased to see them reducing the prevalence of long-term morbidity. Yet these are auxiliary goals. The main point is that many survivors and witnesses of extreme events suffer: afflicted, anxious, depressed, and dismayed, their pain may also become permanent. Morally, such human conditions should not be left unattended.

Similarly, Litz and Gray (2002) observe,

> It would be inappropriate to conclude that as most people adjust to extreme trauma on their own, everyone should be left alone until those most vulnerable to chronic post-traumatic problems seek care on down the line. We also do not deny the suffering of those who develop post-traumatic difficulties by blaming them for some personal inadequacy, which would be horrendously stigmatizing and decrease help seeking. . . . The need to provide supportive, palliative care in the face of disaster has far outweighed interest in, and concern about, evidence supporting the efficacy of crisis intervention strategies.

The desire to ease the suffering of our fellow humans may have overshadowed methodological examination of what we should do. When debriefing appeared to have some success in helping specific populations, the mental health world seized on it and applied it broadly to populations that it may never have been intended to help. The consequences of that overgeneralization are now being widely recognized in the field.

The immediate aftermath of disaster exposure is a period of critical significance when memories of an event are consolidated either productively or pathologically (Shalev, 2000), making early intervention essential. The criticisms and problems associated with psychological debriefing should not discourage early intervention although there is a need for increased sophistication and research-based efficacy evidence in this area. As we complete this text, the debate about the efficacy of debriefing continues. However, some of the other forms of early intervention discussed in Chapters 8 and 9, such as psychological first aid and psychoeducation, are less controversial and have less potential for harm. Let's now leave early interventions behind and move on to the better-supported realm of longer-term treatments for disaster trauma.

References

Bisson, J. I., & Deahl, M. P. (1994). Psychological debriefing and prevention of post-traumatic stress: More research is needed. *British Journal of Psychiatry, 165*, 717–720.

Bisson, J. I., Jenkins, P., Alexander, J., & Bannister, C. (1997). Randomized controlled trial of psychological debriefing for victims of acute burn trauma. *British Journal of Psychiatry, 171*, 78–81.

Busuttil, A. M. C., & Busuttil, W. (1997). Debriefing and crisis interventions. In D. Black, M. Newman, J. Harris-Hendriks, & G. Mezey (Eds.), *Psychological trauma: A developmental approach*. London: Gaskell/Royal College of Psychiatrists.

Cable, D. G., & Martin, T. L. (2003). Effects of public tragedy on first responders. In M. Lattanzi-Licht & K. J. Doka (Eds.), *Coping with public tragedy* (pp. 77–84). Washington, DC: Brunner/Routledge.

Deahl, M. (2000). Psychological debriefing: Controversy and challenge. *Australian and New Zealand Journal of Psychiatry, 34*, 929–939.

Devilly, G. J., & Cotton, P. (2003). Psychological debriefing and the workplace: Defining a concept, controversies and guidelines for intervention. *Australian Psychologist, 38*, 144–150.

Dunning, C. (1988). Intervention strategies for emergency workers. In M. Lystad (Ed.), *Mental health response to mass emergencies: Theory and practice* (pp. 284–307). Philadelphia: Brunner/Mazel.

Dyregrov, A. (1997). The process in psychological debriefing. *Journal of Trauma Stress, 10*, 589–605.

Dyregrov, A. (2003). *Psychological debriefing*. Ellicott City, MD: Chevron Publishing.

Everly, G. S., & Mitchell, J. M. (1999). Critical incident stress management: A review of the literature. *Aggression and Violent Behavior, 5*, 23–40.

Flannery, R. B., & Everly, G. S. (2000). Crisis intervention: A review. *International Journal of Emergency Mental Health, 2*(2), 119–125.

Fullerton, C. S., Ursano, R. J., & Wang, L. (2004). Acute stress disorder, posttraumatic stress disorder, and depression in disaster or rescue workers. *American Journal of Psychiatry, 161*, 1370–1376.

Gist, R., & Woodall, S. J. (1998). Social science versus social movements: The origins and natural history of debriefing. *Australasian Journal of Disaster and Trauma Studies, 1*. Retrieved on May 13, 2005, from an open-access online resource available at http://www.massey.ac.nz/~trauma/issues/1998-1/gist1.htm.

Halberstam, D. (2002). *Firehouse*. New York: Hyperion.

Hilley-Young, B., & Gerrity, E. T. (1994). Critical incident stress debriefing (CISD): Value and limitations in disaster response. *National Center for Post-Traumatic Stress Disorder Clinical Quarterly, 4,* 2.

Kershaw, S. (2005, July 10). As shuttle returns, emotions tug *Columbia* families anew. *New York Times,* pp. 1, 18.

Lindy, J. D. (1985). The trauma membrane and other clinical concepts derived from psychotherapeutic work with survivors of natural disasters. *Psychiatric Annals, 15,* 153–160.

Litz, B. T., & Gray, M. J. (2002). Early intervention for mass violence: What is the evidence? What should be done? *Cognitive and Behavioral Practice, 9,* 266–272.

MacDonald, C. (2003). Evaluation of stress debriefing with military populations. *Military Medicine.* Retrieved September 24, 2005, from www.findarticles.com/p/articles/mi_qa3912/is_200312/ai_n9332602.

Macy, R. D., Behar, L., & Paulson, R. (2004). Community-based, acute posttraumatic stress management: A description and evaluation of psychosocial–intervention continuum. *Harvard Review of Psychiatry, 12*(4), 217–228.

McNally, R. J. (2005). Psychological debriefing does not prevent posttraumatic stress disorder. Retrieved September 24, 2005 from www.psychiatric times.com/p040471.html.

McNally, R. J., Bryant, R. A., & Ehlers, A. (2003). Does early psychological intervention promote recovery from posttraumatic stress? *Psychological Science in the Public Interest, 4*(2).

Mitchell, J. T. (1983). When disaster strikes: The critical incident stress debriefing process. *Journal of Emergency Medical Services, 8,* 36–39.

Mitchell, J. T. (2003). Crisis intervention and CISM: A research summary. Retrieved March 18, 2006, from http://www.icisf.org/.

Mitchell, J. T. (2004). A response to the Devilly and Cotton article, "Pychological debriefing and the workplace." *Australian Psychologist, 39*(1), 24–28.

Mitchell, J., & Everly, G. (1998) Critical incident stress management: A new era in crisis intervention. Retrieved on March 18, 2006, from http://www.istss.org/publications/TS/Fall98/fall98.html#Critical.

NIMH (National Institute of Mental Health). (2002). *Mental health and mass violence: Evidence-based early psychological intervention for victims/survivors of mass violence. A workshop to reach consensus on best practices* (NIH Publication No. 02-5138). Washington, DC: Government Printing Office.

North, C. S., Tivis, L., McMillen, J. C., Pfefferbaum, B., Spitznagel, E. L., Cox, J., Nixon, S., Bunch, K. P., & Smith, E. M. (2002). Psychiatric disorders in rescue workers after the Oklahoma City bombing. *American Journal of Psychiatry, 159,* 857–859.

Pfefferbaum, B., North, C. S., Bunch, K., Wilson, T. G., Tucker, P., & Schorr, J. K. (2002). The impact of the 1995 Oklahoma City bombing on the partners of firefighters. *Journal of Urban Health, 79,* 364–372.

Pulley, S. (2005). Critical incident stress management. Retrieved March 18, 2006, from http://www.emedicine.com/emerg/topic826.htm.

Rando, T. A. (2003). Public tragedy and complicated mourning. In M. Lattanzi-Licht & K. J. Doka (Eds.), *Coping with public tragedy* (pp. 264–274). Washington, DC: Brunner/Routledge.

Raphael, B. (1986). *When disaster strikes: How individuals and communities cope with catastrophe.* New York: Basic Books.

Raphael, B., & Wilson, J. P. (Eds.). (2000). *Psychological debriefing: Theory, practice, and evidence.* New York: Cambridge University Press.

Regehr, C., & Bober, T. (2005). *In the line of fire: Trauma in the emergency services.* New York: Oxford University Press.

Rick, J., & Briner, R. (2004). Trauma management vs. stress debriefing: What should responsible organisations do? *Counselling at Work,* 1–4.

Rose, S., Bisson, J. L., & Wessely, S. (2001). Psychological debriefing for preventing post-traumatic stress disorder (PTSD) (Cochrane Review). The Cochrane Library, issue 4. Oxford: Update Software. Abstract available at www.update-software.com/abstracts/AB000560.htm.

Shalev, A. (2000). Stress management and debriefing: Historical concepts and present patterns, In B. Raphael & J. P. Wilson (Eds.), *Psychological debriefing: Theory, practice, and evidence* (pp. 17–31). New York: Cambridge University Press.

Snelgrove, T. (2005) Psycho-educational debriefings and outcome assessment: A point of view. Retrieved April 15, 2005, from www.ctsn-rcst.ca/PsychoEd.html.

Tucker, P., Pfefferbaum, B., Nixon, S. J., & Foy, D. W. (1999). Trauma and recovery among adults highly exposed to a community disaster. *Psychiatric Annals, 29*(2), 78–83.

Ursano, R. J., McCaughey, B., & Fullerton, C. S. (Eds.). (1994). *Individual and community responses to trauma and disaster: The structure of human chaos.* Cambridge, England: Cambridge University Press.

Weaver, J. D. (1995). *Disasters: Mental health interventions.* Sarasota, FL: Professional Resource Press/Professional Resource Exchange.

11 CHAPTER | Long-Term Treatment: Continuity of Care

We have pointed out throughout this text that most people recover from the trauma of disaster on their own or with help from natural social supports. But some people do not recover easily and develop conditions requiring treatment. Such long-term care could be necessary in the months after the disaster, or it could begin years later. It is of critical importance that resources be available to assist survivors with long-term emotional needs. As North and Westerhaus (2003) explain, "Because posttraumatic disorders often become chronic, mental health resources will need to remain in place to manage the long-term consequences and serve the many who do not seek treatment right away. Applying emergency emotional first aid in the short run only to abandon people in their long-term need will be shortsighted."

Almost by definition, disaster mental health (DMH) workers are focused on early intervention. However, they do make referrals for long-term care and therefore should be aware of the current treatments that are regularly used and available. In this chapter, we review a number of long-term approaches for treating disaster victims, including psychodynamic therapy, cognitive–behavioral therapies including eye movement desensitization and reprocessing and virtual reality exposure therapy, family systems therapy, and group therapy. We also review the effectiveness of pharmacotherapy and briefly discuss working with grieving families. These approaches have all been applied to the treatment of disaster victims suffering from such disorders as posttraumatic stress disorder (PTSD), acute stress disorder (ASD), depression, and a range of anxiety disorders. Bear in mind that these are brief overviews intended to familiarize you with the basic theories and practices involved in each of these therapies. For more detailed presentation, see the following:

> *Effective Treatments of PTSD* edited by E. B. Foa, T. M. Keane, and M. J. Friedman
>
> *Treating Psychological Trauma and PTSD* edited by J. P. Wilson, M. J. Friedman, and J. D. Lindy
>
> *Trauma and Recovery: The Aftermath of Violence From Domestic Abuse to Political Terror* by J. Herman
>
> *Acute Stress Disorder: A Handbook of Theory, Assessment, and Treatment* by RA. Bryant and A. G. Harvey
>
> *Living Beyond Loss: Death in the Family* edited by F. Walsh and M. McGoldrick
>
> *Eye Movement Desensitization and Reprocessing: Basic Principles, Protocols, and Procedures* by F. Shapiro

LONG-TERM NEEDS OF THE TRAUMATIZED PATIENT

Before we discuss specific long-term treatment models, let's define their ultimate objectives. Judith Herman (1992) discusses treatment goals for working with trauma survivors that can apply to long-term goals for survivors of catastrophic disaster:

1. The physiological symptoms of PTSD, depression, or anxiety are mitigated or made manageable.
2. The patient is able to tolerate the feelings connected with the trauma/ disaster.
3. The patient has control over the memories, able to remember them or put them aside at will.
4. The memory is coherent and connected with feelings.
5. The patient's self-esteem is restored.
6. The patient's important relationships are functional and satisfying.
7. The patient's belief system and sense of meaning incorporates the trauma/ disaster.

It is important to note some qualities that differentiate the therapeutic needs of traumatized patients from those with other kinds of problems. One key factor in long-term treatment for trauma is the relationship between survivor and therapist. In her classic work on trauma, Herman (1992) notes that recovery requires a "healing relationship." The central experiences of trauma are disempowerment and disconnection from others, so therapy must be based on the empowerment of the survivor and the development of new relationships. The therapist begins the process of healing and connection by providing a safe and honest relationship with the client. This must occur irrespective of the therapist's specific theoretical orientation.

This essential relationship can be difficult to establish because it requires a level of commitment that many distressed patients are unable or unwilling to make. Research (Regier, Narrow, Rae, Manderscheid, Locke, & Goodwin, 1993) indicates that only about 30% of people with psychological disorders seek treatment at all, and this is true even for people with serious mental illness (Corrigan, 2004). Many patients who do enter therapy do not fully participate once treatment has begun. Patients avoid or discontinue treatment for a number of reasons—some related to trauma and some not. Therapy takes time and energy and can be costly, especially for those without insurance. As we indicated earlier, some people avoid treatment because of the stigma associated with asking for help. There has always been some shame attached to seeking treatment, to a degree that may depend on the individual as well as his or her cultural milieu. For example, as discussed in Chapter 10, the first-responder culture emphasizes strength, self-sufficiency, or comradeship for healing rather than seeking professional help.

This stigma may be even stronger for those seeking help after being exposed to trauma or disaster. "Why am I not strong enough to bounce back from a negative experience?" a survivor may wonder. "I would be embarrassed to think that my friends or family knew I couldn't handle these events." Further compounding some traumatized survivors' resistance to counseling, recall that one of the primary symptoms of PTSD is avoidance. It may be excruciatingly painful for PTSD patients to think or talk about their traumatic experience to the degree that would be expected in therapy. Therefore, therapists should understand that PTSD patients may be especially reluctant to begin treatment. They are prime candidates to discontinue treatment early because of the intensely painful feelings associated with discussing the traumatic events that are a hallmark of their illness.

In general, therapists should be sensitive to the fact that those seeking long-term treatment following exposure to disaster could be feeling reluctant, ashamed, and embarrassed about needing help, as well as fearful of the painful feelings and memories connected with the traumatic event. Patients should be reassured and supported for acknowledging their problem and seeking treatment. There is no "technique" that will provide such reassurance. A traumatized patient will only be reassured and develop trust over time, as the therapist demonstrates some combination of competence, caring and effectiveness.

The therapist also needs to empower the traumatized patient because, according to Herman (1992), the survivor should be the person responsible for his or her own recovery. Empowerment in therapy means that the survivor has considerable control over the therapeutic process. (Note that this is not consistent with a medical model of treatment that puts the doctor squarely in charge of the healing process.) According to Herman, the therapist should become the patient's ally and support, placing all of his or her resources at the patient's disposal. Because the patient asks for help, there is an implicit power imbalance in the relationship. The therapist must be committed to not exploiting this imbalance and must communicate this commitment to the survivor. The therapist also must remain neutral as far as the life decisions of the patient goes, but this does not mean the therapist is *morally* neutral. If the disaster was intentionally caused, the therapist must bear witness to a crime. If a patient lost a loved one in a terrorist attack and is grieving, the therapist acknowledges that the loved one was murdered (Danieli, 1988). The stance and style of the therapist combines intellectual and strategic analysis with deep feeling and empathy.

When working long-term with trauma victims there may be problems in the therapy relationship. Herman (1992) refers to this as the *traumatic transference*. Difficulties in the relationship may be due to a wide range of factors, but a typical issue is that patients seek to take control because they had no control during the traumatic event. Traumatized patients can be doubtful and suspicious. They may scan the therapist, looking for signs of distance or lack of attunement or caring. A patient harmed by a terrorist may direct the helplessness or rage from contact with the terrorist toward the helper. The traumatized patient may shut down or be angry if he or she detects a lack of *mirroring* (understanding and acceptance) on the part of the therapist. On the other hand, the patient may begin to idealize the therapist and think of him or her as all powerful, someone who can offer complete protection. When the therapist is needed in such an extreme fashion, these fantasies cannot be met, and the patient can become disappointed and angry with the therapist. In many cases, it is to be expected that the traumatized patient will have difficulty learning to trust (Herman, 1992).

In addition to the challenges just described, working with trauma patients places another unique demand on the mental health professional: Although all psychotherapy involves listening to painful stories, working with victims of trauma and disaster requires that the therapist be capable of listening to horror stories. As we mentioned in Chapter 3, there is a long history of individual and collective resistance to hearing about and acknowledging traumatic experiences (Herman, 1992). Trauma victims are often highly sensitive to this, recognizing that others do not want to hear their agonizing and excruciating stories that may be filled with ugliness and grotesque images. As a result, the client may be bearing a secret that he or she knows no one wants to share. Therapists need to let the client know that they are willing to listen to the story. This does not mean that they *insist* that the story be told but that they communicate their ability to tolerate it and that they really do want the patient to share the experience. Therapists must be willing to allow the patient to describe and redescribe their experience. Almost every theoretical perspective suggests that healing involves a willingness to listen to the patient tell the trauma story in great depth and detail.

What kinds of stories are you likely to hear? Here are some examples that we have heard in the course of our work with survivors:

A man and two friends were walking in a quiet neighborhood in Brooklyn, New York, when a gas line exploded. The force of the explosion forced fluid out of all of their ears. They all recovered physically but were quite shaken. After a few weeks, when the man did not feel any relief, he called a therapist and asked for help. At the first meeting, he reported that he was experiencing anxiety, but he was reluctant to talk about what had happened or what he saw and felt. "No one really wanted to or wants to hear this story," he explained.

A social worker spoke with a counselor about the work she did during her residency in Israel, assisting groups whose job was to clean up body parts after suicide bombings. She explained that a few days earlier she had to carry a torso from the waist up into an ambulance. When her friends and family, concerned and caring, called her to see how she was, they did not know of the incident, and she did not tell them. "I said I was fine, although I wasn't. I know that they really did not want to know."

A spiritual care worker spent the better part of a year at ground zero in Manhattan during the recovery from the September 11, 2001 attacks on the World Trade Center. His responsibility was to provide spiritual consolation to anyone on the scene and to bless recovered remains. He blessed hundreds of body parts. After a few months, he and many other spiritual care workers became so familiar with body fragments that they were able to assist the medical examiner in the identification process. He said that although good friends and relatives had proclaimed that he could tell his story of what he had seen and heard and smelled, he felt that no one really wanted to know or hear about it. This spiritual care worker was carefully chosen for his assignment and was highly resilient. He functioned magnificently over a long period of time. However, in the quiet setting of a therapy group, he cried and proclaimed his loneliness when he talked about his experience.

A therapist might approach such patients directly, saying something like "I know that what you have been through was dreadful, appalling, shocking, and gruesome. You might want to protect me from the story. You do not need to do that. Whenever you are ready, I would like you to talk about it with me. I can tolerate hearing about it—all about it." Of course, hearing about terrible traumatic events can have an impact on even the most experienced mental health professional, so at the end of this chapter we consider in more detail the impact of doing long-term trauma work on therapists and the need for self-care.

A final note before we move on to specific treatments: In previous chapters, we have discussed the fact that loss is never resolved and recovery is never completed. This is certainly true for survivors of catastrophic trauma. Patients can learn to live with loss and trauma, but milestones or markers may awaken traumatic memories. Births, deaths, marriage, divorce, a child leaving home, anniversaries of the disaster, legal or court proceedings—all can be potential triggers for trauma-related difficulties. Therapists working long term with survivors of catastrophic disaster could encourage the patient to return for periodic "checkups" or "tune-ups" after therapy is concluded. The strength and resilience of the patient is not undermined if the therapist encourages the patient to contact the therapist if trauma memories become too difficult to cope with on their own or with family and friends.

Let's now turn to the various long-term treatments that may be used with disaster survivors. For each approach, we lay out the theoretical model, provide clinical examples, and discuss evidence for the method's effectiveness in treating survivors of disaster (when such specific data are available) or trauma.

PSYCHODYNAMIC APPROACHES

Sigmund Freud's role in the recognition of trauma was recounted in Chapter 3, so here we focus chiefly on the treatment methods that he initiated. In 1893 Freud and his colleague, Joseph Breuer, wrote a paper, which is now a classic in the history of trauma, titled "On the Psychical Mechanisms of Hysterical Phenomenon." In it, Freud and Breuer stated that some patients presenting physical symptoms actually "suffered from reminiscences." Memories of an overwhelming experience from the past, most likely one from childhood, were so painful and socially or personally unacceptable that they were excluded from consciousness and expressed through physical symptoms (Freud, 1925/1963).

It may now seem obvious that stress and emotional factors could produce both psychological and physical problems, but this was a radical idea in the late 1800s, as was the notion that traumatic experiences not "properly processed" or remembered could result in symptoms. Freud and Breuer found that if patients could recall the buried event while under hypnosis, the physical symptoms would dissipate. Freud developed the **cathartic method** so that patients could bring the memory into awareness, allowing them to feel and release the pent-up emotion that caused the symptom. Although Freud soon gave up the use of hypnosis and the cathartic method, these ideas form the foundation of contemporary psychoanalysis.

The goal of psychoanalysis is to bring unconscious conflicts to consciousness as the therapist and patient explore the murky subjective world of the patient and find meaning and language that satisfactorily describe the patient's experiences, in order to bring about insight and understanding. Strengthening and widening the patient's ego—the part of the personality that thinks, plans, and understands—attains this goal. The ego functions to free itself from self-condemnation, judgmentalness, guilt, self-recrimination, and shame (qualities controlled by the superego) and to take control over the impulses of sexuality and aggressiveness (controlled by the id). A person with a strong ego can experience pleasure and joy because the superego is not overdominant, and he or she can stay simultaneously in control and out of trouble because the id's impulses are regulated. According to Freud, trauma weakens the ego, making it more likely that self-condemnation and careless or self-destructive acting out will take place (Freud, 1930/1961). To help a patient, the therapist joins forces with his or her weakened ego, becoming an auxiliary ego. Once the patient's ego is strengthened, he or she is freed from the excessive demands of the superego and in control of the impulses of the id. The person now has the psychological energy to deal with the demands of reality and can love and work— the hallmark of a healthy person.

To accomplish this ego strengthening, the analyst attempts to bring unconscious material into awareness, using the tools of **free association** (the talking cure), **dream analysis** (to reveal unconscious conflicts), and **analysis of the transference** (to discover unconscious conflicts in the patient's changing view of the therapist). Because the buried material is painful, the patient is defensive and resists its uncovering, so the treatment is slow, with more and more painful inner conflicts, memories, impulses, feelings, and thoughts gradually coming to awareness. This process is not easy or pleasant, but as Freud famously noted, "The goal of analysis is to exchange neurotic misery for normal human suffering." The course of treatment in formal psychoanalysis entails four or five meetings a week over many years. Psychodynamic treatment or supportive psychodynamic treatment involves one or two meetings per week and can last months or years (Kudler, Blank Jr., & Krupnick, 2000a).

As we discussed in Chapter 3, Freud initially saw that people suffering from hysteria were not necessarily weak, but they were beset by traumatic memories of external events. Later he simply could not believe that so many of his patients could have been subjected to sexual abuse, and so he de-emphasized the importance of trauma as a cause of disorder and concluded that internal, or intrapsychic, conflicts were the cause of the neuroses. However, most of Freud's followers reinstated the importance of external events as playing a major role in the cause of disorder. The "ego psychologists" (for example, Anna Freud), the "interpersonal psychoanalysts" (for example, K. Horney, H. S. Sullivan), the "object relations theorists" (for example, W. R. D. Fairbairn, D. W. Winnicott), and the "self psychologists," (for example, H. Kohut) all stress the importance of early experience in the development of psychological illness. In the view of these psychodynamic theorists and practitioners, trauma and neglect in childhood are the chief cause of problems in adulthood (Mitchell & Black, 1995).

Of course, the notion that children are highly vulnerable to trauma is certainly consistent with the risk and resilience factors discussed in Chapters 4 and 5. However, the psychodynamic literature tends to focus almost exclusively on traumatic experiences that actually occur during childhood, suggesting that a secure childhood with appropriate parental care can leave one virtually invincible to traumatic disaster stress as an adult. Analysts working with patients who were affected by disaster are still likely to inquire into early childhood experience in which they expect to find the roots of the patient's problems. This orientation may not adequately take into account the overwhelming nature of a disaster.

PTSD and Psychoanalysis

When Freud returned his focus to trauma in the aftermath of World War I, he noted that survivors often reexperienced painful traumatic experiences, or worked them over in their minds. He recognized the importance of this *reliving* of traumatic experience and labeled it the *repetition compulsion* (Freud, 1925/1963). This compulsion presents a particular challenge in using psychodynamic approaches to treat patients with PTSD because, as we mentioned earlier, they have the further burden of actively wanting to avoid their painful memories, thoughts, and feelings and may fear being overwhelmed by the traumatic material.

Jacob Lindy (1996) points out that when treating PTSD with psychoanalytic methods it is to be expected that there will be a repetition of the trauma in the consultation room. The trauma replays itself in the context of the therapeutic process. During the analysis, triggers will set off a trauma response (for example, running water could remind a person of a flood, or sirens from a passing emergency vehicle cause the patient to startle). The patient defends against these experiences in ways that can be observed and discussed, leading to an increased self-understanding. Lindy points out that only gradually will the reenactment become amenable to the therapeutic treatment. At first, the patient's wish to simply escape the memories, the negative feelings, and the treatment predominate. Gradually, the survivor develops the ability to transform the undeveloped sensations, depressive affect, denial, and other feelings into stories of tragedy, loss, and trauma. Together, the therapist and client attempt to find words to express the emotions. For the patient there is likely to be terror at discussing these events with a new person, and there will be complex feelings and experiences including guilt and shame. Many subtleties emerge in the course of an exploration of the inner world of the patient.

Lindy (1996) notes that every person impacted by disaster has a unique experience. Therefore, for every patient the memories, thoughts, and corresponding treatment issues will be different. The subjective experience of each survivor needs to be explored and understood no matter how similar the circumstances may appear to be. He describes a family in which two children, aged 10 years and 4 years, were victims of a devastating flood that killed hundreds and displaced thousands. Twenty years after the flood, the older sister had significantly more symptoms than the younger. Through conversation and exploration, Lindy discovered that the older child was tall enough to look out the window and see the flood approaching. She saw her mother in danger and later saw a dead baby covered with mud. The younger sister was spared these sights and fears. Although both girls were survivors of the same disaster, 20 years later it was the older daughter who sat transfixed in front of her living room window anticipating the next flood, while the younger sister was living a normal life. Survivors of any given disaster are likely to have very different subjective experiences based on their developmental stage (as described in Chapter 6) and their specific circumstances.

As such, it is only through conversation and exploration that the details of the individual's traumatic memories can come to be known and understood. Although the thoughts may be irrational, they still need to be made explicit, processed, and corrected. For example, a 35-year-old man in psychodynamic therapy reported that he had lost a home and his only sibling to a fire when he was 12 years old. In a therapy session, he recalled the many candies and toys that he received from aid workers after the disaster. Although his parents were distraught, he was distracted and excited by his new toys and having "all the candy he could eat." Now, decades later, he felt shame about all the attention he received, as well as shame that he did not act courageously during the fire. He feared that somehow he had done something wrong and even worried that somehow he had caused the fire. The patient came to understand some of his current reactions to sweets, toys, and other of life's pleasures in light of this memory and the guilt he experienced. Although the disaster occurred long ago, significant sequelae needed to be understood.

In general, psychodynamic psychotherapies for the treatment of disaster survivors are not currently considered to be treatments of choice. In addition to being long and costly, there are few controlled studies to support the effectiveness of a psychodynamic approach to the treatment of PTSD; Kudler et al. (2000b) observe that psychodynamic researchers tend to use case reports or clinical studies rather than well-controlled empirical treatment outcome studies.

COGNITIVE–BEHAVIORAL APPROACHES

Dollard and Miller (1950) once suggested that a good therapist is like a good tennis coach, helping the patient learn good habits and unlearn bad ones. In line with this view, **cognitive–behavioral therapy** (CBT) is based on the application of learning theory to the practice of psychotherapy. CBT treatments can include one or several of the approaches listed in this section, each of which place greater or lesser emphasis on classical conditioning, operant conditioning, social learning theory, or more cognitive theories. All view problems or disorders, including PTSD, as learned behaviors and cognitions and see therapy as new learning.

Cognitive–behavioral therapy has its roots in a now classic (and infamous) paper published in 1920 by Watson and Rayner, demonstrating that an anxiety disorder can be learned through classical conditioning. In classical conditioning, an automatic response to a stimulus—for example, recoiling from an electric shock or salivating at the smell of food as in Pavlov's classic example—becomes associated with a neutral stimulus such as the sight of a particular flashing light that signals the onset of the shock or the ringing of a bell that precedes mealtime. After enough pairings of light and shock or bell and aroma, a subject will learn to recoil merely at the sight of the light even when no shock occurs or to salivate at the bell even when no food is presented. The previously neutral signal has become a *conditioned stimulus*.

Watson and Rayner (1920) used this principle to show how a learned fear response could be both long lasting and generalized to other triggers. The subject of their experiment (which would surely never be permitted by today's ethical standards) was "Little Albert," an 11-month-old baby. The researchers first taught Albert to be afraid of a white rat by producing a very loud sound every time the rat was presented. They then observed how his fear generalized to other furry white items, including a rabbit, a fur coat, and even a Santa Claus mask. Initially, the researchers had hoped to demonstrate how such fears could be unlearned through extinction or reconditioning, but due to circumstances that are not fully explained in the original article, they did not get the opportunity to help poor Albert unlearn his fears. Subsequently, other researchers, beginning with Mary Cover Jones in 1924, have amply demonstrated that anxiety disorders including PTSD and ASD can be unlearned by pairing the presentation of the offending stimuli with an anxiety-reducing response. The following paragraphs describe some of the specific methods that have been successful in treating PTSD and other anxiety disorders.

Systematic desensitization, a method developed by Joseph Wolpe (1958), has been used to treat patients suffering from PTSD symptoms. Treatment involves teaching patients to relax physically (Wolpe used the Jacobson method, which involves tightening and relaxing one muscle group at a time) and developing, in consultation with the patient, a graded list of aversive stimuli, ranking anxiety-inducing items from least stressful to most stressful. Once patients are proficient in controlling deep muscle relaxation, they learn to imagine the anxiety-evoking stimuli while in a state of relaxation, beginning with the mildest and working their way up to the most intensive.

For example, a patient suffering anxiety in the aftermath of a flood may be afraid to be near any body of water. When the patient is relaxed, he or she is asked to imagine a low-anxiety trigger, such as a glass of water, for a few seconds. After repeated exposures, the anxiety dissipates and the patient is asked to imagine a more anxiety-producing stimulus, such as a bathtub filled with water. Gradually, higher-level anxiety-producing images are introduced until the patient is anxiety free. Wolpe (1982) offers case studies of how traumatized patients were successfully treated using this method. Systematic desensitization can be used in the treatment of trauma, though it is more commonly used to treat phobias and other anxiety disorders.

Exposure therapy is one form of CBT that is exclusively used in the treatment of anxiety and trauma. It uses careful, repeated, detailed imagining of the trauma (that is, exposure to the memory) in a safe, controlled context to help the survivor face and gain control of the fear and distress that was overwhelming during the trauma. We have previously discussed the fact that the extent and intensity of a survivor's exposure to disaster may be the best predictor of subsequent symptoms; exposure therapy involves "fighting fear with fear." This approach is different from systematic desensitization in that the anxiety-producing stimulus is not introduced gradually, nor is there any relaxation to accompany the images. Exposure therapies have sometimes been referred to as implosive, flooding, prolonged exposure, and directed exposure (Rothbaum, Meadows, Resick, & Foy, 2000).

Stampfl and Levis (1967) describe **implosive therapy** as a treatment that could overcome anxiety and avoidance by forcing clients to confront an anxiety-producing conditioned stimulus. Clients are asked to imagine the traumatic scenes in the present tense, with as much detail and vividness as possible. They are instructed to experience fully whatever anxiety, guilt, or other feelings that are evoked by these scenes. In implosive therapy, the therapist constructs or creates scenes that may be even more terrifying and powerful than the original traumatic experience so that any underlying frightening fantasies and thoughts can be also extinguished. This aspect of implosive therapy distinguishes it from **flooding therapy** in which clients imagine only the *actual* feared stimuli.

Exposure therapies all have in common the practice of exposing patients to the feared stimuli until anxiety is significantly reduced. It has been suggested that exposure to traumatic memories leads to symptom reduction because the patient learns that remembering the trauma does not lead to injury or threat or a loss of control (Jaycox & Foa, 1996). In some cases, patients provide their own narrative by discussing the traumatic experience in the present tense; in other cases, the therapist presents the images to the patient based on information gathered before the exposure takes place. Patients are instructed to focus their attention on the traumatic experience fully, for anywhere from 45 minutes to an hour so that **habituation** can take place, meaning that the conditioned anxiety reaction no longer occurs in response to the stimulus. As a result, sessions can last longer than the standard 50 minutes because it is critical that therapist and client stay with the scene until most of the anxiety has dissipated. A review of the literature examining the effectiveness of treatments for PTSD concludes, "In summary, compelling evidence from many well-controlled trials with a mixed variety of trauma survivors indicates that [exposure therapy] is quite effective. In fact, no other treatment modality has evidence this strong indicating its efficacy" (Rothbaum, Meadows, Resnick, & Foy, 2000).

In most forms of exposure therapy, reproduction of the traumatic material occurs within the patient's imagination in order to target his or her memories, which of course cannot be reproduced in vivo (in real life) (Bryant & Harvey, 2000). But for some patients, imaginal exposure therapy that requires them to remember and retell the story of their traumatic experience presents an impossible problem. Because a primary symptom of PTSD is precisely to avoid such memories or images, these patients may avoid treatment altogether, or if they attempt it they may discontinue it early or avoid getting emotionally involved in the images. New technology may help these patients: **Virtual reality (VR) exposure therapy** is a relatively new treatment that allows patients to experience the illusion of being exposed to a traumatic event. In VR therapy, patients wear headgear that allows them to view computer monitors worn close to their eyes and to receive auditory stimulation as well. Position-tracking devices in the helmet inform the computer when the patient moves his or her head, changing the scene and creating the impression that the individual is truly in the depicted location. With VR therapy, patients cannot avoid the image because it is right in front of them, with the appropriate accompanying sounds. However, the patient can maintain control of the images that are being presented so that a clear distinction can be maintained between the present and the past (Difede, Hoffman, & Jaysinghe, 2002).

Joann Difede and her colleagues at Weill Medical College of Cornell University in New York City developed an approach using VR to treat patients suffering from PTSD as a result of the September 11, 2001 attack on the World Trade Center. Patients put on the headgear and first see the towers from a distance on a beautiful sunny day. The patient regularly reports "subjective units of distress." As the initial distress level decreases, indicating that a patient has become habituated to that level of exposure, he or she next sees a plane flying over the towers. Once the distress level lowers for that image, the patient views the plane hitting the building. New sequences are presented and the patient habituates to each scene. Gradually, sound effects are added so that screams are heard; the building is shown burning and smoking, and people are seen jumping. Eventually, the towers collapse with a cloud of dust. More distressing scenes are only presented with the patient's consent. Difede and Hoffman (2002) report a case study demonstrating how this technique was used with a woman suffering from PTSD in the aftermath of the attacks. During the treatment, she was able to access many horrific memories and thoughts in this virtual world that she had been previously unable to recall. The authors report that with treatment the patient's memories became more detailed but less terrifying.

Though it is still in the early stages of development, it would appear that VR treatment could prove to be even more useful for disaster survivors than for victims of other traumas. A rape or assault survivor would probably have idiosyncratic and specific scenes associated with their particular trauma. Survivors of disaster, on the other hand, may have witnessed many of the same or similar images—the ground shaking from an earthquake, the sounds of hurricane winds or an impending tornado, the sight of a jet hitting the World Trade Center towers. Thus, the computer-generated scenes could be applicable to many patients. More research is certainly merited on this promising approach (Winerman, 2005).

Eye movement desensitization and reprocessing (EMDR) can be considered a type of exposure therapy because patients are asked to imagine a feared or anxiety-producing stimulus as a treatment component. Francine Shapiro (1995) developed EMDR based on the theory that people have an innate tendency to process disturbing life experiences to an "adaptive resolution." When this is blocked by unresolved trauma, Shapiro suggests that patients are most likely to have three types of distorted cognitions: First, the patient takes *responsibility* for the event ("It was my fault; I didn't do enough; I could have done something more or different—proving that I am a bad person; I cannot trust myself"). Second, the patient believes that he or she is in *danger* ("I am not safe; I cannot protect myself"). Third, the patient believes that he or she is trapped and has *no options or choices* ("I cannot succeed; I cannot get what I want; I am powerless"). When the brain's information-processing system is blocked due to trauma so that the patient cannot correct these distorted thoughts, Shapiro suggests that EMDR therapy can lead to an adaptive resolution.

In EMDR treatment, patients imagine the worst part of the traumatic incident at the same time that they think the negative cognition about themselves that best goes with the incident, such as "I am powerless," "I am permanently damaged," "I am in danger." While the patient imagines the scene and thinks the negative self-attribution, the therapist moves his or her hand back and forth in front of the patient's face. The patient is instructed to follow the hand with his or her eyes without moving the head. (The back-and-forth eye movements can be replaced with lights flashing alternately to the left and right or the therapist tapping alternately on the left and right hands of the patient.) Throughout the process, patients report on their thoughts, feelings, and sensations as well as their subjective units of distress. According to Shapiro (1995), this combination of visualization, cognition, and external stimulus unblocks the patient's information-processing system. As this proceeds, the patient reports that traumatic memories are less disturbing.

Early in the therapy, during the preparation and assessment phases, patients are asked to state what they would *like* to believe about themselves when remembering the traumatic event. After the desensitization, when there is little distress associated with imagining the event, the therapist asks the patient to imagine the event while thinking the positive cognition ("I did the best I could; I learned from it; I can trust myself; I am safe now; it is over; I can take care of myself; I have choices").

This occurs with the bilateral stimulation of hand movements or lights until the patient has confidence in the new cognition. This is referred to as the **installation phase** in which the patient can integrate a positive self-assessment with the targeted traumatic image.

EMDR is somewhat controversial within the mental health field, in part because no one, including the treatment's creator, can fully explain why the addition of hand movements might increase efficacy beyond other types of exposure therapy. A review of the empirical literature on the efficacy of EMDR as a treatment for PTSD caused by events such as combat, rape, and a catastrophic hurricane found that EMDR demonstrated positive and often large improvements over control treatments (Chemtob, Tolin, van der Kolk, & Pitman, 2000). Although there is supportive evidence for this treatment approach, the National Institute of Mental Health (NIMH, 2002) concludes that "there is no evidence that eye movement desensitization and reprocessing as an early mental health intervention following mass violence and disaster is a treatment of choice over other approaches." Shapiro (1995) herself notes that patients who were treated with EMDR a few weeks after an earthquake did not benefit significantly from the treatment. She suggests that treatment might be more effective when the memory has had time to consolidate into an integrated whole, which may take 2 to 3 months. Clearly the optimal timing for this (and other treatments) needs further research.

In general, exposure therapy is not without problems. When treatment begins, both therapist and patient must not be faint of heart. PTSD patients are motivated to avoid reminders of the traumatic event, so any treatment insisting that patients confront the event could lead to patient noncompliance. If a survivor knows that he or she must confront the worst aspect of the disaster, some will simply not begin treatment. It has also been pointed out that exposure therapies do not teach people effective coping strategies and can lead to patients dropping out of treatment because the cure can be so distressing. Bryant and Harvey (2000) suggest that therapists should avoid using exposure therapy or that it be used with extreme caution if the patient demonstrates symptoms that include

- Extreme anxiety.
- Panic attacks.
- Marked dissociation.
- Borderline personality disorder.
- Psychotic illness.
- Anger as a primary trauma response.
- Unresolved prior trauma.
- Severe depression or suicide risk.
- Complex comorbidity.
- Substance abuse.
- Marked ongoing stressors.

Nonetheless, Spiegler and Guevremont (2002) conclude that exposure therapies are the most effective treatments for anxiety disorders including PTSD, though they suggest that other behavioral interventions in combination with exposure therapy can improve the treatment. Stress inoculation training and cognitive therapy, discussed next, are two such treatments that can be used on their own or in combination with exposure therapy.

Stress inoculation training (SIT), developed by Donald Meichenbaum (1985), teaches patients the skills to manage anxiety and decrease avoidance. In SIT, therapists instruct patients about the nature of stress and trauma. Patients learn how to cope with stress more effectively through specific skills such as self-acceptance, relaxation techniques, problem solving, communication skills, and using social support systems. Stress inoculation training also addresses the appraisal process that patients use to evaluate stressors. They are taught how to view perceived dangers and frustrations as problems that can be solved and to distinguish those aspects of their situations and reactions that can be changed from those that cannot. They are also instructed on the effective use of problem solving or emotion-focused coping strategies (Meichenbaum, 1996).

Patients practice and rehearse their new coping skills, first with the therapist and later in the real world. To help strengthen these skills, individuals may be asked to help others with similar problems. In most instances, SIT consists of about 8 to 15 sessions, plus booster and follow-up sessions, conducted over a 3- to 12-month period. Stress inoculation training has been shown to be effective in treating sexual assault survivors (Rothbaum et al. 2000). Rothbaum et al. conclude that this approach should be just as effective with other PTSD populations such as disaster victims.

Cognitive therapy, developed by Aaron Beck (1976), suggests that symptoms are caused by distorted and unhelpful thoughts. The therapist uses a variety of methods to produce cognitive change—alterations in the patient's thinking and belief system—to bring about enduring emotional and behavioral change. In this model, the external situation itself does not directly determine how the patient feels; the individual's emotional response is mediated by his or her perception of the situation. According to Judith Beck (1995), cognitive therapy involves the following basic principles:

- Cognitive therapy is based on an evolving formulation of the patient and his or her problems in cognitive terms.
- Cognitive therapy requires a sound therapeutic alliance.
- Cognitive therapy emphasizes collaboration and active participation.
- Cognitive therapy is goal oriented and problem focused.
- Cognitive therapy initially emphasizes the present.
- Cognitive therapy is educative, aims to teach the patient to be his or her own therapist, and emphasizes relapse prevention.
- Cognitive therapy aims to be time limited.
- Cognitive therapy sessions are structured.
- Cognitive therapy teaches patients to identify, evaluate, and respond to their dysfunctional thoughts and beliefs.
- Cognitive therapy uses a variety of techniques to change thinking, mood, and behavior.

The cognitive model asserts that it is the understanding of a situation, often expressed in automatic thoughts, rather than the situation itself that influences one's ensuing emotions, behaviors, and physiological response. People with psychological disorders often misinterpret neutral or even positive situations, and so their automatic thoughts are distorted. After critically examining their thoughts and correcting their thinking errors, they often feel better. Cognitive therapists collaborate with clients to decide which thoughts should be examined based on a determination of how distorted or unhelpful the thoughts might be.

Some of the cognitive distortions or logical errors that patients make can include **catastrophizing,** or thinking of the worst possible scenarios ("What if this is just the first flood or fire in a never-ending chain of disasters that will strike?"); **selective abstraction,** or drawing conclusions from limited evidence ("My neighbor protected his property better than I did; probably all my neighbors did better than I"); **personalization,** or the tendency to see external events as related to the person when there is no basis ("I don't understand why disaster seems to follow me around; I must be cursed"); and **overgeneralization,** or drawing conclusions on the basis of a single episode ("The relief agency did not return my phone call; no one will return my calls") (Beck, 1995).

Cognitive therapists collaborate with patients to identify cognitive distortions and to evaluate and examine the automatic thoughts. Once cognitive distortions are recognized, patients are encouraged to find more helpful and accurate cognitions. Patients are given the homework assignment to record thoughts and their outcome so that they can learn to see the relationship between them. The therapist also questions and examines the validity of the automatic thought with the patient. The therapist might ask the following:

- "How much do you believe the thought?"
- "How did it make you feel?"
- "What did you do after you had the thought?"
- "What are the situations that you associate with the thought?"
- "How typical is the thought? What is the problem solving associated with the automatic thought?"
- "How have you handled this kind of situation?"
- "How would you like to handle this situation?"
- "If this thought were true, what would it mean to you?"

At the deepest level, cognitive therapists attempt to help patients modify their negative core, or underlying, beliefs of helplessness or unlovability.

Cognitive therapy can have a place in long-term treatment of disaster survivors because exposure to a trauma or disaster can contradict the fundamental beliefs of the survivor and contribute to the development of PTSD symptoms. McCann, Sakheim, and Abrahamson (1988) found that trauma can disrupt beliefs associated with safety, trust, power, esteem, and intimacy. In interviews conducted with survivors of the 1993 World Trade Center bombing in New York City, it was apparent that survivors not only had symptoms associated with PTSD, but they also reported that their beliefs about the world, themselves, and others had been altered (Difede, Apfeldorf, Cloitre, Spielman, & Perry, 1997). Those interviewed reported that they saw their lives as "out of control" and said that the world seemed unsafe and other people seemed untrustworthy. They were also angry that their view of a just world had been shattered.

Thus, when working with disaster survivors, cognitive therapists are likely to focus on the patient's appraisals of safety, trust in others, trust in the world, and trust in themselves. For example, Difede and Eskra (2002) applied cognitive processing therapy, a combination of exposure and cognitive techniques, to the treatment of a woman exposed to the 1993 terrorist bombing of the World Trade Center. The woman had been injured in the explosion and was diagnosed with PTSD. The patient doubted her abilities, did not believe that she was safe at work, and saw people as motivated more by evil than good. She saw evil and danger as constant threats. Treatment focused on the patient's view of herself and the world in addition to the PTSD symptoms. It challenged her thinking that catastrophe was imminent, and she began to get a more realistic perspective on the likelihood of any future tragedy. Therapy sessions focused not only on safety but also on her beliefs about trust, power, esteem and intimacy—an approach that appeared to be successful as her symptoms declined over the course of treatment. This anecdotal evidence is supported by several controlled studies that have shown cognitive therapy to be effective in reducing PTSD symptoms (Rothbaum et al., 2002).

As a final note about exposure therapy, Bryant and Harvey (2000) also note the importance of **systemic considerations** that view the patient in the context of his or her family and environment when using this approach. Their concerns seem especially apt for victims of disaster because several members of one family can be impacted by the same trauma. A patient may be reluctant to be immersed in traumatic memories because he or she feels responsible for caring for another family member who is also suffering. It is also possible that a patient who is being treated may go home to a family member who is still certain that disaster will strike again. In such cases, the benefit of the treatment can be undermined by contact with a panicked relative who retraumatizes the patient. As this demonstrates, it is always important to consider family and social relationships—the other people in the life of the patient—even when doing individual therapy. This point brings us to our next major long-term treatment approach, family systems.

FAMILY SYSTEMS APPROACHES

Despite the obvious ways that family relationships impact trauma survivors and vice versa, Harkness and Zador (2001) note that little has been written on the role of family in the recovery process from PTSD. It has also been pointed out that "unfortunately, despite the many suggestions about how to incorporate marital and/or family therapy into comprehensive treatment programs, no controlled studies and very few empirical data exist to address the impact of including such treatment in programs aimed at alleviating the effects of trauma" (Riggs, 2000).

Therapists should always consider the family system when treating individuals, irrespective of the type of problem (Paolino & McGrady, 1978). For example, a therapist who treats a disruptive child without considering siblings, parents, and teachers may have too narrow a focus. Perhaps family members are discouraging or anxious and are impeding the patient's recovery. Perhaps the patient's symptom allows family members to be distracted from their own problems, or it enables family members to receive some financial benefit. From a family systems perspective, the therapist considers **context** in order to best bring about a patient's recovery. Treatment involves a lens that may focus in narrowly on an individual or telescope out to view the wider couple relationship, or even more widely to the extended family and other aspects of the patient's social system. In the following pages, we review a few of the many approaches to family therapy. Although they differ in some respects, they all emphasize the importance of treatment that takes into account how individuals impact and are impacted by one another.

According to a **structural family therapy** perspective (Minuchin, 1974), when the hierarchy or the boundaries of family subsystems become dysfunctional, there are likely to be symptoms in one or more members of the family. A family with a functional **hierarchy** has grandparents supporting parents who are in charge of the children. Functional **boundaries** mean that family members are neither over-involved (enmeshed) nor underinvolved (disengaged) with one another. When stress is introduced in a family with a healthy hierarchy and boundaries, parents can continue to care for and remain in charge of their children, perhaps paying more attention to them while respecting their strength and resilience. In such a functional family, parents know how their children are reacting and are not too distressed to care for them.

But when disaster strikes, the increased stress can disrupt the family struc-ture, leading to symptoms in individuals or creating conflict between family mem-bers. For example, a child might be given too much responsibility, becoming a "parentified" child; or the parents may become overly protective, infantilizing the child; or the couple subsystem may become strained, creating conflict; or a grand-parent and child could collude against a parent they view as incompetent—as someone who couldn't protect them from the disaster. Such disruptions can lead to evident symptoms in one family member, who is described by structural family therapists as the *identified patient*. This term connotes that the family structure as a whole is dysfunctional, but that the rest of the family sees one particular person as having the problem. Structural family therapists try to reshape the family so that the boundaries and hierarchy become more functional. Tactics might involve encouraging parents to maintain their authority in the family hierarchy by remind-ing them that they need to stay calm and reassure their children or by discour-aging a child and grandparent from forming a coalition against a parent. Homework or tasks within the session are assigned to create more functional boundaries and hierarchies.

From a **strategic family therapy** perspective (Haley, 1987), a sequence of interactions among or between family members can maintain a symptom. Thus, a child who is impacted by a disaster might be overindulged by one parent, leav-ing another parent feeling ignored and angry. In response, the second parent is not supportive of the spouse or child. Similarly, from the perspective of **multi-generational family therapy** (Kerr & Bowen, 1988), a symptom requires the par-ticipation of at least three participants: a generator, an amplifier, and a dampener. For example, if a child is frightened by a disaster (generator) and both parents remain calm, the child is likely to recover. If, on the other hand, one parent over-reacts (amplifier) and the other parent underreacts by emotionally distancing him- or herself from the problem (dampener), a triangle is formed, and a symptom is more likely to develop in the child. The current stress caused by the disaster can also combine with historical stressors to increase the likelihood of symptoms (Carter & McGoldrick, 2005).

Strategic family therapists disrupt a negative cycle of interaction by assigning tasks to the family so they do things differently. Multigenerational family therapists (also called Bowen systems therapists) help family members see and understand how their actions impact one another as well as take a more historical perspective. The family in treatment might be encouraged to explore how family members in previous generations effectively coped with similar problems or traumas. They might also keep a lookout for negative or ineffective means of coping in past generations so that they know what patterns to be alert for and avoid.

When stress is high in the aftermath of disaster, some couples pull together while others find themselves in a downward spiral of distancing and anger. In **emotionally focused marital therapy** (EFT), Susan Johnson (1996) argues that everyone has the need to be securely attached to another person. When a couple is in distress, it is because attachment needs are not being met, and there is no secure base. One partner might react to this insecurity by becoming angry, causing the second partner to withdraw—causing the first to be angrier, leading to more withdrawal by the second, and so on. This negative cycle of interaction needs to be observed by the therapist and pointed out to the couple. To repair the couple relationship, EFT therapists provide a safe and accepting stance, helping both partners see how they contribute to the cycle of anger and distancing that leads both parties to feel insecure and distressed. The therapist assists both partners in expressing deeper feelings of vulnerability and loneliness. As partners find new ways to experience each other without the defenses of anger and distancing, each can support the other's dependency needs. Partners thus come to feel safe with and trust one another.

Family Therapy and Disaster

When doing long-term family therapy in the aftermath of disaster, the therapist must first consider *who* in the family is the primary patient or if there is more than one patient. The therapist must also consider the nature of the problem to be treated. Different family members may each be suffering with different problems: PTSD, depression, or anxiety, for example. They might also be reacting to the problems of others in the family (secondary traumatization). Or they might be in conflict with one another. The therapist might consider using a variety of family or couple therapy techniques to treat different problems.

This could involve helping the family help the patient, making the patient the primary focus of the treatment. For example, there are cases in which one person in the family is symptomatic, suffering from PTSD, anxiety, or depression. In such cases, the patient may receive individual therapy at the same time that the family is treated as part of a more comprehensive approach. The family may be given psychoeducation about the patient's condition and may learn how to better support the patient in his or her recovery. Family members learn to become cotherapists in the treatment of the primary patient: "If healing from trauma is about finding positive ways to integrate the past into the ongoing narrative of one's life, then family life provides the setting in which this can be most successfully accomplished" (Harkness & Zador, 2001).

In other cases, the therapist may need to help family members with their own distress, making relatives the focus of treatment rather than the individual patient. For example, the patient could be difficult or "impossible" to live with because he or she is angry or detached. Family members may be frightened, frustrated, and eventually burned out themselves as they struggle to live with the patient, perhaps leading to compassion fatigue (Figley, 1990, 1997) due to the patient's condition. In such cases, family members and the primary patient are in need of treatment. They may require treatment for their own anxiety, depression, burnout, or vicarious trauma, or they may need to learn more effective coping strategies or styles.

Other situations might involve helping family members reduce conflict with each other, making the relationship the focus of the treatment. Sometimes family members are in conflict about how to treat the traumatized patient. More typically, a traumatized survivor will be in conflict with a significant other and will seek treatment for that problem. For cases in which conflict within the family is directly related to the disaster, communication training or marital/couple therapy may focus directly on resolving conflict in the relationship.

Family therapy may be especially useful when more than one person in the family has been traumatized from a disaster. This is a very likely scenario and one that is specific to treating survivors of a disaster as opposed to other traumas. After all, combat veterans or assault victims are less likely to be traumatized at the same time as other relatives, but disasters can traumatize entire families. If a home and possessions are lost in a flood or fire, whole families can be shocked and disturbed; several members of a family may be physically injured in a disaster. If multiple members are traumatized by disaster, there will be many levels of stress and problems. A survivor may suffer with his or her own psychological symptoms and be simultaneously stressed or suffering from compassion fatigue as a result of caring for another family member. At the same time, there may be conflict between individuals. Thus, a family therapist would need to address multiple problems. There may be a need to help resolve conflict, reduce primary trauma symptoms, and address secondary trauma symptoms within several family members in the same family—a daunting task for any therapist.

Although many authors have suggested the use of couple and family therapy, either alone or as an adjunct to individual treatment for PTSD, "the literature on the use of couple and family therapies with survivors of trauma is severely lacking. The lack of empirical support for such treatments means that it is difficult to know if and when they should be used or how they should be incorporated into other treatment programs" (Riggs, 2000). Yet because the impact of PTSD on families is so extensive, Shalev, Friedman, Foa, and Keane (2000) conclude that "it would seem that there is a critical role for marital and family therapy that attempts to achieve a clinically meaningful balance between addressing dysfunctional symptoms and behavior of the PTSD patient and the distress of family members whose needs also require attention."

Assisting a Family With Loss

It has been noted that "coming to terms with death and loss is the most difficult challenge a family must confront" (Walsh & McGoldrick, 2004). Although
death and loss are inevitable aspects of the family life cycle, sudden death caused
by disaster adds the dimension of shock and confusion. Family members are left
without an opportunity to say their good-byes. Trauma and chaos accompany
grief and loss. When death is violent or intentionally caused, whether by an
arsonist hoping to obtain some financial benefit or a terrorist attempting to further a political or social agenda, survivors are particularly devastated. When an
innocent family member, working or commuting or asleep at home, is murdered,
the tragedy is especially hard to bear and may lead to long-term problems.

Walsh and McGoldrick (2004) have adapted Worden's model of stages of
grief to inform therapists working with a grieving family. They suggest that there
are four family tasks involved in mourning the loss of a loved one. Working on
these tasks encourages both short- and long-term adjustment for the family. The
role of a therapist is to facilitate the movement through these tasks.

1. *Shared acknowledgement of the reality of death.* Most mental health
   counselors would agree that it is ultimately not helpful to keep a death a
   secret from a child or vulnerable member of the family. Acknowledging
   the death does not mean that anyone has "gotten over it" or that there is
   some closure, rather that family members are in touch with the reality of
   the loss.
2. *Shared experience of the loss.* In all cultures, throughout the ages, there
   have been traditions that allow family members and friends to come together,
   grieve, and pay their respects to the dead. Sharing the experience of loss in
   whatever ways seem appropriate to family members should be encouraged.
   Ceremonies that allow people to speak and tell stories about the deceased
   provide this opportunity for the sharing of the loss. Trips to the grave serve
   a similar purpose, as do more organized memorials such as the one held annually at ground zero in New York City on September 11. These ceremonies
   let community members and friends honor the deceased and provide support for those in grief. Although families will mourn according to culture and
   tradition, there will also be differences in individual grieving styles within
   the family. Therapists can help family members be tolerant of one another's
   reactions. Therapists can also provide support to family members who are
   frightened by the expression of intense feelings.
3. *Reorganization of the family system.* When a death occurs in the family, all
   relationships undergo realignment. One of the most stressful and disturbing
   aspects of such a major life change is that nothing remains the same. All relationships are altered. Therapists can support family members through the
   many adjustments that occur. For example, when young children experience
   the death of a parent, they can feel burdened and neglected by the surviving
   parent who is in grief. Children sometimes report that when one parent died,
   they felt abandoned by the other just when they needed him or her the most.
   In this situation, therapists can support the surviving parent and attempt to

enlist all possible extended family members to help out so as to mitigate harm to the children.

4. *Reinvestment in other relationships and life pursuits.* The length of the mourning process is quite variable. Even the beginning of the process is not predictable. For example, one widow seemed quite stoic for 2 years after her firefighter husband died on September 11, 2001. Only when her son left for college in 2003, did she begin to mourn. Her husband's dream in life had been for his children to go to college, and when the son began school, all the widow could think about was how her husband could not be present for it. Even when mourning proceeds more typically, anniversaries, holidays, and favorite movies or songs can trigger feelings of loss many years later. Yet over time, family members can learn that the deceased would have wanted them to continue to pursue joy. Therapists can assist family members who feel disloyal if they begin new relationships, helping them sustain bonds with the deceased at the same time that they invest in other relationships and pursuits (Walsh & McGoldrick, 2004).

GROUP THERAPY APPROACHES

Group therapy brings together multiple individuals who are struggling with a shared issue and provides a safe and supportive environment for addressing that issue. A group may meet indefinitely or for a scheduled number of weeks or months. Membership is usually held constant in groups that meet for a defined period to encourage a strong alliance among members. In some open-ended groups, new individuals may be allowed to join, so members may be at different points in their treatment (Foy, Eriksson, & Trice, 2001).

The precise origins of group therapy as an approach to treatment are somewhat unclear, but therapists have experimented with various forms of group treatments since at least the early 20th century (Barlow, Burlingame, & Fuhriman, 2000). Groups gained a wider recognition during World War II, when there was a shortage of individual therapists to assist soldiers suffering from war neuroses (Fehr, 2003). In the 1970s, Vietnam veterans formed "rap groups," while women who had been abused or sexually assaulted formed self-help groups. These groups met to cope with their traumatic experiences, and they did so at a time when officials denied their suffering and there was not yet even a name or diagnosis to describe their condition.

There continue to be leaderless self-help groups for coping with trauma and disaster, but now there are also groups with a clear boundary between therapist and patients (Herman, 1992). Foy et al. (2000) note that, although there are several different approaches to group work with trauma survivors, there are similar features of these groups:

1. Members tend to have been impacted by the same type of trauma.
2. There is the validation and acknowledgment that each member of the group was exposed to the trauma.
3. Group members are encouraged to see their own reactions as normal.

4. The presence of other survivors mitigates against group members dismissing the therapist because he or she did not personally have the traumatic experience.
5. There is a nonjudgmental attitude taken as to how group members coped with the trauma, thus providing an atmosphere of safety and mutual respect.

Foy et al. (2000) describe three broad approaches to group therapy treatment for trauma. *Supportive groups* don't focus on the details and experiences related to the traumatic experience; rather, they encourage an exchange of information and emphasize current coping. The two other approaches, *psychodynamic group therapy* and *cognitive–behavioral group therapy,* are intended to deal directly with the traumatic experience and memories of the event, using some of the method-specific techniques described previously. These approaches have sometimes been described as an *uncovering method* or a *trauma-focused group*.

There is clearly a practical benefit to group therapy's high patient-to-counselor ratio, which may be especially efficient following a disaster when a large number of survivors seek assistance. Beyond that benefit, group treatment is often considered an ideal therapeutic setting for disaster and trauma because survivors can share traumatic material in the environment of safety and empathy provided by other survivors. Patients discover that they are not alone, an experience Yalom (1995) describes as "universality." As group members achieve greater understanding and resolution of their trauma, they often feel more confident and can trust one another. As they discuss and share how they cope with trauma-related shame, guilt, rage, fear, doubt, and self-condemnation, they prepare themselves to focus on the present rather than the past (Foy et al., 2001). Group therapy work can help reverse the isolation that is common to survivors of trauma. It can normalize and validate the survivor's affective and cognitive response to the disaster experience (Stubenbort, Donnelly, & Cohen, 2001). "Because of their inherent heterogeneity, groups provide a context where members can exhibit and address the difficulties that may have motivated their desire for treatment" (Brabender, 2002). Understanding and identifying with the statements and feelings of others can help members accept their own similar feelings and resulting behaviors.

Identifying with another's pain also can reassure a group member that he or she is not alone in suffering:

> Many patients enter therapy with the disquieting thought that they are unique in their wretchedness, that they alone have certain frightening or unacceptable problems, thoughts, impulses, and fantasies. . . . In the therapy group, especially in the early stages, the disconfirmation of a patient's feelings of uniqueness is a powerful source of relief. After hearing other members disclose concerns similar to their own, patients report feeling more in touch with the world and describe the process as a "welcome to the human race" experience. (Yalom, 1995)

Additionally, because a group tends to include members at various points of progress, new individuals are exposed to others with similar problems who have been helped by therapy, which can instill hope that they too can someday improve (Yalom, 1995). Given these strengths, patients who are suffering in the aftermath of disaster might benefit from a combination of individual and group therapy.

This could be especially true for patients who are more comfortable in group settings and for those who prefer receiving support from peers than from professionals.

Organizing and running a successful group requires much skill and experience (Herman, 1992). Group members should be able to relate to one another as equals, learning from one another. At the same time, the group leader or therapist must be certain to protect all group members from **traumatic reenactment** so that members of the group do not act out the roles of victim, bystander, rescuer, and so on. Herman suggests that the tasks of groups may differ according to the stage that participants are in following the trauma. At the earliest stage, groups might focus on safety or on comparing information to be certain that all are receiving the complete array of services available. At a later stage, participants may focus on coming to terms with the disaster. Still later, group members might move on to current interpersonal relationships and activities. They may work at helping one another resume a life in the community with family and friends and work.

In addition to the anecdotal evidence provided by several decades of group therapy, there is some empirical support for the efficacy of group treatments. In one study (Schnurr et al., 2003), Vietnam veterans suffering from chronic PTSD were assigned to a trauma-focused or a present-centered group. After about a year of treatment, about 40% of participants in both groups showed improvement. However, there was a significantly higher dropout rate in the trauma-focused group. Although controlled studies do not yet favor one type of group therapy over another (covering versus uncovering groups), common sense dictates that some patients would benefit more from one approach at a particular time in their recovery. In general, "positive treatment outcomes were reported in most studies, lending general support to the use of group therapy with trauma survivors. Since research on group therapy for PTSD is in its infancy stage, much more research activity is warranted before techniques producing superior outcomes are clearly identified" (Foy et al., 2000).

To learn more about group therapy, we suggest reading Irvin Yalom's *The Theory and Practice of Groups and Group Therapy* (2005). We also refer you to Appendix C, which provides the treatment goals used in a seven-session group therapy model that was developed to treat adults and children who were suffering with both trauma and sudden loss after the crash of US Air flight 427 in 1994 (Stubenbort et al., 2001) as an example of a successful group therapy program.

PHARMACOTHERAPY

It has been suggested that psychopharmacological approaches, or **pharmacotherapy,** should be considered when other approaches to treating PTSD are not effective (Friedman, Charney & Southwick, 1993). Acute hyperarousal or agitation symptoms may be treated with antianxiety drugs, and patients with insomnia may benefit from sleep-inducing medication. In cases of depression or numbing, a selective serotonin reuptake inhibitor (SSRI) such as Prozac or Zoloft may be helpful. It has been reported that these drugs can also reduce the likelihood of alcohol abuse as a form of self-medication for PTSD symptoms.

However, a disadvantage of using SSRIs postdisaster is that they require several weeks to become effective because a certain level needs to be built up over time in an individual's system before the benefits are felt. Still, in a review of empirical studies on the effectiveness of pharmacotherapy as a treatment for PTSD, Friedman, Davidson, Mellman, and Southwick (2000) conclude that the best evidence supports the use of SSRIs as a treatment of choice for PTSD. Since all three symptom clusters of PTSD respond to SSRIs and because depressive symptoms originating soon after trauma may predict PTSD, it is recommended that SSRIs be considered for persistent posttraumatic depression.

Of course, not all survivors should be given pharmacotherapy, especially in the immediate aftermath of disaster when some psychiatric symptoms may arise as a result of head injury, sleep deprivation, intoxication, or drug withdrawal. For these reasons, it has been recommended that medications be withheld for the first 48 hours after a disaster (Young, Ford, Ruzek, Friedman, & Gusman, 1998). When they are prescribed, it is essential for practitioners to educate patients about their medication's side effects and interactions with alcohol, drugs, or other medications. Practitioners should also maintain regular contact with patients in order to monitor side effects and support compliance.

Although medications can help survivors with their more debilitating symptoms, they do not address the underlying traumatic experience that needs to be integrated for a full recovery. Therefore, we believe that pharmacotherapy can best be used as an adjunct to psychotherapy or other therapeutic approaches. Medication may provide some important relief that can enable a patient to begin or continue psychotherapy, but alone it does not provide an ideal long-term solution.

EVIDENCE-BASED PRACTICE FOR LONG-TERM TREATMENT OF DISASTER SURVIVORS

Unfortunately, there are many unanswered questions concerning the long-term treatment of disaster survivors, including the following (Shalev et al., 2000):

1. How does the therapist choose between the various treatment modalities?
2. What can we realistically expect from treatment, and how do we define goals?
3. Can the various treatments be combined? If so, how? Are combined treatments more effective?
4. Do more complex disorders with comorbid conditions (for example, alcoholism, depression) require a different approach?
5. How long should a treatment be offered? What should be the nature of the follow-up interventions?

Attempts to measure the effectiveness of psychotherapy have been conducted for decades, with numerous studies examining the impact of different therapy techniques as well as other variables (Lambert & Barley, 2001). In general, psychotherapy seems to help most people most of the time (Smith & Glass, 1978; Smith, Glass, & Miller, 1980), but the particular approach or type of treatment seems to make little difference (Seligman, 1995). One more recent review

(Wampold & Bhati, 2004) suggests that differences in the treatment approach account for very little of the variance in outcomes. In another review of the major psychotherapy-outcome literature, Lambert & Barley (2001) estimate that the specific therapy techniques used accounted for only 15% of improvement in psychotherapy patients—the same percentage (15%) that was accounted for by expectancy or placebo effects. In contrast, they found that 40% of improvement was due to extratherapeutic factors including "spontaneous remission, fortuitous events, [and] social support," and the final 30% of improvement was due to "common factors, that is, variables found in most therapies" such as the client–therapist relationship.

Despite the evidence that technique does not appear to be a significant factor in determining therapeutic success, much effort has been devoted in recent years to the development of **empirically supported treatments** (ESTs) or *evidence-based best practices* that prescribe the best treatment for a given psychological problem. Interest in ESTs grew after an American Psychological Association task force published a report that encouraged mental health professionals to focus on structured, evidence-based therapies (Task Force on Promotion, 1995). In part, this movement was intended to stem the loss of patients whose insurance companies preferred the concrete efficacy data already offered by pharmacological treatments over the less standardized psychotherapeutic approach (Deegear & Lawson, 2003; Westen, Novotny, & Thompson-Brenner, 2004).

Unfortunately, the quest for external validity in the pursuit of ESTs imposes many restrictions. Treatments generally address one *DSM* Axis I diagnosis with little or no consideration of accompanying personality traits or comorbidities, and participants are selected for their homogeneity (Westen et al., 2004). And the need to standardize the treatments under study—and keep them brief enough in length to appease insurance companies—means that most ESTs are cognitive or behavioral in nature, approaches that may not suit all patients or problems (Deegear & Lawson, 2003). It has been pointed out (Wampold & Bhati, 2004) that a significant problem with ESTs is that they ignore what may be the best predictor of therapy outcomes: individual differences in treatment providers. They also ignore the subjective experience of the patient, which must obviously be taken into account.

Not surprisingly, many in the field have objected to these efforts to regiment treatments, arguing that standardizing therapy ignores the role of the therapist and the therapeutic alliance: "Although efficacy research has gone to considerable lengths to eliminate the individual therapist as a variable that might account for patient improvement, the inescapable fact is that the therapist as a person is a central agent of change. The curative contribution of the person of the therapist is, arguably, as empirically validated as manualized treatments or psychotherapy methods" (Norcross, 2001). It is clear that the person of the therapist is critical to the success of treatment. And if the "self" of the therapist is the primary "instrument" in any treatment, the well-being of the therapist becomes a most important consideration. Therapists doing long-term work with disaster survivors should receive specific training in this specialty and be well supervised. The importance of self-care cannot be overestimated in the practice of psychotherapy, and this is even truer for therapists working with trauma survivors. Therefore, we conclude with another look at the particular pressures faced by DMH practitioners.

THE IMPACT ON THE THERAPIST AND THE NEED FOR SELF-CARE

Although we discussed issues of self-care in Chapter 7, "The Challenges of Counseling in Chaos," we return to them here because they relate to long-term rather than acute care. Doing long-term work with survivors of disaster and trauma is difficult and demanding, risky and rewarding. The risk stems from the fact that trauma is contagious and can be overwhelming. A therapist who is impacted by the trauma stories told by the patient experiences trauma transference or vicarious traumatization. As we discussed earlier, this can pose risks to the psychological and even physical health of the therapist.

All the approaches discussed earlier, with the exception of pharmacotherapy, advocate that the client tell his or her trauma story in detail. But as therapists lead their patients to recall very disturbing imagery as a necessary part of the treatment, they are exposing themselves to the same content and imagery. Listening to horror stories takes a toll on therapists, though this toll is not necessarily incapacitating: Charles Figley (1995) describes **compassion stress** as a natural outcome of knowing about the trauma experienced by a client rather than as a pathological process. The symptoms of compassion stress can include helplessness, confusion, and isolation. When compassion stress is ongoing and severe it can turn into what Figley refers to as **compassion fatigue.** This he defines as "a state of exhaustion and dysfunction, biologically, physiologically, and emotionally, as a result of prolonged exposure to compassion stress" (Figley, 1995).

In an even more persistent reaction, Pearlman and Saakvitne (1995) define **vicarious traumatization** as "permanently transformative, inevitable changes that result from doing therapeutic work with trauma survivors." Therapists' personalities change over time if their practice consists primarily of working with trauma survivors. These changes are not considered to be pathological, but they can be pervasive in the life of the therapist. In extreme cases, vicarious traumatization can damage the feelings, thoughts, memories, actions, and relationships of therapists. This is more likely to occur if the therapist is highly empathic and sensitive, has a previous history of trauma, or is inexperienced. And, according to Herman (1992), therapists working long term with trauma survivors are in danger of succumbing to vicarious traumatization.

Therapy with survivors of trauma can lead to a questioning of faith and can alter one's view of human vulnerability. A therapist may develop a sense of helplessness or lose sight of patient's strength and resilience. There is also the danger that the therapist will assume the role of rescuer and overreach the limits of therapy. Herman (1992) also suggests that a therapist can become overwhelmed by rage at the person who caused the trauma or disaster (if it was human caused), at bystanders, or at other therapists who don't understand nor want to know.

Therapists might also be subject to survivor guilt, bystander guilt, or burnout. Practitioners in danger of burnout or vicarious trauma may defend themselves by avoiding the painful story of the survivor. An overworked and exhausted therapist may change the subject to more mundane topics when the patient attempts to tell a trauma story. The practitioner might withdraw or defend him- or herself from the trauma by not believing the story or minimizing the pain of the survivor. Or therapists might distance themselves from the trauma by being overprofessional or overemphasizing the patient's resilience. Therapists who work long term with trauma or disaster survivors need to protect their own well-being, as well as that of the patient.

To that end, Herman (1992) suggests that when working with trauma survivors, the nature of the therapy contract should be explicit. It should be stated and understood by both therapist and patient that the work is collaborative, with a commitment to the task of truth telling and recovery. The pace should be determined collaboratively so that the patient does not experience a loss of control. It should be expected that there will be an initial presence of shame and guilt and an absence of trust and that these issues should be attended to first. Boundaries must be set about session times and duration and about emergency meetings, though there should also be some flexibility.

Bryant and Harvey (2000) point out that therapists need to be especially cautious when treating more than one person who survived the same trauma. The details of the trauma narratives may be quite different for each survivor, and these differences are highly important to each individual. Therapists treating more than one survivor from a disaster might find it difficult to keep the individual stories clear and distinct. The authors suggest that a therapist might do well to treat only one survivor of a particular trauma or disaster. However, for a therapist doing long-term work in the aftermath of a disaster, treating only one person may not be practical, especially when many members of the community have been affected. If treating multiple survivors is necessary, therapists should be certain to keep detailed notes on the specific experiences of each one.

Because this work is so taxing, the therapist should have a support system in place. This could involve a supervisory relationship and/or a peer supervision group. The therapist should be able to voice clinical concerns and issues and also be able to express emotional reactions. Herman (1992) suggests that the nature of long-term trauma work can easily lead to conflict between professional colleagues. In a therapy setting where the focus is on trauma or disaster survivors, it may be most helpful to have a supervisor who does not work with survivors directly but who specializes in helping the helpers. Such a person could be regularly available to assist and support vulnerable therapists.

Finally, one of the unique aspects of doing long-term work with disaster survivors is that counselors themselves can often be directly impacted by the same disaster as their patients. This makes a support system all the more essential. For example, a system of mutual support was in place for two psychologists, Ann Barnard and Ilene Rothgeb, when Hurricane Marilyn struck the U.S. Virgin Islands in 1995. These women both had private practices in the region and found that in the aftermath of this major disaster they were not only practitioners but victims as well (Barnard & Rothgeb, 2000). They were without power, light, and phone service. Many roads were impassible. Barnard and Rothgeb reported that their offices were hot and humid; their clothes, furniture, and books were damp and mildewed; and they knew that they would be living under austere conditions for weeks and months. They had to prioritize how to take care of themselves, their families, and their regular patients, as well as the many newly traumatized residents in the area. They decided to care for themselves and their families first and to provide care next to their already established patients. They also managed to provide some assistance to the community by doing such things as writing psychoeducational material for local newspapers and offering workshops at several schools. Still, Barnard and Rothgeb acknowledge that they were traumatized themselves. Because disasters often strike whole communities, it is not unusual for practitioners to find themselves, as these women did, undergoing extreme hardship. They reported that they relied on one another for support and perspective.

In another example of therapists being personally affected by disaster, practicing psychologists in the Northeast were surveyed 14 weeks after the attacks of 9/11 (Eidelson, D'Alessio, & Eidelson, 2003). Not surprisingly, it was found that those practicing closer to ground zero were most impacted. These psychologists described significant changes in their personal as well as their professional lives. Of the entire subject pool, 82% reported that their personal lives had been affected, and 72% acknowledged that they were more fearful since the attack. However, we should point out that 54% reported some increase in *positive* feeling about their work, while only 11% reported an increase in negative feelings. These findings suggest that although working with disaster survivors in the therapist's "own back yard" can be difficult, for most the work can be quite rewarding.

Indeed, in the aftermath of disaster, when many in the community feel helpless and are searching for a way to be of use, mental health practitioners can find a constructive role that can last for as long as survivors continue to need assistance. Therapists have the opportunity to learn from patients as they engage in the process of healing. Herman (1992) notes "integrity is the capacity to affirm the value of life in the face of death, to be reconciled with the finite limits of one's own life and the tragic limitations of the human condition, and to accept these realities without despair." Long-term work with survivors of disaster can allow therapists to deepen their integrity.

References

Barlow, S. H., Burlingame, G. M., & Fuhriman, A. (2000). Therapeutic application of groups: From Pratt's "thought control classes" to modern group psychotherapy. *Group Dynamics: Theory, Research, and Practice, 4,* 115–134.

Barnard, A. G., & Rothgeb, I. L. (2000). Rebuilding a private practice in psychology following a hurricane: The experiences of two psychologists. *Professional Psychology: Research and Practice, 31,* 393–397.

Beck, A. T. (1976). *Cognitive therapy and emotional disorders.* New York: International Universities Press.

Beck, J. S. (1995). *Cognitive therapy: Basics and beyond.* New York: Guilford Press.

Brabender, V. (2002). *Introduction to group therapy*. New York: Wiley.

Bryant, R. A., & Harvey, A. G. (2000). *Acute stress disorder: A handbook of theory, assessment, and treatment*. Washington, DC: American Psychological Association.

Carter, E. A., & McGoldrick, M. (Eds.). (2005). *The expanded family life cycle: Individual, family, and social perspectives* (3rd ed.). Needham Heights, MA: Allyn & Bacon.

Chemtob, C. M., Tolin, D. F., van der Kolk, B. A., & Pitman, R. K. (2000). Eye movement desensitization and reprocessing. In E. B. Foa, T. M. Keane, & M. J. Friedman (Eds.), *Effective treatments of PTSD* (pp. 139–154). New York: Guilford Press.

Corrigan, P. (2004). How stigma interferes with mental healthcare. *American Psychologist, 59*(7), 614–625.

Danieli, Y. (1988). Treating survivor and children of survivors of the Nazi Holocaust. In F. Ochberg (Ed.), *Posttraumatic therapy and victims of violence* (pp. 278–294). New York: Brunner/Mazel.

Deegear, J., & Lawson, D. M. (2003). The utility of empirically supported treatments. *Professional Psychology: Research and Practice, 34*, 271–277.

Difede, J., Apfeldorf, W. J., Cloitre, M., Spielman, L. A., & Perry, S. W. (1997). Acute psychiatric responses to the explosion at the World Trade Center: A case series. *Journal of Nervous and Mental Disease, 185*(8), 519–522.

Difede, J., & Eskra, D. (2002). Cognitive processing therapy for PTSD in a survivor of the World Trade Center bombing: A case study. *Journal of Trauma Practice, 1*(3–4), 155–165.

Difede, J., & Hoffman, H. G. (2002). Virtual reality exposure therapy for World Trade Center posttraumatic stress disorder: A case report. *CyberPsychology & Behavior, 5*, 529–535.

Difede J., Hoffman, H., & Jaysinghe, N. (2002). Multimedia reviews: Innovative use of virtual reality technology in the treatment of PTSD in the aftermath of September 11. *Journal of Psychiatric Services, 53*(9), 1083–1085.

Dollard, J., & Miller, N. (1950). *Personality and psychotherapy*. New York: McGraw-Hill.

Eidelson, R. J., D'Alessio, G. R., & Eidelson, J. I. ((2003). The impact of September 11 on psychologists. *Professional Psychology: Research and Practice, 34*, 144–150.

Fehr, S. S. (2003). *Introduction to group therapy: A practical guide* (2nd ed.). Binghamton, NY: Haworth Press.

Figley, C. R. (1990). *Helping traumatized families*. New York: Brunner/Mazel.

Figley, C. R. (Ed.). (1995). *Compassion fatigue: Coping with secondary traumatic stress disorder in those who treat the traumatized*. New York: Brunner/Mazel.

Figley, C. R. (Ed.). (1997). *Burnout in families: The systemic costs of caring*. New York: CRC Press.

Foa, E. B., Keane, T. M., & Friedman, M. J. (Eds.). (2000). *Effective treatments of PTSD*. New York: Guilford Press.

Foy, D. W., Eriksson, C. B., & Trice, G. A. (2001). Introduction to group interventions for trauma survivors. *Group Dynamics: Theory, Research, and Practice, 5*, 246–251.

Foy, D. W., Glynn, S. M., Schnurr, P. P., Jankowski, M. K., Wattneberg, S. S., Weiss, D. S., Marmar, C. R., & Gusman, F. D. (2000). Group therapy. In E. B. Foa, T. M. Keane, & M. J. Friedman (Eds.), *Effective treatments of PTSD* (pp. 155–175). New York: Guilford Press.

Freud, S. (1925/1963). *An autobiographical study*. New York: Norton.

Freud, S. (1930/1961). *Civilization and its discontents*. New York: Norton.

Friedman, M. J., Charney, D. S., & Southwick, S. M. (1993). Pharmacotherapy for recently evacuated military casualties. *Military Medicine, 158*, 493–497.

Friedman, M. J., Davidson, J. R. T., Mellman, T. A., & Southwick, S. M. (2000). Pharmacotherapy. In E. B. Foa, T. M. Keane, & M. J. Friedman (Eds.), *Effective treatments of PTSD* (pp. 84–105). New York: Guilford Press.

Haley, J. (1987). *Problem solving therapy* (2nd ed.). San Francisco: Jossey-Bass.

Harkness, L., & Zador, N. (2001). Treatment of PTSD in families and couples. In J. P. Wilson, M. J. Friedman, & J. D. Lindy (Eds.), *Treating psychological trauma and PTSD* (pp. 335–353). New York: Guilford Press.

Herman, J. (1992). *Trauma and recovery: The aftermath of violence from domestic abuse to political terror.* New York: Basic Books.

Jaycox, L H., & Foa, E. B. (1996). Obstacles in implementing exposure therapy for PTSD: Case discussions and practical solutions. *Clinical Psychology and Psychotherapy, 3,* 176–184.

Johnson, S. (1996). *The practice of emotionally focused marital therapy: Creating connection.* Philadelphia: Brunner/Mazel.

Jones, M. C. (1924). A laboratory study of fear: The case of Peter. *Pedagogical Seminary, 31,* 308–315.

Kerr, M. E., & Bowen, M. (1988). *Family evaluation.* New York: Norton.

Kudler, H. S., Blank Jr., A. S., & Krupnick, J. L. (2000a). Treatment approaches for PTSD: Literature reviews, psychodynamic therapy. In E. B. Foa, T. M. Keane, & M. J. Friedman (Eds.), *Effective treatments of PTSD* (pp. 176–198). New York: Guilford Press.

Kudler, H. S., Blank Jr., A. S., & Krupnick, J. L. (2000b). Treatment guidelines: Psychodynamic therapy. In E. B. Foa, T. M. Keane, & M. J. Friedman (Eds.), *Effective treatments of PTSD* (pp. 339–341). New York: Guilford Press.

Lambert, M. J., & Barley, D. E. (2001). Research summary on the therapeutic relationship and psychotherapy outcome. *Psychotherapy: Theory, Research, Practice, Training, 38,* 357–361.

Lindy, J. (1996). Psychoanalytic therapy of posttraumatic stress disorder: The nature of the therapeutic relationship. In B. A. van der Kolk, A. C. McFarlane, & L. W. Weisaeth (Eds.), *Traumatic stress: The effects of overwhelming experience on mind, body, and society* (pp. 525–536). New York: Guilford Press.

McCann, I. L, Sakheim, D. K., & Abrahamson, D. J. (1988). Trauma and victimization: A model of psychological adaptation. *Counseling Psychologist, 16,* 531–594.

Meichenbaum, D. (1985). *Stress inoculation training.* New York: Pergamon Press.

Meichenbaum, D. (1996). Stress inoculation training for coping with stressors. *Clinical Psychologist, 49,* 4–7.

Minuchin, S. (1974). *Families and family therapy.* Cambridge, MA: Harvard University Press.

Mitchell, S. A., & Black, M. (1995). *Freud and beyond: A history of modern psychoanalytic thought.* New York: Basic Books.

NIMH (National Institute of Mental Health). (2002). *Mental health and mass violence: Evidence-based early psychological intervention for victims/survivors of mass violence. A workshop to reach consensus on best practices* (NIH Publication No. 02-5138). Washington, DC: Government Printing Office.

Norcross, J. C. (2001). Purposes, processes, and products of the Task Force on Empirically Supported Therapy Relationships. *Psychotherapy, 38,* 345–356.

North, C. S., & Westerhaus, E. T. (2003). Applications from previous disaster research to guide mental health interventions after the September 11 attacks. In R. J. Ursano, C. S. Fullerton, & A. E. Norwood (Eds.), *Terrorism and disaster: Individual and community mental health interventions* (pp. 93–106). Cambridge, England, and New York: Cambridge University Press.

Paolino Jr., T. J., & McGrady, B. S. (Eds.). (1978). *Marriage and marital therapy*. New York: Brunner/Mazel.

Pearlman, L. A., & Saakvitne, K. W. (1995). *Trauma and the therapist: Countertransference and vicarious traumatization in psychotherapy with incest survivors*. New York: Norton.

Regier, D. A., Narrow, W. E., Rae, D. S., Manderscheid, R. W., Locke, B. Z., & Goodwin, F. K. (1993). The de facto W.S. mental and addictive disorders service system: Epidemiologic Catchment Area prospective 1-year prevalence rates of disorders and services. *Archives of General Psychiatry, 50*, 85–94.

Riggs, D. S. (2000). Marital and family therapy. In E. B. Foa, T. M. Keane, & M. J. Friedman (Eds.), *Effective treatments of PTSD* (pp. 280–301). New York: Guilford Press.

Rothbaum, B. O., Meadows, E. A., Resick, P, & Foy, D. W. (2000). Cognitive behavior therapy. In E. B. Foa, T. M. Keane, & M. J. Friedman (Eds.), *Effective treatments of PTSD* (pp. 60–83). New York: Guilford Press.

Schnurr, P., Friedman, M. T., Foy, D. W., Shea, M. T., Hsieh, F. Y., Lavori, P. W., Glynn, S. M., Wattenberg, M., & Bernady, N. C. (2003). Randomized trial of trauma-focused group therapy for posttraumatic stress disorder: Results form a Department of Veterans Affairs cooperative study. *Archives of General Psychiatry, 60*, 481.

Seligman, M. E. (1995). The effectiveness of psychotherapy: The consumer report study. *American Psychologist, 50*(12), 965–974.

Shalev, A. Y., Friedman, M. J., Foa, E. B., & Keane, T. M. (2000), Integration and summary. In E. B. Foa, T. M. Keane, & M. J. Friedman (Eds.), *Effective treatments of PTSD* (pp. 359–379). New York: Guilford Press.

Shapiro, F. (1995). Eye movement desensitization and reprocessing: Basic principles, protocols, and procedures. New York: Guilford Press.

Smith, M. L., & Glass, G. V. (1978). Meta-analysis of psychotherapy outcome studies. *American Psychologist, 32*, 752–760.

Smith, M. L., Glass, G. V., & Miller, T. I. (1980). *The benefits of psychotherapy*, Baltimore: Johns Hopkins University Press.

Spiegler, M. D., & Guevremont, D. C. (2002). *Contemporary behavior therapy* (4th ed.). Belmont, CA: Brooks/Cole.

Stampfl, T. C., & Levis, D. J. (1967). Essentials of implosive therapy: A learning-theory-based psychodynamic behavioral therapy. *Journal of Abnormal Psychology, 72*, 496–503.

Stubenbort, K., Donnelly, G. R., & Cohen, J. A. (2001). Cognitive–behavioral group therapy for bereaved adults and children following an air disaster. *Group Dynamics, 5*(4). Retrieved on July 22, 2005, from EBSCOhost.

Task Force on Promotion and Dissemination of Psychological Procedures. (1995). Training in and dissemination of empirically-validated psychological treatments: Report and recommendations. *Clinical Psychologist, 48*, 3–23.

Walsh, F., & McGoldrick, M. (2004). Loss and the family: A systemic perspective. In F. Walsh & M. McGoldrick (Eds.), *Living beyond loss: Death in the family* (2nd ed.) (pp. 3–26). New York: Norton.

Wampold, B. E., & Bhati, K. S. (2004). Attending to the omissions: A historical examination of evidence-based practice movements. *Professional Psychology: Research and Practice, 35*, 563–570.

Watson, J. B., & Rayner, P. (1920). Conditioned emotional reactions, *Journal of Experimental Psychology, 3*, 1.

Westen, D., Novotny, C. M., & Thompson-Brenner, H. (2004). The empirical status of empirically supported psychotherapies: Assumptions, findings, and reporting in controlled clinical trials. *Psychological Bulletin, 130*, 631–663.

Wilson, J. P., Friedman, M. J., & Lindy, J. D. (Eds.). (2001). *Treating psychological trauma and PTSD*. New York: Guilford Press.

Winerman, L. (2005). Fighting phobias: A virtual cure. *Monitor on Psychology, 36*(7), 87–89.

Wolpe, J. (1958). *Psychotherapy by reciprocal inhibition*. Stanford, CA: Stanford University Press.

Wolpe, J. (1982). *The practice of behavior therapy*. New York: Pergamon Press.

Yalom, I. (1995). *The theory and practice of group psychotherapy* (4th ed.). New York: Basic Books.

Yalom, I. (2005). *The theory and practice of group psychotherapy* (5th ed.). New York: Basic Books.

Young, B. H., Ford, J. D., Ruzek, J. I., Friedman, M. J, & Gusman, F. D. (1998). *Disaster mental health services: A guidebook for clinicians and administrators*. St. Louis: National Center for PTSD, Department of Veterans Affairs Employee Education System.

*The trouble with the world is that the stupid are cocksure
and the intelligent are full of doubt.*

Bertrand Russell

12 CHAPTER | New Directions in Disaster Mental Health

In this, our final chapter, we take a close look at the current state of the disaster mental health (DMH) field and at possible future directions. We discuss how communities, practitioners, and the public prepare for disaster. We examine new challenges in DMH, including an international response and the practice of intervening when the trauma is ongoing. We also examine the current backlash against DMH that can be seen in the media and describe what we view as the antidote to it—a focus on ethics and evidence-based best practice in DMH.

It has been noted that in spite of the catastrophic events that defined the 20th century—the two World Wars; the Korean, Vietnam, and Gulf Wars; the Holocaust; genocides in Armenia, Cambodia, and Rwanda; and numerous environmental and technological disasters—the mental health community has been slow to consistently acknowledge the emotional impact of trauma and disaster (Wilson, Friedman, & Lindy, 2001). In retrospect, the study of psychological trauma has a history of episodic amnesia. Periods of awareness and investigation have alternated with periods of forgetfulness (Herman, 1992). This kind of denial or forgetting can result in inadequate preparation for disaster and in inadequate care given to those impacted afterwards. But, fortunately, this tendency to forget appears to be diminishing.

The mental health community now recognizes the importance of early intervention to address the emotional needs of those whose lives are touched by disaster and mass violence, and efforts to increase the effectiveness of those interventions are a current focus of the field. The National Institute of Mental Health (NIMH) report (2002) concluded that "the key components of early intervention include preparation, planning, education, training, service provision, and evaluation of efforts to assist those affected by mass violence and disasters." As a result of this kind of recognition, there are growing numbers of DMH professionals and more of a commitment to assist survivors who have experienced traumatic stress.

Public attitudes also appear to be shifting. The public has always had some desire to know about the psychological impact of disaster, but history suggests that they may have little stamina for such awareness over the long run. After all, the unconscious need to protect oneself from admitting personal vulnerability provides a powerful motive to remain in denial about trauma, catastrophe, and human malevolence. But these days, the culture appears to be at a tipping point with regard to awareness of the inevitable nature of disaster. People are also more accepting that events can overwhelm the psyche of survivors. There is a general acknowledgment that there will continue to be disasters and events of mass violence. There is also a consensus among experts that survivors of disaster will need and benefit from mental health interventions (NIMH, 2002). This is no small step forward. Disasters present a range of challenges to individuals, communities, and mental health practitioners, but the sustained awareness of trauma caused by disaster allows for the possibility of a commitment to preparedness and planning.

PREPARING COMMUNITIES

The increased willingness to acknowledge the inevitability of disasters is allowing mental health organizations to prepare a more organized response. Mental health issues are more likely to be considered as part of a comprehensive approach to preparing for and responding to disaster. As we have mentioned before, key federal, state, and local governments along with private mental health associations, the American Red Cross, spiritual care groups, schools, and hospitals are developing statements of understanding so that when disaster strikes there will be greater clarity about who will provide the mental health response and how it will be organized.

A community that copes reasonably well with individual mental health issues through services provided by government and private practitioners can be overwhelmed when it suddenly finds a whole population traumatized by disaster. Therefore, the mental health system needs to be prepared for an upsurge of needs and demands when disaster strikes. However, preparing extensively at the local level for an event that may happen rarely if ever is not cost efficient. Matching training and preparation to the probability of a particular disaster occurring is challenging but necessary for effective mitigation. Communities need to determine how many mental health professionals to train for disasters in general and for specific disasters that are more likely to occur in a particular region, and they need to have backup plans in place so that they can bring in additional or more specialized help as needed.

This approach is based on the notion of **surge capacity,** which is used by hospital and medical emergency planners who estimate how many cases they can handle in an emergency. The same type of planning can apply to assessing potential mental health needs in the event of a disaster. For example, in 2005 there was extensive flooding in upstate New York that appeared to go beyond the surge capacity of the local mental health response. Communities in the region could not find enough mental health personnel who were trained and prepared to respond to the large scope of the disaster, so they brought in volunteers from the county mental health association as well as from the national level of the American Red Cross. Another example of efficient preparation is the American Red Cross's practice of keeping a roster of specially trained mental health practitioners on call, ready to respond to an aviation incident anywhere in the country on very short notice. Given the unlikely odds of an airplane crash affecting any specific region, it would not be an efficient use of emergency resources to extensively train a local practitioner in the specifics of responding to this kind of incident; instead, specialists are brought in as needed.

Beyond the DMH component, emergency management groups have established a structure for coordinating and managing major disasters, the National Incident Management Structure (NIMS). The intent of Homeland Security Presidential Directive/HSPD-5, which ordered the development of NIMS, is clear: "The objective of the United States Government is to ensure that all levels of government across the Nation have the capability to work efficiently and effectively together, using a [single, comprehensive] national approach to domestic incident management" (www.fema.gov/nims/). To accomplish this objective, all responders at all levels are expected to use the same organizational structures, terminology, procedures, and systems, all the time. The idea is to achieve interoperability among jurisdictions and disciplines. Those who do not train for, exercise, and use NIMS and the *Incident Command System* in their day-to-day operations will be less able to integrate their activities into a system they do not know, have not practiced, and do not use.

To underscore the importance of the nationwide adoption of NIMS, the Department of Homeland Security has directed that all federal preparedness assistance to states and local jurisdictions be tied to compliance with the requirements of NIMS. Beginning October 1, 2005, all recipients of federal preparedness funds had to adopt and use NIMS as a condition for the receipt of certain preparedness assistance funding, which includes preparedness funds from all federal departments and agencies in addition to funds from the Department of Homeland Security. (There is no linkage between postdisaster assistance funds and NIMS compliance.) However, extensive confusion in the coordination of the Federal Emergency Management Agency (FEMA), state, and local responsibilities in the aftermath of Hurricane Katrina in August 2005 makes it obvious that more work needs to be done to prepare for an effective response to complex or large-scale disasters. This operational breakdown provides a vivid illustration of the importance of having a detailed plan in place *before* a catastrophe hits so that recovery efforts are not slowed by confusion or red tape. As the governor of Louisiana's press secretary commented to the *New York Times* days after the storm, "We wanted soldiers, helicopters, food and water. [FEMA] wanted to negotiate an organizational chart" (Shane, 2005).

Despite the progress in the field, mental health providers still need to be better incorporated into a comprehensive response to disaster. There was a consensus among writers of the NIMH report (2002) that "mental health personnel have key roles to play when integrated into mass violence or disaster management teams. These personnel can help coordinate service provisions so that mental health is an integrated element of comprehensive disaster management plans."

PREPARING PROVIDERS

An organization's ability to offer DMH services requires an adequate supply of trained DMH practitioners. This points to the need for graduate mental health programs to offer training in DMH. Much in the way that recognition of the prevalence of child abuse led to mental health licensing laws that required training in recognizing and responding to child abuse, we can envision similar requirements for competency in responding to emergencies and disaster. The New York State Office of Mental Health recently provided DMH training to selected practitioners in virtually every county in the state (Herrmann, 2005).

The NIMH report (2002) states that DMH training can be improved in the following ways:

- Provide training in language that is readily understood, avoiding professional jargon and the pathologizing of normal responses.
- Develop hands-on training approaches that give trainees multiple opportunities to observe, practice, and receive coaching as they attempt to employ various skills by increasing the use of (1) role-play exercises, (2) sample scripts that illustrate skills, (3) narratives describing real-world disasters, and (4) interactive CD-ROM video materials.
- Increase use of videotapes showing aspects of DMH care to give trainees a sense of what really takes place at disaster sites and settings, what they may see, and how these settings typically look and feel.
- Move toward greater specification of training procedures and systemization of delivery of training.
- Develop systems for continuing education of DMH workers.
- Develop methods to evaluate the effectiveness and perceived usefulness of disaster mental health–training procedures.

The NIMH report (2002) also points out that DMH work can bring practitioners into different cultural settings, so any DMH training needs to incorporate units on working with diversity and **cross-cultural differences,** defined as "variations in the meaning or expression of thoughts, feelings or behaviors related to ethnic or religious identity or place of origin. Such differences may influence the validity of assessment, response to treatment, and appropriate ways of interacting with survivor populations" (NIMH, 2002).

Diversity training is important, but so is recognizing the value of offering services within a practitioner's own region. DMH response begins and ends in the local community where residents and mental health practitioners can best understand one another and will be together through the long haul. In the large and diverse state of New York, for example, regional mental health officials often comment that "when you know one county in the state, you know *one* county." They are suggesting that there is so much cultural diversity within the state and that each region is so distinct that effective procedures and policies do not transpose easily from one area to the next. Some counties are subject to regular flooding whereas others may be more prone to urban fires; each county has a different ethnic mix, and so on. When disaster struck a Jewish community in northern New York, state officials thought they were showing sensitivity when they entered the community with a rabbi. Unfortunately, the rabbi was a woman, and the community was Orthodox and did not recognize the authority of female rabbis. This misstep made community members certain their other concerns would not be easily met. In short, whether they come to assist from within the disaster-struck county, from elsewhere in the same state, or from other parts of the country, mental health practitioners must be very sensitive to local customs and culture. National organizations and experts should be sensitive to collaborate with and not take over from the local mental health workers.

PREPARING THE PUBLIC

It is estimated that 60% of the adult population experiences a significant trauma in their lives and that about 1 in 6 experience a natural disaster (McFarlane, 2005). For reasons discussed throughout this book (for example, technological advances, denser populations), we suspect that these percentages will continue to increase. In Chapter 4, we examined what are considered to be **protective factors** in the face of disaster. Social support, good coping skills, material resources, and high socioeconomic class are the kinds of factors that tend to allow survivors to recover from disaster more readily. There is considerable interest in the field of health psychology that focuses on helping individuals to develop a more optimistic attitude and to learn more effective social skills and coping styles that can improve the chances of recovering from disaster.

Resilience is described as a characteristic that allows people to thrive despite severe environmental risk factors (Luthar, Cicchetti, & Becker, 2000). Resilience has been studied in children in the face of war, natural disaster, family violence, and extreme poverty. Children who are talented and intelligent and have faith, high self-esteem, and an easy disposition are more likely to be resilient in the face of adversity (Masten & Coatsworth, 1998). Southwick, Vythilingam, and Charney (2005) identify five basic psychosocial resilience factors in adults: (1) positive emotions (including optimism and humor), (2) cognitive flexibility (including positive explanatory style, positive reappraisal, and acceptance), (3) meaning (including religion, spirituality, and altruism), (4) social support (including role models), and (5) active coping style (including exercise and training).

Bonanno (2004) notes that resilience is different from recovery. In the face of trauma or loss, some people suffer and then recover, while others cope well from the outset and have no need to recover—these people are resilient. Bonanno argues that resilience is more common than most believe and that there can be multiple, often unexpected paths to it. Examining resilience in the face of loss, he found that many people who were bereaved from the death of a spouse exhibited little or no grief, although others did not see them as generally emotionally cold or distant. Their resilience may have been due to factors such as their acceptance of death, their belief in a just world, and the existence of social support. As another example of the commonness of resilience, Bonanno notes that although over one-third of returning Gulf War veterans reported psychological distress within a year of their return to the United States, 62.5% reported no distress. What accounts for the difference in reaction? Bonanno speculates that the personality trait of **hardiness** plays a role. Hardy individuals are confident and committed to finding meaning in life, and they believe that they can benefit from good and bad experiences.

Unexpected paths to resilience that Bonanno (2004) found can include being overoptimistic about oneself (self-enhancement) or repressing and avoiding unpleasant thoughts and emotions—tactics that might not seem emotionally productive but that do evidently help some individuals cope with trauma. Less surprising is the notion that people can cope with extreme adversity through the use of humor and positive emotion. Bonanno's work reminds us that when we think about ways to promote resiliency one size does not fit all and we should certainly not assume that all or most disaster survivors will need professional help.

Consistent with the evidence that most people are resilient in the face of loss and trauma is the finding that many of the survivors who reported suffering symptoms of posttraumatic stress disorder (PTSD) in the immediate aftermath of September 11, 2001, showed a significant reduction in symptoms over time (Galea et al., 2003). Shalev (2004b) points out that this recovery may be due to the fact that there have been no terrorist attacks on American ground since then and to the facts that 1 day after the attacks most parents could find milk for their children, most survivors did not have to relocate, and virtually all were able to contact family and friends within hours of the events. How resilient would the population have been if there had been continuing terror attacks? Would people have become immune, or would they have become more sensitized and fearful? Later in the chapter, we examine how residents in some cultures and countries have been forced to cope with ongoing trauma or disaster. The lasting devastation caused by Hurricane Katrina in 2005 will tragically provide an opportunity to examine this kind of impact within the United States, as survivors cope with indefinite relocation and disruption.

Shalev (2004b) is optimistic about the human capacity to cope even in these most extreme circumstances, not because people are self-reliant but rather because people can help each other. "This is, again, because of mothers who, in the midst of a storm, keep soothing their babies. But wouldn't each of us do whatever it takes to mitigate the effect of stress on friends, families and patients? That is *resilience*: perseverance and soothing human contact" (Shalev, 2004b).

NEW CHALLENGES: PREPARING AN INTERNATIONAL RESPONSE

A truly international response to the mental health impact of disaster is still in its earliest stages. Jean Henri Dunant, the Swiss founder of the Red Cross Movement, referred to psychological distress on the battlefield in 1862, but it was not until 2000 that the European Red Cross/Red Crescent Societies Network for Psychological Support was established. This group attempts to provide the opportunity for the European Red Cross Societies to share experiences, trainings, and practices with special attention to cultural sensitivities on the topic of psychological support (Croq, Croq, Chiapello, & Damiani, 2005).

Other international groups beyond the Red Cross are also turning increasing focus to DMH. The General Assembly of the World Psychiatric Association approved a statement on August 26, 2002, on the implications of disaster for the world community that outlined the following goals:

> The World Psychiatric Association would like to draw the attention of psychiatrists and other mental health professionals, health authorities, decision makers and the general public to the serious and potentially catastrophic psychological and psychopathological effects of disasters. These effects can be diverse in character, intensity and potential for chronicity, but acute stress reactions, posttraumatic stress disorder (PTSD), mood, anxiety and psychotic disorders, and permanent changes in the personality are the ones that, if left untreated, may have the most serious consequences. . . . Disasters . . . produce very serious effects on the population and particularly on children, having a negative impact on the social structure and systems, which increases the effect of the disaster on individuals and populations." (Lopez-Ibor, Christodoulou, Maj, Sartorius, & Okasha, 2005).

International aid groups are now planning for and responding to the mental health needs as well as the material needs of the affected population. There are groups of mental health or psychosocial practitioners prepared to respond to disaster throughout North America, Europe, Latin America, and Asia (Croq et al., 2005). The need for their services is strong: The Red Cross reported that 17 million people living in developing countries were directly impacted by disaster from 1967 through 1991, compared with 700,000 in developed countries in the same period, a ratio of about 166 to 1 (McFarlane, 2005). And people in the hardest hit regions often have the least access to professional mental health care. According to the World Health Organization, the median number of psychiatrists per 100,000 population is as low as 0.20 in Southeast Asia and 0.04 in Africa (WHO, 2005), in contrast with a ratio of nearly 16 psychiatrists per 100,000 population in the United States (Borenstein, 2001). Not surprisingly given these figures, Norris et al. (2002) found that people from developing countries were not only more vulnerable to disaster but also more prone to psychological disorder because they lacked the resources necessary for recovery.

To some degree, the growing international DMH movement has its roots in American traumatology. French researchers note that "the detection and treatment of mental disorders caused by disaster began in the USA, thanks to the advent of the PTSD diagnostic category in the aftermath of the Vietnam War, and the subsequent application of this diagnosis to civilian situations" (Croq et al., 2005). Many international authorities acknowledge that the American diagnosis of PTSD has had a very positive impact on the mental health response to disaster throughout the world (for example, Shalev, 2004a; Shinfuku, 2005). As we discussed in Chapter 5, PTSD is the only *DSM* diagnosis that is more than a description of symptoms. It states clearly that the cause of the disorder is a traumatic event. Receiving a diagnosis of PTSD provides people who suffer with a name for their suffering. It informs them that they are neither defective nor cowardly, nor do they lack character. This has been extremely helpful throughout the developing world.

In recent years, DMH has been included in the international response to numerous large-scale disasters in developing countries. The Turkish government and international aid groups provided psychological assistance to the many victims of the massive earthquake that struck Turkey in August 1999. Six months after the event, which measured 7.4 on the Richter scale and left 18,000 dead and over 50,000 injured, helpers found that 60% of those who lost a relative could be diagnosed with PTSD. Psychiatrists and psychologists were also involved from the very beginning when a massive earthquake struck Algiers in May 2003. Dozens of mental health practitioners worked 10-day shifts throughout the area and in refugee camps (Croq et al., 2005).

After a tsunami of epic proportions killed an estimated 280,000 people in Southeast Asia in 2004, officials from the World Health Organization, UNICEF, and other relief agencies reported that they expected to provide psychological services for *millions* who lost family members, homes, and communities in the weeks and months following the disaster (Carey, 2005). Awareness of the mental health aspects of the disaster was demonstrated in the local as well as the international response to the tsunami: Days after the event, the Associated Press reported that doctors in Sri Lanka worried that many survivors would develop PTSD and other disorders. In the psychiatric hospital ward in the Sri Lankan city of Galle, "Some banged their heads against the hospital wall. Some wide eyed just stared vacantly. Others mumbled 'the sea is coming,' reliving the horrors of the massive tsunami that took their families and homes" (Associated Press, 2005). A psychiatrist from India who was part of a team working in relief camps commented that the emotional and psychological fallout from the tsunami would take years to heal and that survivors who could locate family members swept away by the floodwaters were also particularly at risk for developing complicated grief.

Making a mental health response effective at an international level requires considerable sensitivity. When mental health practitioners leave their own countries to help elsewhere in the world, the problems resulting from cultural differences become more pronounced, especially when practitioners do not speak the local language. In the same way that any intervention must "first do no harm," mental health providers need to be cautioned about creating more problems than they solve if they enter a community without sufficient organization and awareness.

Both the positive and negative aspects of international DMH aid were demonstrated in the aftermath of the 1995 earthquake that devastated Kobe, a large modern port city in Japan. More than 5500 people were killed in 1 day, and approximately 1000 more died as a result of the disaster in the months following the event. In total, it was estimated that the earthquake impacted 2.4 million people. Shinfuku (2005) notes that there may be more stigma attached to psychological problems in Japan than in the West, which may be one reason why there tended to be a large number of stress-related physical symptoms and more postdisaster suicides than are typically found in Western cultures. According to Shinfuku, foreign DMH experts were helpful in the aftermath of the Kobe earthquake because no one in Japan at that time was prepared to cope with the psychological needs of the survivors. Visiting experts were able to explain the importance of mental health needs to local professionals and to the media. However, he provides a cautionary note about the influx of international help that should give pause to anyone thinking of flying overseas to assist survivors of disaster in a foreign country:

> The usefulness of foreign volunteers was difficult to evaluate. A number of international experts on disaster mental health came to Kobe. They put a heavy burden on the small number of local experts, as they needed translators and someone to arrange their visits to the shelters. Some experts in Kobe developed burnout symptoms after meeting with so many foreign disaster experts. (Shinfuku, 2005)

Responding When the Disaster Is Ongoing

Doctors Without Borders, or *Medecins Sans Frontieres* (MSF) as it is known internationally, is best known for delivering emergency medical relief to victims of war and disaster, regardless of politics, race, religion, or ethnicity. The organization began in 1985 with one doctor in a small office and has grown so that they are currently offering services in areas of Africa, the Americas, Australia, Asia, and Europe. MSF responds to wars and conflicts, natural and human-made disasters, treating refugees and displaced people. They also offer long-term assistance to countries with collapsed or insufficient health-care systems. Mental health professionals are now joining the medical doctors in MSF to address the emotional trauma caused by disaster and also by ongoing conditions including periods of war, disease, and famine. Children are often a focus of the psychosocial interventions of MSF because children are most at risk and because families are more likely to allow counselors to enter the family system to assist a child (Michalik, 2004).

As MSF workers have seen, physical trauma caused by war, genocide, famine, and disease also causes emotional trauma. Mental health professionals with MSF assist with global epidemics such as HIV and tuberculosis as well as war and disaster. Their efforts are often specific to a particular region's problems. For example, mental health workers in Rwanda have run group therapy sessions for men who lost limbs to machete attacks, and they have counseled boy soldiers to learn trades and options other than war and fighting. In other areas, MSF mental health workers have assisted rape survivors with individual and group counseling to help them find meaning and to bring about healing. (Although in the United States rape is generally considered to be an individual trauma rather than a disaster impacting a community, there are conflicts in the world where widespread rape is used as a strategy of war.)

Consistent with DMH practice, MSF's interventions often need to be highly practical. For example, in Kosovo in the late 1990s, many people lost their homes, but they would not leave the land. As winter approached, they were in danger of freezing to death if they could not be convinced to move. This was not only a practical and medical problem, but also an emotional one: The survivors had been traumatized and needed psychosocial assistance to help with decisions that could save their lives (de Jong, 2004). Interventions also must be culturally sensitive. For example, in Palestine, a largely Muslim country, a male mental health worker with MSF reported that when he worked with children in their homes, he needed to bring a female translator to be allowed entry if their father was not at home. Throughout many countries, MSF practitioners depend on local resources and utilize native art and music as part of healing rituals (Michalik, 2004).

Responding to an ongoing crisis presents some differences from isolated disasters. Often in the face of drought, famine, epidemic, conflict, and war, the term *posttraumatic stress disorder* has little meaning because the trauma and danger have not passed. As such, MSF and other groups of international trauma experts are attempting to discover ways to be helpful to survivors when there are prolonged adversities and helpers cannot wait to offer assistance until the threat has passed. What they find may apply to more "traditional" disasters as well, especially those that don't necessarily provide a clear end point. Weeks after the Southeast Asian tsunami, aftershocks continued to frighten many residents. After a terrorist attack, there may also be a sense of continuing threat. This creates an additional challenge for mental health workers as they attempt to provide effective interventions amid perceptions of enduring danger.

Some in the field have argued that mental health interventions are not useful until the danger has passed (Brewin, 2003). Yet, there are many cultures where citizens live with a perpetual sense of threat. For example, in many undeveloped countries there are enduring famines and epidemics, and in countries like Israel and Palestine there is ongoing conflict and violence, often targeting civilians. Israel's decades-long experience with community violence offers several lessons in mitigating the mental health effects of suicide bombings and other terrorist acts. First, authorities have found that it is helpful to reduce immediate reminders of the trauma of bombings by engaging in cleanup as soon as possible. Officials expect attacks and prepare to minimize trauma by repairing damaged buildings and even replacing destroyed trees within days (Shalev, 2004a). The public is thus protected from reminders and triggers of the event. Second, officials are committed to providing accurate information about events, including where they occurred and which routes are closed. The media cooperates by providing public broadcasts of accurate and reliable information so that citizens can know immediately whether they should be concerned or reassured. Third, efforts are made to identify victims as quickly as possible. If necessary, DNA testing on corpses is done within hours so that families can be informed right away. This system for rapid identification limits the ambiguity and anxiety about who may or may not have been injured or killed.

How, in the face of ongoing terror, can people possibly continue to thrive or even to function? According to Shalev (2004a), people are resilient in chronically horrific situations for a number of reasons:

- *There is a shift in expectations about security.* If people get home safely, they are pleased. If they hear there is a bombing but with few deaths, they are pleased. The bar for satisfaction lowers, and people adjust.
- *Priorities shift.* Citizens may lose some freedoms, but they are willing to sacrifice them in exchange for a greater sense of safety. There is appreciation for new and simpler pleasures that are achievable and within reach.
- *Routine is a significant factor in promoting adjustment.* People find comfort in being able to read their favorite newspaper, watch their favorite TV show, or talk with those they have always spoken to. Children are helped by a regular wakeup and bedtime habit. Routine helps maintain stability.
- *Necessity contributes to resilience.* There is a need to proceed with life and deal with daily tasks no matter how stressful or dangerous. When people feel that they have to go to work or school, it gives them something to organize their lives around.
- *Life can simply be attractive.* There are pleasures that can be found and experienced in the most difficult circumstances. Those living in the face of trauma and danger can continue to smile and find pleasure in the smiles of others. We must note that not everyone can adjust to threats of violence in these ways. Those suffering with PTSD in particular do not find life attractive. They cannot relax or find pleasure easily. Instead, they experience a chronic sense of fear; they cannot sleep because they cannot experience safety anywhere.

One mental health helper from Holland, working with MSF in Bosnia, reported that his colleagues and friends at home told him his work was not likely to be effective—that in circumstances where trauma and disaster are ongoing and there is no safety, no treatment is possible. The worker was conflicted because he did not want to risk his life in order to simply appear humane. He was only willing to undergo the hardship and risk of this work if clients were truly being helped. One day while he was on assignment, there was a grenade attack on the mental health clinic he supervised in Bosnia. He ordered an immediate evacuation of the clinic, but none of the clients or workers would leave—they refused to have their sessions interrupted. As it turned out, the attack was brief and not repeated, and no one was hurt. The clients' and staff's anger toward the attackers was coupled with a desire to resume the counseling: "How dare you interrupt our sessions?" they asked. Of course, a single anecdote does not prove that treatment is effective during ongoing crises, but the experience clearly demonstrated to the worker that clients did see much value in the program (de Jong, 2004).

If there is insufficient research on early intervention in the aftermath of disaster, there is even less data on evidence-based interventions when there is repeated and chronic trauma. However, as Shalev et al. (2003) note, "The treatment of repeated trauma cannot wait for controlled experiments to be carried out. Thus, somewhat naively we assume that reducing distress and enabling better personal functioning and rewarding human interaction should affect the long-term outcome of traumatic exposure." Effective clinical work while trauma and disaster are ongoing is "an art to be further developed and explored. However there is no reason to abstain from clinically treating those in need, indeed it would be neglectful not to do so" (Shalev et al., 2003).

BACKLASH AGAINST DISASTER MENTAL HEALTH SERVICES

While most DMH practitioners would probably agree with Shalev that efforts to reduce distress and provide supportive human interaction are likely to benefit survivors in the long run, not everyone agrees that mental health interventions should be a high priority in the aftermath of disaster. The argument for a more subdued response is often made out of respect for human resilience or based on a presumed inability to overcome cultural differences. The argument against DMH, however, could also be motivated by the centuries-old denial of the reality of psychological trauma.

In the 2004 movie *Hotel Rwanda,* a cynical television journalist videotapes a massacre a few blocks from his hotel. The hotel's worried manager, Paul Rusesabagina (played by the actor Don Cheadle), watches the tape and becomes encouraged. He is certain that these images, when televised abroad, will force the West to intervene in the ethnic strife destroying his country. But the reporter knows better and simply says, "If people see this footage they'll say, 'Oh my God, that's terrible,' and they'll go on eating their dinners." A decade after the Rwandan genocide, those remarks are painful because he was right.

Although there is a motivation to see and help those affected by disaster, there is also a drive that seeks to keep us distant from the pain of others, an aspect of us that does not want to see or know or remember. Observers may attempt to find comfort in apathy or indifference, and victims can be as distressed by the indifference of observers as by the original trauma itself (Herman, 1992). So, although there is increased recognition of the human suffering following disaster and the victim's need for assistance, there is also an emerging counterposition. It is sometimes described as a skeptical point of view, and it typically concludes that the public and professionals should do less for survivors of disaster because they can take care of themselves.

This backlash has been seen in the popular media, not only on sensationalistic TV news channels, but also in the *New York Times* (for example, "Repress Yourself" by Lauren Slater, 2003; "Bread and Shelter, Yes. Psychiatrists, No" by Sally Satel, 2005), the *New Yorker* magazine (for example, "Getting Over It" by Malcolm Gladwell, 2004), and even in professional journals such as the *American Psychologist* (for example, "Loss, Trauma, and Resilience: Have We Underestimated the Human Capacity to Thrive After Extremely Aversive Events?" by George Bonanno, 2004). As a sample of this view, Slater wrote the following in the *New York Times Magazine* in 2003: "After the twin towers fell there were by some estimates three shrinks for every victim . . . the bearded, the beatnik, the softly empathic all gathered round the survivors urging talk. . . . What actually does help is anyone's best guess—probably some sort of fire, directly under your behind."

This "hands-off" position can include the following kinds of arguments:

- Because aid agencies are corrupt, it makes little sense to contribute to relief organizations.
- The numbers of disasters that occur are exaggerated, perhaps to further a personal or political agenda.
- PTSD is a fictitious diagnosis (Brewin, 2003) used to create a culture of victimization, designed for malingerers and colluding, greedy therapists sometimes described as the "grief industry" (for example, Groopman, 2004).
- Even if there are as many disasters and traumas as are being reported, people are so resilient that they do not suffer because of them.
- Even if people do suffer, they do not suffer for very long because they have a natural capacity for recovery, and this natural recovery does not require any assistance or support (Bonanno, 2004).
- Even if people don't recover and continue to suffer, it is not due to the traumatic event but rather to some premorbid condition in existence well before the disaster occurred.
- Even if this were not the case, people are still better off learning to cope on their own, much as war veterans and trauma victims did for countless centuries before there were psychiatric diagnosis and professional helpers (Gladwell, 2004).
- These helpers will not be effective if they attempt to assist anyone from a different cultural background (Satel, 2005).
- If helpers show a willingness to listen to survivors talk about the traumatic experience, it will worsen their condition (Slater, 2003).

We should acknowledge that there is some grain of truth to all these arguments:

- The PTSD diagnosis is flawed (Brewin, 2003), earlier psychological problems are a risk factor postdisaster (for example, Fullerton, Ursano, Norwood, & Holloway, 2003; Norris et al., 2002), and most trauma victims are resilient and do recover on their own or with help from their natural support systems of friends and family (for example, Litz, 2004; Norris et al., 2002).
- Counselors may not always appreciate the resilience of their clients or the complexity of the cultural issues and differences.
- Pressuring people to talk about a traumatic event when they are not ready is not helpful (for example, Brewin, 2003; Litz, & Gray, 2004; NIMH, 2002).

However, there is ground, too, for skepticism about this hands-off position. We are skeptical of the skeptics. From their perspective, observers of trauma and disaster don't have to do too much. Either survivors are resilient and recover on their own or they don't. From that perspective, the survivor who is not recovering is viewed as lacking the courage or character or resilience that almost everyone else has. If the survivor needs professional assistance, he or she can be viewed as defective. If the victims are from a different cultural background, practitioners should ignore them because they couldn't possibly provide culturally sensitive interventions. If this way of thinking is followed, not only has the survivor been traumatized, but also he or she is next insulted for not being resilient and cheery enough or dismissed as beyond help.

Clearly, we do not agree with the skeptics. Although some in the DMH field may have underestimated the human capacity for resilience, anyone present in the aftermath of a disaster is a witness to human suffering. According to the most recent comprehensive research on the impact of disaster by Norris et al. (2002), an evaluation of 60,000 disaster survivors finds a significant human toll: 50% of survivors suffered moderate impairment, and 39% suffered severe or very severe impairment. Victims from third-world countries were considerably more impacted. This and other research confirms that victims of disaster do suffer and that recovery is tied to a supportive environment.

Therefore, the current emphasis on strengthening resilience and cultural awareness—both very positive developments in the field—should not be conflated with an indifferent hands-off or do-nothing approach. Although it may not be the intended consequence, an overemphasis on resilience can provide an excuse for denial and indifference, and too much emphasis on resilience or its misuse may make some survivors reluctant to seek help. As Shalev (2004b) notes, "The current focus on the resilience of the strong should not be allowed to send us back to an age in which one could be executed for cowardice on the battlefield, an age in which developing a stress disorder was a personal failure."

There may be skeptics who are generally opposed to psychotherapy or any type of mental health intervention, while others are supportive of the profession but committed to pressing practitioners to be sure to "do it right." Whatever their beliefs, those who raise questions about early intervention present a valuable challenge to DMH practitioners, as well as to clergy, community members, and others who provide assistance. If practitioners do not address the cultural issues adequately, underestimate the importance of resilience, or overuse untested or suspect treatment approaches, the cynics are there, ever vigilant, questioning the practice. Which interventions are most effective, when should they be offered, and to which populations? DMH practitioners and other helpers are challenged to provide the evidence that supports their efforts. Interventions do need to be improved, refined, and tested, and healthy skepticism can inform and improve the practice. We believe that the field will benefit most with continued attention given to **ethics** in the practice and to **research that informs practice.**

ETHICS

The general ethical principles of any professional organization represent the ideals that members of the field should aspire to. For mental health workers, this includes ideals such as beneficence and nonmaleficence, fidelity and responsibility, integrity and justice, and respect for people's rights and dignity (Nichols, 2005). Also included in these general principles is the ideal that helpers should strive to contribute a portion of their professional time for little or no compensation or personal advantage.

Maintaining ethical standards is an essential part of professional practice for any mental health practitioner, as the American Psychological Association ethics committee reinforced in 2004: "Psychologists who thoroughly consider the consequences of their actions are better able to effectively weigh competing ethical interests and put client's best interest first" (APA, 2004). In fact, adhering to professional principles may be even more important in times of crisis than in more typical counseling settings because extreme situations, such as those following a disaster, can produce more ethical uncertainty and require more diligent observance of guidelines (Soliman & Rogge, 2002).

Why should this be the case? Consider again some of the challenges of counseling in chaos that we discussed in Chapter 7. Normal standards of confidentiality may be difficult to uphold when working on-scene or in a crowded shelter. Individuals whose lives have been impacted by catastrophe may be extremely vulnerable and unable to meet usual standards of informed consent; they may not have given careful consideration about whether they even want the services of a mental health professional. DMH helpers working in their own communities may find themselves counseling people they know in private life, which creates a dual role conflict that is not generally acceptable. Practitioners also may be struggling with their own responses to a disaster as they try to help others. In all, the situation-driven vulnerability of the clients and the chaotic counseling environment mean that ethical considerations may be even more worthy of attention in DMH than in other forms of mental health.

In the sections that follow, we discuss some of the ethical standards that are directly relevant to the practice of working with survivors of disaster; the actual text of the related sections of the APA Ethics Code are presented in Appendix D. Psychologists working with the APA's Disaster Response Network (DRN) are required to adhere to state law in addition to the APA's general ethical principles. The guidelines note that while participating in DRN activities psychologists might find themselves providing professional services in nontraditional settings. Nonetheless, professional standards remain applicable in all those activities.

Note that although we specifically cite the APA's ethical codes for psychologists these are similar to the codes of all mental health professions. Specific guidelines for other professional associations can generally be found on their respective websites, including:

- American Counseling Association: www.cacd.org/codeofethics.html
- National Association of Social Workers: www.socialworkers.org/pubs/code/code.asp
- American Association for Marriage and Family Therapy: www.aamft.org/resources/LRMPlan/Ethics/ethicscode2001.asp

Competence

Professional competence is primary to the fulfillment of ethical standards (Fisher, 2003), so a basic requirement for providers of early intervention services in the aftermath of disaster is that they have expertise, skills, and training in DMH. The practitioner's training, supervised experience, and continued learning will determine to a large degree the success or failure of the intervention.

The application of a professional base of knowledge should enable the practitioner to provide beneficial help (beneficence) and avoid harm (nonmaleficence). Although competence alone may not guarantee success, it will substantially reduce the possibility of causing harm. For this reason, every mental health organization's code of ethics cautions professionals not to practice outside of their area of training and expertise. This issue has particular relevance for those working in the area of DMH because this is a relatively new field. Training and academic programs for DMH professionals are in the earliest stages of development and are limited both in their scope and availability, but we strongly emphasize the need to seek them out and not to assume that traditional clinical skills will automatically transfer to disaster work without specific training—they will not.

It has been stated throughout this text that although disaster survivors are often in enormous distress, most are experiencing ordinary reactions to an extraordinary event. This basic understanding may not be included as a component of training in general mental health professional programs. Mental health workers are typically accustomed to dealing with long-standing problems in an office setting and are likely to view atypical behavior as a symptom of illness. If practitioners apply this viewpoint in a disaster setting, they might erroneously pathologize typical reactions. According to the NIMH report (2002), the presumption of clinically significant disorders in the early postincident phase is inappropriate except for those individuals with a preexisting condition. Thus, early interventions should address normal recovery, resiliency, and personal growth as well as the special needs of those individuals with enduring mental health problems or disabilities.

Training can also decrease the probability of providers administering an intervention that is faddish, not tested, or even unsafe. For example, providers trained specifically in DMH are more likely to know that evidence suggests that encouraging disaster survivors to recount their traumatic experiences and resulting emotions not only may *not* decrease a survivor's risk of developing PTSD but also may increase that risk for some vulnerable individuals (NIMH, 2002).

The NIMH report (2002) includes the following recommendations regarding the skills, training, and expertise of DMH providers:

1. Individuals providing early interventions or consultations should remain within the scope of their training and expertise, making appropriate referrals when needed.
2. Individuals providing early intervention should be sanctioned by and operate within structures responsible for coordinating disaster response (for example, American Red Cross, DRN). The structure should have quality assurance reviews to make sure that practitioners have proper credentials, expertise, and experience.
3. Providers with the highest degree of training, expertise, accountability, and responsibility should be selected to provide those interventions that may have the highest potential for unintended harm. These interventions would include triage, mass education via media, leadership consultation, and interventions that require detailed recall of traumatic experiences.

4. Mental health professionals—and others sanctioned to provide early inter-
    ventions—should avail themselves of high-quality, empirically defensible
    training that confers competence in specific interventions and strategies for
    responding to mass violence and disasters. Organizations with experience
    and expertise in providing such responses should collaborate to provide this
    training.
5. Additionally, specialist education, training, and certification programs should
    be developed so that they can be sanctioned or validated by professional bodies
    or organizations. This will ensure quality standards that are in the interest of
    service users and providers as well as the organizations that provide such staff.

Competence Working With Human Differences

Mental health practitioners should be trained to provide culturally effective, evidence-based interventions (Mollica et al., 2004). Effective clinical interventions
require assessment and treatment that will vary according to the client's ethnic
and cultural background, history of prior pathology, coping responses, and risk
and resilience factors (Flynn & Norwood, 2004; Norris et al., 2002). Thus, it
is important to understand how a culture shapes individuals' responses to a disaster as well as their receptivity to psychological services.

As a DMH practitioner making home visits or doing outreach from an emergency response vehicle or at a shelter or in a service center, you will likely find
yourself working with survivors from many diverse cultures, so you need to
obtain as much information as possible about the cultural issues of the impacted
population before going into the field. The American Red Cross typically provides such information in an extensive orientation session when workers arrive
at headquarters. We should also note that there may be emergency situations in
which the practitioner will need to do the best he or she can without adequate
preparation. It is clearly stated in the APA Ethics Code (Section 2.02) that "in
emergencies, when psychologists provide services to individuals for whom other
mental health services are not available and for which psychologists have not
obtained the necessary training, psychologists may provide such services in order
to ensure that services are not denied. The services are discontinued as soon as
the emergency has ended or appropriate services are available."

The "Guidelines for International Training in Mental Health and Psychosocial
Interventions for Trauma Exposed Populations in Clinical and Community
Settings," which were developed by the Task Force on International Trauma
Training of the International Society for Traumatic Stress Studies (Weine et al.,
2002), are a good example of the work being done to advance the provision of
culturally sensitive, respectful, and knowledgeable help to all who need it and
to prevent and avoid ethical violations.

Personal Problems and Conflicts

Despite their best intentions and efforts, DMH workers are subject to the occupational hazards of stress, compassion fatigue, burnout, and vicarious traumatization, as we discussed in Chapters 7 and 11. Beyond helpers' personal needs to

protect themselves from harm, it is the ethical responsibility of DMH workers to monitor their own physical and emotional status and to be aware of any conditions that might negatively impact their ability to serve their clients. Exhausted or traumatized helpers are temporarily impaired and cannot provide the assistance and support required in their professional roles. They also may be in personal danger of developing significant problems following the disaster.

As noted earlier, NIMH strongly recommends that providers of early intervention operate within the structures of organizations responsible for disaster response. These sponsoring agencies have a mandate to provide supportive, active supervision. Supervisors within these organizations are responsible for assigning appropriate tasks to assure that clients' needs are met, while monitoring the staff for any type of impairment. Supervisors must take precautions to be sure that inexperienced or less skilled practitioners do not take on responsibilities that they cannot perform effectively or that might overwhelm them. Supervisors should be especially careful to gauge their own stress levels. A supervisor who notices that he or she has no patience and is in a state of chronic irritation may not be effectively supporting workers. Professional colleagues, in addition to their other duties, must be responsible to and monitor each other.

Yet, acknowledging personal limits while doing DMH is always difficult. Practitioners witnessing the catastrophic aftermath of a disaster may feel compelled to work until the "job is done." Helpers who push beyond their limits do not provide consistent quality service, and if they are burned out or exhausted, they may not be able to recognize their own difficulties. Peers operating within an organized structure can provide invaluable support, encouragement and feedback to each other. For this reason, peer feedback and supervisory advice is essential.

Informed Consent

Informed consent, meaning the formal acknowledgment that a client understands the nature and limits of the therapeutic relationship, may seem to be difficult to obtain amid the chaos of a large disaster. However, the ethical guidelines make clear that standards should never be overlooked even if they are difficult to follow. We have observed that it is *not* common practice at disaster sites for mental health professionals to obtain informed consent when delivering psychological first aid, particularly if they are distributing food or water or blankets. In such cases, mental health professionals may not be acting in their role as mental health workers but rather as general disaster workers. Even when mental health workers approach survivors to ask how they are doing, they may be acting more as general helpers than as mental health providers.

The ethical guidelines do make it clear that practitioners should never be practicing surreptitiously. When helpers enter their role as mental health professionals, they should obtain informed consent and discuss the limits of confidentiality. When professionals are practicing counseling or therapy (for example, discussing stress reactions or coping skills with a survivor), they should identify themselves as mental health workers or counselors and be certain that the client wants such services. Mollica et al. (2004) recommend that mental health care providers make a special effort to guarantee informed consent during a complex emergency because the normal standards of practice may be disrupted.

Does it always make sense for mental health workers to introduce themselves to all survivors in their professional capacity, or is it preferable to wait until they are actually performing mental health services? The issue of optimal timing for seeking informed consent requires additional consideration and research. Public officials working with mental health professionals could cooperate on public awareness campaigns that could help facilitate informed consent through ethically responsible public service announcements explaining available services.

Maintaining Confidentiality and Discussing the Limits of Confidentiality

The same rules that govern confidentiality in all mental health disciplines and settings apply to disaster work. The DRN requires that all psychologists providing services in the aftermath of a disaster inform clients of the limits of confidentiality; other organizations that respond to disasters, including the American Red Cross, also have scrupulous rules regarding confidentiality. For example, release forms are required to obtain permission to share confidential information in order to provide advocacy, secure resources, and perform other services to benefit survivors.

Protecting client privacy and maintaining confidentiality in a disaster setting can be very difficult. When providing mental health services on the street or in a shelter or service center, there are no soundproof offices in which to provide mental health services. Often friends and neighbors can directly observe the interaction between a DMH worker and a client. However, providers should make every effort to consider privacy issues. You might attempt to find a more private location within a shelter or walk with a client to get away from a crowd. Helpers should also be aware of the presence of cameras and try to avoid them.

The ethical responsibility to maintain confidentiality extends beyond the disaster recovery site. The desire to talk about personal experiences and feelings related to a catastrophic event receiving public attention is normal, but practitioners must protect the confidentiality of disaster survivors by not speaking about them with family or friends. However, it is ethically acceptable and advisable to discuss your experiences with your supervisor or colleagues in the response organization.

Finally, providers should not speak to the media unless they are designated to do so by the organization they are working for. Mental health workers should be sensitive to the fact that disasters are breeding grounds for rumor and misinformation. The public has a right to accurate, credible information that will assist them during the disaster and postdisaster recovery phase, but this flow of information needs to be handled in a controlled way to ensure accuracy (Robinson, 2000). Great care is taken by organizations such as the American Red Cross to ensure that a designated Red Cross representative familiar with the operation and with Red Cross protocol provides all information shared with or through the media. Within the APA, the Practice Directorate's Public Relations

Office works with DRN to determine how to best inform the public regarding professional responses to a disaster. Generally, a formal press release is developed and distributed to the media to provide helpful information regarding planned professional responses, as well as information educating the public on how to manage psychological stress related to the disaster.

Multiple Relationships

The APA ethics code prohibits members from working with clients when a relationship exists outside the professional helper–client relationship or when the helper has a relationship with someone close to the client. This standard can be extremely difficult to uphold in a disaster situation because early responders often live in the communities in which the disaster occurred. Local responders tend to know the needs and resources of their own community and therefore can be very effective. However, under these circumstances, there is a high likelihood that volunteers will know many of the survivors receiving services. According to the ethical guidelines, all individuals receiving services must be protected from any harmful effect the professional contact might potentially create. If a survivor is a neighbor or member of the community and is known to the provider, he or she should be offered the opportunity to work with another counselor.

This does not mean that the provider should decline to provide services to a familiar person in need. Lazarus (1994) cautions against overrigid adherence to dual-relationship guidelines, which he believes were created in response to increased concern regarding litigious action. In his view, the ethical guidelines can prohibit effectiveness when taken too far. In fact, he writes, "The worst ethical violation is that of permitting risk management to take precedence over humane intervention." As a possible solution to the sometimes unavoidable multiple-role conflict in DMH, Welfel (2002) recommends providing only brief and less intense services to those individuals with whom there may be community ties. He suggests that longer-term counseling should be limited to those individuals with whom there is no connection or relationship.

Which brings us to the final role issue of referring survivors for longer-term treatment. Professional and organizational guidelines do not allow self-referrals; in other words, you may not suggest that a survivor who you encounter in disaster response work should become a client in your own practice. If a disaster victim is in need of ongoing assistance, appropriate referrals can be made using the protocol established by the agency in charge. Participating in a disaster relief effort in order to promote the clinician's private practice is a bit like ambulance-chasing lawyers rushing to an accident to hand out their cards. Such practices may be illegal and are certainly unethical.

Advocacy

As part of their code of ethics, psychologists recognize that special safeguards may be necessary to protect the rights and welfare of persons or communities whose vulnerabilities impair autonomous decision making. These principles are consistent with the contribution made by mental health professionals to advocate on behalf of those who have been traumatized or psychically injured. Without such advocacy, there would be no general field of trauma studies (Bloom, 2000), let alone a specialty of DMH.

Advocacy recognizes that victims of trauma are likely to be blamed as responsible for their own victimization. Some might question why the Jews did not leave Germany or if the rape victim could have worn less provocative clothes. Some question why those abandoned in New Orleans after Hurricane Katrina did not evacuate when warned. Advocacy means recognizing that the less powerful are more vulnerable to disaster and that recovery is more difficult because they have fewer resources to support it. Mental health professionals have an ethical responsibility to promote social justice or at least to make sure that the most vulnerable are not blamed for being victimized.

RESEARCH AND INFORMED PRACTICE

In addition to strict adherence to ethical standards, we believe that developing practices with a stronger base in empirical evidence will help strengthen acceptance of the field of DMH. According to the APA guidelines, psychologists' work should be "based upon established scientific and professional knowledge of the discipline" (APA Ethics Code, Section 2.04). Yet the discipline currently offers less scientific research than we would like to see.

As we have discussed throughout this book, DMH is a new science as well as an art, born out of the increasing instance of catastrophe. Targeted interventions during a time of immense stress can have significant consequences for the long-term health of survivors, but this needs to be demonstrated to all, including the skeptics and the cynics, through well-controlled research studies. Participants of the NIMH (2002) workshop made the following recommendations:

1. There is an ethical duty to conduct scientifically valid research to improve prevention, assessment, early intervention, and treatment in order to enhance outcomes achieved by early interventions.
2. The Institute of Medicine, in collaboration with the Office of Human Research Protections, should be encouraged to develop a strategy for educating the broader research community (including institutional review boards) about the ethical necessity of conducting rigorous research on sensitive topics related to mass violence and trauma. Ideally, this strategy will encompass guidance on determining what types of research are appropriate and when, given the existing knowledge base on early interventions.
3. Early intervention policies should be based on empirically defensible and evidence-based practices. An ethical duty exists to discourage the use of ineffective or unsafe techniques.

There is a long and often not so proud history of treating trauma, as we saw in earlier chapters. We must learn from this history that treatments that reach wide acceptance can become overformulaic, applied to survivors regardless of their individual needs. Shalev et al. (2003) warn that treatment should be neither dogmatic nor excessively flexible. In this book, we have provided positive descriptions of early interventions such as psychological first aid (PFA), psychoeducation, and cognitive–behavioral therapy (CBT). But we caution the reader that these approaches should be seen as guidelines and not as a recipe for doing DMH.

Protocols, or treatments with rigidly established steps and guidelines, may be attractive because they provide a uniform and consistent approach to helping. For example, the practice of critical incident stress debriefing (CISD) gained adherents and popularity in recent years because of its clarity and the way in which it could be applied across situations and populations. It is now clear that for the CISD protocol to be effective there must be some flexibility in its application and that it should not be applied to all populations and in all situations. DMH researchers and practitioners should be skeptical of any new protocol such as PFA or CBT if there is no flexibility in treatment.

The primary allegiance of the practitioner must never be to a theory, method, or protocol but should always be to the client or survivor. As an example of misplaced adherence to standardization, Dr. Edna Foa, a major figure in the treatment of PTSD with CBT, and some of her associates posted guidelines on the Internet for treating September 11, 2001 survivors shortly after the attacks occurred. They wrote that only those who continue to suffer extreme impairment *3 months after the attack* should be referred for treatment. Although this may have been a helpful corrective to the practitioners who thought that the entire country needed immediate and extensive psychotherapy, there were some survivors who might have benefited from treatment without waiting 3 months. Any survivor who is in distress or disabled by traumatic events deserves to be observed, evaluated, and treated, and the care provided should be determined on a case-by-case basis (Shalev et al., 2003).

At the same time that research is needed on almost every aspect of DMH, mental health practitioners must still attend to the immediate needs of survivors: "How does one balance clinical demand to provide an intervention with the inadequacies in the empirical evidence-based knowledge of effective early interventions for trauma?" (NIMH, 2002). This difficulty is exacerbated by the ever-changing nature of disasters that have unfolded recently, from unprecedented large-scale terrorist attacks to a tsunami and a hurricane that each wiped out entire communities. There is no evidence-based best practice for treating large displaced populations within the United States, yet in the aftermath of Hurricane Katrina this is a population that must be helped. The assistance we offer should be consistent with research findings but not limited by what we do not know because survivors cannot wait for the data to catch up to their needs.

A FINAL NOTE ON NEW DIRECTIONS

Experts in the field of DMH and emergency management continue to plan for worst-case scenarios, and the destructive power of new disasters continues to exceed those plans. The attacks on 9/11, the four consecutive hurricanes in Florida in 2004, the Southeast Asia tsunami of 2004, and 2005's Hurricane

Katrina in the Gulf Coast region challenged the preparations and even the imaginations of the experts. Apparently, the worst-case scenarios that are used for purposes of planning may not be catastrophic enough.

Throughout this book, we have attempted to outline our view of where the field of DMH is headed, including a commitment to planning and preparedness at both the national and international levels, as well as a commitment to research and ethics. But we also acknowledge that this field is characterized by great uncertainty and unpredictability. As we both helped with preparations in the spring of 2001 for a worst-case scenario of two planes crashing into residential areas of New York City, neither of us was adequately prepared for what occurred just a few months later on September 11. We found that just as our city and country were under attack, so were our imaginations. The events of that day contributed to shaping the field of DMH, and subsequent events will continue to alter that emerging shape as we learn from their impact on survivors. As we completed the draft of this book, Hurricane Katrina left us with images that once again shattered our assumptions about the world. This field will continue to adapt and evolve in response to future events, including disasters that cannot possibly be foreseen or controlled—and you may be a part of that change.

You might be coming to DMH from any of a number of related fields: psychology, social work, social services, nursing, psychiatry, or pastoral care, among other possibilities. Whatever your background, the most essential quality you will need as a DMH practitioner is a willingness to be with and assist people who are in pain. As a disaster worker, you will see things that most people would rather not see. You will work in chaotic, sometimes exhausting conditions, and you will need to take special care to avoid burnout or compassion fatigue. But you will also have the opportunity to play a meaningful role in a growing field. Most significantly, you will have the opportunity to be with and assist survivors at what may be the most important time in their lives.

References

APA (American Psychological Association). (2004). Ethical principles of psychologists and code of conduct. Retrieved June 16, 2004, from http://www.apa.org/ethics/code2002.html.

Associated Press. (2005, January 5). Tsunami survivors worry psychiatrists. *New York Times*.

Bloom, S. L. (2000). Our hearts and our hopes are turned to peace: Origins of the International Society for Traumatic Stress Studies. In A. Y. Shalev, R. Yehuda, & A. C. McFarlane (Eds.), *The international handbook of human response to trauma* (pp. 220–250). New York: Kluwer Academic/Plenum.

Bonanno, G. A. (2004). Loss, trauma, and human resilience: Have we underestimated the human capacity to thrive after extremely adverse events? *American Psychologist, 59*(1), 20–28.

Borenstein, D. (2001, March 2). Psychiatry: Composition and trends. *Psychiatric News*. Retrieved September 6, 2005, from http://www.psych.org/pnews/01-03-02/pres3a.html

Brewin, C. R. (2003). *Posttraumatic stress disorder: Malady or myth?* New Haven, CT: Yale University Press.

Carey, B. (2005, January 4). After food and shelter, help in coping with unbearable loss. *New York Times.*

Croq, L., Croq, M., Chiapello, A., & Damiani, C. (2005). Organization of mental health services for disaster victims. In J. J. Loperz-Ibor, G. Christodoulou, M. Maj, N. Sartorius, & A. Okasha (Eds.), *Disasters and mental health* (pp. 99–126). West Sussex, England: Wiley.

de Jong, K (2004, November 17). Presentation on The Hidden Scars of War: Providing Mental Health Care in Times of Conflict, at New York University Medical Center, New York.

Fisher, C. (2003). *Decoding the ethics code.* Thousand Oaks, CA: Sage.

Fullerton, C., Ursano, R. J., Norwook, A. E., Holloway, H. H. (2003). Trauma, terrorism, and disaster. In R. J. Ursano, C. S. Fullerton, & A. E. Norwood (Eds.), *Terrorism and disaster: Individual and community mental health interventions* (pp. 1–20). Cambridge, England, and New York: Cambridge University Press.

Flynn, B. W., & Norwood, A. E. (2004). Defining normal psychological reactions to disaster. *Psychiatric Annals, 34,* 597–603.

Galea, S., Vlahov, D., Resnick, H., Ahern, J., Ezra, S., Gold, J., et al. (2003). Trends of probably post-traumatic stress disorder in New York City after the September 11th terrorist attacks. *American Journal of Epidemiology, 158,* 514–524.

Gladwell, M. (2004, November 8). Getting over it. *The New Yorker.*

Groopman, J. (2004, January 26). The grief industry. *The New Yorker, 30.*

Herman, J. (1992). *Trauma and recovery: The aftermath of violence from domestic abuse to political terror.* New York: Basic Books.

Herrmann, J. (2005). Disaster mental health: A critical response. Rochester, NY: University of Rochester. Available at http://www.centerfordisastermedicine.org/index.html.

Lazarus, A. (1994). How certain boundaries and ethics diminish therapeutic effectiveness. *Ethics and Behavior, 4,* 259–261.

Litz, B. T. (Ed). (2004). *Early intervention for trauma and traumatic loss.* New York: Guilford Press.

Litz, B. T., & Gray, M. J. (2004). Early intervention for trauma in adults: A framework for first aid and secondary prevention. In B. T. Litz (Ed.), *Early intervention for trauma and traumatic loss* (pp. 87–111). New York: Guilford Press.

Loperz-Ibor, J. J., Christodoulou, G., Maj, M., Sartorius, N., & Okasha, A. (Eds.). (2005). *Disasters and mental health.* West Sussex, England: Wiley.

Luthar, S. S., Cicchetti, D., & Becker, B. (2000). The construct of resilience: A critical evaluation and guidelines for future work. *Child Development, 71,* 543–62.

Masten, A. S., & Coatsworth, D. J. (1998). The development of competence in favorable and unfavorable environments: Lessons from research on successful children. *American Psychologist, 53,* 205–220.

McFarlane, A. C. (2005). Psychiatric morbidity following disasters: Epidemiology, risk, and protective factors. In J. J. Loperz-Ibor, G. Christodoulou, M. Maj, N. Sartorius, & A. Okasha (Eds.), *Disasters and mental health* (pp. 37–63). West Sussex, England: Wiley.

Michalik, M. (2004, November 17). Presentation on The Hidden Scars of War: Providing Mental Health Care in Times of Conflict, New York University Medical Center, New York.

Mollica, R. F., Cardozo, B., Osofsky, H. J., Raphael, B., Ager, A., & Salama, P. (2004). Mental health in complex emergencies. *Lancet, 364*(9450), 2058–2067.

Nichols, W. C. (2005). Ethical issues in practice with couples and families. *Family Psychologist, 21*(3), 4–7.

NIMH (National Institute of Mental Health). (2002). *Mental health and mass violence: Evidence-based early psychological intervention for victims/survivors of mass violence. A workshop to reach consensus on best practices* (NIH Publication No. 02-5138). Washington, DC: Government Printing Office.

Norris, F. H., Friedman, M. J., Watson, P. J., Byrne, C. M., Diaz, E., & Kaniasty, K. (2002). 60,000 disaster victims speak: Part 1. An empirical review of the empirical literature, 1981–2001. *Psychiatry, 65,* 207–260.

Robinson, P. (2000). The policy–media interaction model: Measuring media power during humanitarian crisis. *Journal of Peace Research, 37*(5), 613–633.

Satel, S. (2005, March 29). Bread and shelter, yes. Psychiatrists, no. *New York Times.*

Shalev, A. (2004a, October 27). *Living in an age of terror: Creating spiritual and psychological resilience.* Paper presented at New York University, New York.

Shalev, A. (2004b). Commentary on "A national longitudinal study on the psychological consequences of the September 11, 2001 terrorist attacks: Reactions, impairment, and help-seeking." *Psychiatry, 67,* 174–177.

Shalev, A. Y., Adessky, R., Boker, R., Bargai, N., Cooper, R., Freedman, S., Hadar, H., Peri, T., & Tuval-Mashiach, R. (2003). Clinical interventions for survivors of prolonged adversities. In R. J. Ursano, C. S. Fullerton, & A. E. Norwood (Eds.), *Terrorism and disaster: Individual and community mental health interventions* (pp. 162–188). Cambridge, England, and New York: Cambridge University Press.

Shane, S. (2005, September 5). After failures, government officials play blame game. *New York Times.* Retrieved September 5, 2005 from http://nytimes.com/2005/09/05/national/nationalspecial/05blame.html.

Shinfuku, N. (2005). The experience of the Kobe earthquake In J. J. Loperz-Ibor, G. Christodoulou, M. Maj, N. Sartorius, & A. Okasha (Eds.), *Disasters and mental health* (pp. 37–63). West Sussex, England: Wiley.

Slater, L. (2003, February 23). Repress yourself. *New York Times Magazine.*

Soliman, H., & Rogge, M. E. (2002). Ethical considerations in disaster services: A social work perspective. *Electronic Journal of Social Work, 1*(1), 1–21.

Southwick, S. M., Vythilingam, M., & Charney, D. S. (2005). The psychobiology of depression and resilience to stress: Implications for prevention and treatment. *Annual Review of Clinical Psychology,* 255–291.

Weine, S., Danieli, Y., Silove, D., Van Ommeren, M., Fairbank, J. A., & Saul, J. (2002). Guidelines for international training in mental health and psychosocial interventions for trauma exposed populations in clinical and community settings. *Psychiatry, 65*(2), 156–164.

Welfel, E. R. (2002). Ethics in counseling in psychotherapy: Standards, research, and emerging issues (2nd ed.). Pacific Grove, CA: Brooks/Cole.

WHO (World Health Organization). (2005). *Mental health atlas—2005.* Retrieved September 6, 2005, from http://www.who.int/mental_health/evidence/atlas/.

Wilson, J. P., Friedman, M. J., & Lindy, J. D. (2001). Treatment goals for PTSD. In J. P. Wilson, M. J. Friedman, & J. D. Lindy (Eds.), *Treating psychological trauma and PTSD* (pp. 3–28). New York: Guilford Press.

A Sample Common Reactions Document

This handout was produced by one of the authors for their workplace in the wake of the attacks of September 11, 2001.

COPING WITH THE AFTERMATH OF TERRORIST ACTS

Our community has experienced a "larger than life" event. The landscape of our city has been altered, and the effects are far reaching. Some people have lost loved ones. Many more are sharing their sense of loss and horror that has resulted from this attack. Our sadness and outrage over others' loss and our sense of threat are real and should be respected.

Our daily lives and schedules have been changed, and we are operating under trying circumstances. This disruption and dislocation only adds to the stress of our loss and the disaster itself. It is possible to feel that things will never be the same.

We are living through events that are emotionally stressful and troubling. They would challenge anyone's ability to cope. As this disaster recovery continues, the experience may wear more heavily on everyone's resources and emotions.

Below are some reactions that people can experience to this event, immediately or weeks later. Although these thoughts, feelings, and actions can be very upsetting, it is important to

337

remember that they are common and shared reactions to an abnormal, disruptive situation and that they should lessen with time.

COMMON REACTIONS

- Flashbacks or "reliving the event"
- Feeling withdrawn, disconnected, or numb
- Jumpiness, a tendency to be easily startled
- Nightmares, difficulties in falling or staying asleep
- Irritability, anger
- Changes in appetite
- Feelings of anxiety or helplessness
- Pain or tension in one's body
- Nervous energy or hyperactivity
- Tendency to overwork
- Lapses of memory
- Headaches
- Questioning your spiritual or religious beliefs
- Fatigue, world weariness
- Tendency to self-medicate (overindulgence in alcohol or other substances)
- Inability to concentrate
- Extremes of emotion
- Feelings of terror, fear, and disbelief
- Lowered productivity
- Inability to remove yourself from the event, emotionally or physically
- A lack of interest in usually enjoyable activities
- Guilt
- Heightened concern for personal well-being
- Being tearful or crying, sometimes for no apparent reason
- Increased conflicts with family/colleagues
- Isolating yourself from others
- Feeling depressed or blue
- Avoidance of places or activities that evoke the event
- Heart palpitations, dizzy spells (see your doctor if you experience these)

Coping Tips

Recovering from this sudden, violent event will take time. Acknowledge that you're going through a stressful time. Begin by recognizing the need to take care of yourself on different levels.

- *Take care of your physical well-being.* Make time for yourself. Remember to eat, to rest, and to get some exercise, even if it as simple as going for a brisk walk. Get a massage, soak in a long, hot bath, and enjoy little things. Although it may be difficult to enjoy yourself at a time like this, it is important to strengthen your bonds with the people you love. Try to keep in place familiar routines such as regular meal times and other family rituals. These will help you to feel as though your life has some sense of order. *Take breaks from your pain.*

- *Be gentle with what you may be feeling.* When you can, allow yourself to feel all your feelings over what has happened. Avoid walling off your pain, which can seem automatic at a time like this. Talk to others about how you feel. Understanding what you are feeling and making an effort to work through it will help you overcome your pain. Make a connection between this event and your response. Don't be afraid to seek counseling.
- *Accept practical support from others.* Don't let yourself become isolated. Include your circle of friends, coworkers, and family in the healing process (they'll sense something is on your mind anyway). This can be a stressful time for them, too, and they may also need some help getting through it. Help others by sharing your experience.
- *Search for meaning in this event.* This may be a difficult task. Put this event into some kind of perspective. Ask the questions that don't have easy answers: "How could someone do this?" "Why does it always happen to good people?" Don't expect to be the same as before. Things have changed and, chances are, you may have changed, too. You may never forget this event. That's why it's especially important to find a way to understand this event and make it part of who you are.
- *Forgive yourself and others when you act out because you are stressed.* This is a difficult time, and everyone's emotions are closer to the surface. Try to cut down on responsibilities in other areas of your life until you've had some time to recover from this crisis.

APPENDIX

Internet Resources for Helping Children Cope With Disaster

http://www.fema.gov/kids/	Child-oriented website on disasters developed by the Federal Emergency Management Association. It contains information on different types of disasters, how to prepare for them, and how to cope.
http://www.redcross.org/ disaster/safety/guide.html	Brochure developed by the American Red Cross: *Talking About Disaster: Guide.* Check the Red Cross home page (http://www.redcross.org) for additional information and breaking news on disasters.
http://www.apa.org/ practice/ kids.html	Website developed by the American Psychological Association (APA). Contains a fact sheet, "Helping Children Cope: A Guide to Helping Children Cope With the Stress of the Oklahoma City Explosion." Useful for a wide range of disasters. Check the APA home page (http://www.apa.org) for additional information and breaking news.
http://www.aacap.org	Website of the American Academy of Child and Adolescent Psychiatry. Contains many fact sheets for children

	and families, including how to help children cope with disasters. Contains disaster-related information for children from the Virginia Disaster Stress Intervention at James Madison University, Harrisonburg, VA.
http://www.jmu.edu/ psychologydept/4kids.htm	This website provides adults with information to help children cope with natural disasters and violence.
http://www. disastertraining.org	Website for the Center for Mental Health Services. Contains information for communities and reference lists for practitioners on disaster interventions.
http://www. mentalhealth.org	Website for the Center for Mental Health Services. Contains information for communities and professionals.
http://www.ncptsd.org	Website for the National Center for PTSD. Includes manual for DMH services.
http://www.aap.org	Website for the American Academy of Pediatrics. Contains disaster intervention information for pediatricians.
www.nasponline. org/NEATcrisismain.htl	Website for the National Association for School Psychologists. Contains disaster information in many languages that can be used by teachers or parents.

Based on La Greca, A. M., & Prinstein, M. J. (2002). Hurricanes and earthquakes. In A. M. La Greca, W. K. Silverma, E. M. Vernberg, & M. C. Roberts (Eds.), *Helping children cope with disasters and terrorism* (pp. 107–138). Washington, DC: APA Press.

Treatment Goals for a Cognitive–Behavioral Group Therapy for Adults and Children Following an Air Disaster

The following list presents the goals used in each session of a structured, seven-session group therapy model that was developed by a group of mental health professionals to treat adults and children who were suffering with both trauma and sudden loss after the crash of US Air flight 427 in 1994. To learn more about the program, we refer you to the original article:

> Stubenbort, K., Donnelly, G. R., & Cohen, J. A. (2001). Cognitive–behavioral group therapy for bereaved adults and children following an air disaster. *Group Dynamics, 5*(4). Retrieved on July 22, 2005, from EBSCOhost.

THE CHILDREN'S GROUP

Session 1: Introduction, Definition of Purpose, and Establishment of Group Rules

Treatment objectives were the following:

- Strengthen group cohesion.
- Normalize survivors' distress reactions and establish fellow members as a comparison group for gauging one's own reaction.

- Strengthen members' perception that the group is a safe place for disclosing and exploring members' painful reactions to their traumatic losses.
- Increase tolerance for trauma-related material.
- Begin converting the relationship with the lost loved one from an interactive relationship to one of memory.

Session 2: Psychoeducation to Further Normalize the Experience and Increase Coping Skills

Treatment objectives were the following:

- Increase understanding and challenge misconceptions about death.
- Increase coping skills surrounding loss through the identification of feelings.
- Increase coping skills surrounding the trauma through a shared discussion regarding learning about the trauma and death of the loved one.
- Strengthen the members' perceptions that the group is a safe place for discussing feelings.
- Strengthen group cohesion and normalize reactions to loss as members share experiences.

Session 3: Coping With Traumatic Death

Treatment objectives were the following:

- Continue to increase tolerance by exploring thoughts and feelings about death.
- Continue to increase group cohesion and to normalize thoughts and feelings related to the trauma through shared discussion.
- Begin identifying, challenging, and reframing cognitive distortions regarding expectations about the future.
- Begin the process of moving on in life.

Session 4: Strengthening Group Cohesion Through the Exploration of Loss and Unfinished Business

Treatment objectives were the following:

- Increase group cohesion through collaborative exercises.
- Continue to normalize distress reactions and to use members as a comparison group for gauging one's own reactions.
- Facilitate empathic response among group members.
- Continue to increase tolerance through exposure and through the use of cognitive reframing.

Session 5: Continuing to Explore Loss and Unfinished Business

Treatment objectives were the following:

- Continue strengthening group cohesion.
- Continue normalizing of thoughts and feelings.

- Continue correcting distortions regarding trauma-related material.
- Continue increasing tolerance for trauma-related material.
- Begin the process of placing the deceased in memory.
- Address the upcoming holidays and the impact that the recent loss may have on these holidays.

Session 6: Increasing Coping Skills

Treatment objectives were the following:

- Continue to increase tolerance through feelings identification.
- Increase coping through thought stopping and cognitive correcting.

Session 7: Group Closure and Moving On

Treatment objectives were the following:

- Emotional and cognitive processing of the holidays.
- Facilitate closure and moving on.
- Challenge and correct faulty cognitions relating to perceptions about the future.

THE ADULT GROUP

Session 1: Introduction, Definition of Group's Purpose, and Establishment of Group Rules

Treatment objectives were the following:

- Promote trust between the facilitators and the group members.
- Strengthen members' perceptions that the group is a safe place for disclosing and exploring members' painful reactions to their traumatic losses.
- Promote group cohesion.
- Normalize survivors' distress reactions and establish fellow members as comparison group for gauging one's own reactions.
- Increase tolerance for trauma-related material.

Session 2: Adjusting to the Environment in the Absence of the Lost Loved One

Treatment objectives were the following:

- Establish a check-in period.
- Continue to strengthen group cohesion.
- Continue to increase tolerance for trauma-related material.
- Begin converting the relationship with the lost loved one from an interactive relationship to one of memory.

Session 3: Coping With Traumatic Death

Treatment objectives were the following:

- Increase members' understanding about traumatic stress reactions.
- Continue to normalize survivors' distress reactions.
- Continue to increase tolerance for trauma-related material.
- Increase members' understanding of children's posttraumatic and grief reactions.

Session 4: Strengthening Group Cohesion Through the Exploration of Loss and Unfinished Business

Treatment objectives were the following:

- Promote an understanding of unfinished business.
- Continue converting the relationship with the lost loved one from an interactive relationship to one of memory.
- Increase tolerance and expression of trauma- and loss-related feeling states.
- Introduce anger management training.

Session 5: Identifying and Building Ongoing Support Structures

Treatment objectives were the following:

- Continue increasing tolerance for trauma-related material.
- Identify extended support systems.

Session 6: Relocating the Deceased to Memory and Moving On

Treatment objectives were the following:

- Address the upcoming holidays and the impact that the recent loss may have upon these holidays.
- Identify needs regarding holiday coping.
- Begin to address closure.

Session 7: Group Closure and Moving On

Treatment objectives were the following:

- Conduct emotional and cognitive processing of the holidays.
- Facilitate closure.
- Facilitate tolerance and moving on through the experiences of guest speakers.

D

Disaster Mental Health–Relevant Articles From the American Psychological Association Ethics Code

The entire APA Ethical Principles of Psychologists and Code of Conduct can be downloaded from the organization's website,

http://www.apa.org/ethics/code2002.html

COMPETENCE

Psychologists provide services, teach, and conduct research with populations and in areas only within the boundaries of their competence, based on their education, training, supervised experience, consultation, study, or professional experience. (APA Ethics Code 2.01)

COMPETENCE WORKING WITH HUMAN DIFFERENCES

Where scientific or professional knowledge in the discipline of psychology establishes that an understanding of factors associated with age, gender, gender identity, race, ethnicity, culture, national origin, religion, sexual orientation, disability, language, or socioeconomic status is essential for effective implementation of their services or research, psychologists have or obtain the training, experience, consultation, or supervision necessary to ensure the competence of their services, or they make appropriate referrals. (APA Ethics Code 2.01.b)

PERSONAL PROBLEMS AND CONFLICTS

(a) Psychologists refrain from initiating an activity when they know or should know that there is a substantial likelihood that their personal problems will prevent them from performing their work-related activities in a competent manner.

(b) When psychologists become aware of personal problems that may interfere with their performing work-related duties adequately, they take appropriate measures, such as obtaining professional consultation or assistance, and determine whether they should limit, suspend, or terminate their work-related duties. (APA Ethics Code 2.06)

INFORMED CONSENT

(a) When psychologists conduct research or provide assessment, therapy, counseling, or consulting services in person or via electronic transmission or other forms of communication, they obtain the informed consent of the individual or individuals using language that is reasonably understandable to that person or persons except when conducting such activities without consent is mandated by law or governmental regulation or as otherwise provided in this Ethics Code. (APA Ethics Code 3.10)

MAINTAINING CONFIDENTIALITY

Psychologists have a primary obligation and take reasonable precautions to protect confidential information obtained through or stored in any medium, recognizing that the extent and limits of confidentiality may be regulated by law or established by institutional rules or professional or scientific relationship. (APA Ethics Code 4.01)

DISCUSSING THE LIMITS OF CONFIDENTIALITY

(a) Psychologists discuss with persons (including, to the extent feasible, persons who are legally incapable of giving informed consent and their legal representatives) and organizations with whom they establish a scientific or professional relationship (1) the relevant limits of confidentiality and (2) the foreseeable uses of the information generated through their psychological activities. (b) Unless it is not feasible or is contraindicated, the discussion of confidentiality occurs at the outset of the relationship and thereafter as new circumstances may warrant (APA Ethics Code 4.02).

MULTIPLE RELATIONSHIPS

(a) A multiple relationship occurs when a psychologist is in a professional role with a person and (1) at the same time is in another role with the same person, (2) at the same time is in a relationship with a person closely associated with or related to the person with whom the psychologist has the professional relationship, or (3) promises to enter into another relationship in the future with the person or a person closely associated with or related to the person.

A psychologist refrains from entering into a multiple relationship if the multiple relationship could reasonably be expected to impair the psychologist's objectivity, competence, or effectiveness in performing his or her functions as a psychologist, or otherwise risks exploitation or harm to the person with whom the professional relationship exists.

Multiple relationships that would not reasonably be expected to cause impairment or risk exploitation or harm are not unethical.

(b) If a psychologist finds that, due to unforeseen factors, a potentially harmful multiple relationship has arisen, the psychologist takes reasonable steps to resolve it with due regard for the best interests of the affected person and maximal compliance with the Ethics Code.

(c) When psychologists are required by law, institutional policy, or extraordinary circumstances to serve in more than one role in judicial or administrative proceedings, at the outset they clarify role expectations and the extent of confidentiality and thereafter as changes occur. (APA Ethics Code 3.05)

Resource List for Disaster Mental Health Helpers

The following list includes many of the organizations and agencies that DMH helpers may encounter in their professional work, as well as informational resources that provide material about emotional reactions and practical needs following disasters.

GOVERNMENT AGENCIES

Department of Health and Human Services (DHHS)

DHHS is the government agency responsible for protecting the health of all Americans. Responsibilities include public health, biomedical research, Medicare and Medicaid, welfare, social services, and more.

> 200 Independence Avenue, SW
> Washington, DC 20201
> Phone: 202-619-0257
> Website: http://www.hhs.gov

DHHS information about disasters and traumatic events can be found here:

> http://dhhs.gov/emergency/index.shtml

Department of Veterans Affairs (VA)

The VA provides benefits and services to veterans and their dependents, including medical and mental health-care assistance. Local facilities nationwide can be located at

http://www.va.gov/directory

The VA also operates the National Center for Post-Traumatic Stress Disorder, which was created in 1989 in response to a congressional mandate to address the needs of veterans with military-related PTSD. The center's mission is to advance the clinical care and social welfare of America's veterans through research, education, and training in the science, diagnosis, and treatment of PTSD and stress-related disorders. Its website offers information and other resources concerning PTSD:

http://www.ncptsd.va.gov

Federal Emergency Management Agency (FEMA)

FEMA, which is a part of the U.S. Department of Homeland Security, is the primary government organization in charge of disaster preparation and response. FEMA also initiates proactive mitigation activities, trains first responders, and manages the National Flood Insurance Program and the U.S. Fire Administration. FEMA's general contact information is

500 C Street SW
Washington, DC 20472
Phone: 800-621-FEMA
Website: http://www.fema.gov

More specific contact information can be found at

http://www.fema.gov/feedback

National Institute of Mental Health (NIMH)

NIMH, part of the U.S. Department of Health and Human Services, works to reduce the burden of mental illness and behavioral disorders through research on mind, brain, and behavior. The Institute conducts and disseminates research on numerous aspects of mental health, including the impact of trauma and disasters.

6001 Executive Boulevard, Room 8184, MSC 9663
Bethesda, MD 20892-9663
Phone: 866-615-6464
Fax: 301-443-4279
Website: http://www.nimh.nih.gov

U.S. Department of Justice: Office for Victims of Crime (OVC)

The OVC is a component of the Office of Justice Programs, U.S. Department of Justice. It provides leadership and funding on behalf of crime victims, including victims of terrorism and mass violence.

810 7th Street NW
Washington, DC 20531
Phone: 800-851-3420
Website: http://www.ojp.usdoj.gov/ovc

State Emergency Management Offices (SEMOs)

SEMOs are the state-level agencies that provide government response to disasters. A complete listing of contact information for specific state offices and agencies of emergency management, as well as state emergency managers' e-mail addresses, can be found at

http://www.fema.gov/fema/statedr.shtm

Substance Abuse and Mental Health Services Administration (SAMHSA)

SAMHSA provides information about various aspects of mental health and substance-abuse issues for providers, consumers, and the media. Two departments may be particularly helpful for DMH helpers:

Center for Mental Health Services
Emergency Mental Health and Traumatic Stress Services Branch
1 Choke Cherry Road, Sixth Floor
Rockville, MD 20850
Phone: 800-789-2647
Fax: 240-276-1844
Website: http://www.mentalhealth.samhsa.gov/cmhs/emergencyservices

Disaster Technical Assistance Center
7735 Old Georgetown Road, Suite 600
Bethesda, MD 20814
Phone: 800-308-3515
Fax: 800-311-7691
Website: http://www.mentalhealth.samhsa.gov/dtac
E-mail: dtac@esi-dc.com

NONGOVERNMENT AGENCIES

American Red Cross

Since 1905 the American Red Cross has been mandated by the U.S. Congress to respond to disasters across the nation, providing shelter, food, and health and mental health services to address basic human needs.

American Red Cross National Headquarters
2025 E Street, NW
Washington, DC 20006
Phone: 202-303-4498

Local chapters can be located at:

http://www.redcross.org/where/where.html

Information about taking the American Red Cross Introduction to Disaster Services Training course, which is required in order to provide DMH services in association with the American Red Cross, can be found at

http://www.redcross.org/flash/course01_v01/

Doctors Without Borders

Doctors Without Borders is an international independent medical humanitarian organization that delivers emergency aid to people affected by armed conflict, epidemics, natural or human-made disasters, or exclusion from health care in more than 70 countries.

U.S. Headquarters
333 7th Avenue, 2nd Floor
New York, NY 10001-5004
Phone: 212-679-6800
Fax: 212-679-7016
Website: http://www.doctorswithoutborders.org
E-mail: Elizabeth.lee@msf.org

International Federation of Red Cross and Red Crescent Societies (IFRC)

The IFRC is the world's largest humanitarian organization, providing relief assistance for international emergencies regardless of recipients' nationality, race, religious beliefs, class, or political opinions.

PO Box 372
CH-1211 Geneva 19
Switzerland
Phone: +41 22 730 42 22
Fax: +41 22 733 03 95
Website: http://www.ifrc.org
E-mail: secretariat@ifrc.org

Pan America Health Organization (PAHO)

PAHO has 35 member governments in the Western Hemisphere. It also serves as the regional office for the Americas of the World Health Organization (WHO). PAHO/WHO works through the Ministries of Health and in the area of disaster reduction, with the health sector disaster programs in these ministries. The health sector includes security systems, the Red Cross, private medical services, nongovernment organizations, and others, who are also included in technical cooperation activities.

525 23rd Street, NW
Washington, DC 20037

Phone: 202-974-3000
Website: http://www.paho.org

Petfinder

Petfinder is an online search database of animals that need homes. It is also a directory of over 9000 animal shelters and adoption organizations across the United States, Canada, and Mexico.

Website: http://www.petfinders.com/disaster
E-mail pets@petfinder.com

UNICEF

UNICEF, the United Nations Children's Fund, works internationally to protect the rights and development of children, including children affected by disasters. UNICEF headquarters can be contacted at

UNICEF House
3 United Nations Plaza
New York, NY 10017
Phone: 212-326-7000
Fax: 212-887-7465
Website: http://www.unicef.org

Contact information for other international branches can be found at

http://unicef.org/about/structure/index_worldcontact.html

World Health Organization (WHO)

WHO, a United Nations agency, works internationally to decrease disease or infirmity and to improve physical, mental, and social well-being.

Avenue Appia 20
1211 Geneva 27
Switzerland
Phone: +41 22 791 21 11
Fax: +41 22 791 3111
Website: http://www.who.org

OTHER DISASTER MENTAL HEALTH RESOURCES

American Psychiatric Association

The American Psychiatric Association is a medical specialty society with more than 35,000 member-physicians who work together to ensure humane care and effective treatment for all persons with mental disorders.

1000 Wilson Boulevard, Suite 1825
Arlington, VA 22209-3901

Phone: 703-907-7300
Website: http://www.psych.org
Email: apa@psych.org

Disaster-specific information can be found at

http://www.psych.org/disasterpsych

American Psychological Association (APA)

The APA is a 150,000-member scientific and professional organization that represents psychology in the United States.

750 First Street, NE
Washington, DC 20002-4242
Phone: 800-374-2721 or 202-336-5500
Fax: 202-336-5797
Website: http://www.apa.org

The Disaster Response Network is a pro-bono service of the APA and its membership that provides information on identifying and managing traumatic stress. Information about the Disaster Response Network can be found at

http://www.apa.org/practice/drnindex.html

International Critical Incident Stress Foundation, Inc. (ICISF)

ICISF is a nonprofit foundation dedicated to the prevention and mitigation of disabling stress through the provision of education, training, and support services for emergency services professionals.

3290 Pine Orchard Lane, Suite 106
Ellicott City, MD 21042
Phone: 410-750-9600
Fax: 410-750-9601
Website: http://icisf.org
E-mail: info@icisf.org

International Society for Traumatic Stress Studies (ISTSS)

ISTSS is an international multidisciplinary, professional membership organization that was founded in 1985 to promote advancement and exchange of knowledge about severe stress and trauma and to advocate for the field of traumatic stress.

60 Revere Drive, Suite 500
Northbrook, IL 60062
Phone: 847-480-9028
Fax: 847-480-9282
Website: http://istss.org
E-mail: istss@istss.org

National Association of Social Workers (NASW)

NASW, the largest membership organization of professional social workers in the world, works to enhance the professional growth and development of its members, to create and maintain professional standards, and to advance sound social policies.

750 First Street, NE, Suite 700
Washington, DC 20002-4241
Phone: 202-408-8600
Website: http://www.naswdc.org

National Board for Certified Counselors (NBCC)

NBCC is an independent, nonprofit credentialing body for counselors. It maintains a register of certified counselors. The Disaster Relief Resources links counselors with the American Red Cross for training and volunteer work. It also maintains a register of counselors willing to provide pro-bono counseling following a disaster.

National Board for Certified Counselors
Disaster Relief Resources
3 Terrace Way, Suite D
Greensboro, NC 27403-3660
Phone: 336-547-0607
Fax: 336-547-0017
Website: www.nbcc.org/resourses
E-mail: nbcc@nbcc.org

National Association for School Psychologists (NASP)

The NASP represents school psychology and the provision of mental health and educational services for all schoolchildren.

National Association for School Psychologists
4340 East West Highway, Suite 402
Bethesda, MdD 20814
Phone: 301-657-0270
Fax: 301-657-0275
TTY: 301-657-4155
Website: www.nasponline.org/NEAT crisismain.htl
E-mail: Generalinfo@NASPWeb.com

National Voluntary Organizations Active in Disaster (NVOAD)

NVOAD coordinates planning efforts by many voluntary organizations responding to disaster in order to avoid duplication and to provide more effective service when disasters strike.

PO Box 151973
Alexandria, VA 22315

Phone: 703-339-5596
Fax: 703-339-3316
Website: http://nvoad.org

Natural Hazards Research and Applications Information Center

The Natural Hazards Center, which is operated by the University of Colorado, works to advance and communicate knowledge on hazards mitigation and disaster preparedness, response, and recovery among researchers, practitioners, and policy makers. The center also supports and conducts research and provides educational opportunities concerning disasters and other hazards.

482 UCB
Boulder, CO 80309-0482
Phone: 303-492-6818
Fax: 303-492-2151
Website: http://www.colorado.edu/hazards
E-mail: hazctr@colorado.edu

Index